ALSO BY MAUREEN ORTH

Vulgar Favors

the importance of being

Famous

behind the scenes of the
celebrity-industrial
complex

MAUREEN ORTH

HENRY HOLT AND COMPANY | NEW YORK

Henry Holt and Company, LLC
Publishers since 1866
115 West 18th Street
New York, New York 10011

Henry Holt® is a registered trademark of
Henry Holt and Company, LLC.

Library of Congress Cataloging-in-Publication Data
Orth, Maureen.
    The importance of being famous : behind the scenes of the
celebrity-industrial complex / Maureen Orth—1st ed.
        p.   cm.
    ISBN 0-8050-7545-3
    1. United States—Social Life and customs—1971–
2. Celebrities—United States.   3. Popular culture—United States.
4. Mass media and culture—United States.   5. Fame.   I. Title.

E169.02O75 2004
920'.009'045—dc22   2003056890

Henry Holt books are available for special
promotions and premiums.
For details contact:
Director, Special Markets.

First Edition 2004

Designed by Paula Russell Szafranski

Printed in the United States of America

10   9   8   7   6   5   4   3   2

For Larry McMurtry, my first writing mentor,
and
For Wayne Lawson, my wonderful editor

CONTENTS

the importance of being

Famous

I Love Laci:

Laci Peterson: Welcome to America's
Number One Reality Soap Opera

August 2003

Few in the horde of journalists covering the Laci Peterson murder case—the number one reality soap opera in America—have ever set foot in Gervasoni's bar. Yet this friendly, 1950s-style saloon in Laci's hometown of Modesto, California, has become the hangout of choice for two of the story's most prodigious propagators, David Wright and Michael Hanrahan of the *National Enquirer*. The highly organized pageants of grief and speculation that big criminal cases have become in the United States—particularly on cable television—are the perfect petri dishes for Wright and Hanrahan to develop their stories in. Says Wright, a Brit and a twenty-seven-year *Enquirer* veteran, "The Peterson story has broken perfectly. The tabs kept Laci going during the Iraq war, and as soon as the war finishes, her body washes up."

By liberally spreading cash all over this community of 203,000, the dapper, silver-haired operators, both in their sixties, have broken many of the scoops claimed by better-known reporters and newscasters. The *Enquirer* has local private investigators on its payroll and keeps at least two reporters in Modesto at all times. After the paper gleefully reported in May that it had "penetrated the ongoing investigation," the Modesto Police Department began an internal scrutiny of the force. But if you ask Hanrahan who his source on the force is, he'll say, "That's not the way it works. Cops all have girlfriends, sisters, uncles, mothers." It's not just the cops' closest who can't resist, though. Even the families of the victims get in line: Laci's father, Dennis Rocha, sold his story, along with family pictures, to the *Enquirer's* sibling publication the *Globe*—which outbid the *Enquirer*—for $12,000.

In this increasingly frenzied and downscale news era, the weekly tabloids—which were once considered beneath contempt by the establishment press—are must-reads for everyone in the media. And their methods have paid off in more tangible ways, too. According to Steve Coz, former editorial director of American Media, which publishes the *National Enquirer, Globe,* and *Star,* every Laci Peterson cover has increased sales of each of the three weeklies by as many as 300,000 copies.

At four P.M., while giant satellite trucks jockey for curb space, Hanrahan greets the bar's owner, Gary Gervasoni, as an old friend and orders his first vodka and soda. Gervasoni's, just a few blocks from the Stanislaus County Courthouse, is a popular spot with locals. Before the murder, Laci's stepfather, Ron Grantski, used to drop in. It's just the sort of entrenched-in-the-community place that *Enquirer* reporters favor to find out which doors to knock on. They also trawl certain restaurants and churches.

Today a tough-looking construction worker in shorts and sneakers pops in to ask whether something he has come across is worth anything. Hanrahan says the man has contacted the *Enquirer,* which routinely pays $500 per tip, because he believes he has uncovered a satanic mural in a house he is remodeling. Leading him over to a booth, Hanrahan pulls a notebook out of his back pocket and starts writing.

Anything smacking of satanic cults is big, since Mark Geragos, the attorney for Laci's husband, Scott (who stands accused of murdering her and their unborn baby), promised to find the "real killers." It was Geragos who started the search for a brown van seen in Laci's neighborhood. According to Geragos, the vehicle supposedly had some connection to a satanic cult. He added that he was also trying to locate a reluctant female witness who had valuable information. Whether the woman was linked to the van was not made clear at first.

The *Enquirer* reporters, who are convinced of Scott Peterson's guilt, tell me that Geragos is "all smoke and mirrors." The *Globe* ran a story earlier saying that the police had already checked out the brown van. As for the mysterious woman, she had contacted the *Globe* as well as the police, but then her ex-husband told the former that she had a history of mental illness and multiple-personality disorder.

Nevertheless, partly because the prosecution has played the case so close to the vest and partly because of the media feeding frenzy, the defense has had ample opportunity to cast doubt on Peterson's guilt. Geragos has filled the void and the media's desperate need to provide alternative scenarios. Former judge Robert G. M. Keating, dean of the New York State Judicial Institute, told me, "Defense lawyers often try to throw out red herrings in hopes that some member of the jury someday will say, 'Hey, what about that dragon somebody saw?'" In this case, the strategy has worked, particularly since cable news channels have to fill the air 24/7. A Fox News poll taken early in June showed that fifty-eight percent of Americans thought that Scott Peterson was involved in his wife's murder. A month earlier the number had been sixty-seven percent.

Earlier that same day, May 29, about one P.M. eastern daylight time, NBC chief legal correspondent Dan Abrams excitedly announced a bombshell on MSNBC: he had "exclusively obtained" a partial copy of the addendum to the sealed report on the autopsy of the remains of Laci's baby. (Official sources later confirmed the authenticity to the Associated Press.) The document revealed that the fully formed fetus had been found with a piece of plastic tape wound around its neck one and a half times, "with extension to a knot near the left shoulder." There was also a "post-mortem tear" going from the baby's right shoulder to the right lateral abdominal wall. Until then, the baby's separation from Laci had been assumed to be the result of "coffin birth," in which the built-up gas in the mother's decomposing body expels the fetus. Now, suddenly, there was the tantalizing idea that the baby might have been cut out of Laci's womb.

This news, combined with Geragos's remarks about satanic cults, sent the media pack racing: thirty minutes later, the cult idea was being discussed on Fox cable by Linda Vester and Rita Cosby, who gave no credit to Abrams. Meanwhile, Abrams reappeared with a lawyer who scored the case, as it now stood, like a tennis match: "Advantage defense!" At three P.M., Pat Buchanan and Bill Press abandoned national politics to focus "almost exclusively on the breaking news first reported here on MSNBC by Dan Abrams." By four o'clock, CNN had announced that the prosecution, citing "numerous leaks to the media today," had sent out a press release requesting that the judge make public the full autopsy report. At five P.M. both Wolf Blitzer on CNN and Lester Holt on MSNBC were discussing the feeding frenzy. MSNBC editor in chief Jerry Nachman characterized the story as "crack for us in the business . . . we can't stop ourselves."

His words proved prophetic. Fox's Geraldo Rivera, who claimed—two hours after Abrams's scoop—also to have the full addendum, was back at eight P.M. But now, on Bill O'Reilly's show, Rivera was going out of his way to pooh-pooh the new information. He said that the addendum did not support material "spun earlier by sources friendly to the defense."

In David Wright's opinion, "This cable thing is like Fleet Street in the old days. One paper would have a scoop, and the other papers would trash it but be free to follow it up." He was right: it was all Laci all the time throughout the evening—on Chris Matthews's *Hardball*, *Hannity and Colmes*, *Larry King Live*, *Scarborough Country*, and *On the Record* with Greta Van Susteren. The flurry kept on the next day, May 30, when *Good Morning America* announced that ABC had seen the autopsy report "in full exclusively." Charles Gibson noted that, according to the findings, Peterson's cervix was closed; he had been assured by an expert, he added, that "this can happen." Soon local newspapers in California were quoting coroners closer to home who said that the plastic tape was most likely debris caught around the baby's neck and that the cut may have been made by a boat propeller.

That night the *Enquirer* reporters introduced me to a local criminal-defense investigator sitting at the other end of Gervasoni's bar. Alan Peacock, who wasn't working for either side, handed me his business card, which read, "Fruits and Nutz," a play on Modesto's largest cash crops—not counting sensational criminal cases that include, pre-Laci, the murder of Modesto native Chandra Levy. Absolutely free of charge, Peacock gave me a rundown on the defense's satanic-cult theory; it's proving remarkably accurate as the story has played out since.

Peacock explained that ten years ago he had worked on a murder case, in nearby Salinas, involving members of a satanic cult. All were convicted and remain behind bars, but the mere existence of the previous case gives Geragos and company an opening to speculate that individuals from the satanic group are still around. "If I'm a criminal-defense attorney, I'm going to get someone to sell the public, to get people to look a different way," Peacock explains. "If I can identify a suspect or a vehicle that law enforcement doesn't want to deal with or account for, I can put out a call for the occupants of a brown vehicle." In fact, there were reports of a brown van in Laci Peterson's neighborhood at the time she disappeared. The police claimed that it belonged to landscapers, but Peacock says the occupants were not identified and witnesses reported that the vehicle had no lawn mowers or rakes in it. Peacock also told me the defense had found out about the people in the van from the police files and had figured that the authorities had not looked hard enough for them.

"The defense also put out a call for a young woman who had floated through a rape-crisis center. She claimed she was raped by two women while the men [in a brown van] watched, ten days before Laci disappeared," Peacock says. The woman also asserted, "according to the defense theory," that "if you want to see the other part of this sacrifice, keep a close look at the newspapers and read about it Christmas Day." Peacock added, however, that she wasn't the only woman to make such a claim. "There was a prior point in April in Merced [a town about forty miles from Modesto] where a woman spoke of a similar circumstance—a similar night with a similar group of people. Police wrote her off as a kook, but the defense always needs kooks."

Peacock mentioned, too, that one of the van's occupants allegedly had a tattoo on his arm—"666," supposedly a satanic symbol—and that the defense leaked this information. He said that the whole idea was "to draw attention away from Scott Peterson and give the public someone different to look for. . . . They are satisfied the cult is the way to go." Since Peacock told me this, the defense has leaked more details. Scott Peterson's lawyers are seeking a man named Donnie with a "666" tattoo and a woman who was raped and who later reportedly told a rape center employee that her attackers said she could read about the rest of the ritual on Christmas Day.

Saying he admires Geragos's manipulation of the media, Peacock suggested that it was half of a two-part defense strategy. If the trial takes place in Modesto, Peacock believes, Geragos—after doing his work on the media and with the satanic-cult theory—can sit back and let Kirk McAllister, Scott Peterson's original Modesto attorney, take the lead. "Kirk is the one who can step in with a lot of credibility with the locals." (In January 2004 the trial was moved to San Mateo, California.)

Less than two weeks later, on June 12, Judge Al Girolami issued a far-reaching gag order to stanch the flood of leaks and speculations. It prohibits all involved lawyers and their staffs, court and law-enforcement employees, and potential witnesses from discussing the case or releasing any relevant documents, photos, or information. But it seemed more than a little late. The show, by now, was in full swing. By this time even the supporting cast was hiring celebrity lawyers who had logged plenty of camera time.

One part of the fallout from a story of this magnitude is its impact on ordinary people suddenly thrust into the spotlight. A prize example is Amber Frey, the twenty-eight-year-old massage therapist from Fresno, who was also Scott Peterson's mistress. Frey is the most important witness in the prosecution's case, because Scott Peterson told her he was unmarried when they met, about a month before Laci disappeared.

(Their affair was so intense that Frey sent out Christmas cards with the couple's picture on them—one of the pictures the *Enquirer* paid dearly to acquire.) For the prosecution, Frey provides the motive for Laci's murder.

Shortly before Laci disappeared, Scott corrected his previous explanation, telling Amber that he was a widower. In fact, he did not admit he was the husband of Laci until twelve days after she disappeared. Earlier, Amber had thought Scott's story that he would be in Europe for Christmas fishy enough to get a private-investigator friend to check him out. Now, she went right to the police and told them all she knew. She also wore a wire for the prosecution, and, as the *Enquirer* first reported in May, Scott told her that he had not killed Laci but knew who had. This was something he never told the police.

Amber Frey is the single biggest interview a reporter can get—except Peterson himself. But she refuses all offers and has received no money for her information. In February, the *Enquirer* published seminude pictures of her from 1999 with braces on her teeth (she had signed away the rights years before). Because of those pictures, her credibility in a courtroom will certainly be under attack, and she can expect to be pilloried by the defense. To provide a queenly foil for Mark Geragos, Frey has retained well-known, impeccably groomed victims'-rights lawyer Gloria Allred of Los Angeles, who sometimes makes the networks come to a studio of her choosing for the sound bites she so frequently gives out. As one lawyer put it, "The quickest way to get a broken leg is to get between Gloria Allred and a camera."

The rare onscreen opportunity she missed was a crucial one. On June 5, Fox's Van Susteren dramatically lowered the ethical bar and invited Larry Flynt of *Hustler* magazine to discuss the negotiations he was going through to acquire the topless pictures of Amber. (Van Susteren kept flashing the photo with a red banner over the breasts.) Referring to Frey's work, Flynt slandered both Amber and her profession by saying that a masseuse is "just a glorified term for a hooker." Van Susteren refused to comment to me for this article, but the next night she began her program by telling Allred, "It's no secret I am a fan of Amber's" and "I imagine it's pretty tough on her." Equally surprising, Allred responded to the previous night's vulgarity by complimenting Van Susteren: "You're a very sensitive person to recognize this."

Watching all this from Fresno was one of the most colorful characters in the story, Ron Frey, Amber's gruff, voluble father, a fifty-one-year-old general contractor with a fondness for tying the media in knots. Without telling him that Flynt was going to be on the show, he says, Van Susteren's staff had begged him to call in. He had previously called in to Rita Cosby's show on Fox News in February to denounce David Wright when the *Enquirer* first published the pictures. But he is now on friendly terms with Wright, who made the nearly one hundred-mile pilgrimage from Modesto to Fresno in an attempt to persuade Ron to ask Amber if she would accept $100,000 for an exclusive interview plus pictures of her and Scott. "She sat there and said, 'It just doesn't seem right.' That brought tears to my eyes, when you see a kid do that," Ron Frey told me during my own pilgrimage to Fresno.

I have since learned that when Amber's name surfaced last winter, a number of producers and reporters, hoping to catch her visiting her dad, embedded themselves for up to two weeks at a time in Ron Frey's eighty-one-year-old mother's house, where he lives. First he made some of them promise, on network letterhead, not to repeat or report anything they saw or heard there. Frey claims he still has the letters in his safe. "CBS, Diane Sawyer's staff—they'd all be sitting here all day long," he said. "They were here so much they know my dog's name, my mother's name. They would talk about my little dachshund, who is kind of smart. He dresses himself, but they never got to see that."

"Pardon me?"

"My little dog puts his own shirt on. Larry King's producer, after the war, called me up awhile back, and she said, 'Do you want to do the show? And your mother? And your little dog, Buddy?' See, they know." Setting me straight on Amber's supposed makeover, Frey explained that his daughter had first appeared on camera with no makeup and messy, dirty-blond hair. That, he said, was because the *Enquirer* had revealed her affair with Peterson, and she had to hide from the media in the ladies' room at work until the Modesto police took her to a hastily called press conference. At the subsequent news conference, at which she named Allred as her attorney, she was back to her normal platinum blond. Or so says her father. Since his ordeal began, Frey has put on thirty-five pounds, much of it while dining out with the media. He has received more than five thousand phone calls from reporters, on several lines. At first his construction workers helped him answer the calls, which he carefully logs, "but they won't do it anymore." He adds, "I was down to one cigarette a day; now I'm back to a pack." This admission came after he told me, "I put in nine hours of work yesterday and six hours on the phone last night answering the media."

Frey got additional media attention after the *Modesto Bee* and the *Fresno Bee* published a letter of his praising the courage of his daughter as well as of his son, Jason, a captain in the United States Army in Iraq, for doing their duty for their country. The letter prompted the *Today* show to float the possibility of putting Ron and Amber on a satellite phone with

Jason on Father's Day. But when Amber declined, the conversation was placed on hold.

Apart from the statements Amber Frey made when she came forward and when she retained Allred, the only time she has spoken to the press was to denounce her onetime close friend Sherina Vincent for selling photos she had taken of Amber and Scott at a Christmas party to *People* magazine. Vincent is suing *People* for failing to crop a picture of herself in the background of one shot and for not paying her the full $15,000 she claims she was originally offered. (One of the pictures, it seems, also showed up on Fox News and in the *New York Post*.) "That's appalling that she's doing this," Amber Frey told the *Fresno Bee*. "She doesn't want her picture in the magazine, but it's OK that she sells the photos and profits off me, Laci Peterson and her baby?"

"Here we go—whatever it is, whoever it is." After saying that, the tall TV cameraman outside the Modesto courthouse on the day Geragos made his first appearance shoved me, politely, out of the way. Around us, I counted eighteen cameras mounted on tripods, three handheld cameras, and eleven satellite dishes on the street—in other words, it was a relatively quiet day. Off to the side, however, an ambulance was at the ready, lights blinking, because word had just come out that a woman inside had fainted. All the news reporters were clearly hoping that it had been Jackie Peterson, Scott's mother, who usually carries a breathing aid with tubes in her nose. She had appeared frail as she entered the courthouse earlier. When, suddenly, the doors swung open and a flushed, heavyset woman was carried out on a stretcher, the cameras stopped whirring. You could hear the sighs of disappointment.

When Jackie Peterson did emerge, on her feet, she said of Geragos: "God sent him our way." Before God intervened, Geragos had been a regular on CNN's *Larry King Live*, where he declared that finding Laci's body so near to where Scott had been fishing was "devastating" to Peterson's case. There were rumors that the Petersons, who are well-off, had put one of their imported cars—a Jaguar—up for sale to help pay for their son's defense. Geragos, like Allred, is a real Hollywood character; for him a day without flashbulbs and microphones is like a day without prayer for the pope. Once hired, he immediately took charge, down to the smallest details. Even the awful tie Scott Peterson wore the first day in court with Geragos had been chosen so that the defendant would not appear designer-slick. Although Geragos is known to be highly considerate toward the media, he can also be tough. Sandy Rivera of NBC, visiting at the Petersons' house near San Diego, was once close to network Nirvana—five minutes from finishing copying the videotape of Laci and Scott's wedding—when Geragos telephoned, heard what was happening, and ordered her to stop. Days before Judge Girolami issued the gag order, I asked Geragos if he thought the judge would do so. He laughed and said, "That would be so futile."

The networks each have white tents, which are spread out across the street from the courthouse. The scene is like a giant media bazaar, with numerous talking heads selling their wares over the airwaves. Until recently, a local denizen with some radio experience knocked on the doors of the satellite trucks daily to ask if any man-on-the-street sound bites were needed.

Modesto's resources have been severely taxed by the TV-and-press crowd, and the city plans to ask the California legislature for money from the state—which is broke—to help bail it out. Detective Doug Ridenour of the Modesto Police Department, which has about seven detectives on the case, told me they have received thousands of calls from the media and more than ten thousand leads, hundreds of them from psychics. It costs money to follow up on all these tips—many from obsessive, lonely people glued to the media drama and hoping to be drawn into its feverish embrace.

More than four hundred media professionals have signed up on a Web site sponsored by the Stanislaus County Sheriff's Department. Created by a twenty-year-old named Scott Campbell for $95, it allows everyone to see the latest court documents, displays a photograph of a cell like Scott Peterson's, and answers frequently asked questions about the defendant. "I even get requests to interview the inmate who cuts his hair," the sheriff's spokesperson, Kelly Huston, told me. Sheriff Les Weidman said that TV people lurk outside the jail in hopes of catching a released inmate who might pass on a smidgen about Peterson. About sixty other inmates have been awaiting trial on murder charges in the Stanislaus County jail, he added, some of them for as long as three years. "We have a guy who allegedly stabbed his wife and unborn child not that far away from Scott. He ended up on page 2 in the local-news section."

To give some idea of the mass interest in the story, the official Laci Peterson Web site has received more than 20 million hits since January. "Every time we put [the story] on, the ratings spike," Fox News's Bill O'Reilly told me. "It's the only thing keeping Larry King on the air. We do Laci Peterson every fifteen minutes and see the numbers go up. It's a story that resonates with women particularly." Wendy Whitworth, executive producer of *Larry King Live*, countered, "I don't determine what I do according to Fox." Van Susteren, who has virtually turned her show into the Laci Peterson hour, is getting more than double the ratings of her main competitor, Aaron Brown on CNN, who specializes in hard news.

Granted, the cable audiences are small—usually fewer than a million—but Laci's story is also a staple of network news in the morning and network magazine shows. The total number of hours devoted to the Peterson case represents a good part of the most fought-for time on the airwaves. Moreover, the depths to which those involved sometimes sink to get the story or to become part of the story have a pernicious influence across mainstream media. "It's gotten out of hand, the reliance on the tabloids for stories," said NBC's Dan Abrams. "It's just happened—it's a new phenomenon." (In the interest of full disclosure, I am married to Tim Russert of NBC News.)

Others point out, however, that cable gives networks such as NBC the opportunity to have it both ways. "Tom Brokaw can still be clean and pure on the network, and MSNBC can be as greasy as they want, and they can say, Hey, this is just cable," noted Tim Daly, a Stockton-based reporter for the ABC-TV affiliate in Sacramento, who is alarmed at the level of coverage of a single story. "We are not naive enough to say that Laci Peterson is not news, but is it news every day? The answer is no."

Other local TV people in Modesto and outlying markets complained to me that unsubstantiated rumors about the case were too often making it onto the air. "I've done stories about all the false rumors just to dispel them," said Gloria Gomez, who is also based in Stockton, for KOVR, the CBS affiliate in Sacramento, and who got an early interview with Scott Peterson. Yet recently her station broadcast as its lead story the unconfirmed account of a man who said that two years previously he had played golf with someone who *might* have been Scott Peterson. According to the source, the possibly Peterson golfer said he had gotten married too early and did not want children. The story was repeated to me by a local cabdriver—a potential member of the jury—as proof of Peterson's guilt. One night the panels of lawyers on Larry King and Greta Van Susteren made much of a potential witness, who had appeared on the shows, named Michael Chiavetta. A neighbor of Scott and Laci's, he said he had seen the Petersons' dog in a nearby park the morning of her disappearance. He believed he might also have glimpsed Laci herself in the background. I later learned that he has one glass eye.

Having dinner one night in Modesto, I didn't pay much attention to a blond woman at the bar chatting and laughing with friends. But I did recognize one of the women with her as Kim Petersen, who is a controversial figure in the story. Petersen is Modesto's high priestess of grief management, the media handler for the Rocha family, including Sharon Rocha, Laci Peterson's mother. Nobody gets near Rocha without Petersen's okay. So, in one of those surreal scenes that materialize in small towns with big stories, I suddenly realized that the blond woman a few feet away from me was Sharon Rocha, watching Van Susteren interview two of Laci's close friends over at the media bazaar. Rocha herself had been on the night before.

Stacey Boyers, one of the young women being interviewed, had known Laci since third grade and her mother, Terri Western, had run the Laci Peterson volunteer center. Boyers complained that she was forever being told by TV people: "Let us see you crying. Try to talk about the intimate moments, and when you start to lose it, don't stop. Put your arm on your friend and hold on." Traditionally, news programmers have interviewed people who could advance a story. But that is no longer the rule. There have been endless lengthy interviews on the Laci case that are virtually content-free. "Our mission is different," Michael Reel, a producer with CBS News, told me. "It's not being factual; it's a different genre. We see people going through tragedy in the midst of the storm."

Boyers and the Rocha family continue to be amazed at the callousness of some of the reporting on television. One night on Jay Leno's show, Geraldo Rivera, referring to the continued dredging for the remains of Laci and the baby, said, "Every tuna in San Francisco Bay is going to be looking for lunch." Rivera also took credit for announcing which limbs were missing from Laci's body—information that had appeared in the *Contra Costa Times* a month earlier. Kim Petersen called a press conference to announce that Sharon Rocha had been shocked to hear, without warning, about the tape around baby Conner's neck. But when I asked Phil Griffin, head of prime-time programming at MSNBC, whether he thought the families should get a heads-up, he said, "If you did that, you'd spend all your time trying to reach people to tell them. If you found out new information about Bill's relationship with Monica, should you call up Hillary to let her know? I don't think it's our job."

Ironically, Sharon Rocha chose to tell of her anguish over what Dan Abrams of NBC first revealed about the condition of her grandson's body to another NBC interviewer, Katie Couric, early in June.

Petersen is a former third-grade teacher who learned grief counseling on the job as a volunteer in the 1999 Yosemite National Park slayings, in which a mother, a daughter, and a friend were murdered. Later she became head of the Sund-Carrington Memorial Foundation, which was set up by the family of one of the victims to help find missing persons whose families cannot afford to pay for assistance. She is a typical, though high-ranking, member of the professional support staffs now on duty during media dramas, and has also worked with Chandra Levy's parents. On the walls of her office she has smiling pictures featuring herself with a devastated Susan Levy, mother of Chandra, and in the company of Stone Philips of NBC's *Dateline* and other media celebrities. She frequently appears on *Larry King Live* and the *Today* show.

In a highly competitive atmosphere such as Modesto, a gatekeeper like Petersen is closely watched, and Petersen has found herself under intense scrutiny: many reporters feel that she gives them short shrift in favor of more famous names. The *Modesto Bee*, which has been a model of probity on this story, makes a practice of rarely mentioning her name. Early last January, when Laci was still considered missing, Kirk McAllister, Scott Peterson's original attorney, received a three-page anonymous letter signed by "select members of the local and national news media." It condemned Petersen for "unprofessional bias towards select 'favorite' news organizations" and for "inappropriately spreading rumors and innuendo about Scott Peterson." (Petersen says the letter contained "blatant lies," adding, "I wouldn't ever care to do another media interview if my job didn't require it.") In June the Associated Press ran a story stating that much of Petersen's energy and devotion went to the cases of well-off families, such as the Rochas and the Levys, "that don't even meet one of [the Sund-Carrington Foundation's] basic criteria." Petersen's response: "We help any family that needs our help."

Whether she is liked by everyone or not, Petersen has amassed a unique power base by keeping the media from suffocating shell-shocked families. She handles ninety-five percent of the Rochas' mail and instructs family members on where to go, media-wise, for the largest audiences. She warns devastated families to expect to be questioned like suspects by the police. "I explain I want to reach as many people as possible in as few mediums as possible," Petersen told me. "These families aren't sleeping or eating. They age tremendously." As for the media's ethical violations, Petersen feels they come with the territory. "When you get into a high-profile case, the dynamics and people's motives are deplorable."

Unlike O. J. Simpson, who never gave an interview before his arrest, Scott Peterson gave four—one to Diane Sawyer on ABC's *Good Morning*

America and the others to local TV reporters Gloria Gomez, Ted Rowlands of Fox's KTVU in Oakland, and Jodi Hernandez of NBC's KNTV in San Jose. Peterson falsely claimed to Sawyer that he had told the police immediately about Amber Frey. (He later called Sawyer and reversed his statement.) He also said that there had not been any other women in his life while he was married, although there are already unconfirmed reports of at least two others. Anything in those interviews that conflicts with what Peterson told police investigators will be fair game for the prosecution at his preliminary hearing.

I've learned that, after Laci's disappearance, Peterson seemed a curious figure to those who saw him every day in Modesto before he left to spend most of his time in southern California. "He was very controlling—he had his guard up," said Rowlands. "He was very careful who he talked to, and he didn't want the camera on him at all, probably because he didn't want Amber Frey to see it—he had a couple of things going." Others were struck by his lack of emotion. Gloria Gomez recalled, "I said, 'You haven't mentioned anything about the baby.' 'It's very difficult' is all he said." Rita Cosby of Fox described Peterson as "numb and unemotional—more passionate about his golf game."

Apparently, however, Peterson could get quite animated, as he did about his desire to have a pet psychic flown in. "She claimed she could be with McKenzie [the Petersons' dog] for a day and be able to tell us what happened," said Terri Western, then director of the volunteer center. "He said, 'Let's bring her out.'" When the idea was vetoed, Scott said he would break the news to the psychic, adding: "I'm also letting you all know that if she's had to pay for her flight, and it's nonrefundable, I will be reimbursing her." Since then, several of Laci's friends who appeared on television showing little support for Scott have received identical letters from him. Western paraphrased what he had written to her daughter Stacey Boyers: "It's hard for me sitting in this cell knowing it's Laci's birthday; we had a tradition that we would fly a kite on her birthday. So if you get a chance, I'd really like for you to go fly a kite."

As I prepare to leave this surreal environment, Mark Geragos continues to predict vehemently that the "real killers" will be found. "It's clear she was abducted—that's the only thing that makes sense," he told me. "It's only a matter of time forensically and we'll find out who did it." Geragos said that a number of women had been abducted by "some pretty sick people out there," and that "we've got subpoenas out for records on various people." When I asked him how he knew that the brown van the police had picked up a second time to check out was the brown van that the defense had talked about so extensively, he said, "We don't necessarily." It will be tested again by the defense.

Not surprisingly, Geragos says he "doesn't mind" the media circus, but he admitted, "There is no way you can justify the coverage of this case. . . . It's a circle jerk." He wants to move the trial out of Modesto, where polls indicate that an overwhelming number of people think Scott Peterson is guilty. His change-of-venue strategy would argue that the media overkill is confined to cable TV, so if potential jurors haven't watched cable, don't live in Modesto, and weren't exposed to courtroom cameras during the preliminary hearing, there could be a chance of impaneling an untainted jury.

I found it interesting to learn, a mere three days after my conversation with Geragos, that Judge Roger Beauchesne had written that the defense had not produced evidence indicating that it was actually investigating any other suspects. In response, Mark Geragos asked the court to remove Beauchesne from the case.

If those covering the Laci Peterson case want to grade themselves, all they have to do is follow the preliminary hearing, when the prosecution will present some of the actual evidence—the facts. Then the world will be able to see just how much of the endless speculation is valid. To take just one example, I would like to know the truth about a mop taken from the Peterson house. The *National Enquirer* stands by its story that blood and vomit were found on it. A local newspaper reporter told me only blood was found, and Gloria Gomez said the mop had nothing at all on it. "Half the stuff you hear you don't report, because you can't substantiate it," Ted Rowlands told me. "I think a lot about what I've reported. Some of it will be true, some will be off. It will be really interesting to find out."

In the interim, the media's frenzied scramble to keep the Laci Peterson case on the air shows no abatement. One day a reporter from a local channel asked if he could interview me as a member of the national media covering the case in Modesto. "You want to do a story on me doing a story on you?" I asked incredulously. "Why?" "Because there is nothing else to report today," a cameraman blurted out.

Part I:

The DNA of Fame

Notes from the Celebrity-Industrial Complex I

As the Laci Peterson case proves, you don't have to be famous anymore to be famous. A media tornado can strike anywhere now, shaking up everyone in its path. Unlike O. J. Simpson—a football star and TV celebrity before his wife's murder—Laci and Scott Peterson were completely unknown. They were attractive looking (a top requirement for TV coverage) but did not appear destined for fame. Their story was not an obvious blockbuster, either; unfortunately, it's not that rare for husbands to be accused of killing pregnant wives. But the couples aren't usually so telegenic. "They didn't have any tattoos," a TV reporter told me about the Petersons—as if this said it all.

What Laci and Scott did have were media-savvy friends who knew how to get TV airtime during the Christmas news lull when Laci vanished. Those friends had pictures and video, too—enough images to engrave the missing woman's passage from little girl to bride to radiant expectant mommy right on to our collective cortex. So now Laci has become an icon, a kind of star—mainly because the restless media is constantly trolling for the newest bait to hook the audience. Today, becoming famous has more to do with feeding the insatiable media beast than with the person. Or the story. Or the talent. Or the impact.

You could say that the publicity mill has always operated that way, starting with William Randolph Hearst's newspaper empire. But these days the dimensions are different: "The media"—now a morass of cross-pollinating companies—is far bigger and its appetite for higher ratings, higher profits—*more, more, more*—affects stories, stars, and also the truth. We live in a global era of extremes: extreme media presence, extreme stories, extreme recognition. Everybody's out for some action—and those who succeed know how to stoke the flame. The omnipresent world of celebrity—which now bridges entertainment, politics, and news—is dominated by expert, expensive stage managers who understand the DNA, the very chemistry, of fame and how to create it. They can tilt coverage and cameras any way they choose. The Internet can put any rumor into play whether or not it is accurate. Reality now is something to be created, played with, adjusted for maximum appeal. Welcome to the world of the reality soap opera, where celebrity sells everything, where complicated news stories are served up in entertaining ways and then get made into movies—where it's harder and harder to tell fact from fiction.

My work in this book comes from a topsy-turvy climate—a war zone of media monsters and million-dollar spin. It is a different, hyped-up, star-obsessed, more intense, and more artificial reality than when I began my career, in the 1970s, observing and writing about lives lived in the spotlight of politics and entertainment. With cable TV, the Internet, and the ballooning size of the media conglomerates, there is more need for content and airtime to fill. But what do we get? A lot less meaning and a lot less real product. Politics is often served up as scandal. News is more and more centered on the latest sensational drama. Stars edge out coverage of world events with breathless reports about their latest deals and endorsements. We get scoops on who is behaving badly with ditzy heiresses who sleep around, who dropped which agent, who wore what designer's dress and jewelry to transform herself into a human billboard on the red carpet. Call it a subliminal message about money, consumption, and a seemingly unattainable lifestyle. But the fact is, fame has come uncoupled from achievement and is an end in itself.

One need not look further than page one of the distinguished *New York Times* to see how far celebrity coverage has come and how it dominates. In the last year or so, page one of the *Times* has featured such previously unthinkable stories as the deaths of singers Aaliyah and Celia Cruz, not to mention the mauling of Las Vegas liontamer Roy Horn of Siegfried and Roy, and an analysis of the career of Britney Spears. Where will it all end?

"Why do I know that Lenny Kravitz has a shark swimming under his glass bedroom floor but have no idea what music he has put out since

1995?" a friend asked me. Why are millions who have never watched *Sex and the City* so well acquainted with the clothes, shoes, and baby-in-the-stroller outings of Sarah Jessica Parker? Why did so much about Bill Clinton's sex life overshadow the fact that we were in increasing danger from terrorists?

When we look for information about public figures today, we get trends, clothes, pets, marriage partners, significant others, workouts, how the "crib" is decorated, the details of plastic surgery and rehab, an endless parade of lifestyle and process. No longer do we get context, or content. Nor do we hear much about their work. Now, if you are a star—if you are Cameron or Justin or Demi—your life, or some reasonable facsimile of it, becomes your greatest performance, replayed endlessly in a series of fast cuts on video news shows. Shopping, clinging on crowded dance floors, appearing at awards ceremonies: all of these photo opportunities keep you visible and marketable, and frequently overshadow whatever talent or skill you may possess. But this fixation on process is not limited to Hollywood stars. Increasingly in sports we learn about contract disputes and money paid rather than points scored; in politics it is the horse race, the performance, the contest handicapped by the political consultants, instead of what the politician stands for.

Joan Didion once wrote an influential essay in the *New York Review of Books* in which she argued that in Hollywood in the seventies, deal making was becoming the true art form. Now, however, the values of Hollywood are pervasive and the art form is spinning a lifestyle that gets stars and all sorts of celebrities in the media and keeps them hot. Then comes the deal. The work itself is a pretty low priority, particularly considering time spent at the gym and plastic surgeons. Today the personality is nothing without the posse, the portfolio, the designer duds, the relationship, the stuff. With mainstream media going downmarket to meet the tabs whose format and style increasingly set the pace, it is the lifestyles of the richer and more famous that have become the art form. As shame takes a holiday, process is all.

In this book, I want to take you inside the world of those willing to sacrifice everything, including, sometimes, their lives, to be famous. I want to show you the workings of the celebrity machine in several arenas (news, Hollywood, politics) so that you gain insight into the lives of the driven people who have come to dominate so much of what passes for journalism and entertainment.

This book is an informal tour of what I call the Celebrity-Industrial Complex: the media monster that creates the reality we think we see, and the people who thrive or perish there. My challenge, as a reporter in this environment, is to bring the story back alive, accurately, to find the key that unlocks the personalities, the story, or the crime. I don't mind digging in grubby places. My early experience as a Peace Corps volunteer in Medellin, Colombia, prepared me to fit in at any level. I am also more than willing to pore through thousands of pages of court documents, or whatever is necessary. Often there are scores of highly paid obfuscators in the path of the story. They increase the thrill of the hunt. Willing subjects with high-paid lawyers often get court records sealed; law-enforcement authorities cover their mistakes; any number of spinmeisters or fawning acolytes steer reporters clear of the truth. That is their job. Mine is to find the reality behind the facade. What are the circumstances behind person X's behavior? What is the motivation? Who is the actual human being hiding behind the make-believe life? A huge "Made for TV and Tabloids" bubble surrounds the famous and infamous today. My job is to pierce it, pull it back.

For example, in the Laci story, Scott Peterson's attorney Mark Geragos— a seasoned practitioner who represented Winona Ryder after her shoplifting arrest and is now defending Michael Jackson—clearly earns his salary and knows how to play the media big-time. When he took over Peterson's defense, he needed to provide a little drama to divert attention from the fact that there were no suspects in Laci's murder besides his client. Voilà— satanic cults. It was the devil-worshipers who did it! Call in the cameras. Talk about the old razzle-dazzle. Except now it's more dazzling than ever. And the reality is getting lost. Geragos's demonology had the thrill of a horror movie. Unfortunately, it had as little credibility. Still, legal professionals on TV endlessly discussing satanic cults—and legitimizing Geragos's claims—became part of the story that the public absorbed. Reality and entertainment merged right before our eyes.

In writing about Laci Peterson, I intentionally made the process—the story of the story—my subject. As a lone reporter, I didn't stand a chance to compete with the phalanx of video and print teams who had been camped in Modesto for months. Or with the tabloids who pay big money for scoops. Paying for sources is obviously a practice forbidden to me and other mainstream journalists, although the standards continue to change. In such real-life sagas as those of Laci or Private First Class Jessica Lynch—elevated to heroine status after beefed-up claims of her emptying her gun on her attackers in Iraq—the old rules of serious journalism are under siege.

Media conglomerates have a lot of power and many ways to broker deals. Once-patrician CBS News, now owned by giant Viacom, was so gung-ho to get the first TV interview with former Private Lynch (who admits she has no memory of what happened to her) that, in exchange for Jessica's first televised words, Viacom was prepared to offer a package deal, with elements drawn from all branches of its corporate domain—a book deal from Simon & Schuster; a movie deal, presumably from Paramount Television; an hour-long MTV appearance; and a concert with Columbia recording artists in her hometown in West Virginia. Where does journalism end and entertainment begin?

Because the rules of journalism are bending so dangerously, we need to know how the Celebrity-Industrial Complex actually functions in a major story, like the Laci Peterson case. In my Laci piece, I tried to take my readers beyond the screen to highlight the contrast between the on-the-ground "reality" of the media bazaar, with its talking heads, and the much smaller, more controlled picture you see at home. How the case avalanched into the national consciousness, how "the wildness of celebrity" distorted the events—these, to me, were the untold parts of the story. And they had to be explained.

If we are going to worship celebrity, let's have a clear idea of who is up on the altar. Celebrity culture, which now extends beyond the arts and sports into politics and business, has become such a huge area of interest with so much monetary and cultural impact that it demands as much investigative reporting as the White House or Wall Street. But it has yet to get it regularly. That is unfortunate because, increasingly, big businesses and parts of the government such as the Pentagon have learned to use their own celebrities or manufactured ones like Jessica Lynch as go-betweens with consumers, the public, and voters. Familiar faces, everyone now seems to realize, not only attract large audiences; they provoke sympathy, trust, and identification.

Stories on so-called personalities like Martha Stewart can reveal the world of big business (or in her case, bad business). Yet, too often, mainstream journalists ignore the larger dimensions and sobering aspects of these stories, letting the tabloids take the lead as readers drown in fatuous or sinister spin. As a result, a lot of rather revealing truths get overlooked. I have found it no easier to peel away the layers of a story like Michael Jackson's or untangle the complicated finances of Hollywood money manager Dana Giacchetto than to tackle "more serious" subjects like the connection between terrorism and drugs or the latest White House scandal, which I have also covered.

The FBI wiretap investigation into now-jailed private investigator

Anthony Pellicano—who figures prominently in my Michael Jackson stories—and the kind of work he did for some of Hollywood's most prominent lawyers has been treated seriously. But what about an analysis of Elizabeth Smart or Jessica Lynch, stories that blanketed the airwaves for months and whose lives were made into supposedly factual TV movies that ran against one another during the November sweeps of 2003? Not far from the surface of each are truths to be told about American values, the media, and—in Lynch's case—the way the American government has sold the war in Iraq to Americans.

The tale of the kidnapping of fourteen-year-old Elizabeth Smart has always drawn the cameras, probably because of her pristine beauty. She even played the cello. However, shortly after she was found alive and physically unhurt, the media mob actually backed off the angelic-looking girl, who was abducted from her bed in Utah by a polygamist drifter. A zone of privacy seemed to have been established by the media after it was learned that Smart's abductor and his wife, who had kept the girl for nine months, were both being charged with sexual assault. It appeared as if there might actually be some limits to what the media was willing to report and the public's prurient interest. After all, Elizabeth was just a kid who had been through a very traumatic experience.

Yet within eight months, the actions of Smart's own family changed everything and the story again became fodder for the celebrity-industrial complex: Elizabeth's Mormon parents appeared to be cashing in with lucrative book and TV movie deals that thrust the little girl back into the limelight. (Even her uncles wrote a book.) The Smarts justified their actions by explaining they had no choice but to go public: Why should they let someone else beat them to it? Someone who wouldn't tell "the truth"? So began another wave of coverage. So much for privacy. *TV Guide* even reported that Elizabeth—now generally portrayed as miraculously recovered from her complicated ordeal—was puzzled about why she was not allowed to play herself in the TV movie based on her harrowing experience!

Jessica Lynch also became instant myth and, despite my sympathies for the young soldier, that's what her story turned out to be—mostly a myth. Yet even since her story has been mostly discredited, the press has been reluctant to focus on how Jessica and the media themselves were used by the Pentagon and the White House to rally the country behind the war when the news was getting worse. Instead, even serious journalists seemed much more eager to jump on the bandwagon, sentimentalize the events surrounding Lynch, and continue the sham.

The fairy tale began with a page-one story in the *Washington Post,* based on anonymous military sources. According to these sources, Private First Class Lynch, caught in a gun battle in Nasiriyah, had fought fiercely— emptying her rifle on the Iraqi enemy. In the course of attempting to resist, she was shot at and stabbed. The next installment came nine days later with her dramatic rescue from an Iraqi hospital by U.S. commandos and Navy SEALS, who reportedly blazed in with guns and video cameras, knocking down doors.

Jessica's return was trumpeted as the first successful rescue of a POW since World War II. We learned that the Americans had been alerted to Lynch's whereabouts by an Iraqi lawyer, whose wife was apparently a nurse at the hospital where Jessica was held. We were told that he had seen a badly injured Lynch being slapped across the face by her military captors and had risked his life to alert the U.S. command to where she was being held. He and his family were brought to the U.S. and he got a book deal that became the basis for the NBC TV movie about Lynch.

On the home front, this amazing story of a pale wisp of a country girl, barely twenty years old, naturally attracted sympathy. Her family, her neighbors, her hometown of Palestine, West Virginia, practically her entire state, became staples of the 24-hour news cycle for weeks. Jessica Lynch's name appeared more times in the press than General Tommy Franks, who was in charge of the military effort.

But the international media, notably the BBC, began questioning the facts. The English discovered that U.S. force had not been necessary in Lynch's rescue: the Americans had been told outside the hospital that there were no Iraqi fighters inside. But the White House did nothing to correct the gross exaggerations and the Pentagon did not make it easy for the press to get the truth. (The *Washington Post* did not correct its erroneous reporting for over two months.) The myth of Jessica was simply too useful to the powers that be. A subsequent army investigation revealed that Lynch was not shot at or stabbed at the time of her capture. Her weapon had jammed and the fight in which she was captured ensued because her convoy had taken a wrong turn. Jessica herself said she spent the battle with her arms around her shoulders and her forehead on her knees, praying for her life. Beyond that, she has no memory of how she sustained the multiple fractures that have compromised her ability to walk. Nor does she know what transpired during the three hours or so it took for her to get to the hospital.

All these holes in the story didn't prevent it from being told and retold and sold and resold. In a further spin of the saga, Alfred Knopf, her venerable publishing house, launched her book, *I'm a Soldier Too*, with the news that Lynch *might* have been raped—a detail that the Pentagon had not seen fit to include after she was examined in Germany where she was first taken to recover. Again, Jessica says that she does not remember. Knopf, however, needed "new revelations" to launch the title. The *Philadelphia Inquirer* reviewer even accused the publishers of using "rape as a marketing tool."

Lynch, who was awarded the Bronze Star which is given for meritorious service, usually under fire, has displayed exemplary courage in her determination to stay alive and to walk again. But she has, understandably, had a complicated time negotiating the minefield of the media wars. She did not endorse the TV movie based on the book written by the man who allegedly helped save her life. In fact, she has largely ignored the Iraqi lawyer and she denies his claims that she was slapped by fedayeen soldiers. (She does remember her time in the Iraqi hospital.) Other sources say that the man's wife was not a nurse there, as he claimed in his explanations for his presence at the facility. This adds yet another dubious aspect to this now near-legendary but incredibly suspicious tale of heroism. When NBC aired the movie based on the doctor's book, they were forced to include a disclaimer because of the disputed facts.

Not surprisingly, Lynch suffered a backlash among fellow soldiers. Someone seeking to discredit Lynch sold topless photos of her to *Hustler* publisher Larry Flynt.

Lynch now admits she was used by the military in a public relations gambit, but has been honest enough to say that she has enjoyed the attention. After her big media week in New York to launch her book, Lynch told the Charlottesville, West Virginia, AP that she's "no longer the same little girl who grew up in Wirt County."

So, obviously, in the worlds of entertainment and politics, there are many skillfully maintained obstacles to truth.

The unceasing demands of filling the airwaves and print 24/7 have created a level of confusion—often a giant media mush—to penetrate, as well as a whole new set of requirements for those hapless souls caught in the maelstrom. If you become an accidental celebrity, take a loan and strap yourself in. You'll need a media handler who can help craft sound bites, a grief counselor who also books TV shows, an agent, a contract lawyer, a ghostwriter, an accountant, security guards, Capitol Hill contacts (should there be need for the passage of a relevant law), a suitable wardrobe, and a good haircut (for public appearances).

You'll also want several phone lines to handle media requests, someone to receive the solicitous knocks on the door from network bookers of guests (and to open the personal letters from Katie Couric, Diane Sawyer, and Barbara Walters), vases for bouquets from would-be interviewers, a functioning Web site, a crew to answer the e-mail, and another sort of counselor for when all the attention fades.

And it will. That's how it works now. The media moves on. The day before Laci Peterson's memorial service, I spoke to the family of Chandra Levy, the murdered Washington intern whose affair with Representative Gary Condit had generated similar media hoopla during the summer of 2002. Coincidentally, the Levys are also from Modesto, and they were full of genuine sympathy and compassion for the Petersons. Mrs. Levy remained an emotional wreck. She and her family were conflicted about attending the Peterson memorial; they didn't want to take any of the attention away from Laci's family. A few days later, a TV producer told me that when Mrs. Levy—who for nearly two years could virtually command the American airwaves—knocked on the doors of one of the big network satellite trucks in front of the Stanislaus County Courthouse during the Laci circus, hoping to read a poem she had written about her daughter, she was abruptly turned away. The scorch of fame can be brutal, but the chill of the aftermath is an even stranger, more bitter sensation.

Many who survive never acknowledge feeling the slam of the door on their faces; they just scope out a different entry and kick their way back in with new variations on what they're saying or selling. To keep the party going, new stories have to be at the ready. So if you want to extend your notoriety or sustain your bankability, you'd better have variations in the pipeline to keep the cameras satisfied. Change your politics, your hairstyle, your lifestyle—perhaps even your sexual preference. Decide you're the scarred child of some parental transgression. Recover a memory. If you alter your story completely, not to worry—hardly anyone will remember the ones you told before, will they? That's a question that everyone who thrives in the public eye has to consider.

For famous people in any field, an encounter with a journalist represents risk—a potential gash in the careful public portraits they are painting of themselves. They try to minimize their unguarded exposure and set the stage to their advantage. I used to joke about chronicling a lot of low people in high places. And they are often used to getting their way in print. Whereas I walk into an interview alone, my media-savvy subjects have usually been prepared by one or an entire retinue of expensive advisors. Everything from the place of meeting to the time of day is calculated. This is the big league, and the players are pros at games of control. In this book, I often set the scenes as I attempt to bring the cast of characters surrounding my subjects into the picture. It's instructive at times to show you the entire environment that surrounds these people. That is essential to providing a true sense of their complicated world.

This book endeavors to reveal and contrast the various stages of fame and power. Sometimes you actually luck out and get an interview with an extraordinary person at a particularly revealing moment. In rereading the chapter on Tina Turner, I am amazed by the level of candor that Turner—at perhaps the summit of her hard-won struggle to reclaim her life—displayed. She sat down and talked frankly, offering personal information and, I think, connecting with the millions of people who would read her words. So many conversations with stars today occur in the presence of handlers over, say, a single lunch. The celebrities are surrounded by people running around with clipboards and walkie-talkies and things in their ears and mikes in their mouths—as if the event were the invasion of Normandy. (A friend of mine, who observed the scene, said that it took a full twenty-five minutes for a dozen security people and handlers to orchestrate, in his pregubernatorial days, Arnold Schwarzenegger's walk from the door of a private Beverly Hills party to one of his three waiting SUVs.) I was able to be around Tina Turner long enough before the interview, watching her work in various locales, so that by the time we sat down to talk, she trusted me.

A vulnerable moment can also be especially productive. How a public person leaves the Big Tent is usually as important as how he or she enters, often more so. I obtained the first interview with Margaret Thatcher after her fall from power. The Iron Lady had ruled the British government for eleven years, and the sudden loss of all that authority and the perks that accompanied it was harsh. She told me her life was shattered, and the admission made headlines all over Britain. Yet Lady Thatcher bowed to no one. After losing her status as perhaps the world's most powerful woman, she stood by her principles, despite the fact that they, along with the imperiousness of her personality, had led stalwarts of her own Conservative Party to oust her from office. How to manage the next stage—how to stay famous, powerful, and influential without the office—was key. America offered promise: Britain was sick of Thatcher but the United States was not. Her friends were concerned that her greatest blind spot was her son, Mark, who had taken over the management of her affairs. Many of her friends and close associates, I felt, spoke to me in hopes she would see the light.

At a memorable point during my work on Thatcher, one of her less-discreet intimates told me that by the end of her time at 10 Downing Street, the woman who once commanded the world stage had become "slightly potty" and had "lost touch with reality."

You might be surprised how often this happens.

Proud Tina: Tina Turner

"Nothin' evah is nice and easy."

May 1993

The Rainforest Foundation benefit at Carnegie Hall on March 2, 1993, started out as one of those preachy-hip, politically correct, dead-in-the-tundra New York evenings. The stage was littered with stars—Dustin Hoffman, James Taylor, Sting, George Michael, Ian McKellen, Herb Alpert, Canadian rocker Bryan Adams—but even though Tom Jones woke up the audience by belting out "It's Not Unusual" Vegas-style, the white boys were mostly in the tepid zone.

Then came the hurricane. "Ladies and gentlemen, Miss Tina Turner." *Yes.* The queen mother of rock 'n' roll, fifty-three years old, with the body of a vamp, came running out in a tight black leather cat suit with tails and high platform boots. Her hair (piece) was a flying wedge of layered copper, and her powerful voice pierced the darkness like lightning: "When I was a little girl . . . I had a rag doll." Tina Turner was singing her classic "River Deep, Mountain High," her trademark legs swathed in leather, her moves sinuous. None of her bountiful energy had dissipated in the twenty-seven years since she first sang the song, and her little trademark Pony steps proved she could still coochie-coochie up to the guys.

James Taylor leapt to his feet and started shaking a tambourine, singing backup. Hoffman and McKellen joined him. Pretty soon, Turner had relegated all the superstar males to an adoring chorus. Afterward, Hoffman told her, "You've added ten years to my life."

"The first time you see Tina is mind-boggling," Keith Richards tells me. To Mick Jagger, she was "so gutsy and dynamic." Turner has long been an icon-mascot to the British supergroups, particularly the Rolling Stones, and even today she is revered more in Europe, where she makes her home with her younger German boyfriend, than in the States. Turner got her first wide exposure to young white audiences in the 1960s, when she and her former husband, Ike Turner, toured with the very youthful Mick and company in England.

Richards remembers that watching Ike and Tina, whom the Stones had idolized from records, was "kind of like school for us." At that point, "we were one little blues band," suddenly surrounded by "all these beautiful black chicks in sequins running around backstage, and these fantastic musicians to learn from." Every night, he says, "we'd do our little bit and then we'd watch Ike and Tina and the Ikettes, and we said, 'Wow, this is show business!' They made us realize you got to do more than just stand there and play the guitar." He adds, "To me it was all just Tina Turner. Ike didn't see it that way. To him he was a Svengali, who wrote the songs; he was the producer and Tina was his ticket. He saw himself as Phil Spector, as the driving force behind the star. I saw him as the driving force behind a lot of things. It was the first time I saw a guy pistol-whip another guy in his own band." Richards concludes, "Ike acted like a goddamned pimp."

To the outside world, however, Turner appeared oblivious. "That was when I was just being led blindly, because I didn't care about anything," she recalls. "I was just getting through this period." She was so immersed in Ike's reality that she didn't have any idea who Jagger was. "I had never seen a white person with lips that big anyway, so I didn't know who he was or what race he was." The one thing she realized, however, was that "he liked black women, liked to play around with them."

She and Mick became fast friends. "He says, 'I like how you girls dance. How are you doing that stuff?' We would all get up with Mick, and we would do things, and we would laugh, because his rhythm and his hips and how he was doing it was totally off. It wasn't teaching him; it wasn't dance classes. This is what we did backstage—we played around. . . . Afterwards Mick came to America doing the Pony. Well, I didn't tell people I taught him. I said we would just sit around during intermissions and have a good time."

"Later on, when Tina finally got real big, and she still looked incredible, guys would talk about her image sexually, just as a woman," Richards says. "But the Tina I knew was different. Tina was somebody to take care of you. Out on the road somebody would always be sick, and she would say, 'Take care of yourself, you have a cold, here's the VapoRub, keep your scarf on, do your coat up.'"

"I am a fun person, and when I'm onstage, I act," Turner notes. "I like to tease to a point. I'm not teasing men. I am playing with the girls—you know, when all the girls get together and everybody gets up and they get a little cigarette and champagne and they do little things. That's the same thing I do onstage when I'm performing for the girls and then for the guys." She is insulted that people would assume otherwise. "I am not a vulgar, sexy person onstage. I think that's how people perceive me, because I have a lot of vulgar videos where they want me to do the garter-belt thing."

It's more than that. Who can forget Turner doing dirty things to a microphone when she sang "I've Been Loving You Too Long," a song she now hates, or Turner belting out the immortal words in her version of "Proud Mary": "We nevah, evah, do nothin' nice and easy. We always do it nice and rough"?

"She has this sensual persona, but her private mores are so old-fashioned, so traditional," says Bob Krasnow, the Elektra Entertainment chairman who still remembers the time in the 1960s when he first walked into the Turners' house in Baldwin Hills, in Los Angeles, expecting Tina to be a hot number. "She was in the kitchen with a wet rag, down on her hands and knees wiping the floor, wearing a do-rag on her head."

Today, Tina Turner is nervously steeling herself for the release of the film based on her 1986 best-selling autobiography, *I, Tina,* written with Kurt Loder. The movie, *What's Love Got to Do with It,* stars Angela Bassett as Tina and Laurence Fishburne as Ike. The sound track—Tina's old standards plus three new songs—will come out just in time for her grand concert tour of America and Canada this summer—the first time she's toured the United States in six years.

Turner is clearly testing the waters. "I don't believe that I can go and stand and sing for the people," she tells me. "I can't stand the idea of just standing there like Barbra Streisand or Ella Fitzgerald or Diana Ross. I have never been that kind of performer. I have been in rock 'n' roll all my life. You can't be a rock 'n' roll old woman. You can be a rock 'n' roll old man." "If there's anybody around who can grow up and still be a rock 'n' roll woman, it's got to be Tina," says Richards, now forty-nine himself. "She's in the same position I and the Stones are. It's out there to find out. The area's open."

Turner likes to spend money—oodles of it. She doesn't look at price tags. She often buys duplicates of her designer clothes in case the cleaners wreck something. She collects antique furniture, owns a house in Germany, and is renovating another in the south of France. She drinks Cristal champagne, drives a Mercedes jeep, and indulges herself with massages, facials, psychic readings, and holistic cures. Since 1984, when "What's Love Got to Do with It" soared to number one on the pop charts and her *Private Dancer* album spawned three additional hit singles and swept the Grammys, she's sold 30 million records. On her last European tour, in 1990, she filled stadiums and played to 3.5 million people, outdrawing both Madonna and the Rolling Stones. So she's hardly hurting.

But not long ago her accountant told her, "You've been having a good time." If she wanted to keep the perfumed bubble bath filled to overflowing, it was time to go out and strut her stuff, for millions of dollars, while the movie was playing and the sound track was being released. Not that she feels particularly like singing onstage—doing that every night is associated, in her mind, with hideous memories of beatings and indentured servitude. She'd rather act. "I think it's more classy to be an actress than to be a rock singer. But you don't make as much money. I ain't no dummy. I know that."

So Turner has moved from Europe and rented a furnished house in Beverly Hills, in Benedict Canyon, a Mediterranean-style house that's all white stucco, beamed ceilings, and bleached wooden floors, with hillsides of daisies. She greets me at the door in a long tan sleeveless knit shift and brown suede Chanel ballet slippers. We go on a tour of the house, which is lovely, low-key, and tasteful. The most interesting part is an enormous walk-in closet the size of a bedroom, filled with ten pieces of Vuitton luggage, about sixty pairs of shoes, and racks and racks of designer clothes, mostly in neutral colors, which she coordinates and tends herself. Inside the big closet is a smaller, cedar closet, in which a wig identical to the auburn layered short cut she has on is suspended from a wire hanger, like a spider dangling from a thread.

The house is quiet, and filled with fragrant white roses and tuberoses. It's a place where Turner can be a lady. Refinement is something she has always aspired to. "I patterned myself from classy ladies. I take as much from them as I can, but I take it naturally, because I'm not going to be phony about it. I'm not going to walk around in Chanel suits or Gucci suits—that's a little bit too much, because that's not my nature. But watching my manners, caring about not being overdressed at the wrong time—it matters how I carry myself—that's what I'm concerned about as far as being a lady. Nobody would ever think that Tina Turner is a lady. I am."

Even in her bleakest years, when living meant driving up to six hundred or seven hundred miles a day, 365 days a year—when she might be onstage singing with two black eyes and blood "whooshing into my mouth"—she dreamed of her idol, Jackie O. "The first time I met her, I was nearly in tears," Tina recalls. "In those days I wasn't thinking about anybody in my circle or the clubs where I was. I was thinking that nobody was at the level of what I wanted in my life—you understand?" Even stardom, when it came, did not make much difference. "It was not my priority." Not at all. "Music life was not attractive," she observes. "It was dirty. It was a chitlin circuit—eating on your lap. And that's why I say I was always above it. Why I don't know, but I knew I didn't want it. I'd rather go and clean a white person's house, where it is nice, than sing in dirty old places and deal with Ike and his low life."

Today, of course, things are different. Turner speaks of "classy ladies" acknowledging *her*. "I see a lot of ladies these days in places like Armani, and even those ladies come over and say, 'You look so good.'" Does that make her feel good? "To be accepted by another class of people? I am going to say yes, absolutely."

But love, too, does have something to do with it. Erwin Bach, the "very private, conservative," thirty-seven-year-old managing director of the giant EMI recording company in Germany, with whom she shares a house in Cologne, has been Tina's boyfriend for six years. "He doesn't like to be discussed, because he's a businessman," she says. "It took three years for us to get together—it wasn't one of those run-and-jump-in-bed situations."

They met when he was sent by the record company to give her a jeep to drive around Germany in. She didn't even know his name, and for two and a half years he had no idea, when their paths crossed occasionally, that she was smitten. "Oh yeah, first sight. It's an electrical charge, really, in the body. The body responds to something," Tina explains. "Heart *boom-bama-boom*. Hands are wet. But I said no." Then again, she thought, why not?

"Something happens to you when you're secure as a woman. I began to feel, Well, I'm fine. If I don't really find anybody, I'm okay. It's just those times when you start running the streets, and seeing couples and loving, and watching those movies where there's a lot of love, you miss being cuddled." It wasn't until Bach went to Los Angeles for a visit while Tina was at her house in Sherman Oaks that she included him in a friend's birthday party at Spago. "Afterwards everyone came to my house, and something magic started to happen. Of course, I was attracted. By then I'm sure he knew that I was. . . . I made sure I sat next to him. Because I was also analyzing him, too." She wanted to know that he wasn't into drugs or heavy drinking. "After everyone left, I think we exchanged a few kisses. We started to talk, and I asked him about what his record company is like." Then he pulled away, saying, "'Private life is private life.' So I didn't really push.

"What I did do, to actually get him, was I stayed in Switzerland. I rented a house in Gstaad." She had a house party at Christmastime in 1987 and invited Bach and some mutual friends. That did it, although since then, because of their work, they tend to be apart more than they are together. "It's the first time I've ever had a real comfortable relationship. I'm not threatened. He's not jealous." There are no marriage plans, but she is friendly with Bach's parents, who have retired to the country and don't speak English. (She has struggled to learn German, to no avail.) "I believe they would prefer if Erwin had a German girl or a white woman. But when they met me, well, it's the usual. Everybody likes Tina."

For good reason. There's a warmth and utter guilelessness to Tina Turner, plus an awesomely strong constitution—although her independence and sense of security have been won at a high price. Physically, at fifty-three, she is in superb condition. And just because, "in California, everyone goes under the knife," doesn't mean Tina does. She was hurt when the director of the movie implied that she must have had work done on her face. "I pulled my hair back. I showed them there were no scars. I pulled my ears. I said, 'Look, this is me.' . . .

"I almost wish I wasn't wearing a wig, because then you can see there are no scars," she tells me. "They don't take into consideration that I've been singing and dancing—and that's exercise—thirty-five years. It's got to do something. I have muscle. From control." To prove her point, Turner leaps off the sofa where we've been chatting and begins to pull her knit shift up, up, up those fabulous tawny legs, up past the knees, the thighs—"I still have little-girl legs"—up past her old-fashioned white panties to the just slightly thicker waist, up, up over the taut breasts. She's wearing no bra. With her shift now around her shoulders, she turns to the side to show off the profile of her high, rounded bottom. At that moment Roger Davies, her Australian manager, strides into the room. "Oh, Roger!" she gasps, and quickly lets the dress fall.

What's *really* remarkable about Turner's face is how few scars it bears from the years of beatings she took. The one operation she had to have was for a deviated septum, to open one nostril because it had been punched in so much. Ike Turner struck her on a regular basis for sixteen years, with everything from shoes to coat hangers to walking canes; once he put a burning cigarette to her lips and also threw boiling-hot coffee on her face. He cracked her ribs. He made her perform with jaundice, with tuberculosis, nine months pregnant, and three days after having a baby. Following her one suicide attempt, in 1968, when she thought she had timed her overdose of Valium to take effect *after* a performance so that Ike wouldn't lose the night's receipts, he tried to revive her, saying, "You wanna die, motherfucker, die!"

"She was scared to death of him—everybody around him was, in his own little cult," says Ike and Tina's longtime road manager, Rhonda Graam, who is today Tina's assistant. "It was almost like a hold he had on people."

"This was always just bruised," Turner tells me, pointing to her jaw. "This was always just torn apart, because it hits the teeth," she says, showing me the inside of her lower lip. "So the mouth was always distorted, and the eyes were always black. If you look at some of the earlier pictures, my eyes were always dark. I couldn't get them clear. I thought it was the smoke or whatever. But Ike always banged me against the head." She is kneeling on the sofa now, clutching a pillow, leaning her face in close to mine. When she pushes up the bangs of her wig, you can see a tiny part of her fuzzy white hairline. "I said the same thing—how could I have survived? Only once I got knocked out. Only once. And that was when I got this," she says, and runs her finger along the outer tip of her right eye, where there is a scar about a half inch long. "Yeah, black eyes, busted lips—somehow I just ignored it, but people knew. I thought that they thought it was a car accident. I made something up in my head in terms of the public."

Along the way there were many people who witnessed Ike's mistreatment of Tina, but no one ever intervened. Krasnow says the horror really began after Ike discovered cocaine, in the late 1960s. "The whole thing took this huge turn for ugliness. Tina was the focus . . . but the whole world suffered. In those days there was no Oprah Winfrey, no publicity dealing with abuse, no abuse hot lines. Tina was out there on the road with B.B. King and Chubby Checker by herself. She was the only woman in this world . . . a demeaning man's world."

Turner hates talking about being beaten, and she can't stand the idea that people consider her a victim. She rejects that label and wants nobody's sympathy. One minute she's defiant on the subject: "I tried to explain it to Disney [for the movie]." Lost cause. She says they see "a deep need—a woman who was a victim to a con man. How weak! How shallow! How dare you think that was what I was? I was in control every minute there. I was there because I wanted to be, because I had promised."

The next minute she says, "Okay, so if I was a victim, *fine*. Maybe I was a victim for a short while. But give me credit for *thinking* the whole time

I was there. See, I do have pride." In fact, she's stymied. "I've got to get somebody else to say, 'Yes, Tina, I do understand, and there are no buts.'" Finally, there is a moment when Turner begins to pace, and her eyes fill with tears. "What's reality sometimes is not exactly real. Because you keep saying, 'What did I do?' You get on your knees every night and you say the Lord's Prayer, and you say, 'Somebody must send some help to me, because I've never done a thing in my life to deserve this.' And that's when I started to chant."

Anna Mae Bullock never knew anything but domestic strife. She was the result of an angry, unwanted pregnancy, and by the time she arrived, on November 26, 1939, her mother and father, the majordomo of a cotton plantation in Nutbush, Tennessee, were fighting constantly. One day her mother just took off, and for years never bothered to contact her two young daughters.

"My mother was not a woman who wanted children," Turner says. "She wasn't a mother mother. She was a woman who bore children." Her father tried to cope for a while, but then he, too, split. "I was always shifted. I was always going from one relative to another. So I didn't have any stability."

Ann considered herself too gawky to be desirable. "I was very skinny when I was growing up. Long, long legs and nothing like what black people really like. I must say that black people in the class where I was at the time liked heavier women." She was living part-time with a white family, doing cleaning for her board and going to high school—just singing along to the radio—when her mother arrived to take her to Saint Louis, where she was working as a maid.

Ann first laid eyes on Ike Turner when she was a junior in high school and went out to a club one night with her sister. She was seventeen, he was twenty-five and a badass star in East Saint Louis. Ike Turner and the Kings of Rhythm were the biggest deal around, but, Tina says, "he had a bad reputation. He was known as 'pistol-whipping Ike Turner.'" Although she knew he had "an uncontrollable temper," he was also exciting. After months of begging him to let her sing, she finally grabbed the mike one night during a break and blew his mind with her voice. "I wanted to get up there with those guys," Tina remembers. "They had people on their feet. That place was rocking. I needed to get up there with that energy, and when I got there, Ike was shocked, and he never let go."

Ike Turner, a preacher's son whose father was shot by whites who accused him of playing around with a white woman, had already walked from Mississippi to Tennessee and been recorded by Sam Phillips of Sun Records—the first company to record Elvis Presley—when he met Ann

Bullock. Today, Ike Turner is credited with recording one of the first rock 'n' roll songs, "Rocket '88," in 1951, but he never got anything for it.

At first, he and Tina were just friends, and he confided to her that he felt small and unattractive, that he was constantly abandoned, and that his songwriting and publishing rights were being ripped off. "My problem, little Ann, is people always took my songs." Wide-eyed, Tina—who was well aware that he had women, both black and white, in every neighborhood in St. Louis, that he beat those he was closest to, and that he kept guns and bragged about having robbed a bank—promised that *she* would never leave him; she would help him make it to the top. "That's why I had no say," she declares. She would deeply regret her promise, but she kept it for nearly two decades.

"Ike had some kind of innate quality about him that you really loved him," Turner says. "And if he liked you, he would take the clothes from his back, so to speak." Tina makes it clear that "I was there because I wanted to be. Ike Turner was allowing me the chance to sing. I was a little country girl from Tennessee. This man had a big house in St. Louis, and he had a Cadillac, money, diamonds, shoes—all of the stuff that a different class of blacks would look up to."

Tina got pregnant by one of Ike's musicians and had a baby boy, Craig, in 1958. The musician, however, left before the baby was born, and Tina worked in a hospital during the day while continuing to sing at night. After club dates, she sometimes spent the weekends at Ike's house, where she had her own room. "Then he offered me more money, because one of his singers had left. That's when the relationship started. I cannot tell you how wrong it felt."

Sex with Ike and shame, it seems, were always linked in Tina's mind. The first time he touched her, she felt like a victim of child abuse. The second time, she was seeking refuge in his room because two musicians had threatened to rape her. "Something was going on—maybe the feeling he could protect me." She was hooked. "That's the kind of girl I am. If I go to bed with you, then you're my boyfriend." She hastens to add, however, that "it wasn't love in the beginning; it was someone else who I found to give love to."

Ike had a common-law wife, Lorraine Taylor, who was pregnant at the time, but he took care of Ann, too. "He was giving me money for singing. He went out and bought me clothes. I was having a dental problem, and my mother didn't have money at that point for dental work. He corrected all that. And then I was a little star around him. I was loyal to this man. He was good to me." But she was not attracted to him physically.

"I really didn't like Ike's body. I don't give a damn how big his member was," Tina says blithely. "I think that must have been very attractive to a lot of white women. I swear, the first time I saw Ike's body, I thought he had the body of a horse. It hung without an erection, it hung with an erection. He really was blessed, I must say, in that area. . . . Was he a good lover? What can you do except go up and down, or sideways, or whatever it is that you do with sex?"

Well, you can get pregnant, and a year later Tina was pregnant by Ike. Lorraine—who had previously threatened Tina with a gun—shot herself instead, and survived. But by then, Ike and Tina's first hit, "A Fool in Love," was climbing the R&B charts. Along the way, "Ike did pull a few strings. . . ." He changed Ann's name to Tina—she says it reminded him of Sheena the jungle queen from the TV series—without consulting her, and she hated it. Worse, on the road everyone thought the two were married.

When their baby, Ronnie, was born in 1960, Ike didn't take her to the hospital—he slept through the delivery. That was just the beginning. When Ronnie was about two, Ike and Tina moved to California. Lorraine had left Ike by then, and, without warning, she sent the two sons she had had by Ike to live with their father. Tina was suddenly mother to four boys under the age of six. (Until Lorraine's boys were in their teens, they didn't know Tina was not their real mother.)

But Tina was not around very much: Ike was obsessive about work and had Tina and the band and various Ikettes out on the road year-round. It was a rough, cash business; Ike didn't believe in banks. He had a safe in the house, a safe in the car, and lots of guns to protect him. When Tina was allowed to go shopping, he would peel bills off a big wad. They put out dozens of records, and some became hits, but they never made the top ten, only the rhythm-and-blues or soul charts. Nevertheless, Ike and Tina were becoming hip, cult favorites, regularly booked into the Fillmore West. Within five years, Ike himself was able to book them where few black acts like theirs had been before, including Vegas. At the International Hotel they were in the lounge, and Elvis Presley was the headliner.

They had married in 1962, in Tijuana, primarily, Tina says, because another woman who had been married to Ike before Lorraine was after him for alimony. "As far as I'm concerned, I've never been married," Tina explains. For about five years, she "was caught in his web." But about 1965, when she came home from touring alone to find that Ike had moved another woman into the house with the children, she felt defeated once again, and began to consider leaving.

"I had gotten to the stage where I started to think that I didn't want to be Ike's wife, and I didn't care about the money," Tina recalls. "I was thinking the whole time, how could I fulfill my promise and get out of it all right?" In 1966, Phil Spector paid Ike $20,000 to let Tina record "River Deep, Mountain High." She was thrilled to be able to really sing. "Nobody wanted me to sing in those days. They wanted me to do that screaming and yelling." Although the song is considered a rock 'n' roll milestone and became a huge hit in England, it bombed here. Yet however much Tina may have wanted to go off on her own, she didn't, for fear that "Ike would kill" anyone who tried to wrest her away.

She was trapped. "I had to get out of there because whatever I was doing didn't matter anymore." She told Ike that she wanted only a business relationship. "He would really fight harder then, because he thought he was losing control." As Rhonda Graam notes, "He was afraid she'd leave him. He would keep the fear going."

And Ike continued to make demands on Tina. Right up until the day she left him, he expected her to massage him, give him manicures and pedicures, and have food ready for him at all times. Sometimes, after beating her, he'd force her to have sex with him. "Sex had become rape as far as I was concerned. . . . That was not my style."

Tina tried to leave once, but Ike caught up with her at a terminal where her bus stopped. A suicide attempt had also failed. But the following year, 1969, Ike and Tina toured in the United States once again, with the now-humongous Rolling Stones. What really kept Tina going, she says, was her belief in what psychics told her: "One day you will be among the biggest of stars and you will live across the water." In the interim, she chanted more and more every day: *Nam-myo-ho-renge-kyo.*

In California in the late 1960s and early 1970s, this particular chant, the mantra of a controversial Buddhist sect, Soka Gakkai, was touted as a way to achieve goals as well as inner harmony. A woman Ike brought to the house one night shortly after Tina's suicide attempt turned her on to the chant. She remembers, "I never let go of the Lord's Prayer until I was sure of those words."

Gradually Tina became convinced that chanting was her path to salvation. She was thrilled in 1974 to accept her first movie role, the Acid Queen in Ken Russell's *Tommy* (she did not know at the time that acid was a reference to LSD), and hoped for more roles in films, but they did not come. She played Aunty Entity in *Mad Max beyond Thunderdome*, with Mel Gibson, but turned down a leading role in *The Color Purple*, saying it was too much like real life to her. Today she still says, "I feel there is a calling inside me to act."

Finally, in 1976, Tina Turner felt strong enough to get away. Ike, she realized, was never going to give her their house, which she had long wanted and felt she deserved. The children would soon graduate from high school. Meanwhile, Ike was involved with the nonsinging Ikette, Ann Thomas, who had had his baby and was traveling everywhere with Ike and Tina. By then, Ike was doing so much coke that he would stay up for three or four days at a time, and his preferred mode of travel was to sleep on airplanes with his head on Ann's lap and his feet on Tina's.

In early July they flew to Fort Worth to perform a date at the Dallas Hilton. Because Tina was wearing a white Yves Saint Laurent suit on the plane, she refused some chocolate Ike handed her. He kicked her, and later battered her again and again with his hand and shoe in the back of the limo. This time something clicked. She understood. "I knew I would never be given my freedom. I would have to take it."

She astounded Ike by fighting back. "When someone is really trying to kill you, it hurts. But this time it didn't hurt. I was angry, too." Tina remembers "digging, or just hitting and kicking. By the time we got to the hotel, I had a big swollen eye. My mouth was bleeding." She refused, however, to cover the blood, as he directed her to. Ike was in sad shape himself. He had been up for days, strung out on coke; when they got to the room, she massaged his head, as she often did, until he passed out. Tina waited for his breathing to tell her he was asleep. "My heart was in my ears."

She recalls thinking, Now is the time. You are headed toward dealing with what you're going to have to deal with, with this man. "I ran down the hall, and I was afraid I was going to run into his people—his band and his bodyguards. So I went through an exit and down the steps. I was so afraid. . . . Went through the back door, and I remember throwing myself up onto trash cans just to rest, just to feel I had gotten away. Then I composed myself and thought, Now what? I started to run fast, just run."

She had thirty-six cents and a Mobil credit card.

"I needed to call somebody with money. My family didn't have the money for a ticket. That's the whole thing always. I didn't know anybody with money. They were all Ike's people."

Tina's life away from Ike began when the manager of the Ramada Inn across the freeway from the Hilton gave her a suite for the night. Ike did not take her leaving passively. For the next two years, people who had helped her escape were threatened, and their houses and cars were set afire or shot into. Tina was unwavering, however; she even lived on food stamps for a while. In 1978 their divorce became final. Tina took nothing, because she didn't want to be tied to Ike in any way. What she did come away with was an astounding debt, since she had walked out on a performance. In addition, Ike always booked them solidly for months in advance, so Tina was held liable for the missed dates.

Michael Stewart, the former head of United Artists, one of the many record companies Ike and Tina had been under contract to, lent Tina money to develop an act; he began booking her in cabarets and hotels, where she performed in feathers and chiffon in a disco-inferno act. She also did guest shots on *Hollywood Squares* to pay the rent. "Tina never complained," Stewart said, adding that he knew she would be okay. At the height of her in-the-depths period, he took her to a movie premiere, "and you would have thought I was with Madonna today. The paparazzi swarmed. She was a celebrity."

"Tina was probably half a million in debt when I took her on," says Roger Davies, her current manager. To work off what she owed, she performed in such places as Poland, Yugoslavia, Bahrain, and Singapore. Davies tried hard to get her a record contract, but Ike's reputation cast a pall. As Tina explained, Davies would tell her, "I can't get you a record now, Tina. Whenever I say Tina, they say Ike." In 1981 the Rolling Stones came to her rescue, and she opened a few dates of their American tour. After a magic night at the Ritz club in New York in 1983, with Keith Richards, David Bowie, and Rod Stewart in the audience, her record company, Capitol, finally agreed to proceed with plans to have her cut an album. At the end of that year, she hit it big in England with the single "Let's Stay Together." Then she made *Private Dancer*. The rosy future the psychics had predicted was coming true. Meanwhile, after eleven arrests, Ike Turner finally ended up in jail in 1990, and served eighteen months for cocaine possession and transportation, among other charges.

"I never had no bad thoughts about women. I think about women just like I think about my mother. And I wouldn't do no more to no woman than I would want them to do to my mother." Ike Turner is giving a bravura performance on the phone from his new home base, Carlsbad, California, outside San Diego, where he is putting together an all-new Ike Turner Revue, with Ikettes he has scouted in local karaoke bars. He's sixty-one now, and Tina is a sore subject. "Did I hit her all the time? That's the biggest lie ever been told by her or by anybody that say that. I didn't hit her any more than you been hit by your guy. . . . I'm not going to sit here and lie and say because I was doing dope I slapped Tina. Because it's not the reason I slapped her. If the same thing occurred again, I'd do the same thing. It's nothing that I'm proud of, because I just didn't stop and think."

Ike has been out of jail—"It was the best thing that ever happened to me"—since September 1991. (According to one friend, he tried unsuc-cessfully to marry four different women in jail so that he could have con-tact visits.) Today he's off drugs, lives with a thirty-year-old blond singer named Jeanette Bazzell, and says he's getting his own TV movie together to tell *his* story. "Whatever happened with Ike and Tina—if we fought every day—it's just as much her fault as it was mine. Because she stayed there and took it for whatever reason she was taking it," he asserts. "Why would she stay there for eighteen years? You know, I feel like I've been used. . . . Didn't nobody else grab her and put her where I put her at." Ike also denies that he hurt Tina as much as she and others say. "You know, if somebody throws coffee on your face and your skin rolls down your face, it should be some burns there, shouldn't it? Well, you look at her face real good. When you talk to her, say, 'What kind of surgery did you have on your face?' . . . I know damn well she didn't," Ike maintains. "She ain't did shit to her skin."

His desire for all those other women, he says, can be traced to his childhood. Ever since he was "a little nappy-headed boy" in Mississippi working in a hotel, "I would see white guys pull up with their little white girls in their father's car with the mink stole, and I'd say, 'Oh boy, one of these days I'm going to be like that.'" That he succeeded with women beyond his wildest imaginings is Tina's fault too, he says. "I blame Tina as much for that as I blame myself. Because she always acted like it didn't bother her for me being with women. . . . She'd be pissed off about some girl or something, and she would lie and say she wasn't. . . . We had fights, but we was together twenty-four hours a day, and so, other words, she feels more like an employee than a wife, because I would tell her what words to say, what dress to wear, how to act onstage, what songs to sing. You know, it all came from me. . . . There is no Tina in reality."

It's a glorious L.A. Sunday afternoon in March. Tina Turner is bouncing in and out of a chair in an upstairs den flooded with light, giving away her beauty secrets. "I do something about my life besides eating and exercis-ing and whatever. I contact my soul. I must stay in touch with my soul. That's my connection to the universe."

"What are you?" I ask.

"I'm a Buddhist-Baptist. My training is Baptist. And I can still relate to the Ten Commandments and to the Ten Worlds. It's all very close, as long as you contact the subconscious mind. That's where the coin of the Almighty is." Every morning and evening, Turner, who keeps a Buddhist shrine in her house, prays and chants. "I don't care what they feel about me and my tight pants onstage, and my lips and my hair. I am a chanter.

And everyone who knows anything about chanting knows you correct everything in your life by chanting every day," she says. "People look at me and wonder, `You look so great—what is it you do?' What can I tell them except I changed my life?"

People often ask Turner if she will ever preach or teach. Yes, she says, but not yet. After the tour, she is planning to put together a lifestyle cassette detailing her dance steps and holistic cures. Basically, for Turner, it comes down to this: "I was a victim; I don't dwell on it. I was hurt. I'm not proud of being hurt; I don't need sympathy for it. Really, I'm very forgiving. I'm very analytical. I'm very patient. My endurance is very good. I learned a lot being there with that very sick man." Like Ike, she wouldn't change the past. "I am happy that I'm not like anybody else. Because I really do believe that if I was different, I might not be where I am today," Tina says. "You asked me if I ever stood up for anything. Yeah, I stood up for my life."

UPDATE: Tina Turner told me when this story was published that she figured she had a few more years on the concert circuit to make some money and then she was going to retire to Europe, travel, take it easy, and live the good life with her German boyfriend. She has been true to her word. In the fall of 2003, she was mobbed at a rare United States appearance when she showed up in New York for the movie premiere of *Brother Bear*, a Disney animated feature in which she sang a part of the sound track. At sixty-four, she was wearing a mini skirt and high boots and it was those legs that still became a legend most.

No Way to Treat a Lady: Margaret Thatcher

"I have never been defeated by the people."

June 1991

For Margaret Thatcher, it was a throwback to the glory days. Here she was in the White House private quarters, reveling in a lavish dinner party in her honor, basking in the golden glow of twenty-four-inch tapers, gazing out over the perfect pink and fuschia roses floating in crystal bowls, the centerpieces on six tables for ten diners. Only hours earlier, in the East Room of the White House, George H. W. Bush had awarded her the Presidential Medal of Freedom, the country's highest civilian honor. He had praised "the greengrocer's daughter who shaped a nation to her will," and concluded, "Prime Minister, there will always be an England, but there can never be another Margaret Thatcher." From that exquisite high, she had raced up to the Queen's Bedroom to change into a long black pleated skirt and brilliant red-and-black brocade jacket for a cocktail party at which America's most powerful leaders would rise to pay her homage. It was as if the colonies had not yet heard the news of her unceremonious sacking as prime minister by the members of the Conservative Party. Barbara Bush rose to toast the new baronet, Sir Denis Thatcher. "They broke the mold when they made you, Denis. . . . As the spouse of a powerful leader, you do it better than anyone."

Sir Denis graciously thanked his hosts and quoted Mark Antony upon entering Cleopatra's bedroom: "I did not come here to talk."

The evening was, quite simply, divine. Margaret Thatcher was in the inner sanctum of power—surrounded by old chums from summits and visits to Camp David—who had gathered for the express purpose of administering massive doses of adulation to the former Iron Lady. Then suddenly the spell was broken. One of the heroes of the day, Secretary of Defense Dick Cheney, actually uttered the as-yet-unspoken name: John Major. How could he? So what if the new prime minister was Mrs. Thatcher's handpicked choice? She gave no indication of distress, of course, but the sudden mention of her successor jolted more than a few guests to focus on the ghastly fate that had befallen her only a few months before. As one guest remarked, "It was as if he had spilled something dirty on the tablecloth."

Even when life was beautiful, it was cruel. Exceedingly so. As usual, Mrs. Thatcher's son, Mark, was part of the problem. Now, while acting as her personal manager as she planned a career in international relations, he was facing a firestorm of criticism from her friends and former advisors that would soon erupt in a London *Sunday Times* headline: MARK IS WRECKING YOUR LIFE.

To add insult to injury, while Thatcher was polishing off her chocolate mint soufflé with President Bush, one of the safest Conservative seats in Britain—Ribble Valley—was going down to defeat in a by-election upset. And the disaster was being blamed on Margaret Thatcher and her legacy, the hated poll tax.

Let the longest-serving British prime minister in the twentieth century eat cake in America. At home, she was eating crow.

"The pattern of my life was fractured," Mrs. Thatcher said the next day in the residence of the British ambassador, referring to her surprise resignation. Dressed in a crisp spring suit and her ubiquitous pearls, she plumped all the pillows on the sofa in the decorous drawing room, then sat down, balancing a porcelain teacup in the palm of her graceful hand. "It's like throwing a pane of glass with a complicated map upon it on the floor," she said, "and all habits and thoughts and actions that went with it and the staff that went with it. . . . You threw it on the floor and it shattered." And the pieces? "You couldn't pick up those pieces."

As though some answer might be found amid the debris, Thatcher began to recite her daily and seasonal rhythms as prime minister. Mondays, "we went down to the House of Commons for preparations for questions at two o'clock," she said. "Questions at the House were on Tuesday and Thursday, so on Mondays and Wednesdays we saw foreign statesmen. There were a certain number of overseas events—the economic summit, two European councils. All of this structure happened;

you geared your clothes-buying to external visits and your conferences. You geared your hair to when you were in the House, etc., and then you had a certain amount of entertaining. In June there was the Trooping of the Color, a whole range of engagements throughout the year which became the pattern of my life." All gone after nearly twelve years, on ninety-six hours' notice. She paused. "Sometimes I say, 'Which day is it?' I never said that at Number 10."

"She is like a great athlete suddenly confined to a wheelchair," says Christopher Wall, the Conservative Party press officer who was on loan to Thatcher for her United States trip. As another Thatcher loyalist, Sir Peregrine Worsthorne, who edits the right-wing *Sunday Telegraph* editorial page, observes, "In a sense she hasn't come to, yet, from the concussion—everything was so brutal and sudden. She's pretty shell-shocked still. The Iron Lady has a very emotional side. People underestimate the extent to which she was shattered by this."

The day after Mrs. Thatcher lost a Conservative leadership battle and decided to resign in the interest of party unity, Worsthorne got a call from Thatcher's press secretary, Bernard Ingham: "The prime minister would like to say good-bye." Arriving at 10 Downing Street, Worsthorne was stunned by what he found. "I went round thinking there'd be a long queue of people waiting to say farewell. I found myself *alone*. I expected to stay fifteen minutes, which would be quite normal. After an hour, I ran out of conversation. She was very short on people." On the way out, Worsthorne ran into Thatcher's journalist daughter, Carol. "She had a basket on her arm from the supermarket, 'bringing Mummy's supplies' of cold chicken or something for dinner. It was very disorienting."

Tory Party leadership transitions are known to be less than genteel, but this ouster seemed a classic illustration of the axiom that she who lives by the sword shall die by the sword. Here was a prime minister famous for her prodigious recall, who routinely exhausted her aides with her energy, who every night, no matter the hour, relished "doing her boxes"—reading the documents in the locked red containers, filled with confidential papers from every ministry, that were delivered by dispatch riders who would roar through town to deposit them on her doorstep at 10 Downing Street. Here was a phenomenal woman who was devoid of hobbies or interests off the world stage, who once said that taking vacations tends to cause colds. "She wanted us to be like the Japanese," grumbles one political observer. Here was the leader who had bestowed Thatcherism on England. And if you were not with her in the dismantling of the welfare state and the charge toward privatization, you were mushy, a "wet." Anyone who couldn't keep up or who displeased her was ruthlessly sacrificed. "In the United States, she has this reputation as a chaste, saintly figure," says Andrew Stephen, Washington bureau chief of the London *Observer.* "In fact, she's knifed every Cabinet minister she's ever had in the back. That's how she survived eleven years."

A favorite instrument of torture was Ingham, her powerful press secretary, who would leak to the reporters on the Parliament beat that certain unsuspecting ministers were in trouble. His penchant for denigration earned him the sobriquet the Yorkshire Rasputin from one of the ministers, John Biffen. Biffen, himself later axed, would add, "He was the sewer, rather than the sewage."

But now it was Thatcher who was instantaneously, irrevocably out. "She thought she was unassailable," says Thatcherite columnist Frank Johnson. "It was hubris. She was brought down by the fault of her virtues—her enormous bravery in battling the most powerful opponent of all, the European Community."

Others take a less charitable view: "She'd become slightly potty by the end and lost touch with reality," says one observer. Thatcher's opposition to a united Europe, and the poll tax—the hated per capita levy that replaced property taxes to finance local government—certainly helped make her hugely unpopular; in April 1990 her approval rating was 23 percent, the lowest for a prime minister in memory. By November she was stuck at just 26 percent. Many in the Tory Party were, as Mrs. Thatcher put it, "running scared," convinced she would cause them to lose the next election. When the votes were counted in a challenge to her party leadership by her former defense minister Michael Heseltine, she had a clear majority. But under the convoluted Tory leadership formula, she would have had to submit to a second ballot. Rather than do so, she stepped down.

"I have never been defeated by the people," she said no fewer than five time during our interview. "I've never been defeated in an election. I have never been defeated in a vote of confidence in the Parliament, so I don't know what that would be like." This last was spoken as if she were flicking an imaginary crumb off her bodice. Moreover, Thatcher refused to concede that the poll tax was an error, and declared that she would have won a fourth election had The People decided.

"I'd still be there if I had my choice," she said at one point. "I did not have my choice, so I decided to do the best thing for my party for the future. . . . And I knew I'd still have a good bit of influence."

There was little humor in her predicament. For months after leaving office, Mrs. Thatcher seemed uncharacteristically frozen in indecision.

Her friends tried to cheer her up with a luncheon at David Frost's, a week-end at the grand manor house of trade-and-industry minister Lord Hesketh, a party at the home of the millionaire novelist Jeffrey Archer, with a cake in the shape of the Order of Merit. Even John Major was said to be concerned; when he came to Washington for talks with President Bush before the Gulf War, he told her American friends, "Be sure to look up Maggie—she's down." Those who made the trip found her worried about money: Somehow Denis's comfortable retirement and her son's reputed millions weren't going to be enough. Had the leader who had slashed benefits during her three terms become dependent on the perquisites of public office? By American standards, former prime ministers don't get much: an annual pension of roughly $45,000. As long as Thatcher kept her seat in the House of Commons, she was also entitled to her MP's salary of $37,000, one constituency secretary, a small basement office, and a $19,000 cost-of-living allowance. Then, just before Easter, acting on complaints about her financial straits, Major delivered a golden egg to the woman the London *Times* had dubbed "the priestess of self-help"—an additional $53,000 a year to all former prime ministers, effective immediately. "It's very welcome and I'm extremely grateful," was Thatcher's comment.

Yet the thing she wanted most they couldn't give her—her power back. And no wonder she was so distraught about the whole mess. First, there were 65,000 letters to answer; they had come from all over the world in the weeks after her resignation. But she had no real staff, only a borrowed office and a few volunteers who showed up to answer the phone. Then there were her living arrangements—her Georgian manse manqué, on a golf course behind an iron gate in the village of Dulwich, about half an hour southeast of central London in light traffic, was too far away. She had to find a convenient pied-à-terre. (Henry Ford II's widow solved this problem, lending her an apartment in Eaton Square.) Invitations to speak poured in, but who could sort through them? How much should she charge? Literary agents were desperate to deliver bids worth millions for a quick kiss-and-tell. Could she sell them on her notion of a serious historical examination of her era? How should she position herself?

"She could have put together a blue-ribbon panel of British business-people who would have helped her organize her office, get a staff, and get it all done," says Charles Price, former United States ambassador to the United Kingdom. "There were plenty of dynamic people around to help." But she never got back to them. Several friends suspect they know the reason. "She has put all her affairs in the hands of her son, Mark Thatcher; he's very stubborn and thinks he knows everything," one associate noted. "We know he's wrong, but who the hell is going to mix in? Everyone is scared to death to confront her about it."

One story making the rounds in London recently was that Mark Thatcher enjoys referring to President Bush as George. All his adult life, in fact, he has seemed to be very much in a hurry to make it big, and more than willing to trade off his mother's name to do so. "He's for use," says a powerful member of the Texas establishment. "The word is, if you want to use him, you can use him." Mark himself once said, "I suppose I was the slowest learner in the family, the last to realize that because of Mum's success, everyone would have their eyes that much closer on me, their expectations that much higher." Today if you want to get to Mrs. Thatcher, then one way or the other you must go through Mark. He is her adored child, the light of her life. But to most of those outside the family who are close to Mrs. Thatcher, he is known as "that dreadful son."

"The son is a fly in the ointment," agrees the famed literary agent Irving Lazar, who says he offered to advise Mrs. Thatcher on her memoirs "even if I wasn't the agent," but never got to meet her. "The son thinks he can be the agent," Lazar says. "He's decided he knows all about publishing, and he's an amateur. He overestimates the value of the book, and what's worse, when he had the chance to strike, he didn't."

"We are not dashing into the memoirs," says Mrs. Thatcher briskly. "We're making quite certain the memoirs will be a vigorous intellectual, historical record of what we did and what happened."

Several months is not enough time to rebuild a life, Mrs. Thatcher admits, but in true Thatcherite fashion she is gamely making the attempt: "You have to create a new pane of glass—we are building up new habits." One of those habits—and the best way to keep glamour alive, of course— is to travel to the United States, where the money and adulation that are so lacking at home are plentiful. America and Maggie Thatcher is the story of milk and honey meeting iron and silk. Certainly at the $2,500-a-plate March of the Glittering Mummies that was Ronald Reagan's eightieth-birthday party in Beverly Hills in February 1991, Mrs. Thatcher was the superstar—even when it was difficult to see who came through the metal detector first, Ricardo Montalban or Cesar Romero, Phyllis or Barry Diller, Dinah Shore or Ed Meese, Rupert Murdoch or Eva Gabor, and, dead last, Elizabeth Taylor, all cleavage and curls and with her latest thirtyish escort in tow. Not to mention Thatcher's holding hands with Nancy Reagan herself, indulging in photo ops with Merv Griffin and Dan Quayle, listening to Liza Minnelli sing "New York, New York" to a bunch of people who despise New York, and watching Ronald Reagan lean over to blow out his candles and get frosting smeared all over his tux—well, it certainly beat getting slagged off by Neil Kinnock. And Mrs. Thatcher, sparkling in gold brocade and black velvet, did get the longest standing ovation of the night.

But the next morning the world, and Thatcher's diminished status in it, intruded rudely. What was supposed to have been a carefree breakfast with Vice President Quayle in Century City, in Hollywood, became a full-scale news conference when word arrived that terrorists had fired three mortar rounds at the British Cabinet meeting being held at 10 Downing Street. Mrs. Thatcher, in a navy suit with brass buttons that looked like a military uniform, was ready with a statement, handwritten on a scrap of paper. She then found herself in the ludicrously unnatural position of ceding control of the event to Quayle and watching him grope with reporters' questions. There were moments when she actually rocked up on her toes, clenched her fists, and bit her lip, as if to silence herself. Finally, a question implying that British and United States imperialism was the cause of anti-American sentiment in the Persian Gulf pushed her over the edge. When she was asked to give her views, she blasted, "I think all comment should be directed to criticism of Saddam Hussein, who started a brutal war on the second of August and has been prosecuting it ever since." She glared at the offending reporter. "Criticism should be directed towards him, not those who are standing against aggression."

Once again, she had flattened the opposition. Is that why Americans loved her so? Is that why, on Capitol Hill, when tourists spotted her, they broke into applause? "I don't know, but I'm eternally grateful they do," she remarked. It certainly didn't hurt that she was breathtakingly well informed, the cerebral half of the heralded Thatcher–Reagan alliance. Reagan might have been able to get away with watching *The Sound of Music* on TV the night before an economic summit instead of reading his briefing book, but for Mrs. Thatcher, work was her entertainment.

"Reagan was particularly appreciative of having Thatcher in his corner during his early ventures onto the world stage, when his inner confidence may not quite have matched his fortress of convictions," writes Lou Cannon in the definitive political biography *President Reagan: The Role of a Lifetime*. The former national security advisor Robert McFarlane agrees: "She was quite good at reinforcing him when he needed it, and made a point of giving him credit for something he hadn't said," McFarlane observes. "She was truly conscious of his limitations, but she adored his constancy—they both understood the power that derives from constancy." Mrs. Thatcher was also masterful at having her way with the president. "I wouldn't say she exploited him," says McFarlane, "but she knew how to play upon his lack of knowledge and his chivalrous nature. To be in a room with her really *stirrrrrs* you," he adds. "She is a performer, an overwhelming presence. I couldn't be around her without just feeling . . . passion is the wrong word, I guess. She could move men and she knew it. Oh yes!"

Denis Thatcher had a more succinct explanation: "With Ronald Reagan," he told an American friend, "it takes awhile for the penny to drop." Yet even when they knew they were being had, the Yanks couldn't get enough of her. Both Charles Price and Robert McFarlane remember the Christmastime visit in 1983 when Margaret Thatcher was flying to Washington from the Far East. After landing at Hickam Air Force Base, near Pearl Harbor, in the middle of the night, she announced she wanted to visit the battle site. Of course, said the meet-and-greets, they'd get her a car. "That won't be necessary," she replied, fishing a flashlight out of her purse and setting off on foot.

Hours later, at Camp David, she had Star Wars on her mind. "Her real purpose was to rein Reagan in before he did serious damage to the alliance—the Europeans were very alarmed by SDI," says McFarlane, referring to the formal designation the White House used, Strategic Defense Initiative. "She and two aides sat across the table from the whole array of the top people in the administration," says Price. "'Look here, Ron,' she said. 'I think we may face considerable turmoil in the alliance. . . . I think you should make a statement today.'" Mrs. Thatcher dived into her handbag once again. "I brought one." With minor tinkerings, says McFarlane, it became the communiqué that was issued shortly afterward.

But by the time George Bush assumed office, in January 1989, Margaret Thatcher had, in the words of a senior American official present at the meetings between the two, "lost the ability to listen." She lectured Deputy Secretary of State Lawrence Eagleburger for twenty minutes at a time "and didn't even seem to hear his answers." At a meeting in Colorado in 1989, when Bush tried to engage her in a political bull session, she answered him "as if she were turning on a cassette tape." She was asked to relax and she did somewhat, eventually, but by then the Americans, while still respecting her intellect, generally considered her "difficult and imperial." ("She always talks too much when she's nervous," explains a friend.) Nevertheless, Margaret Thatcher is widely viewed to have bolstered Bush's resolve to send troops to the Gulf, since the two of them happened to be in Aspen together when Saddam Hussein invaded Kuwait, and she was also in the Oval Office when the defense secretary, Cheney, called to tell the president that King Fahd would allow American troops on Saudi Arabian soil.

At the Medal of Freedom ceremony, Bush himself alluded to Thatcher's help and her lack of self-doubt. He remembered telephoning her, not long after Saddam Hussein had sent forces into Kuwait, to say that he was planning to allow a single Iraqi vessel through the naval blockade the allies had imposed. She "agreed with the decision, but then added these words of caution—words that guided me through the Gulf crisis. Words I'll never forget as long as I'm alive," said the president. "'Remember, George,' she said, 'this is no time to go wobbly.'"

When she herself was thrown off balance, Margaret Thatcher turned to the person she has always trusted most, her husband. "If you want any help, you ask for it at home. If you've got any problems, you take them home. That's what family life is about." Mrs. Thatcher sat up straight and stressed every consonant. "It is the home always to be there—always certain that you can find there, no matter what happens, affection and loyalty. . . . Home is where you come to when you have nothing better to do.

"Denis is absolutely marvelous," she went on. "We are a very close-knit family." In addition to the Thatchers' thirty-seven-year-old twins, Mark and Carol, there's Mark's congenial wife, Diane—a former Kappa Kappa Gamma at Southern Methodist University and the daughter of a car dealer—and their two-year-old son. Carol, a freelance writer and, friends say, the one with the sense of humor, has stayed in the background, while her mother has put Mark in charge of everything and found solace with the affable Sir Denis. Now seventy-six, he is "the mainstay of my life," said his wife, and, according to Lord Hesketh, "the bedrock on which the whole cathedral sits." As former Conservative Party treasurer Lord McAlpine notes, "The dynamic of their relationship is simple: it's just love, true affection, romance—they love each other. He's enormously protective of her."

When asked to speak in personal terms about Denis, however, Mrs. Thatcher fielded the question with English reserve. "Denis is on several boards, which he is extremely conscientious about—all the board papers are thoroughly analyzed before he goes to board meetings. He's run the family business. He knows what it's like when you are committing your own money. . . . He's a crack accountant and he also always has been mad keen on certain sports and living up to certain standards in those sports." Golf, she said, which Sir Denis plays with left-handed women's clubs, is his favorite. "He's very, very pro-golf," she said in her best instructional tone, "because when it comes to playing professional golf, the standards of the game are some of the highest standards in sports. There are *no* histrionics."

Denis has been celebrated in British pop culture in the play *Anyone for Denis?* in which he is "mad keen" on golf chiefly for the libations of the nineteenth hole, and in the hilarious "Dear Bill" letters in *Private Eye*, in which an old buffer never far from gin meltdown partakes in and reports on a daffy right-wing world. In fact, Denis Thatcher is far right in his views—he has always been an avid advocate of trade with South Africa and has called the BBC "a viper's nest" of "outrageous bloody pinkos." (A female dinner partner remembers him referring to the Indians as "wogs.") And during his wife's tenure, Denis, like his son, had the propriety of several of his business dealings questioned.

For many years Denis was a consultant for a building group, IDC, involved in civil engineering. His most controversial intervention on the firm's behalf came to light when his letter to the government's secretary of state for Wales—about delays in building permits on an IDC project—was published in the British press in 1981. The message from Denis Thatcher, on 10 Downing Street notepaper, prompted the secretary to scrawl to his staff in the margin, "The explanation better be good and quick."

Also in 1981, Denis and Mark Thatcher became embroiled in a controversial building contract in Oman. Mrs. Thatcher was making an official visit there while a British construction company, Cementation International, was bidding on a billion-dollar university complex. Mark, a consultant for Cementation, showed up as well. His mother lobbied on behalf of the company, and after it won the contract, Mark reaped a sizable fee. For his part, Denis was chairman of a company that had a fifty percent interest in a bid to subcontract to Cementation. After the *Observer* broke the story in 1984, Mrs. Thatcher and her government were criticized in Parliament for the striking conflict of interest. Later the *Sunday Times* revealed that Denis was a cosignatory on the bank account in which Mark's fee was deposited.

These days, Denis, who spends one week out of four in the United States, is in business with some heavily investigated characters. One of his major ventures—he serves as deputy chairman—is with Attwoods, a British waste-management concern that draws substantial profits from an American subsidiary, Industrial Waste Services, in Miami. When Attwoods acquired IWS in 1984, it was owned by Jack R. Casagrande and Ralph Velocci and some of their relatives. As part of the sale, these family members received Attwoods stock, and Casagrande and Velocci have joined Denis on the Attwoods board. The two come from three generations involved in the garbage trade in New Jersey and New York, where another company Casagrande has an interest in was charged with price-fixing and illegal property-rights schemes. A 1986 report from Maurice Hinchey, chair of the New York State Assembly Environmental Conservation Committee, stated that organized crime is "a dominating presence" in the state's garbage industry. FBI reports refer to IWS's business dealings with convicted mob associate Mel Cooper, now serving twenty-five years in prison for racketeering. Cooper ran a garbage-equipment leasing operation in New York that was alleged to be a front for loan-sharking operations connected to the Gambino, Genovese, and Colombo crime families.

In 1986, IWS was convicted in Florida of conspiracy in a criminal antitrust case and fined $375,000. Also that year, Casagrande and Velocci were investigated, but not indicted, in an alleged bribe of the mayor of Opa-Locka, Florida, for that city's garbage contract. The following year a civil suit was brought against IWS, Casagrande, and several other defendants for allegedly defrauding Marion County, Florida, in a garbage-conversion scheme. In 1991, IWS and Casagrande were part of a $2.2-million out-of-court settlement.

Hinchey claims that Scotland Yard, at least, did inquire about Attwoods and IWS. "I've seen documents from British authorities," he says. "They knew about these things and were frustrated about it." Yet British investigators apparently did not contact others who could have aided them.

If Denis has successfully deflected criticism of his business transgressions, his son has not been as fortunate. In fact, almost nobody has a very kind word for Mark Thatcher. "Mark gets a bit of a bum rap," says John O'Sullivan, the *National Review* editor. "He doesn't have immense charm. He's not winning." Indeed. He's the son who mixes with international arms traders; the wheeler-dealer, the suddenly wealthy son who travels with a butler and, in 1990, bought a $3.5 million London town house with up-to-the-minute security; the inept son who got lost in the desert for six days on the Paris-to-Dakar rally when he wanted to be a racecar driver, causing his mother her first public tears (and prompting former German chancellor Helmut Schmidt to comment privately, "It's the first time I ever realized she was a woman"); the arrogant son who got his mother in hot water over the Oman deal; the boorish son who used to pull out a walkie-talkie in the middle of dinner parties to chat with his bodyguards. Mark once told the cultivated billionaire Walter Annenberg that he was setting his table with the wrong glasses for red wine and that his golf course was "Mickey Mouse."

"I think Mark is extremely bright and loyal to his mother," says former trade representative Richard Fisher, who befriended Mark in Dallas. "I think he realizes that great people can serve and then be forgotten and their offspring amount to nothing. The Churchills basically live in poverty by Texas standards. He will take good care of his mother." Recently, when Fisher hosted eighteen for dinner in Mrs. Thatcher's honor in Dallas, he toasted her "as a wife and mother first, then as the greatest prime minister since Churchill." "Richard," she replied," "you have finally got your priorities right."

"I see something else," Fisher continues. "I think she's a loving mother, and, if anything, there is a sense of loss that in her career she didn't spend enough time with her children. I wouldn't call it guilt, but she works very hard to love her two kids."

When asked directly about Mark's role in her life today, Thatcher was not at all pleased. "He is helping make some of the arrangements, and he is a very, very good businessman. He's a born businessman, as indeed my husband was. He built up his own business and he managed to sell part of his interest in it." When pressed about just what sort of business Mark was in, she reluctantly answered, "It's a big concern for security—the best possible kind of home-security systems." Asked about his qualifications to handle her affairs now, she lost her patience. "Look, my children are not children anymore," she said. "They know about life. I find he is one of the most businesslike people I deal with. You want something done, he does it quickly—there's no 'Oh, well, I'll do it tomorrow.'"

The day after she received the Medal of Freedom, Thatcher was introduced by Federal Reserve Board chair Alan Greenspan to members of five right-wing think tanks at the posh Four Seasons Hotel in Washington. She delivered (gratis) a rousing forty-five-minute address on Europe and advocated the economic equivalent of NATO. Imagine crossing Reagan's TelePrompTer technique with her brains—for these thirsty hard-liners, her words went down like vintage champagne. Anyone who had thought she might modify her views on opposing a common European currency or a European superstate as a result of her downfall would have been deeply disappointed. "Utopian aspirations," she informed her rapt audience of right-wing stars, "have never made for a stable polity."

Her next stop, Dallas, seemed more of a favor to Mark, who made sure she was wined and dined by the civic elite. At one dinner, she took issue with the CEO of the *Dallas Morning News*, who, in a discussion about social inequities, dared to mention the notion of class structure. "Any reference to class distinctions is a Marxist concept," Thatcher told him. Although she was now able to command a cool $60,000 per speech—

$20,000 more than Henry Kissinger gets—she made yet another speech for free to a room full of wowed million- and billionaires. During the question-and-answer period following, she referred to the special relationship between Britain and the United States: if it ever faltered, she promised in jest, "I may come back."

"She's invigorated, in very good form," says John O'Sullivan, but "she wished she were in office." And yet, he says, "when she was in power, there were always constraints—she couldn't develop a positive agenda. With the reception she received from that Washington speech, she realized she could be this new world figure—a female Kissinger," he enthuses. "There are still remnants of official caution, but I could see her shaking it off. In another six months she'll be unrecognizable. She'll just get more outspoken."

In Lord Hesketh's view, "she's going through a period of enormous boredom." Nevertheless, loyalists like Hesketh maintain, one must never count Margaret Thatcher out. "She was destroyed by the poll tax and her views on Europe. The chattering classes—the media, the dons, the Pinters—they're absolutely blinded by their hatred. Because they don't like her, they say she's gone. Exit, stage right. That's a great advantage to her."

"If she aspires to be an influence in British politics, and I think she does," says Robert McFarlane, "there is a need for a pause. If she'll just tap her foot for a while, they'll come her way. They'll realize what a giant she is."

"My role now is to go round the world saying, propounding, what I believe in, and to help those reaching out to democracy," Mrs. Thatcher declares. In the United States, she's already got millions on her side. Deep in Orange County, the denizens are still talking about the penetrating speech they recently heard from her. "After all," said one matron, "she is the most powerful woman who ever lived."

UPDATE: Margaret Thatcher's revelation to me that her life was shattered hit like a bombshell and made huge headlines in England and was reported widely in the United States. In advance of the article, however, *Vanity Fair's* British press release featured one of Thatcher's statements ("Home is where you come to when you have nothing better to do"), seemingly implying that she hated the prospect of going home. That was not what she had meant, but this interpretation was subsequently pounced upon by the British press in a controversy that lasted for days and included spirited letters, defending the article, to the London *Times* and other publications by *Vanity Fair's* then editor, Tina Brown. On the other hand, I received congratulatory calls and letters from some of Thatcher's close associates telling me how accurate they felt the article to be and saying that they thought it would help her. Senator Daniel Patrick Moynihan totally surprised me by including the article in the *Congressional Record* with the comment "Fleet Street could do no better, indeed not half so well." Lady Thatcher, of course, was not pleased.

The following Christmas, Simon Doonan, the witty British creative director for Barney's department store in New York, who had not yet launched his successful writing career, used my article as the basis for one of Barney's holiday windows. His depiction of the Iron Lady in a skirt of dangling chains and belt buckle reading "Tory Toy" was truly outrageous. She was pictured ironing Sir Denis Thatcher's boxer shorts, and on the mirror of her iron dressing table was scrawled, "I have never been defeated."

In the summer of 2000, when Steve Forbes was running for the Republican nomination for president, my husband and I were lucky enough to be invited to a dinner in Nantucket, on the Forbes yacht, for Lady Thatcher and Sir Denis, who, during his wife's toast, banged his hand on the table saying, "Hear, Hear," in a manner that reminded me of the *amens* shouted in black congregations. He died in the summer of 2003, and by all accounts, Margaret Thatcher, who was as devoted to him as he had been to her, has felt his loss keenly; she no longer makes public appearances and has suffered a series of small strokes. Sir Denis's motto during his wife's tenure was "Always present, never there." That night at my table he was highly entertaining, explaining that, of course, "Princess Diana was mentally unstable. She's a Spencer and they have been mad since the thirteenth century!" For her part, Margaret Thatcher had lost none of her aplomb. She was perfectly coiffed and after dinner spoke as forcefully as ever. I concentrated on Sir Denis and was deeply grateful that Lady Thatcher seemed to have no recollection of me whatsoever.

Part II:

Reinventions, Second Acts, Grand Finales

Notes from the Celebrity-Industrial Complex II

I have been covering famous, powerful people since the 1970s, when I became the third woman writer at *Newsweek* and my beat was pop music/Hollywood. In those days—quaint now, despite the counter-culture's sex, drugs, and rock 'n' roll—an entertainment or sports celebrity getting a cover from *Newsweek* or *Time* was a fairly rare achievement. Prime space was reserved for icons, and the magazines did not want to dilute their own significance by putting undue emphasis on entertainment figures.

My first cover story was Bob Dylan, my second Stevie Wonder. The fifth brought down the house. When Bruce Springsteen, still a personally awkward but brilliantly talented twenty-six-year-old, landed on the covers of the two newsweeklies at once, the outcry over excessive publicity actually hurt his career. People screamed overload. As *Newsweek*'s writer, I had to deal with a lot of the brickbats and accusations of hype. Springsteen's people, who originally pushed for both covers, suddenly worried that their client's genuine talent would be overlooked in the shuffle. Can you imagine how much attention it takes these days before the agents get worried? Overexposure is par for the course now; there's no sense that today's stars are supposed to last. A constant stream of new names is necessary to keep the wheels turning and the dollars flowing.

When I started out, access to stars was fairly simple. A famous person who wanted a cover would accept the reporter or writer assigned as well as the photographer. Control wasn't negotiable, and publicists weren't treated like power players. Cover shoots lasted a couple of hours, and the subject mostly wore his or her own clothes—racks of designer offerings and flown in stylists were reserved for fashion shoots. In terms of the story, the subject made himself or herself available along with costars, friends, and family. There was a fairly free give-and-take; reporters weren't trying to entrap or play gotcha, but neither were the articles bland or devoid of content.

Now so much celebrity reporting has become boring, because cooperation from stars often involves negotiations worthy of Colin Powell, including a series of demands to be met, questions not to be asked, insistence on quote approval, and other stipulations. Some magazines and TV programs agree to the stipulations because stars draw audiences. But the interviews used to be more of a conversation: once, during work on a cover story on Francis Coppola for *Godfather II,* I told the director an anecdote I had heard from a friend whose uncle was mafia don Joe Bonnano. Disguised as a raving Howard Hughes (with unkempt long gray hair and grown-out, dirty fingernails), the Don-on-the-lam had advised my *Newsweek* pal Peter Bonventre: "Listen, kid. Keep your friends close but your enemies closer." I told Coppola the line, and he liked it so much he had it looped into the movie.

Even a few years later, things were different with Coppola. One of the themes running through this book is the way people who are made into celebrities lose any sense of reality. Inside the big room, a lot gets distorted. And it starts when the rules that govern mere mortals stop applying. Coppola was always treated like a cross between the Dalai Lama and Cecil B. DeMille. Three years after the deserved, ecstatic reception of *Godfather II* had increased his creative genius quotient, I basically conned my way onto the very closed set of his film *Apocalypse Now* in the Philippine jungle.

I arrived by canoe two and a half hours from the nearest town after a nineteen-hour flight to Manila from New York. The shoot was hell: among other disasters, leading man Martin Sheen suffered a heart attack and a typhoon destroyed sets. Coppola had become so driven, so catered to, so possessed by his desire for authenticity that just about anything seemed possible out there. Prop man Doug Madison had reached the point where he thought nothing of driving four hundred miles to fetch a special army knife. (He also made a connection with a supplier of real corpses.) At one point, when Coppola asked Dean Tavoularis to come up with a thousand blackbirds, the baffled production designer considered making cardboard beaks for pigeons and dying them black. By the time I arrived, the crew had started to resemble the out-of-control GIs the movie was about. The making of the movie become a modern myth of mono-mania.

At one point, Coppola, on some sort of bizarre whim, I guess, told me that I could use one quotation of his in my story—whichever one I wanted. But only one. The more I thought about it, the more ludicrous and arbitrary this admonition became. On my last day in the jungle, we were on a PT boat with the crew about a half hour up the river from the main location. Everyone was anxious—the first shot of the day kept get-ting postponed. As it got later and later, I knew it was almost time for me to go. So I thanked Francis, who was dressed in rumpled white Mao paja-mas, for the fascinating experience. I added (naively and honestly) that I thought I had a really good story but could not guarantee a cover if he held me to his one-quote rule.

Hearing this, Coppola flew into a rage and began to denounce me in front of the entire crew. He was so furious that he threw a $7,000-camera lens into the river and ordered our boat turned around so I could be thrown off. I felt worst for the crew, who would lose precious hours of the day's shoot. Ultimately, I did not write a cover story. I did, however, report that the $15,000 the film company paid the pilots the first day of the big helicopter scene was pocketed by the officer of the Philippine air force in charge (then under the corrupt dictatorship of Ferdinand Marcos), and every day thereafter the pilots made demands for money before they would fly. This detail showed just how complicated it was to make the movie in this location and I was told caused Coppola trouble with Marcos's government. Although the *Newsweek* story was essentially posi-tive, Coppola did not speak to me for years.

I tell these stories to illustrate the differences between then and now and maybe to point out what has been lost. In my early days, stories about famous people focused mostly on their achievements, the content of their work, and the way it got done. Michael Jackson dangling his baby from a hotel balcony would have been considered a tragedy or an oddity, but the scene would not have been replayed hundreds of times a day on TV at the moment when the country was preparing for war. But now, with so much entertainment just pap and politicians' insights boiled down to sound bites, we tend to home in on the drama of the stars' and politicians' private lives. Their "reality" has become the soap opera, the big show, even if it's clearly a rigged-up carnival. We barely need the movies or the speeches. (Would Nicole Kidman, who has proven herself to be a serious actress, be getting all those terrific parts if she hadn't also been made into mass-marketable tabloid fodder as the former Mrs. Tom Cruise?) But which parts of the well-crafted little dramas that public figures invent for public consumption are in fact real? We tend to think of manufactured biographies and stories rigged for publicity as the province of MGM and the golden years of Hollywood. But it still goes on and the techniques of those who are part of the star-making machinery are more sophisticated than ever.

The key to staying in the public eye, of course, is the ability to continually fascinate and surprise. Elizabeth Taylor—the Madame Curie of Fame Extension—made herself into a living-and-breathing soap opera with her serial husbands and health crises. Michael Jackson, who regularly employs crutches and wheelchairs to spark sympathy, has attempted to follow suit. Liza Minnelli's short-lived marriage to David Gest, not to mention his charges of her battering him, got the world to pay attention. Sharon Stone's near-death experience with a brain aneurysm became instant material for a TV interview. These maneuvers may catch the cameras, but if they're not accompanied by stellar work, or if the figure is not sympathetic to begin with, these attention-grabbing occasions can create an aura of opportunism around those they are meant to enshrine. When President Lyndon Johnson raised his shirt for photographers in order to bare his scar from an operation, the public was repulsed. Similarly, Al Gore's invocation, at the Democratic convention of 1996, of his sister's untimely death from lung cancer mostly backfired.

Monica Lewinsky's desire for the limelight and her surreal confusion over how to attain it may be emblematic in today's environment. In another time, she might not have harbored the delusion that her hug with Bill Clinton as she stood in that rope line in her black beret, or their affair, had made her some kind of star. At the height of the Whitewater scandal, I met Monica one night in Washington. When she heard I was with *Vanity Fair*, it became clear she wanted to be photographed for the magazine. Her eagerness to be immortalized in this once-humiliating situation suggested that—like her lawyer at the time—she had acquired a case of advanced attention addiction. Like so many, Lewinsky had lost any sense of the distinction between fame and infamy.

Not everyone resorts to extreme behavior to catch the public's eye. Some people just deliberately become a little racier than they usually are. The designer Karl Lagerfeld, my most enjoyable assignment ever, allowed me to observe him preparing two new collections in Paris. Lagerfeld takes delight in verbal zingers and provocative pronouncements intended to get him into print. He assumes you get the irony. In 2002 he lost ninety pounds and radically transformed his image. The man who once appeared daily in baggy black Japanese pajamas, wielding a fan, was suddenly wearing tight-tight blue jeans and making his haute couture clothes so skinny that even the models could not fit into them. Kaiser Karl has kept himself front and center on the highest perch of snobby chic for over two decades, no small feat. But there is a sense of aloneness about him, as there so often is with unique and fantastically successful people. Lagerfeld seems to spend a great deal of time on his own in the rooms where he reads, sketches, sends faxes, and dreams up his next metamorphosis. He is a truly sophisticated chameleon. But others rely on less subtle sorts of transformations to maintain the public's attention.

Reinvention is tricky, and I have observed the masters. To repeatedly transform yourself, you have to be shameless—you can't take half-measures if you want to be continuing camera fodder. But beyond the old Liz and Cher remakes, what we are seeing today in the celebrity-industrial complex is a more drastic kind of reinvention. In politics and in entertainment, star figures are allowed to walk away from their pasts. Arnold Schwarzenegger's overwhelming victory in the California recall campaign, despite the fact that more than a dozen women came forward to complain that he groped or humiliated them, indicates that star power and the yearning to identify with a celebrity can erase the past. But Arnold is just the tip of the iceberg. I am constantly confounded by the ease with which famous people simply ignore the truths of their earlier lives. Of course, these vanishing acts owe a great deal to the millions of dollars paid to experts skilled at making the public forget. The sheer volume of lifestyle stuff whizzing from the Internet, the newsstand, and TV also makes it virtually impossible to keep up. Still, it unnerves me to see what people get away with.

My personal champion of reinvention is Arianna Stassinopoulos Huffington, a onetime California gubernatorial candidate in the 2003 recall election—as an Independent—and surely the most ruthlessly focused and opportunistic woman I have encountered. Many of Arianna's past incarnations seem to have drifted away, like the fog off Malibu. She just keeps slipping in and out of selves, and no one takes the time to plow through her messy discard pile.

Huffington arrived in the United States a virtually penniless Greek immigrant after being a skilled debater at Cambridge University. Her rise to prominence there was fueled by a relationship with an older man who had wide media and political contacts. Later, in New York, she crashed onto the social scene determined to find a rich husband. She dated media mogul and real estate developer Mort Zuckerman and former California governor Jerry Brown. (In those early years, she espoused liberalism.) She made her name as an author, writing biographies of Maria Callas and Picasso, although she has been sued for plagiarism once and accused at least two other times.

At the time I was tracking Arianna in 1994, she was pushing her then husband, Michael Huffington, in a race for the United States Senate. (They are now divorced, and he has come out as a bisexual—something she denied to me.) An awkward, fiscally right-wing member of Congress from Santa Barbara, Michael spent $28 million of his own inherited money to run for the Senate. Despite her history as a liberal, Mr. and Mrs. Huffington campaigned as conservative Republican followers of House speaker Newt Gingrich, who was then receiving huge attention from the media. Arianna, particularly, was an enthusiastic cheerleader for Gingrich's right-wing agenda, hosting parties to promote his Contract with America. In articles and columns she urged Gingrich to run for president. "There is a moral imperative for him to fill the leadership vacuum," she wrote.

After her husband lost the Senate race and proved himself not ready for prime-time politics, the couple divorced. Arianna got the cold shoulder from the Bushes after her hero Newt Gingrich fell from power. No problem. She went to Los Angeles, picked up a populist message (attacking SUVs), and became a gubernatorial candidate as a Hollywood liberal darling and now attacks big money interests in campaign finance. Comedians Al Franken, Bill Maher, and Harry Shearer gave her fundraisers, and she got contributions from Aaron Sorkin (creator of *The West Wing*), Dustin Hoffman, Candice Bergen, and Barbra Streisand, as well as the heads of Warner Bros., Universal, Miramax, and MTV.

During his former wife's campaign for the governor's seat, Michael Huffington accused Arianna of using his generous, nontaxable child-support payments for their two daughters to finance her born-again political career. The *Los Angeles Times* reported that Arianna, who lives in a Brentwood mansion and wrote *Pigs at the Trough* (about corporate fat cats and their tax loopholes), paid no state income tax and less than $800 in federal taxes. She also hired a tobacco and gaming lobbyist to run her campaign. Her leapfrogging political identity was duly mentioned in the media, but there was no in-depth coverage of many of the complexities that have defined Arianna's very public life—including her alleged plagiarism and her controversial marriage—not to mention her longtime guru, whom Michael Huffington refers to as his former wife's Achilles' heel.

For years no one has bothered to probe Arianna's allegiance to the bizarre Santa Barbara New Age guru John-Roger, who calls himself the

Preceptor Consciousness and considers himself above Jesus Christ. Among Roger's followers, Arianna has attained the level of Soul Initiate, the highest rung of his belief system, which requires invoking his name in prayer three times a day. According to numerous fallen-away members of Roger's circle (who observed her with him for years), he has always encouraged his disciple's quest for fame and power. Although she shied away from paying taxes in 2002, she contributed $6,800 to John-Roger.

Then there is the Queen Mother of All Reinvention. I met Madonna, who was given to me as a cover assignment, in 1992, and of course I was curious. Madonna's drive matches Arianna Huffington's, but there is where the similarity ends. I once quipped that I had no idea what the nuns did to Madonna in the second grade, but whatever it was, she has been making us all pay for it ever since. At the time of our meeting, I found a tough, middle-class, ex-Catholic girl who craved to be really, really bad so that she could be noticed even more. I also found a woman who represents, perhaps more than anyone else, one of the truths about fame today. It is not only hard to get famous; it is even harder to stay cutting-edge. The pursuit and nurturing of fame is a job that can occupy the seeker twenty-four hours a day, seven days a week—and that doesn't count doing the actual work. Fame takes endless maintenance, fine-tuning, damage control. It is a never-ending task, and Madonna has tackled it with a steely determination and zeal.

During our interview, I got the first look at what turned out to be the biggest misstep of Madonna's career, the publication of her book *Sex*, in which she posed—in the book's more innocent pages—as a nude hitchhiker. Interestingly, after the embarrassment of *Sex*, it was suggested that the only way for Madonna to come back from the debacle would be to do a 180-degree switch and have a baby. In other words, transform herself once again.

Now, she is married and the mother of two, and it has been with some amusement that I have watched her trajectory from the sex book to her latest literary effort—her first children's book, which she debuted in London while wearing a dowdy floral print dress fit for a 1950s British mum. This outing took place a mere three weeks after some parts of the media—perhaps reduced to a state of nostalgia by the singer's dominatrix boulevardier getup—treated her smooch with Britney Spears at the 2003 VH1 music awards as a revelatory moment in our culture. (Come on. This was a gathering of rock 'n' roll stars, not a DAR convention. Are we really to believe that this pale attempt at titillation left Marilyn Manson and Tommy Lee in a state of shock? I mean, let the record show that Barbara Walters, herself a champion at staying on top, kissed actress Julianne Moore on the mouth during an interview about four months before the Madonna-Britney smooch. Is Madonna now taking her cues in the steam-heat derby from a woman who once shared a desk with Harry Reasoner?)

Like Michael Jackson, who is the same age, forty-five, Madonna is having a hard time holding on to a younger audience. Each of her last CDs has sold fewer than the one before. Now she appears to be pioneering the art of being at least two people at once. You can see her in garters on VH1 and I would not be surprised to see her appearing next on *Sesame Street*. Stars have nine lives—at least, many during the same week. Past realities and identities are easily erased. In the celebrity-industrial complex, reinvention and transformation are games that must be mastered and, increasingly, no one is noticing just how radical these metamorphoses are becoming.

The Diva Lets Her Hair Down: Madonna

"I will not feel this pain in my heart."

October 1992

Madonna and I are sitting side by side on her navy silk art deco sofa looking at *Sex*. The perfume of decaying gardenias permeates her steamy New York living room, a space that has, despite a Fernand Léger over the fireplace, the solitary feel of a deserted, if elegant, 1930s hotel lobby. Wearing ragged cutoffs and looking exhausted, her face blotchy and without makeup, she barely resembles the star auteur who flashes and slashes her way through the 128 pages of *Sex*, perhaps the dirtiest coffee-table book ever published.

I am not allowed to turn the pages. She turns them. Madonna must be in control, despite her command: "Pretend I'm not here." Taking a break from twelve-hour days in the recording studio, she is allowing me a first peek at what she hopes will be the worldwide publishing phenomenon of the year—her latest reinvention of her go-for-broke image: Pansexual Madonna, in your face hard, if not hardcore.

"She has a nipple ring? She pierced her nipple?" I ask weakly about a woman in one of the first images. "Everything in their bodies is pierced," Madonna says of her two costars in the first section of *Sex*. The book is billed as the enactment of Madonna's private sexual fantasies, brought to the page by her longtime collaborator, the photographer Steven Meisel. Just to get things rolling, her first supporting actors are two unnamed, tattooed, and bare-breasted lesbian skinheads, who answered a casting call for the book and whose appearance would probably cause Don King's hair to go straight up to heaven.

"She's showing me her clit ring. That's why I have that expression on my face," Madonna says. Her *egad!*-I'm-caught look in another pose, she assures me, "is supposed to establish the humor of the book." Nobody is smiling, however, in the many bondage images of Madonna—her fondling and sucking threesomes with the two women, complete with masks, knives, and whips. "This is pretty scary," I say of a photo of one of the skinheads holding an unsheathed stiletto right under the crotch of Madonna's black bodysuit. "It's meant to be funny, not scary," Madonna replies curtly. In other words, it's your fault, dear reader, if you can't see it as fun.

Of course, we all know that the thirty-four-year-old Ms. Ciccone has never been one for a gradual buildup to shock. She seems to have a deep, complete understanding of its value. "She is someone who has a highly charged sexuality, and, unlike most people, she neither disguises it nor is ashamed of it," says Nicholas Callaway of Callaway Editions, the quality publishing house that is producing *Sex* for Warner Books. "She exhibits, explores, and displays it, and feels no compunction about doing so publicly. She also realizes it can be very profitable."

Sex, he adds, "is a real high-low book, ranging from high to low constantly in content, form, and material. It's a microcosm of what her career has been, a series of changing roles."

Sex was shot in various locations, but mainly in New York—in a downtown sex club called the Vault, in the Chelsea Hotel, in Meisel's studio, and at the Gaiety, a male burlesque theater. The word went out that Madonna was looking for people. "I said, 'I'm doing a book on erotica, like my erotic fantasies,'" recalls Madonna. "I wasn't too specific." In fact, according to Callaway, "sometimes she brought people in, and within minutes of first meeting her, they found themselves without their clothes on, French-kissing Madonna."

Madonna's persona in the book is Dita Parlo, a name taken from an old French movie Madonna became enamored of. Dita is known as "the good-time girl," and nowhere is her penchant for arousal more in evidence than in the photos shot in Miami Beach, where Madonna staged public nudity scenes, playing "the housewife left alone too much." On any given day in Miami, Madonna would ride around in a convertible until the right locale presented itself. She would pull up to a gas station, for instance, hop out in nothing but black lace leggings, and start pumping gas. Meisel would immediately start taking pictures while art director Fabien Baron shot super-8 film for a future video. One night Madonna, wearing only a fur coat, ordered a slice of pizza, and when it was served, she threw off her coat and began to eat. "Customers really didn't seem to mind I was naked," Madonna says, "but the woman who owned the pizza parlor turned on an alarm to summon the police, so we kind of got out of there pretty fast."

Madonna's fantasy of being nude in public places was fulfilled when she started hitchhiking one afternoon in nothing but a pair of spiky black pumps and carrying a purse. Nobody recognized her. "A lot of cars just passed me by, believe it or not." One cyclist, however, got right up close and "fell off his bike."

The resulting photo album of the star who flaunts what others choose to hide is certainly unprecedented. But let us not neglect the debut of the writer here. Madonna's whimsical aphorisms, such as "My pussy has nine lives," and essayettes on the splendors of sex with other women are also part of the package, included, it would seem, to counteract the harshness of some of the images. In one lighthearted poem she says, "Her body was a weapon, not a fatal weapon / More like a stun gun / More like a fun gun / She did it to remind everybody she could bring happiness or she could bring danger / Kind of like the Lone Ranger." There are also a series of "Dear Johnny" letters, which depict Johnny, a fictitious character, and Madonna sharing a girl called Ingrid, "a friend," Madonna says, in real life.

"I don't have the same hang-ups that other people do, and that's the point I'm trying to make with this book," Madonna says, scrunching up waiflike in a corner of the sofa.

Madonna's celebrity is unique in that it apparently depends as much on repugnance as on acceptance. Her fame frame, unlike that of most other megastars, rests on people who love to hate her—while monitoring her every move—and on others who hate to love her, as well as on the traditional adoring fans. Perhaps it's not surprising that even academics are doing a brisk trade in Madonna-ology. This fall the pop star's major competition in the book world is a collection of essays entitled *The Madonna Connection: Representational Politics, Subcultural Identities, and Cultural Theory* (Westview Press).

She'll take it all. Anything, it seems, even derision, just not to fade away. Certainly there is no shame, and there never has been. In 1984, Madonna's fame exploded with "Like a Virgin"; at the same time, a negative cover story appeared in *Rolling Stone,* recalls Liz Rosenberg, her longtime publicist and close friend. "We found out then it was because people both hated and loved her. Suddenly everyone had to take a stance on Madonna." Rosenberg quickly adds, "I love when people really hate Madonna—Madonna does, too. She'd rather have that than apathy."

These days, however, with *Sex* on the horizon, the affable Rosenberg is holding her breath. "I've been at this point in Madonna's career before," she says with a sigh. Rosenberg, who is head of publicity for Warner Bros. Records, has already gone through at least half a dozen other controversies over Madonna, involving vulgarity, blasphemy, and sexual explicitness, from "Like a Prayer" to "Justify My Love" to *Truth or Dare.* The scandals seem to come along every year or so. Still, Rosenberg seems shaken by what she has seen in *Sex*. "There's a lot to hate in that book," she admits. She also worries for Madonna's security. "Psychos might see there's a message in it for them."

But from Madonna's so-far-unerring point of view, *Sex* is her hedge against staleness, her latest ploy to remain the leader of the pack, to be downtown and artsy—more Andy Warhol than Marilyn Monroe. "She has to reinvent herself every time out, and if she misses the wave, she's history," says the prominent music-business attorney John Eastman, who handles such stars as Paul McCartney and Billy Joel. "She's a phenomenon rather than a deep creator." So, like, just when you thought Madonna might be stuck catching pop flies in her cap and sliding into second with her tender number one summer hit "This Used to Be My Playground," from *A League of Their Own,* wailing in the background—*pow!* We are introduced to the Naked Marketeer.

Consider her global plan. *Sex* will be the biggest international launch of a book ever: on October 21, 750,000 copies go on sale simultaneously in Japan, Britain, France, Germany, and the United States, in the appropriate languages. The book retails for $50 a copy, so the profit on the first printing alone could run to $20 million. More than two million copies of her album *Erotica* will be released at the same time. Together, she says, they are the work she's most proud of to date. The videos will not be far behind.

Naturally, hype has dictated that *Sex* be a work conceived in tightest secrecy; it has already survived a theft broken up by an FBI sting, and it is hitting bookstores in a vacuum-packed Mylar bag that has to be cut open. To keep the heavy breathing hot, Madonna wants no copies of the book displayed outside the Mylar bag, and the package carries a label warning that *Sex* is for adults only. She is arrogant enough to want consumers to buy her sight unseen, so to speak.

Then, in late January, Madonna will perform simulated sex and masturbation on two thousand screens across the country in Uli Edel's courtroom drama, *Body of Evidence,* for which she was paid $2.25 million, a modest sum considering her celebrity but not in light of her track record onscreen (eight movies and only three commercial successes: *Desperately Seeking Susan*, *Dick Tracy*, and *A League of Their Own*, in which she has a minor role). *Body of Evidence*, which costars veteran actors Willem Dafoe, Joe Mantegna, and Anne Archer, is the less-than-heartwarming story of a psychotic sex fiend who is accused of murdering the rich old man she's involved with by screwing him to death. A studio executive says it's about "hard sex—there's no loving here." Madonna made even big Hollywood players gasp when the dailies were shown. "All of us were really shocked watching these sex scenes. You never quite expect to see this behavior in a star," an executive notes. By way of explanation he can only offer, "She has not conquered movies yet; it's an obsession with her." But what is she really up to? In the view of one Hollywood observer, "She's out to desensitize us and demystify sex."

"They're going to edit a good performance out of her," says someone who was on the set of *Body of Evidence*. According to Madonna, she found simulating sex on camera more difficult than she had imagined. "It's hard enough to bare your soul in front of the camera. But it's even harder, I think, to be baring your ass at the same time." Immediately following the movie's United States premiere, Madonna, a frequent insomniac who seems almost pathologically driven, will personally promote it internationally. Does she ever slow down? Not really. "After two weeks of being naked simulating sex with Willem Dafoe on the hood of a car," she says, "I just want to go home for a week and not take my clothes off."

Freddy DeMann, Madonna's manager, speaks very quietly and pads around in soft velvet slippers, but these are the sounds of money talking. Together, he and Madonna are planning to build an entertainment colossus. "I already have an empire," says Madonna—and you wouldn't necessarily bet against them. A self-described "Brooklyn Jewboy," the tanned, fifty-three-year-old DeMann, who once managed Michael Jackson, is one of a small, tight knot of people who have been with Madonna since the beginning, almost a decade ago.

When the breadth of Madonna's worldwide celebrity is measured, people such as DeMann, who recognized early on the power of MTV and videos, as opposed to radio airplay, to sell Madonna's image; Liz Rosenberg, who taught her to cultivate the media, not hide from it; and Seymour Stein, the godfather of New Wave music and the head of her longtime label, Sire Records, have to be included on the yardstick.

DeMann in Los Angeles and Rosenberg in New York are the grown-ups, the surrogate parents, who freely admit they devote more time to Madonna than to their own families. "My husband has to compete for my time with Madonna," Rosenberg says. "At the very moment my husband proposed to me, I said, 'Yes, I'll marry you, but I have to go on Madonna's tour.' Before I met her," Rosenberg continues, "I had a premonition I'd meet an artist who'd play a big part in my life, that I'd be very devoted to." Then Madonna walked in, in rags again, with one hundred rubber bracelets up her arm. "I loved her energy. She was an original. . . . I was a big believer." But back then, no self-respecting pop-music writer was about to give space to a little one-hit dance diva.

Rosenberg finally got a reporter from *Newsday* to interview Madonna; at that first interview, the great manipulator gave all her answers while looking at Rosenberg. Today, it's amazing to think she ever needed coaching. "I had to tell her to look at the writer instead of me." How about today? "She's brilliant and frustrating and part of the fabric of my life at this point. I have to tell her to eat—I'm like her Jewish mother." Rosenberg even admits that "I dream about her constantly." But the one thing Rosenberg won't do for Madonna is leave Warner Bros., where she supervises the publicity for one hundred other recording artists, to go to Maverick, Madonna's recently established multimedia, multimillion-dollar company.

Last April, after a solid year of negotiations overseen by Freddy DeMann and orchestrated by the attorney Allen Grubman, Time Warner announced a joint venture with Madonna that included her own record label, also named Maverick, and a two-book deal with Warner Books (*Sex* is the first), as well as a music-publishing company, plans for HBO specials, and TV and film divisions. The deal is so complex and operates on so many levels that, DeMann says, assigning zeros to its value is just pure speculation, since all figures—such as the $60 million that has been thrown around in the media—will depend on how the eventual products perform. Certainly, Maverick is being given more than sufficient start-up money by Time Warner, which it must recoup in a few years or, Madonna says, she must pay back out of her music royalties.

"Warner's didn't hand me this money so I could go off and go shopping at Bergdorf's. I have to work. I have to come up with the goods," Madonna says. "The deal with Warner's isn't necessarily about me. It's about developing other talent. There's tons of talent out there, and the idea of finding it and nurturing it and shaping it and giving it life is very exciting to me." To that end, Maverick has recently signed its first act, Proper Grounds, five Los Angeles–based black "anguished rock rappers," according to DeMann, who was busy all summer hiring executives to head Maverick's various divisions. Naturally, Madonna is keeping close tabs on *everything*. "There's the bands I have to go see and the tapes I have to listen to, and there's the publishing deals I have to approve of, and there's the employees that I have to hire to run the company and the interviews that have to take place and the scripts I have to read for movies that I would like to act in. And there's the books I'd like to read that I would consider buying to make movies out of as a producer, and the list is endless."

She currently has a script in the works on the life of the dance pioneer Martha Graham to star in. Dino De Laurentiis, who produced *Body of Evidence*, wants Madonna to play Marilyn Monroe in *The Immortals*, Michael Korda's fictionalized, if exploitive, version of the famed actress's last days. But Madonna feels that playing Monroe, from whom she has borrowed so much, is "probably a stupid idea."

A manuscript of *The Immortals* is on a shelf right above her desk, directly under a beautiful Picasso portrait of a woman in a blue hat. Madonna now has an art curator to advise her on what to acquire. Rosenberg says, "What does Madonna want to do when she grows up? She wants to be Peggy Guggenheim." But there is so much else to do first.

"I don't believe Madonna's taken a full week off in nine years," says DeMann, and her commitment to work was surely part of the investment return Time Warner granted the Maverick deal. "She's willing to defer a relationship, throw having children aside—perhaps forever—in the elusive search to be a celebrity," says a high-ranking Time Warner executive who knows Madonna. "She's willing to defer everything for this. For more covers of magazines. More just feeds on itself. It's like an addiction. Sometimes, in business, you like people to give up everything."

Neither DeMann nor Rosenberg pretends that Madonna is happy. Even De Laurentiis says, "She's a very lonely woman. She needs love and affection from the people." "I encourage her to sit back, reflect, enjoy the success, but it's really tough for her," says Rosenberg, adding, "She's not good at that." "I don't know to what extent she enjoys life," says DeMann. "Nothing will ever be enough," Freddy DeMann declares. "Never."

"So what are you going to do when you get older, Madonna? Time Warner waits for no woman. Are you going to be going on fifty and still get up onstage and shake your booty, like Cher? What happens when your body goes?"

"Then I'll use my mind."

On location for *A League of Their Own* in Indiana, Madonna chafed at the length of the shoot and used her time off the set to write. By the time she left the film, she had firmed up the original concept for *Sex*. Then she sat down with Meisel for what she describes as "meeting after meeting." Throughout the process, Madonna was the hawkeyed producer, hiring

French-born Fabien Baron, art director of *Harper's Bazaar*, to design the book, and later bringing on, as her editor, the writer Glenn O'Brien, whom she knew from his days as an editor at *Interview*. Madonna herself went over all twenty thousand frames that were shot. It took her four weeks. "Ninety percent of the time her eye was right on the button," says Baron, who adds, "America is too Puritan. Sometimes you have to slap people in the face to have them change."

Baron didn't want anything that would resemble a normal book. The metal covers, he declares, are "aggressive," whereas the cardboard inside is "warm. It's like layered." As you open the candy-bar wrapper, you can think of it as "unwrapping a sex toy," Baron says. He licks his lips. *"Schlurp!"*

Enter Nicholas Callaway, who has produced two elegant coffee-table books on Georgia O'Keeffe, as well as last year's admired volume of Irving Penn's photographs. It was his job to mass-produce 750,000 copies of a complicated, handmade-looking art book printed in five colors and five languages, on several different kinds of paper, and including an eight-page comic strip—the kind of book, he says, for which ordinarily you "might expect to see only 250 copies made." For the covers, he tells me, "We ordered three-quarters of a million pounds of aluminum. You can stamp a number on each one." The packaging required heat-sealing. As to opening the Mylar bag to get to the book, Callaway says, "We wanted there to be an act of entering, of breaking and entering." It took a MacArthur Fellow, the printing and publishing wizard Richard Benson, to figure out how to produce the desired quality on a three-story-high, ultraspeed press that would churn out 25,000 impressions an hour instead of the usual 5,000 for such books. So instead of taking six months to print, the whole book is being produced in a record fifteen days.

The FBI agent in Los Angeles had spent one day last June being coached on how to talk like an oily tabloid editor. Now it was night at the Sunset Marquis Hotel, and he and a reporter from the British tabloid *News of the World,* as well as Gavin de Becker, Hollywood's leading safety and privacy consultant, who is employed by Madonna and many other stars, were waiting for the man with the stolen pictures.

Sex had been shot under the strictest security. Anybody remotely involved in the project was obliged to sign a statement of confidentiality and forbidden even to speak of its contents. Fabien Baron himself had installed a special alarm in his studio, where he hid the book layouts in a closet every night. But late last May, de Becker—who never publicly talks of client matters but was authorized by Madonna to speak to *Vanity Fair* about this case—heard from a source in "the tabloid community" that someone in New York was trying to sell a batch of explicit pictures from the book. The person had contacted *News of the World*. Asking price: $100,000 minimum.

"We negotiated a deal with *News of the World*," says de Becker, who made it clear that if the paper tried to publish the pictures it would be sued immediately. One of Madonna's legion of lawyers faxed the same message to seventeen other publications around the world. The British tabloid set up a meeting with the contact in Los Angeles in exchange for permission to print a story about the incident, and the United States attorney in Los Angeles participated in the sting. "If we could arrange to get the guy in the right place," said de Becker, "they would nab him."

After receiving an airline ticket, a forty-four-year-old New York man flew to Los Angeles. De Becker had an agent on the plane and others at the airports, but nobody knew what the man looked like. Fortunately, he contacted the *News of the World* reporter in the correspondent's hotel room—which was wired—and duly showed up with forty-four perfect prints in a box. De Becker, who was monitoring the conversation, said the man balked when he saw the FBI agent, who was posing as an editor— the New Yorker's meeting was to have been with the reporter only—but he calmed down when the agent showed him $50,000 in cash and said he had to go get the rest of the money.

When the G-man returned to the room, he flashed his badge and took the man into custody. Ironically, the alleged source for the photographs was a woman who worked at the New York photo lab that was processing the pictures. She is still at large. "I wanted them to arrest the girl," Madonna says. "But now they can't find her, and the FBI is, like, on to the next case."

Naturally, such drama brought down paranoia and suspicion among the fifty or so people connected with the book until the mystery was solved. "All this security made everything a lot slower," says Baron. Paranoia struck several more times in the following weeks, once in London and once in New York, where Bob Guccione and *Penthouse* got into the act. A couple claimed to have found copies of the pictures on a bench in Central Park. Guccione, who Madonna says would have liked to serialize the book in *Penthouse*, agreed to help out, and had his staff set up a meeting. When the couple walked into Guccione's office, they were met by a detective from the New York City Police Department. But the man and the woman had a foolproof story: they had had no idea how to return the pix, so they thought it best to hand them over to Guccione. "Please get them to the right people," they said.

It is a hot Sunday afternoon. Madonna is violating her rule of not working weekends to do this interview. But work is work is work. She is in a long navy column of a dress, her white bra and bikini underpants showing through, and is wearing high-heeled open-toed sandals and little makeup or jewelry. She is surprisingly small in person and not an overwhelming physical presence. The electricity is conserved for the camera or the stage.

She is alone in her apartment overlooking Central Park West, and she gives the impression of being quite alone, although there are always reports of girlfriends and bodyguard boyfriends floating around. (The most recent names in the gossip columns are those of Jimmy Albright, a handsome fellow in his mid-twenties who works in security, and a former model–nightclub owner, John Enos.) Her hair is wet on the ends, scraggly, and the part is wide and dark. As usual, she has been pushing herself hard, and in fatigue she tilts on that thin edge where street chic can all of a sudden look trashy. She sits rigidly as we speak, and rarely if ever smiles, but her compelling eyes often spark. There is an icy coolness about her that cuts right through the heat. This is strictly business—all business.

"Sex is not love. Love is not sex," Madonna proclaims. "But when they come together, it's the most incredible thing."

"What do you think the proportion is of their coming together?"

"For me? A lot. I would say I probably very rarely in my life had sex with someone that I didn't have real feelings of love for. Because ultimately I can only allow myself to be really intimate with someone if I really care for them."

She is quick to respond, smart, and confident of her ability to answer. When a question bothers her, she inadvertently bites the knuckles of her hands, almost as if she were trying to jam her fist into her mouth. And if she is truly holding something back, the black elastic that's meant to keep her hair in place gets twisted around and around her fingers.

The one subject on which Madonna actually appears vulnerable is that of having children. She says the sight of beautiful children while she's running in the park fills her with longing. It doesn't help that both her former husband, Sean Penn, with whom she was seen holding hands on the set of *Body of Evidence*, and her most famous recent former lover, Warren Beatty, have become fathers lately. "I think it's amusing that every time I break up with somebody, they get married and have a baby with somebody," Madonna says as she begins curling her hair elastic again. She speculates, "Maybe they feel emasculated by me." She grabs one hand with the other in an effort to stop the twisting. "Sean wanted to have a child. And we talked about it all the time—Warren and I. Um, it just wasn't the right time. For them either. You know, everything is about timing."

Madonna calms her hands. "I think about having children all the time. There is a part of me that says, Oh God, I wish that I was madly in love with someone and it was something viable, something I could really think about. But I don't idealize childbirth, and I don't want to just go get knocked up by somebody," she adds. "I think it's important to have a father around, so when you think about that, you have to think, Is this person the right person?"

Suddenly the tiny part of Madonna that clings to being the good little Catholic girl she was brought up to be comes forward. "I think that there is merit in praising family values, and I think that in this day and age there's a lot of fatherless children, and I think that if children had fathers as role models—um, I don't know—I think it's important to have a father, okay? And a mother. On the other hand, to condemn someone for making that choice [single parenthood] is irresponsible."

As the oldest daughter in a family of eight children, including two half-siblings, who were born after her mother died and her father remarried, she was the rebellious little girl who was constantly called on to help care for the younger kids. In therapy now, she can see that her obsessive drive and perfectionism are a need to control what she could not control in early childhood and what subsequently caused such pain. She also admits that her need to dominate stems from "losing my mother and then being very attached to my father and then losing my father to my step-mother and going through my childhood thinking the things that I loved and was sure about were being pulled away." The fact that, even today, her engineer father refuses to acknowledge her celebrity on her visits home must make her desire to shock and succeed all the more powerful.

"I didn't have a mother . . . and I was left on my own a lot, and I think that probably gave me courage to do things," she explains. "I think when you go through something really traumatic in your childhood you choose one of two things—you either overcompensate and pull yourself up and make yourself stand tall, and become a real attention getter, or you become terribly introverted and you have real personality problems.

"The courage part comes from the same place the need for control comes from, which is, I will never be hurt again, I will be in charge of my life, in charge of my destiny. I will make things work. I will not feel this pain in my heart."

UPDATE: As part of the 2003 MTV Music Video Awards production number in which Madonna created an obviously manufactured media controversy by kissing younger stars Britney Spears and Christina Aguilera, she had her seven-year-old daughter, Lourdes, onstage. The little girl was dressed in what looked like a white First Communion dress. But she also wore a special accessory—the same signature "Boy Toy" belt buckle that Madonna wore, so famously, when she first became a star. Lourdes was scattering rose petals, paving the way for Material Mom in a black satin bustier to come on and try to shock us one more time. It was the same awards stage on which, twenty years before, I had watched Madonna writhe around on the ground in her "Like a Virgin" veil, at the very first MTV Music Video Awards, a performance that more or less put her on the pop culture map.

This time Britney and Christina were made to writhe around on the ground in the bridal outfits, while the Big M stayed upright. The whole number seemed geared to making the audience remember just who brought all this sexual titillation stuff to the music business in the first place. Madonna, who recently appeared in ads for the Gap, wants to remind the public of herself at this particular juncture as the sales of her last album, *American Life*, were disappointing. The video for the album's first single had to be shelved: it was considered antiwar at a time when American troops were invading Iraq. She is also recovering from being basically ripped to shreds for her (non)acting ability in her last film, *Swept Away*. The movie was directed by Guy Ritchie, the Englishman ten years her junior whom she married and for whom she bore a son (Rocco).

True to her voracious self, Madonna has now more or less appropriated Ritchie's career, is trying unsuccessfully to speak with his accent (they live in London), and has submerged him in Kaballah, the Hollywood New Age version of Judaism, which involves decoding ancient mystical texts in order to live life "according to the laws of the universe."

What we are supposed to believe now is that Madonna cares beyond herself, that her family has grounded her. As she told Edna Gunderson in *USA Today*, "Our job is to navigate through this world while understanding the only thing that matters is the state of our soul."

Indeed. Madonna has spent two decades in the limelight and it remains to be seen whether she can ever gracefully take a bow or whether she will navigate her way to some previously unattained level of celebrity surrealism.

Recently, she gave an interview to the London *Sunday Times* magazine, in which the interviewer, Ginny Dougary, described a strangely off-putting and dark ambiance around the superstar who hardly seemed in the best of moods. "What followed was any journalist's idea of a nightmare," Dougary wrote of her experience after Madonna had second thoughts about some of the interview questions. The journalist described confrontations with five different sets of Madonna's representatives—United States and United Kingdom publicists and publishers and her book agent—and four weeks of complaints and threats that Madonna would no longer deal with the *Times* of London "unless they had full approval and control of the interview." In the end Dougary says, they did not.

Today Madonna, who has launched a whole line of merchandise tied to her children's books, distances herself from the *Sex* book a bit, implying that it represents her less-evolved, less-spiritual self: "Was I really trying to liberate people? Or was I being an exhibitionist and basking in the glory of being a diva and being able to do whatever I wanted?" she asked no one in particular in the *Sunday Times* interview. "I think it was, 'What am I gonna get out of this? How much money will I make? How much attention will I get?' It was very self-involved and that's kind of where I was then."

Today, however, she would have us believe things are quite different. Her concerns are global, and in the 2004 primaries she endorsed Democratic presidential hopeful and retired general Wesley Clark. Madonna has always liked a tough guy. But she made the general fly across the country to meet her. And she had him audition at a ninety-minute dinner.

The Emperor's New Clothes: Karl Lagerfeld

"I was spoiled. I hated the idea of being a child. They all had slave parts. I had no need for company."

February 1992

The pudgy little hand is pounding the Louis XV table, rattling the delicate porcelain and threatening to upset the shimmering vermeil flatware. "I'd prefer to have my success before me now, not behind me for twenty years, like other people." Karl Lagerfeld's piercing eyes are minus their usual cover of tinted glasses, although his Chanel makeup is on. "My past should only be addressed the minute I'm not part of it anymore and I stop doing what I'm doing," he says vehemently.

The referent names are not so much as whispered over lunch in German-born Lagerfeld's ornate Paris apartment, but two nights earlier the world-wide fashion elite and all of Paris society turned out for the opening of a forty-year retrospective of the work of Hubert de Givenchy. And in June, Valentino had commemorated his thirty years in fashion with a multi-million-dollar bash in Rome. "I hate this idea"—*bang*—"as if all those people are going to their own funeral"—*thump*—"I think it's a nightmare"—*whack*—"the worst habit"—*whack, whack*—and "it's strange it's only done by not very trendy designers, eh?"

A few minutes earlier, the subject was Yves Saint Laurent, who is widely considered in Paris to have slipped precipitously of late but whose image is carefully controlled to make it appear he is in torture for his art. "Look, you want his life? Of course not, eh? I mean, I hear Yves is suffering, but you cannot suffer and bring out the same collection every six months." Then, between bites of hot fish salad and sips of Diet Coke, he continues. "I stopped seeing him already fifteen years ago, because they [YSL and his powerful partner, Pierre Bergé] all changed completely, but I don't like to talk about those people. I am uninterested, because they're not very trendy anymore, so really, huh . . ."

For the ponytailed, fifty-three-year-old Lagerfeld, not to be trendy is a most unfortunate condition: it signifies that you are B, and the *B* word, in the heady sphere of KL, also signifies banishment. The most powerful designer of the moment states his fashion philosophy with a final *bang*. "When luxury goods become an institution, then they are Boring."

Nobody watching the witty Lagerfeld at work deconstructing Chanel just before he showed his spring collection in Paris would immediately think institutional. It was more likely that Coco, who died in 1971, was rolling over in her grave. Her simple chain belts now had three descending tiers hung with a big fig leaf that banged right against the G spot. Her famous ropes of pearls were being reinvented in two new sizes: Ping-Pong ball and golf ball. There were Chanel cutoff jeans in bright-colored denim for $400 and quilted bags in traditional blue denim that the staff whispered would be fobbed off on the Japanese; her tasteful suits were in clingy stretch fabric, or shown in terry cloth for the beach, and worn with Minnie Mouse platform heels with cork soles. And just in case there was not enough product ID, Chanel's quilted eye shadow came in a compact shaped exactly like the top of the famous perfume bottles.

"I'm an intelligent opportunist," Lagerfeld proclaims. "In fashion you have to be. Pierre Bergé says about me, 'He's not a designer; he's a mercenary.' I like the idea of doing things you're not supposed to do." In sixteen collections a year—for Chanel, Fendi, his own signature line, and Trevira fabrics, Lagerfeld labors ceaselessly to land on the charts in a field even more fickle than pop music.

He has been wildly successful. "When Lagerfeld took over the Chanel collections, they had one foot in the grave and the other on a banana peel—it was Seconal City," says Marian McEvoy, editor of *Elle Decor*, who used to cover them. The old-line Chanel dressed the wives of industrialists and French ministers. Today, according to Barbara Cirkva, who heads the Chanel boutiques in the United States, "the average age of the customer has dropped from the mid-fifties to between thirty-five and forty-five." There are Chanel boutiques in Nashville and Oklahoma City and on the island of Guam. Clearly, Chanel has become the upscale uniform of choice. "I never thought for one second I could bring it that far," Lagerfeld confesses. But he has—in trademark *C*s. As *Women's Wear Daily* publisher John Fairchild declares, "Karl Lagerfeld is the designer today with the most influence, the only designer who could bring Chanel to such a peak."

The man traffics in trends—if you sneeze, you might miss one. Who would have guessed a few years ago that he could get women to run around in Chanel jackets with nothing but leggings on the bottom, or that MTV's "Downtown" Julie Brown would be sent to Paris to review his latest signature Karl Lagerfeld collection—lean, transparent, and tight? ("I dunno, Karl," said Downtown Julie, who was dressed in black velvet short-shorts trimmed in fur, black fishnet stockings, and a strapless black lace bra. "That look was a bit more than I could wear.")

"He's got to destroy Chanel, in a way," observes *International Herald Tribune* fashion editor Suzy Menkes. "Otherwise, he just becomes a caricature of her." Says Lagerfeld, "Only the minute and the future are interesting in fashion—it exists to be destroyed. If everybody did everything with respect, you'd go nowhere."

That's how Lagerfeld answers the critics who say his recent work for Chanel—which borrows liberally from downtown hookers and hustlers as well as from uptown debs on drugs, in tank tops and tulle ballerina skirts—is vulgar. His assertion also anticipates the skeptics who wonder if the high-flying Chanel, which employs legions of lobbyists, lawyers, and detectives to protect it against counterfeiting, isn't becoming so successful there's a risk of being knocked off and devalued, à la Louis Vuitton. Lagerfeld begs to differ.

Maybe you are longing for those chic-of-the-week, $1,000 Chanel motorcycle boots?—exact replicas, except for the trademark Cs, of the $70 variety he appropriated from the look of S&M boys in leather bars fifteen years ago. But in Lagerfeld's head they are already gone, out. When a model started to wrap a plastic chain around her thigh backstage at his recent Chanel show in Paris, he stopped her. "Of human bondage? No, we did that before." He was two collections ahead with—are you ready?—quilted clogs for the enchanted forest. The theme was back to nature, "but not boring ecology." Lagerfeld had his models carry sheaves of wheat, the symbol of abundance, wrapped in $650 iridescent-bead necklaces that probably cost less than $50 to make. "Here, carry this," he said to one of the most beautiful girls in the world just before she went down the runway. "It means money—that's all they care about anyway."

The next day the *International Herald Tribune* ran a photograph of one of Chanel's simpler new, longer-length suits ($2,260), paired with a basic tank top ($545), bobby socks, two-tone pastel Jay Gatsby golf shoes ($660), and *really* pared-down accessories, meaning there were only six pieces of costume jewelry on the model, including the poured-glass earrings ($745) and the chain belt with dangling *C*s ($1,000). To buy the whole outfit would cost $9,290. Lagerfeld is convinced it will all sell out. Why? It's not just that Chanel strictly controls the amount of its inventory so that there will always be pent-up demand; Lagerfeld also understands the importance of creating fantasy.

"The reason American cars don't sell anymore is that they have forgotten how to design the American Dream," he says. "What does it matter if you buy a car today or six months from now, because cars are not beautiful. That's why the American auto industry is in trouble: no design, no desire." Similarly: "Give me the name of one trendsetting actress. They are all sloppy and they all talk too much. They're all into political causes. Maybe that gives them a nice feeling, but people want dreams, too."

"Still, Karl, do you really think women are going to spend $1,500 on a little Chanel terry-cloth jacket?"

"Oh yes."

"Why?"

"Ah, this is the mystery of fashion."

Tricycles are strewn across the cobbled courtyard on the Rue de l'Université; twenty children, all family of the elderly American-born countess who rents to the designer, leave them lying about. Normality ends there, however, and the private world of Karl unfolds. It begins as soon as the door to his wing of the *hôtel particulier*, or private mansion, is opened and the first whiff of powerful potpourri hits—the eighteenth century envelops, a moment of perfection for French civilization, the spirit of which Lagerfeld says is "the only real constant in a life based on change."

Once up the majestic marble staircase, one is surrounded by damask and gilt, tapestries and canopies, priceless objets from all three Louis. No wonder Lagerfeld used to powder his ponytail and often still wields a fan. It must be hard to stay out of high heels. Lunch is supposed to be at 1:30, but time in this rarefied atmosphere is only to be used, not observed, and when the door to the study is still *fermée*, the maid never so much as knocks.

Would Madame de Pompadour and Voltaire feel at home here? Undoubtedly, if they and other Enlightenment-era ghosts wanted a place to haunt, these dark rooms would be ideal. Certainly the twenty imposing paintings on the walls of the smallish salon provide endless fascination, particularly the one of Christ just down from the cross with bare-breasted guardian angels protecting him from Roman soldiers (its original owner was Marie de Médicis, wife of Henri IV). To further tantalize, there is just a glimpse through the open doorway to a blue bedroom with a gilded sleigh bed, once owned by a grand duke, and walls covered in silk-velvet *frappé*, made in Lyon according to the records and machinery that exist from two hundred years ago. Then, suddenly, out of nowhere, blasts the old R&B song "It's in His Kiss."

Lagerfeld's universe is one of luxury and irony, lived at a level of European opulence and breadth no American could possibly muster.

Is he rich?

Very. He was born rich.

Then, is he different from . . . ?

Very.

The iconoclastic philosophe of fashion lives at once frozen in time and at the cutting edge of the *moderne*; the software in Karl Lagerfeld's computerlike brain never shuts down. "Style is about defining things, and Karl has to define things all the time," says the writer Joan Juliet Buck, who was close to Lagerfeld in the 1970s. "It's like a search-and-destroy mission for stuff, ideas, shapes, colors, correspondence. Karl can outlast anybody in terms of coming up with stuff."

He is also a very wealthy freelancer, collecting hefty salaries from Chanel and Fendi and sharing in profits from his own line and from the licensing of his name for several top-selling perfumes. He couldn't care less that KL—which, defying recessionary times, has increased by fifty percent in the last year, to about $20 million—may be sold to the British Dunhill Holdings. (The firm also owns Chloé, where Lagerfeld got his start.) Perhaps it's because he's always had money that the pride of ownership holds no interest. "My currency is my work," Lagerfeld says. "I don't want to have an empire; I don't like people dependent on me. I prefer to have a success like this," and he makes an upward, wavelike curve, "not like this," and he slices the air vertically.

Imagine, then, a creator with a keen nose for business whose work spans the globe, yet who disdains the telephone as well as vacations. Imagine that in addition to meeting his sixteen fashion deadlines a year he may, at any given time, be spending a half-million dollars on a single chair to add to his collection of eighteenth-century furniture—one of the most extensive in the world—or renovating one of his seven meticulously furnished houses and apartments, or designing sets for operas and illustrating children's books, or taking all the photos for the Chanel and Karl Lagerfeld advertising campaigns.

But perhaps Lagerfeld's greatest love is books; the eighteenth-century ideal of the cosmopolitan mind and intellectual control is foremost. His discipline is to awake before dawn to begin his strenuous mental aero-bics, the voracious reading of biographies and history, art magazines and newspapers in several languages (as a result, says Buck, Lagerfeld knows all the gossip about all the dead people in the world). Next, he begins his voluminous correspondence, each note and then fax after fax handwrit-ten to a worldwide network—"I have my own secret service." They keep him informed up to the nano-nanosecond.

"Karl is at the center of an extraordinary cobweb. People write to him and tell him things; the world comes to him," says his close friend Princesse Laure de Beauvau Craon, the director of Sotheby's in Paris. "He prefers to be alone. He likes his own company, which must be very enter-taining." The puns and word games flow in four idioms: German, the mother tongue; French, the language of the adopted country; English, picked up as a child because the dialect of northern Germany "was very similar to English"; and Italian, because "to those of us from the north, the Mediterranean represents danger."

The first work shift for Lagerfeld lasts from dawn until lunch (which is always taken at home, and usually alone, in a dining room with a giant television screen). In preparation for the second half of his day, Lagerfeld will spend the morning in a fresh white piqué robe, sketching alone in his study while listening to music that ranges from one of Proust's favorite composers, Reynaldo Hahn, to Japanese Muzak, to the latest top ten. (He has been known to drop by a music store and buy three hundred cassettes at a time.) A lot of his detailed sketches will go right into the garbage can; sometimes two weeks will pass without his delivering anything to his top-notch design teams, who by then are on the verge of despair.

But they have learned to adapt to his late-afternoon, early-evening, sometimes even dinnertime arrivals. Meanwhile, his minions keep busy. Lagerfeld creates a team that can bring him not only the best craftsman-ship but also the New. Several leggy, dark-haired girls are among his muses—twenty-eight-year-old Antoinette Ancelle, an exotic, pale-skinned beauty from a tiny village in Burgundy, is his current inspiration at Karl Lagerfeld, and she doubles as his button designer: she combs the flea markets, on the lookout for specimens and ideas. Ancelle admits that "it's pretty hard to have a private life" with the hours Lagerfeld keeps, "but one adapts to him or makes another life. I don't say much to him, because he knows me very well—you don't have to speak much for him to know you." Still, having seen many employees come and go during her five years with Lagerfeld, she keeps a certain distance. "To be close, it's like fire. The fire, it's very pretty, but get closer and closer and at one moment you get burned up and finished. *Moi*, I warm myself, but I never burn."

.   .   .

Lest anyone think he's simple to read, Lagerfeld is extremely generous with those he cares for. A number of women he knows receive dresses gratis, he has made lots of wedding gowns for free, and he says he has even given away sable coats from Fendi. "I throw money out the window. I vaguely know how far I can go, that's all. I like overspending, because you stay more alive—you're ready for the battlefield once again." Of course, there are times when cynicism overwhelms munificence. "Here, take this," he once said, throwing an antique Mme Grès dress at a point midway between Paloma Picasso and Anna Piaggi, the eccentric Italian he has often sketched, and watching as they lunged for it.

Still, lavishing gifts is almost like breathing. At an hour when the rest of Paris has barely had its café au lait, Lagerfeld's discreet manservant, Brahim, will start ordering the lush bouquets and the thoughtful books that will be sent to that day's favored, usually in pairs, for the city house and the country house. "Karl Lagerfeld is the least selfish designer I know," says John Fairchild. Then Brahim will chauffeur certain pieces of the correspondence around town in the big, dark-gray Bentley. ("Thank God we still have chauffeurs who can deliver our notes," said Liliane de Rothschild on the day she received her nineteenth bouquet of the year from Lagerfeld—her butler keeps a list.)

Undoubtedly, Lagerfeld will also contact his old friend Patrick Hourcade, his private curator, who shares his passion for the eighteenth century but who is also fast becoming the ice-skating impresario of France. "Actually, Karl is most interested in a very short period at the end of the reign of Louis XV, just before Louis XVI, after the first trip of Madame de Pompadour's brother, the Marquis de Marigny, to Italy," Hourcade earnestly recounts. The two have spent seventeen years perfecting the garden of Lagerfeld's castle in Brittany, and now that the castle is undergoing renovation, they have constructed a perfect scale model of forty rooms, complete with precisely labeled furnishings.

Lagerfeld has also been drawn back to Germany of late and is renovating a house in his native Hamburg, on the Elbe River not far from the posh Baurs Park area, where he spent his youth. All his nonfashion profits go to German children's charities, and he is designing, for free, the interiors for a luxury hotel in Berlin. (In exchange, he gets an apartment for life, including room service.) Nonetheless, he doesn't harbor much hope for the renewed nation: "Germany cannot be what she used to be, because there are not enough Jewish people. My mother always said there was some sparkle only the Jewish culture could bring. Germany without Jews is a boring, materialistic country."

Of all his residences, it is the one in Brittany that has captured his soul. Lagerfeld's mother is buried in the private chapel there, as is Jacques de Bascher, his flamboyant, aristocratic, and closest friend for nearly twenty years. De Bascher died of AIDS in 1989, at thirty-seven, and his death has left a gaping hole in Lagerfeld's life—he still cannot speak of Jacques without bursting into tears. In the wake of his death, Lagerfeld, who says he has never been decadent—"I'm not one who can get lost"— rarely even socializes; these days he stays home and reads and watches videos far into the night. He has also completely changed the way he dresses, exchanging his lifelong uniform of perfectly tailored Parisian suits, shirts, and ties, no matter the season, for looser black mourning-like garb of Japanese design.

Jacques de Bascher was an infamous character who looked like a 1930s movie star, dressed like a nineteenth-century dandy, and was kept by Lagerfeld, whom de Bascher called Mein Kaiser, although the two never lived together and, according to Lagerfeld, were never sexually intimate. He says it was *amour absolu, detached from all the problems— money, family, physical relationship—that can ruin a relationship.*

Many found him utterly charming, others unsavory and creepy. "He was the wildest person in the West," says Lagerfeld of Jacques. "But this was like a double life—a kind of Mr. Hyde and Dr. Jekyll, and I had nothing to do with that. If I had had the same kind of life, I wouldn't be here anymore, because he died from that."

"Karl has all the qualities of the virgin," says Gilles Dufour, the studio director of Chanel and Lagerfeld's collaborator for twenty-five years. "He has great discipline. He does not need people around to be happy—he's very much into his dreams, his fantasies, and his books." He is afraid of one thing in his life: betrayal," says his close friend and "private curator," Patrick Hourcade. "As soon as he discovers people do things behind his back, he closes the curtain."

"Karl has always been about being above human emotion, human frailty, the chatter and passions that consume us," Joan Buck adds. "He could look at Jacques's excesses from above, in a princely fashion—he himself was too grand."

When asked if he considers himself happy, Lagerfeld responds, "Happiness, in my sense, doesn't say anything, you know. The only person I really cared for died, so—poof—I don't care." Suddenly Lagerfeld emits an involuntary sob, but he goes on waving his hands as if to drive the grief away. "But it also gives you a kind of freedom—now I'm ready for everything because I've got nothing." His face, which usually radiates mischief and energy, is a terrified mask of tears and pain.

"I'm not a family-minded person, and he was the only thing that gave a kind of sense to things. . . . But the strange thing is, it wasn't physical—it had nothing to do with that. . . . No, it was like family without the burden of family, and he brought to my life a kind of sparkle nobody else ever will. Maybe there is one person in life for you and that's all."

"I was born to be alone." Lagerfeld says a fortune-teller first told him so when he was only eighteen, but he knew it already. As a child he preferred to sketch than "to play with the peasants." He wouldn't need anybody else, the fortune-teller prophesied: "'There are things you can have and things you cannot have. One cannot have everything, and nobody can adjust as well to that as you.' She told me, 'You can never have a normal family life, so whatever the standard image is of happiness, family, friendship, *bonheur* [happiness], for you it doesn't work. Stay alone—watch the world—you can get everything if you are ready not to conform. Stay away from everything that is normal life.' Strange, eh?"

Of course, there was nothing terribly normal to begin with. Lagerfeld was actually born Lagerfelt, in Hamburg, in 1938, when his German mother was forty-two and his Swedish father was over sixty. "I was treated like a grandchild in a way." His parents were rich, cerebral, and cultivated. His mother had been married in a Vionnet gown, and he was told she was the first woman in Europe to get an aviator's license, although he never saw her fly. She mostly smoked and read and played the violin three hours every morning—until one day she stopped forever.

At dinner his parents would discuss, in French, things not meant for small ears, but their favorite sport was arguing about the history of religion—both his parents were Catholic, a decidedly minority religion in northern Germany, and both had fallen away. "When my father became very old, he resented that, because she pushed him out of the church," Lagerfeld says. "He thought he would never die, because his parents had lived to be nearly a hundred and it was his dream to survive my mother. He hated the idea of her living happily, spending his money without him—he couldn't stand that idea."

The money came from controlling fifty-seven percent of the condensed-milk market in Europe—Lagerfeld's father had gotten the concession from Carnation after World War I. The Germans wouldn't buy cans with an American label, so he changed the name to Glücksklee, or Cloverleaf, and then bought a 1,200-acre country estate, Bissenmoor, where Karl and his "much older" half sister, from his father's first marriage (his wife had died), were sheltered from World War II. Lagerfeld no longer speaks to his sister: "She did not behave well after my father's death in 1967, and I never saw her again."

As a war baby, Lagerfeld was much more than privileged. "We went through the worst period of the war without knowing it—this was something my parents achieved that was unbelievable," he recalls. It didn't seem off that there were fifty-six refugees sharing the house with the family. The Frenchwoman who became Karl's French tutor when he was five was only one of many who tended to him. He grew up hearing the story that at four he demanded a valet to dress him and at Christmas dinner a few years later, he screamed and would not stop, because his parents had bought him a copy of the wrong eighteenth-century portrait. (He got the one he wanted, of Frederick the Great at a court dinner, and it still hangs over his bed at Le Mée, his house on the outskirts of Paris.) When he asked his mother to read him children's stories, she told him he would have to learn to read himself, and he did. When he entered the nearby school, he shot ahead two grades.

"I was spoiled, I hated the idea of being a child," says Lagerfeld, who can't really recall any childhood friends. "They all had slave parts. I had no need for company—I had the feeling the world was mine and nobody could say anything." What young Karl really loved to do was sketch. "I was born with a pencil in my hand, and I can't remember ever wanting to do something other than what I do today." Sometimes he would sneak into the attic to pore over old *Vogues* and sniff around the huge trunks belonging to his father's first wife. "I was interested in what people used to wear—I loved to look at old photos. I had the feeling I was born too late— the twenties and the thirties were better times."

At first he thought he would like to paint portraits, but that idea was quashed by Mater. "My mother said this was ridiculous, but 'if you want to learn to paint, you will learn to paint. You are totally ungifted for music.'" He also credits his mother for his rapid-fire speech. "She told me, 'I can't bear to hear your ridiculous stories; finish them before I get to the door.'" It was also thanks to her that he never smoked: "'When you smoke, you often see the hands, and as yours are not very beautiful . . .' Well, you can imagine what this did to a fourteen-year-old boy. I never touched another cigarette." His mother was, of course, "bored to death" in the country, and she remained bored when she and her husband moved to Hamburg, which was nothing compared with Berlin, where she had lived before marrying.

Perhaps Lagerfeld's boredom phobia can be traced to those early days. Yet, in recounting these tales, he seems unaware of how demanding his mother sounds to his listener. "Maybe she was severe, but things were done in a very light way, eh? I wanted to please her because she hated everything second-rate."

Certainly, she didn't suffer fools gladly. Many years later, after her son had become a famous designer and she was living in the castle in Brittany he has since inherited from her, a television-commercial producer demanded to know why there was a little wooden plank overhanging the small pond in front of the house. Lagerfeld's mother, who by this time had striking white hair and dressed in long skirts over slacks, with delicate blouses and a monocle hanging around her neck, threw open the downstairs windows and proclaimed, "It is there in case the goldfish want to get out and take a walk in the garden." She then slammed the windows shut.

Karl was fourteen when he announced he wanted to leave Hamburg—a port city on the Elbe, near the North Sea, which billed itself as "the door to the world"—to go to Paris and become a designer. "You are not snobbish, my son," his mother commented dryly, "for you want to be a *fournisseur* [supplier]." Says Karl: "I was allowed to try whatever I wanted, but I had to prove I was serious about it—there was no freaking out."

Arriving in Paris and never having liked the shape of the *l* and *t* together at the end of his name, Karl created "Lagerfeld" at customs, and that was that. Less than two years later, he won a prize from the International Wool Secretariat for designing a coat. Saint Laurent, seventeen, won the dress prize, and the two have been competing ever since. "You have to understand that, to the French, Yves Saint Laurent is a god," says the fashion journalist Christa Worthington, "but Karl Lagerfeld is a German."

The youthful Karl, so well bred, was horrified by the tawdriness of the *fournisseur*'s existence in those days. The designer Balmain hired him and made his coat, but life in the haute couture was not as he had imagined. "I thought the people were quite cheap, the intellectual level very low," says Lagerfeld, who by then was deeply interested in history, literature, and languages. "The minute you left the gilded salons, it was the worst—mean, vulgar, filthy. People were treated like dirt. But I wanted to stay in Paris and so I said, Shut up, don't think about anything, because you are here in Paris to learn."

Learn he did, and in the process became a kind of high-style hit man, taking aim at both ends of the market, designing shoes, fabrics, furs, china, pencils. His creations always started with a sketch and Lagerfeld always worked freelance; worrying about the bottom line would encroach on his freedom. In 1963 he was one of four hired by Madame Aghion and her financial partner, Jacques Lenoir, to design a pioneering line of luxury ready-to-wear for Chloé.

The four designers competed furiously until there were three and then only two, Lagerfeld and Graziella Fontana, who worked side by side for seven years until Lagerfeld, having mastered Fontana's technique of tailoring, triumphed in 1972 in a kind of lace leukemia: "Karl could do Graziella, but Graziella could not do Karl," Lenoir once explained to *Women's Wear*, diagnosing the competition as a case of "the white corpuscles eating the red."

"I am not a Woodstock person," Lagerfeld says in utter seriousness. "For one thing, in the sixties I hated the smell." So when Saint Laurent, as a full-blown couturier, was taking the Mao jacket from the barricades of 1968 and turning it into the height of chic, all the while becoming French society's darling, Lagerfeld was at the center of a younger, more outré group. The designers were still good friends then—they went shopping for art deco objets together, and both knew Andy Warhol—but it was Lagerfeld who played the role of the bored German aristocrat in *L'Amour*, Warhol and Paul Morrissey's version of *How to Marry a Millionaire*, with Donna Jordan and Jane Forth. As the rival camps asserted themselves in the mid-1970s, Karl was considered the fun one, looser and more accessible. And there was no majordomo playing gatekeeper, as Bergé did for Saint Laurent.

It was Lagerfeld, in a semiprivate show for one of his shoe lines, who sent the black model Pat Cleveland down the runway in nothing but his shoes and a pink feather in her pubic hair. And Lagerfeld who encouraged his older Italian muse, Anna Piaggi—whom he sketched again and again in male and female costumes from all periods of history—in her sartorial excesses, which featured baskets of dead fish on her head and feathery pigeon carcasses at her waist. But he could also be cruel. Another of his acquaintances he used as a model once was a Beatnik artist, the late Shirley Goldfarb; Lagerfeld had her on the runway, it seems, just to make fun of her. Then she did something to displease him and he said, "Ugly is one thing, stupid is another, but ugly and stupid is too much." She was sent away. Observes Marian McEvoy: "All monsters of creation are monsters in other ways."

Lagerfeld was an encyclopedia of retro who reworked fantasies of the past for Chloé—a postmodernist before the term was coined. He haunted the flea markets for antique designer clothes and fabrics; he poured over old magazines and photos and learned the histories of hundreds of Art Deco brooches. He collected old Vionnet, Poiret, and Mme. Grès dresses (never Chanel), and made over the twenties and thirties or the eighteenth century—whatever, it was all referential. When Chanel beckoned, Lagerfeld had already grasped the fantasy and possessed the background and research to understand how to remake "Mademoiselle."

The timing was perfect. "The growing yuppie movement needed status symbols," says Allan Mottus, who publishes a newsletter on the beauty-and-cosmetics business. "There weren't a lot around and Chanel was one of the great ones."

Says the *Herald Tribune*'s Menkes, "In my view the American woman longs for a uniform. You don't see so much Chanel on the streets in Europe. You do in Hong Kong, which is another aspirational society."

Lagerfeld's renowned ability to perform for the press is another, inestimable advantage. Explaining the Chanel marketing strategy, American Chanel President Arie Kopelman puts "the support of the press" second only to "the clothes on the hanger." "I've found over the years that Karl's very easy to deal with," says Fairchild Publications president Michael Coady. "He understands the role we play, at least, and he rides the ups and downs—he's always been less emotional about coverage than most." Is there a moment when Karl Lagerfeld, who once hosted a live TV talk show in Germany, is at a loss for words? Never. "He's good for the whole business, because excitement swirls around him," says Bergdorf's Tansky. "He loves to create controversy. . . ."

UPDATE: Karl Lagerfeld corresponded with me in handwritten letters, delivered in engraved oversize envelopes, and also in handwritten faxes. After this article appeared, he wrote me a long letter saying he thought the story was "great" and quoted one of his favorite models at the time, Linda Evangelista, who told him that the piece made him seem "human but invincible."

Today Karl Lagerfeld has vanquished all rivals—not only managing to stay on top in fashion and continuing to design for Fendi and his own label in addition to Chanel but also photographing album covers for groups like the Rolling Stones and doing fashion spreads for magazines. He also owns a publishing house and bookstore on the Left Bank in Paris.

Much of his success, I believe, rests on his intellectual curiosity spiced with a healthy dollop of showmanship that emphasizes both braininess and an ironic moral superiority. In his spring 2004 collection, he featured models in tiny silver bikini bottoms wearing T-shirts that said "4 Slim People Only," playing up his recent weight loss once again and his self-control. He also remains an avid collector. Last spring, Lagerfeld moved 100,000 of his books into a new underground library in Biarritz, and just as he shed those ninety pounds in 2001–02, he rid himself of his prized decorative arts collections, garnering over $20 million for his eighteenth-century furniture and objets, sold by Christie's at auction in 2000, and more than $7 million in 2003 for his art deco treasures sold at a Sotheby's auction. Thus space is cleared to concentrate on the next wave of acquisitions. To commemorate the 150th anniversary of Steinway, Lagerfeld has also designed a piano. The hits just keep on coming.

Desperately Striving Susan: Susan Gutfreund

"It's a ballbuster, n'est-ce pas?"

November 1991

In Tuscan and Turkish villas, in Nantucket and Southampton cottages, in Venetian castles, in Provence, not to mention *le tout* Paris, London, and New York, global chicdom was abuzz and atwitter, enthralled, incapable of changing the subject: Would Jayne Wrightsman and Annette de la Renta drop her? The Rothschilds, at least, were hanging in. Poor, poor Susan, her former clique gleefully clucked.

Her infatuation with all that glittered finally came to symbolize the fool's gold of an era. Today, Susan Gutfreund is learning just how swiftly those who live by the "in" die by the "out." Not surprisingly, some of the worst sneers over the fate of the onetime flight attendant are coming from her fellow mountaineers, all of whom scaled high society's slopes with a tenacity Sir Edmund Hillary might admire. Hypocrisy endures.

Susan Gutfreund behaved as if she was born to conquer, and pursued her fantasy of life at the top—over the top—with total abandon. Now the extravagant world she created with such obsession may be teetering on the brink of collapse. But, clearly, she is not about to crash without her Chanel flotation gear firmly in place. "Girls like me are like a tea bag," Ahmet Ertegün says Susan told him. "You don't know how strong we are until we get into hot water."

Talk about heat. The pot is boiling over as the financial scandal that has disgraced her husband escalates almost by the day. In August, as

Susan was ensconced on Nantucket with their six-year-old son, Jean-Pierre (né John Peter), paying homage to the wealthy grande dame Jane Engelhard, the Wall Street bombshell hit: the mighty Salomon Brothers Inc., headed by John Gutfreund, admitted to violating the bidding rules at Treasury bond auctions. Had he reported the violations as soon as he was told about them, the much-feared Gutfreund would have been a hero. But he didn't, and today the man once dubbed the King of Wall Street is a target of five civil and criminal investigations by everyone from the United States attorney for the Southern District of New York to the Securities and Exchange Commission. He may face jail time. Salomon is, for the present, being run by its majority shareholder, straight-arrow billionaire Warren Buffett, who joined the board of directors in a stunning, unprecedented move to cut Gutfreund off from help with his legal fees or any other perks. (Gutfreund's response was completely in character: according to the *Wall Street Journal*, he said, "Apologies don't mean shit.")

Salomon traders have already organized a betting pool on which month Susan will file for divorce. No matter that it was the husband's behavior that has been called into question, it was at Susan that the gilded ones aimed jokes, most playing off her famed Francophilia, in evidence long before she learned to speak French properly:

"What did Susan say after John told her what had happened?"

"It's a ballbuster, *n'est-ce pas?*"

They laid it on as lavishly as Susan had in her early nouveau period at River House in New York, when she served caviar as an appetizer, chili for the main course, and floating islands for dessert. They claimed that she couldn't understand what all the fuss was about, that she insisted, "What John did is no worse than going sixty in a fifty-five-mile-per-hour zone."

In some circles, it was even suggested that Susan Gutfreund's hunger for luxury, her fabulous faux pas, her escape to Paris to hang out with the Rothschilds and the Agnellis, made her somehow responsible for her husband's downfall—she distracted him and blew him off course. The merchant princes of Paris, however, where Susan is considered *adorable* and where wives remain more in the background in business, beg to differ. "John Gutfreund is a big boy," asserts Baron Élie de Rothschild. "If I get in a mess, it's *my* fault, not my wife's. If I do something dishonest, *I've* made a horse's ass of myself. If you're the wife, you stick with him and say, 'You've been a stupid ass.'"

So how did Gutfreund get into this mess? I ask Baron Élie's cousin Baron Guy de Rothschild: "I think it's pride," Baron Guy practically whispers. "You think you're the king, that nobody can touch you—you can do whatever you want. It happened to Napoléon, it happened to a lot of big men. . . . It had nothing to do with Susan."

Indeed, it is too easy to view Hungarian-and-Spanish-descended Susan Kaposta Penn Gutfreund as a mere striver about to get hers. Her diligence, her devotion to elevation and to acquiring the knowledge of her betters, are simply too intense. "If some of these women didn't care about style, they could run countries," says one social observer. Those who know Susan best seem to divide into two groups: the offended, who consider her irredeemable, pretentious, and absurd, and the sympathetic, who see her as irrepressible, generous, and charming. The latter are only amused that she told a *New York Times* reporter she was born in England in a thatched cottage, perhaps not realizing that the reporter would also call her father and learn that he was a retired air force pilot and that Susan, the only daughter in a family with five sons, was born in Chicago and raised "all over the place." Her supporters smile on hearing that she informed an admirer of her embroidery-covered walls in New York, "Oh, I did that when I was at the convent boarding school."

Susan Gutfreund comes right out of a great American tradition that harks back to Henry James and Edith Wharton. Past goddesses of self-invention like Wallis Simpson and Grace Kelly had, of course, a little polish to start with. But for the marvelous late-twentieth-century specimens, like Susan, the less baggage the better.

"These women *became*," says the *nouvelle observatrice* Barbara Howar. "They don't have a background—only a beginning and an end."

John Gutfreund was not Susan's first rich husband. That honorific goes to John Roby Penn, an indulged, spirited Fort Worth playboy about twenty-five years older than she who is now married to his eighth wife. Roby and Susan met when she was in her twenties, working as a flight attendant for Pan Am. It seems that Penn, who never had to work, got on her plane and wouldn't get off until she accepted his proposal.

The socially prominent Texas women in Penn's circle, such as Mrs. Elton Hyder, Mrs. Percy Bass, and the immensely wealthy Mrs. Charles Tandy, all of whom Susan courted, found her to be fresh, friendly, and "absolutely precious," says Mrs. Charles Stephens, a member of one of Fort Worth's first families. "Once you met Susan, she never forgot your name. She hit here like a whirlwind—that's Susan's personality."

The newlyweds settled in a big house on a canal in Fort Lauderdale and also frequented Palm Beach and Fort Worth. It was a backgammon-tennis kind of life, and Susan was surrounded by big Texas money. She began to indulge her love of expensive flowers and generous gift giving. Some pegged "Social Susie" as a climber, but, "for Susan, entertaining and creating beautiful things is an art form," her former mentor Martha Hyder says in her defense. "She's a big learner and I have an admiration for that. How can you criticize that? That's the American Dream—someone comes along and learns and picks the very best."

The marriage, however, did not last long and ended somewhat bitterly. According to knowledgeable sources, Roby Penn got hold of a newspaper photograph of the emperor of Japan on a visit to Chicago; in the background was his wife—who had told him she was visiting her parents that weekend—with a prominent Texan whom he knew. After the divorce, Susan began to drift between Texas and New York, one of those attractive women at liberty who might be seen at Le Club. A New York businessman remembers encountering Susan one Thanksgiving on her way to Aspen, even though she didn't ski. Why go? he asked. "Because that's where you find someone who's rich and available, and I'm looking for a husband."

As it happened, she found him in Manhattan, on an arranged dinner date.

Their bed at River House was a concoction of white laces, and there was a button you could push that moved it into myriad positions. It is probably fair to say that John Gutfreund, fifty-one at the time of their marriage in 1981, had never slept in such a bed before he met the earthy and sensual Susan, who was then thirty-five. The studious son of a meat-truck company owner in Westchester, he went to Oberlin when he didn't get into Harvard, majored in English, and didn't date much. He married a woman who cared nothing for fashion or high society and who bore him three sons. They divorced in 1979, and through it all John Gutfreund, a lifelong Democrat who was a major fund-raiser for George McGovern, never worked anywhere other than Salomon Brothers. B-o-r-i-n-g.

"After meeting Susan, he did a real 180-degree turn," says Billy Salomon, son of one of the firm's founders, who recruited Gutfreund and later had a bitter falling-out with him. "He was just like a man who had never had good sex before. It drove him bananas, he went bonkers, he loved it—he would even sit people down and tell them about it." Salomon pronounces the fever a case of raging "male menopause."

Not only did Susan make the former wallflower spend money; she got him to get up and boogie. They hired the socially correct decorators Mica Ertegün and Chessy Rayner; the Gutfreunds were invited to Thanksgiving in Barbados with the Ertegüns and Jerry Zipkin and Lord Weidenfeld, who took it upon himself to explain to the bride the subtleties of when to say "house" and when to say "home." The education of Susan was in full bloom, mostly in lavish displays of orchids, which became her signature. Susan, in fact, gave a whole new meaning to the expression "say it with flowers"—she would send $700 orchid trees just to decline a dinner invitation. In 1983 the Gutfreunds went so far as to rent Blenheim Palace, the duke of Marlborough's ancestral seat, for a Salomon ball—one entered the great hall to find a forest of green and a different flowering tree at each table. But all anybody seemed to talk about was the invitations: "Mr. and Mrs. John Gutfreund. At Home. Blenheim."

In the early 1980s, the banner of society in New York was being passed from those who exalted art and the avant-garde to a new crowd that doted on commerce—and what were parties for, anyway? Susan Gutfreund formed an alliance with the social realtor Alice Mason and was thrilled to be friendly with Françoise de la Renta, Oscar's late first wife, who had shrewdly recognized that these nouvelle party girls could be great for the dress business.

Susan's most important role model, however, was the currently legendary Jayne Wrightsman, who came out from behind a perfume counter to marry her very rich and controlling late husband, made herself an authority on eighteenth-century furniture—endowing rooms at the Metropolitan Museum in the process—and secured a spot on the socialite All-Stars by helping Jackie Kennedy to refurbish the White House.

"I remember the Duke of Windsor telling Jayne, 'We have lived with these things so long *we* don't talk about them,'" says fellow traveler Rosemary Kanzler. Undaunted, the Wrightsmans bought other people's taste and collections and shared their newfound knowledge in much the same way Jayne's protégée later would—leading an art authority to say of Susan, "She copies copycats."

Billy Salomon, for one, was dumbstruck by the transformation he observed in John Gutfreund, once so tight with a buck that he would complain if a partner spent $100 for dinner with an important client at the restaurant "21." Imagine the irony, then, when just a few years later, Susan apologetically told their guest, the very chic international hostess São Schlumberger, that as it was Sunday night, they would have to take her to dinner on—horrors—the West Side. And where did they pull up? Twenty-one West Fifty-second Street.

"I suppose some change began in 1979, after I got divorced," Gutfreund told *Institutional Investor* in an interview earlier this year. "At that time so much of my life was extremely structured. . . . Then I met Susan and . . . my horizons opened up."

And how. After observing the Gutfreunds one New York evening when

Susan implied coquettishly that her favors would be withheld if her husband failed to authorize the purchase of an expensive antique clock, Donald Trump quipped, "She's doing surgery on his wallet."

The new Mrs. John Gutfreund's diamonds were never as big as the Ritz, her only important painting was one of Monet's water lilies—as the art snobs in Paris will tell you, Monet painted a lot of water lilies—and she hung it smack-dab in the foyer with orchid trees climbing alongside it. Nevertheless, Susan was making her mark, learning about decor and becoming a kind of homebound special-events producer. The jaded jet-setters who came to view Susan's buffets, with spun-sugar fruits and bird-cages made out of pasta, dismissed these painstakingly plotted affairs as the work of a "frustrated set designer." But others appreciated the trouble she took in an apartment that was ocean-liner modern, with little touches of eighteenth-century froufrou thrown in. "Susan never wanted to shock," says her impeccable friend Deeda Blair. "She wanted to be noticed." Blair adds that Susan once told her that arranging an exquisite centerpiece was like "playing in a dollhouse."

And Susan was always eager to share what she had learned. Barbara Howar recalls sitting with Barbara Walters at a New York dinner party one night when Susan wafted by and said, "If you all ever want to know anything about trompe l'oeil painting, I'd be happy to tell you." Says Howar, "It was not intended to be funny." Howar, impressed by her friend's generosity and her full-tilt southern style, says Susan thought quite ingenuously that, in marrying John Gutfreund, and all the institutional power that came with his being the chairman and CEO of Salomon Brothers, she had been given a charge. "She thought that by landing him, she had a carte blanche that allowed her to operate like nobody else. What she did she did well. She cared about John and made him happy." But she also "went overboard," says Howar, "and whatever she did was all right with him."

The Gutfreunds tried to keep up despite the fact that their $35 or $40 million was only a tenth of what some of those they socialized with were worth. Who could forget the lawsuit over Susan's insistence on installing a winch on her neighbors' roof at River House to hoist a twenty-two-foot Christmas tree up the side of the building and into her two-story apartment? And her practice of turning out the light above a door that led to the neighbors' penthouse, apparently because she wanted visitors to think she lived on the top floor—combined with her habit of telling guests to "come to the penthouse"—led her alienated neighbors, Mr. and Mrs. Robert Postel, more than once to encounter strangers, including the designer Hubert de Givenchy, stepping off the elevator into their living room.

"We had a procession of masseurs, masseuses, piano tuners, someone delivering two thousand orchids for her ceiling," Robert Postel says. But nothing quite compared with the two A.M. visitation by a group of formally dressed guests, one of them carrying a harp. Postel, clad only in his Jockey shorts, told them, "Sorry, it's not my time to go."

What becomes a legend most? Clearly not River House. By the time John Peter was born, in August 1985, the Gutfreunds were already planning to move to grander quarters. Once the correct module on Fifth Avenue was found, for $6.2 million, Jayne Wrightsman intervened. The job of decorating the Gutfreunds' Gotham château would be undertaken for millions more by the incomparable eighty-seven-year-old Henri Samuel of Paris, who would be brought out of retirement for the commission. He did not disappoint, and created a Louis-Louis habitat fit for a close personal friend of Marie Antoinette's. Susan flew bands in from Paris for after-dinner entertainment in the winter garden, graced with an English porcelain fireplace. It was such fun to hop the Concorde to buy a $100,000 eighteenth-century Russian desk. The *antiquaires* loved her. In the words of one, "She became a great *animatrice* of the market." Thus began the *ici* and *là* of Susan's Parisian period.

"I think she came to Paris as a kind of revenge on New York—to punish New York, to get even," says one French noblewoman. Flanked by the protective cachet of Wrightsman and Samuel—charter members of an exclusive *petit* Parisian tribe of eighteenth-century passionists that also includes Karl Lagerfeld, Liliane de Rothschild, Hubert de Givenchy, and Princesse Laure de Beauvau Craon, director of Sotheby's in Paris—Susan began to soak up the rites and cultural language and to set her sights far beyond those of such New York socialites as Ivana Trump, Gayfryd, and Carolyne. "Some friends asked if we could give a party for them," Élie de Rothschild recalls of Susan's orchestrated entrance. "Of course, everybody knew Gutfreund in business, and Henri Samuel and Givenchy also gave parties."

Although Gutfreund preferred New York to Paris, he supported his wife in her European pursuits. It wasn't long before she coveted her own showplace, and Givenchy came to her aid, asking if she would care to purchase the former servants' quarters of the elegant building he would also buy into on the Rue de Grenelle, in the Septième Arrondissement, near the French Assembly. Once again Samuel was called in to supervise the decor. For her Parisian sojourns, Susan Concorded over frequently, with child and nanny, and installed herself in a $1,000-a-day suite at the Ritz. When at last her four-floor jewel, with its *intime* dining room and newly excavated ceramic-tile garage equipped with car wash and fax, was completed, she was ready to take on the City of Light.

Quickly the stories of her ingratiating extravagance began to make the rounds. Liliane and Élie de Rothschild heatedly deny that Susan gave the baroness letters written by Marie Antoinette worth around $14,000 and that Liliane returned them. But Liliane, who did receive an elaborate eighteenth-century beaded bag once used by French noblemen for gambling, says she considers Susan "like a daughter. She had lovely linens embroidered in Spain for me with my initials and lily of the valley. And years ago she gave me this paper, the Helmsley cipher."

"The Helmsley cipher, madam?"

"For the choke."

"The Heimlich maneuver?"

"Yes, yes. Thanks to that, it saved my life. I've put it up in all my children's homes. I'm most grateful."

For Baron Guy de Rothschild, who was fascinated by the works of Will Rogers, there were out-of-print editions for his collection; for Lagerfeld, delicate, golden eighteenth-century scissors. The item caused a minor uproar, since a gift of scissors suggests the severing of friendship. "But all I had to do was give her a coin back and it was finished," Lagerfeld explains genially. Did he also give her free dresses? "Of course, as I cannot wear them myself."

Many were charmed by Susan's passion for all things French. "During one lunch, she gave us a little course in the eighteenth century and we listened—it was all so fresh to her," says Princesse de Beauvau Craon. "It would fascinate people she had the fortitude to do so—she was exotic for Paris, something new. The bottom line, as the Americans love to say, is that they were a success." As a woman who runs one of Paris's most exclusive salons observes, "Even the rich like to eat other people's caviar."

There was the 1988 party for sixty for Wrightsman—Susan, with the help of the celebrated party planner Pierre Celeyron, filled the first floor of Ledoyen restaurant with eighteenth-century antiques to re-create a period salon, while the tables were laden with silver-framed photos and books the guests had written. For John's sixtieth-birthday celebration, at the Musée Carnavalet, the tableau was a re-creation of an *orangerie* of Louis XV, exactly as described by the king for an outdoor fete, down to semicircular tables placed around a boxed orange tree banked with woven camellia leaves. That party took at least "two months and fifteen meetings" to plan, according to Celeyron. "She is very fussy, but she's right."

A year later, Susan threw another big bash, at a château near Fontainebleau, Vaux-le-Vicomte, originally constructed by Louis XIV's finance minister. (The locale would prove ludicrously portentous: when the king arrived to see such beauty, he called his minister a crook and eventually threw him in jail.)

But when the parties ended, the French always returned to the business at hand. "I have a feeling a lot of people the Gutfreunds saw here made a lot of money with him," says Lagerfeld, echoing a sentiment heard again and again in Parisian society. "Yes, the Agnellis and the Niarchoses and the Livanoses—why not?"

Evidently, the Agnellis had only a vague idea of who the Gutfreunds were until Gianni Agnelli was hospitalized in New York in 1983 for coronary-bypass surgery. Suddenly, day after day, huge bouquets from Susan and John Gutfreund arrived at the hospital. Once the connection was made, she pursued the legendary playboy on two continents and he got big presents.

One Parisian remembers a dinner with Gianni Agnelli and Susan: "Before the dinner Susan was so emotional, she was panting like a girl before her first big dance. And then when he got up to toast, as he went around the room, he also talked about her. For her that was the sublime moment, all that that could represent as refinement. She was so happy. Then I began to see that money for her was serving a way of life—it wasn't just money for money's sake."

"When she first arrived in Paris, she was the gauchest American on high heels," says a stylish expatriate. The social gatekeepers had a field day with her. She made her introduction to the arch-X-ray Jacqueline de Ribes, only to be rebuked for presuming to use the familiar *tu* form with her. "My dear, in France you don't *tutoyer* people you just met," de Ribes reportedly said. Susan, an onlooker noted, abandoned propriety and burst into childlike tears.

But Gutfreund was undeterred. She felt, if not fulfilled, then at least that she had found her spiritual home in France. She gave her all to the effort of remaking herself, impressing even the worst snobs by learning to speak the language well, and adding three more *f*s to her repertoire—fine French furniture. To those she deemed worthy, she was attentive and kind, so much so that many of her friends in France cannot understand why people in the United States would want to be mean to her. "For us, she is very American in the best sense—open, free," says the art dealer and socialite Philippe Boucheny. "Perhaps in the beginning it's difficult and you have to fight. Then when you reach a certain point, a real quality of heart appears. I am always surprised at the intensity of the competition of New York society."

"I feel she wanted to create a fantasy in which she was the queen and

John was the backer of the show," says a young member of European royalty. "Sometimes I thought I saw a touch of madness in her, as if she lived a fantasy life. The power of imagination is fascinating because, for Susan, for a time, it really did become reality."

UPDATE: In the wake of the Salamon Brothers scandal, Susan Gutfreund assumed a much lower profile. Her husband was fined $100,000 for his role in the Treasury-bond trading scandal and banned from ever leading a brokerage house. But even a decade later, in 2002, the *Journal of Business Ethics* produced a scathing paper denouncing Salomon Brothers' "unethical organizational culture under the leadership of John Gutfreund"; thus Susan Gutfreund has been denied the grand stage to mount the tableaux starring herself and the crème of international society she once ardently pursued.

The Gutfreunds still maintain the lavish apartment on Fifth Avenue that was decorated by the late Henri Samuel, a pied-à-terre in Paris, and a rented house outside Philadelphia, where Susan, now an interior decorator, pursues her passion for early-American furniture. Last year she announced in *Women's Wear Daily* that she and her teenage son, John Peter, planned to launch a line of eco-friendly jogging suits made from soybean and bamboo fabrics, which proves that Susan is no longer biting off more than she can chew.

Cult Favorite:
Arianna Stassinopoulos
Huffington

*"I can be cruel. Of course, I'm trying to
improve myself every day."*

November 1994

Fueled by his father's money, Texas millionaire Roy Michael
Huffington Jr. is trying to buy his way into 1600 Pennsylvania Avenue in
1996, after brief stops in the House and the Senate. He hasn't quite made
it to the latter yet. That's why the first-term member of Congress from
California, who moved to Santa Barbara from Texas only four years ago,
is setting his own sort of record: he's on his way to spending more money
(perhaps $25 million) on a Senate campaign than anyone in history. But
that's only one part of the story, and it's not the interesting part. That
would be his wife.

"If anyone thinks she hasn't seen herself in the White House yet, then
they don't know Arianna Stassinopoulos Huffington," says Peter Matson, a
former literary agent of the Greek-born, Cambridge-educated author.
"Michael was searching for himself, and Arianna found him," says a friend.
"My illustration for them is 'Driving Michael Huffington': Arianna wearing
a cap behind the wheel and Michael sitting in the backseat looking perfectly bewildered."

Yet Huffington has already managed to win once with the help of his
wife, who frequently spoke in his place. In 1992 he spent $5.2 million—
$43 a vote—in a mostly Republican district, in a slash-and-burn cam-
paign for the House seat. Now, in the process of spending five times that
amount against Democratic incumbent senator Dianne Feinstein, he's

rapidly depleting his $70-million share of the money from the sale of Huffco, the oil-and-gas company his father created. And he's running the entire campaign on TV, with everything he says scripted. He doesn't even have to talk to the media or to the voters.

"He's a media projection. When the cameras go away, nothing is there," says political reporter Nick Welsh of the *Santa Barbara Independent,* in which Huffington is routinely referred to as "the alleged congressman." Indeed, Michael Huffington could easily become the Chauncey Gardiner of the 1990s—the man who says nothing to great acclaim. "Huffington has never stood up for anything: I've never seen a position paper, a press conference, even an ad where he's said anything," declares the Santa Barbara County Republican activist Hazel Richardson Blankenship. "Once in a while you can actually get a complete idiot elected to the U.S. Senate, and it could happen again."

I caught up with Michael Huffington and an aide in the hall outside the congressman's Capitol Hill office on the day he reversed his earlier support for the crime bill and voted to block it from getting to the floor for final consideration. Having tried in vain to set up an interview, I introduced myself and said, "Do you remember me? We met at a party?"

"Yes, I do."

"I'd like to ask you just a couple of questions."

"No questions, sorry."

"Just one or two."

"None, thank you, we're getting ready to have lunch."

"But you're just walking along here."

"Will you excuse me, please. I'm with a gentleman."

"Can you just tell me what the most important thing in your Senate campaign is?"

At this point, Huffington called to a congressional guard: "Officer, this lady is bothering me. Would you mind asking her to leave?"

"Is this how you treat the press when you're running for the Senate?" I asked. "Is there a time when we can talk?"

"No."

Michael Huffington's behavior in Congress is considered strange by many ex-staffers I talked to. "He never communicated with us," said one. In the words of another former aide, "We said, 'God, where's he coming from?' I don't know if he has thoughts. A very large number of his policies are reflections of his wife's attitudes." Before a vote that caused Huffington to waffle on his pro-choice position and vote against federal funding for abortions for poor women, he called Arianna from the cloakroom off the floor of the House. "On any big decision, you'd go in and talk to him and leave, and then you'd see his phone light go on, and he'd call Arianna to ask her," says another ex-staffer. "Walking from his desk to your own, you could count 3, 2, 1, and Arianna was on the line."

Huffington is so secretive that he keeps a shredder next to his desk and once directed a staffer to shred an office copy of the *Congressional Record* because "it was nobody's business" how he voted. "You never had to prepare anything for him, because he wasn't going to do anything," says a former legislative aide. For a time all press releases went through Arianna, who played the enforcer. Although Arianna denies that she has ever threatened anyone who worked for them, one Washington aide who left claims that Arianna told her, "You ever say anything about us and I'll come back and try to pin things on you." There's been similar intimidation in California. "Arianna and Michael Huffington know how to threaten people with 'You'll never work in this town again,'" says Blankenship. They exerted pressure, for example, to have Jerry Cornfield, the *Santa Barbara News-Press* reporter assigned to cover Huffington, replaced; they complained about him to the editor and refused to acknowledge his queries. Cornfield soon left the paper.

Since he announced his bid for the Senate, Huffington has not held a single formal press conference, will not release his tax returns, and does not go to bat against the government on behalf of companies in his district, even if his failure to act means the loss of hundreds of jobs. And the general lack of scrutiny of political figures in California, coupled with the services of expensive, high-powered handlers such as Ed Rollins, Mike Deaver, former Reagan speechwriter Ken Khachigian, former Reagan pollster Richard Wirthlin, and Larry McCarthy (the creator of the infamous Willie Horton commercial in the 1988 presidential campaign), has kept Huffington from exposing himself or from being exposed. In one unscripted foray, Huffington told a reporter that he thought his chances of winning southern California were good because he was on the Los Angeles Music Center board. He seems to feel that his wealth is a protective shield, but it also shields him from reality. He told a staffer, "I don't want anyone working for me who needs a paycheck."

Two young men in Huffington's office felt compelled to leave after he hugged them against their will. In front of two witnesses, he told one, "It looks like you need a hug." The man said no and left the room "to start all over," but when he returned, Huffington hugged him anyway, despite his protests. When the incident was reported in the *Los Angeles Times*, Huffington responded, "saying it 'was not a big hug,' and the staffer never got one after that. 'I like to hug people. I'm a hugger. So is Bill Clinton.'"

Chad Westover, a former Huffington aide who witnessed the incident, said he felt that "it was not an embrace" but "more of a management technique." However, Westover said, "from that point on," the staffer and the member of Congress "just didn't click." The young man left a short time later, after Huffington criticized his work.

When Huffington hugged the other aide, the two men were alone. The then-twenty-three-year-old staffer says that, without warning, Huffington came from behind his desk after reprimanding him and said, "Let's hug." The staffer tried to resist; Huffington hugged him nevertheless. After that, he says, Huffington's attitude toward him became cold.

Huffington's support of abortion for those who can afford it and of gays in the military often causes him to be labeled a moderate. In fact, he is extremely conservative about economics: his mantra is that government is bad—just say no to it. He's even been said to advocate the gold standard. When I called a number of Huffington's Republican colleagues in California and on the House committees on banking and small business for comment on his abilities, none would call me back. Democrats on those committees with Huffington described him as courtly and pleasant, but essentially a cipher. "On the Hill he's almost a nonpresence. . . . He sort of floats through the place," says New York representative Charles Schumer.

"He shouldn't be running for the job," says an outspoken Republican conservative, longtime Ronald Reagan pal Barney Klinger. "He's *not*—his wife is. He doesn't have the intelligence to run for the U.S. Senate, but his wife does, so she's running through him."

Huffington did not carry Santa Barbara County, where he lives, in last June's Republican primary. Where the couple is best known and most closely observed, feelings toward the Huffingtons run very high. "The hatred of him is beyond hormonal here," says Nick Welsh. The Huffingtons live in a $4.3-million Italianate mansion in Montecito. Arianna employs about a dozen staff members, and the turnover is rapid. "He's obviously so busy he's not terribly involved," says Barbara Coventry, who likes to be called consultant, rather than tutor, to the Huffington children—Christina, five, and Isabella, three. Instead, Arianna's mother, Elli, a follower of the late Indian philosopher Krishnamurti, holds sway, along with Arianna's sister, Agapi, who has taught a course, How to Be a Goddess, to local women. The servant problem has been acrimonious and unceasing, although Coventry says that things have improved. Not so at their Washington residence, where Arianna hired ambassador to France Pamela Harriman's former servants, some of whom fled within a few months, after being treated "like slaves."

"We were joking about making a T-shirt that said, I QUIT THE BITCH," says a researcher who was diverted to menial tasks. She says she was in tears many times. "Arianna was so cruel—mean and nasty to everyone in the house." According to former employees in Santa Barbara, Arianna issued orders over a speakerphone from the bathtub, kept a lock on the refrigerator, threw frequent tantrums, and sent the children's bodyguards to the store for her Tampax. Worse still were slurs overheard by the staff about "stupid and lazy" Mexican help at a time when Huffington was targeting Latino voters in his district.

By the same token, almost everyone I spoke with remarked on what a charmer and world-class flatterer Arianna can be. "I've seen her charm people right down to their socks," says Hazel Blankenship. Marcy Rudo, one of the principal researchers Arianna hired to work on her biography of Picasso, traveled with her through the south of France to interview sources. "She was dazzling. I saw her operate, melting the most reticent, unwilling-to-speak people. I saw her disarm them totally," Rudo told me. "She has a determination that's beyond most human comprehension. . . . I felt I had been lady-in-waiting to a Mack truck."

There is definitely a quality to both Huffingtons that allows them to go after what they want unaffected by the impression they leave behind. The pervasive sense is that everyone and everything is of use.

Not surprisingly, a key part of Michael Huffington's political platform neatly coincides with the thesis of his wife's latest book, *The Fourth Instinct: The Call of the Soul.* The book asserts that humankind's hunger for spirituality is as great as its drive for survival, sex, and power, and that if we would all get beyond the empty striving for materialism, give vent to our better nature, and volunteer to help the poor more, the wasteful welfare state we live in would be eliminated.

Michael told Charlie Rose on his talk show, "People are ready for something beyond materialism." But his debut speech on having volunteerism replace welfare—delivered to a group of black entrepreneurs in San Diego—was a disaster.

Since volunteerism is meant to be a cornerstone of Huffington's Senate campaign, I asked Arianna where she personally had volunteered. Her response was that she volunteered "very regularly." I had been told that she was seldom seen at her children's preschool in Washington, and, in April, Michael announced to the Los Angeles *Times* that he couldn't recall where he had volunteered before last New Year's, when he gave out food in two shelters, except to do fund-raising for his alma mater, Stanford. But, to me, Arianna mentioned her church and Storyteller, a nonprofit

Santa Barbara organization that cares for homeless and abused children during the day. I was hardly prepared for the reaction I got from Liliana Hensel, the executive director of Storyteller.

"No, she has never volunteered here. In three years, no one has ever seen Arianna but twice, and both times she brought a TV crew with her. It was self-promotion, nothing more. She's never given a penny to us and never even worked with the children," said Hensel. "The board as well as myself feel the same way about her. We don't want our name used in connection with her. . . . It's using needy children in a needy situation for political gain, and it's really disgusting." Hensel went on to say that several months earlier she had gotten a call from Michael Huffington's secretary, asking if he could stop by at one o'clock. "I said wonderful, but the children would be napping then, and I didn't want any TV cameras or press. . . . She called me back in fifteen minutes. He had found another agency. Is that blatantly telling you something?"

I got a similar reaction from Barbara Tellefson, the executive director of the Santa Barbara Council of Christmas Cheer, which runs the Unity Shoppe, where the poor can shop for food as well as clothes and toys made by senior volunteers. Tellefson, who supervises more than four thousand volunteers, was asked if Arianna could visit with a TV crew for "a video essay" to promote her book in which the Unity Shoppe is mentioned. Although Arianna once chaired a fund-raiser for the charity and Michael made a $10,000 donation, Tellefson was stunned when the video aired. It clearly gave the impression that the Unity Shoppe is an offshoot of Arianna's Partnership for the Children. "I received many calls from local people," said Tellefson. "They were shocked and upset with the way Mrs. Huffington and her film editors created the illusion that the work of the Unity Shoppe was a result of her efforts, and that it is her dream to have a pilot program for other cities implemented by a Partnership for the Children."

"They're scary," one of Michael Huffington's former legislative aides told me. "They're scary because it's a process taking place in *America*. Democracy for the average guy isn't there, because these guys buy elections, and they buy them on ego."

To Arianna Huffington, there are two kinds of people who serve in public life: leaders and managers. Managers are the grunts who tinker with the process. Feinstein, whom Michael Huffington told to "get a life" the night he won the primary, "is a manager," says Arianna when we meet in a coffee shop near her home: "Dianne Feinstein was quoted saying, 'Government is my life,' and that's part of the problem. Government should not be a politician's life." Her husband's transcendent vision is "much more radical. . . . Michael is a thinker and a leader. We're not going to turn things around with managers. Managers reshuffle the deck chairs on the *Titanic*. That's what she's doing."

"You're thinking about a radical new vision in which government plays a completely different role?" I ask.

"Absolutely, where the concept of citizenship is redefined to include involvement in the community." She adds, "Most people in the last thirty years, when they are confronted with a problem, ask the question, 'What is the government going to do about it?' We need to start asking ourselves the question, 'What am *I* going to do about it?' . . . I have given six speeches on the subject, in which I develop this theme." And now Michael is running on it.

Arianna Stassinopoulos first became noticed in her undergraduate days at Cambridge. As the first foreign-born woman president of the Cambridge Union, the venerable debating society, she was led into a romance and ongoing affiliation with a reigning cultural figure of the time, the pundit Bernard Levin, whom she met as a fellow quiz-show contestant. An avid disciple of the late discredited guru Bhagwan Shree Rajneesh, Levin long wrote Arianna's toasts for her and still advises her on her books.

"Even then," says a Cambridge classmate, "she was ambitious beyond measure." Soon Arianna was launched into British society and the great beyond, eventually becoming the author of six books. (She has been accused of appropriating parts of three from other writers.) In our interview, to which she has volunteered to come in place of her husband, many of the techniques she learned on the debating fields of Cambridge are put into play.

For example, I try to pin her down on why Michael will not release his income tax returns. At first, Arianna avoids answering: "He has done everything that is required by law." Next, it is Feinstein's fault: "He feels that he has released everything that is legal. He feels Dianne Feinstein has attacked him for not paying his taxes." Then she implies that the problem is mine for having asked the question. "I think that maybe you have made up your mind."

Arianna claims that she has no input whatsoever into Michael's congressional office, that she merely helps out with strategy in his campaigns: "These are all illusions, [that] all these things in his congressional office go through me—it's just totally unreal and untrue." She does not know that I have just spoken to her supporter Donald Smith, the executive director of the Western Commercial Space Center at Vandenberg Air

Force Base, which is in Huffington's district. Smith, who has had extensive dealings with Huffington's office, told me what everyone else ended up saying when I asked about Arianna's role: "She's locked into everything he does. She's the one doing most of the talking for him."

Arianna, in fact, disputes almost everything I have been told about her. She even claims not to have a large turnover of servants. Haven't *I* ever dismissed anyone? she asks me, adding that people also accused Jackie Kennedy of having problems with the help. "I can be cruel," she finally admits. "Of course, I'm trying to improve myself every day and get better and be better—at whatever I'm doing." Life, to her, is like "being on a train and going home to God. . . . And outside the train, everything that happens to my life is scenery. Some of it is beautiful scenery. Some of it is ugly scenery . . . but the train moves on."

In Paris in the late 1970s, Arianna Stassinopoulos was ordained a minister in the Church of the Movement of Spiritual Inner Awareness (MSIA), which its followers consider a New Age church but which others describe as a mind-manipulating cult. In her ordination, Arianna, who attained the highest level of secret initiation, Soul Initiate, swore devotion to a curious divinity. The document of ordination reads: "We do this through the order of the Melchizedek Priesthood, the Office of the Christ, the Mystical Traveler, Preceptor Consciousness, and into God. This delineates for you the divine line of authority."

In other words, the instigator of a Senate campaign advocating traditional values has long been beholden to a most untraditional form of religion, led by a guru who considers himself more powerful than Jesus Christ. MSIA ministers believe that the Mystical Traveler, the chosen one of God on earth at any given time, is now John-Roger, the founder of MSIA. The Preceptor Consciousness, embodied on the planet only every 25,000 years and therefore higher than Christ, is personified by John-Roger. Soul Initiates such as Arianna are required to pray by chanting the secret names of God that John-Roger gives them. They either follow the rules or renounce the ministry, which is fully accredited in California and allows them to perform weddings and baptisms.

Arianna, who has followed the diminutive John-Roger all over the world for two decades, has never renounced her ministry. She told me, "That's not necessary. Because to me a ministry is something of being of service . . . not about performing baptisms and weddings." When I asked Arianna if she still chants the names of God that John-Roger gave her—a dead-bang giveaway, according to former MSIA members, as to whether someone still believes—she replied, "These are sacred questions. . . . I pray. I'm not going to discuss how I pray."

Records filed with the California attorney general show that between July 1990 and June 1993, Arianna Huffington contributed $35,000 to the Foundation for the Study of Individual and World Peace, formerly the John-Roger Foundation. John-Roger, or J-R, the sixty-year-old former schoolteacher from Utah based in Los Angeles, was born Roger Hinkins but metamorphosed, during a nine-day kidney-stone–induced coma, into a self-proclaimed god. He has been accused in various media exposés, notably in the *Los Angeles Times* in 1988, of mind control, electronic eavesdropping, and the sexual coercion of male acolytes—charges he denied. He encourages his three thousand or so followers to tithe—to give ten percent of their income to him. Former member Susan Roberts remembers Arianna, during an MSIA retreat in upstate New York in 1987, standing up and saying, "'Dahlings, if you want to marry a rich man like I did, then *tithe!*' Everyone whooped and hollered."

John-Roger has told his followers that they have the power to change weather patterns and dismantle nuclear weapons. Yet Arianna has always defended him, although now she minimizes how close they have been and insists, in interviews about John-Roger's multimillion-dollar empire, that there is "nothing that you join."

"Of course there's something to join. You have to enroll in discourses in order to be an Initiate of the Traveler," says Roberts. "She's a very lying woman."

Perhaps now that Arianna is courting Christian conservatives, touting her Greek Orthodox religion, and appearing with televangelist Robert Schuller on his Sunday-morning show to extol her husband's advocacy of prayer in the schools, her allegiance to John-Roger is definitely something to keep hidden. "If the Christian right knew what MSIA was about," says Dodie Brady, "they wouldn't be endorsing Arianna and Michael Huffington."

Arianna told me that John-Roger is merely "a friend," that "there is nothing I participate in," that "I have not spent many years in his training," and that "he has never been a guru—nobody's been a guru to me." She points out that there is no acknowledgment of him in her current book. But former followers of John-Roger with whom I spoke were incredulous at these denials. Jim Brady, once the head of John-Roger's Insight training seminars in the Northeast, told me that in 1986, when Michael Huffington worked for the Department of Defense, Brady was called by Arianna, as a fellow MSIA minister, to bless her rented house in

Georgetown. "It was just the two of us. It took about an hour, and you have to pray first, invoking John-Roger: 'Light of the Mystical Traveler, Preceptor Consciousness, be with us now.' I blessed every room, from all the way down to the wine cellar up to her office on the top floor." Arianna denied that any blessing ever took place. When I pressed her repeatedly about whether John-Roger was higher than Jesus Christ, five times she refused to answer directly and professed not to know what I meant about the Preceptor Consciousness. "That part of it doesn't interest me."

"Arianna," I said, "I have talked to people who believe that you have been in a cult for over twenty years." She gave me another nondenial denial: "Well, did I do anything ever that made you think that I am a member of a cult?" I mentioned that I had been told that she recruited people and J-R paid her to do this, which she also denied, although many of the social elite of New York and Los Angeles had met John-Roger at dinner parties she threw. Art-book dealer Dagny Corcoran, for instance, told me that on a number of occasions she was seated between J-R acolytes, and that of course she met John-Roger. "It was like trying literally to sell things to your friends. I'd never had that happen to me."

Arianna was key to John-Roger, who, says another former follower, "can read what drives you and feed it. . . . Her purpose fit hand in glove with J-R's." Not only was Arianna passing along stock tips gleaned from the financier David Murdock, one of the rich men she was trying to land at the time: she was also able to introduce John-Roger to such people as Peter Jennings; her close friend Barbara Walters, later a bridesmaid at her wedding; and the actor Raul Julia.

In exchange, John-Roger allegedly paid consulting fees to help support her costly, over-the-top, debt-ridden lifestyle. One of his checks to her was for $10,000. "I was there in his bedroom when they discussed the money for Arianna," says Victor Toso, one of several former members who have charged they were pressured to submit to sex with J-R. But Arianna flatly denied receiving any such payments, and says she lived off lecture fees and her sizable book earnings.

Peter McWilliams, a best-selling author who split from John-Roger only last March and who is embroiled in a lawsuit with MSIA, remembers many times when Arianna publicly shared intimate details of her life with Michael. According to McWilliams, Arianna would complain that Michael didn't want to pay for a big mansion in Santa Barbara because he preferred Texas. At one retreat, he says, Arianna beseeched the guru to tell her how to get her husband to impregnate her again. "And John-Roger would answer these questions," says McWilliams, "something like 'You know, dahlin', we made a deal here . . . and if you're looking for romance in the bargain, you're being stupid.'"

Several of the nine sources I spoke with who had been with Arianna in MSIA told me that John-Roger guided her every step in her pursuit of Huffington, including how to negotiate their prenuptial contract. "He was perfect. He was rich and he had no point of view, so she could mold him," says a source. "It happened incredibly fast." Before and after every date, Arianna would check in with the guru by telephone, to see "what would God do next." McWilliams says, "It was like the Machiavelli brothers telling the princess how to win the war." For his own amusement and that of "the guys" who tended him, J-R would put Arianna on the speakerphone so that they could all hear the travails of her sex life, which she also "shared" in retreats and seminars.

Before Huffington, Arianna had made plays for former California governor Jerry Brown, est founder Werner Erhard, developer and publisher Mort Zuckerman, and billionaire David Murdock. But her major crushes were Erhard and Brown. "She very much wanted Jerry. She was a liberal Democrat then," says a close friend at the time. "She felt he could become president with her behind him."

Arianna Huffington has been accused of plagiarism in her best-selling biographies of Maria Callas and Pablo Picasso, and I have learned that she also "borrowed" heavily for her 1983 book, *The Gods of Greece*. Two previous Callas biographers felt their material had been lifted. One, Henry Wisneski, said he did not care. The other, the late Gerald Fitzgerald, according to sources close to Arianna at the time, received a substantial settlement, although Arianna has maintained that the amount was only "in the low five figures."

When *Picasso: Creator and Destroyer* was published in 1988, it outraged the art world. With the help of Picasso's former mistress Françoise Gilot, Arianna painted a portrait of a cruel sex addict and genius. According to Lydia Gasman, an art historian at the University of Virginia, Arianna tried to ingratiate herself with Gasman even before the book came out. Gasman's widely hailed four-volume doctoral dissertation on Picasso had not yet been published as a book, but it was easily available on file in typescript. (Picasso's principal biographer, John Richardson, praises Gasman as having "done more to unlock the secrets of the artist's imagination than anyone else.") And Gasman was planning to issue her life's work under the Yale University Press imprint.

On the eve of publication of Arianna's Picasso biography, according to

Gasman and her husband, Daniel, Arianna started calling them. She also sent Gasman a letter saying that she had quoted her and that "each quote is fully attributed in the Source Notes in the back of the book."' Gasman gave the book a cursory once-over and sent Arianna a note. Later, however, after she had given *Picasso* a more careful reading—it cites her only twice in the source notes, and not at all in the acknowledgments—she was horrified. "What she did was steal twenty years of my work."

"She used it as a data bank," says Daniel Gasman, who teaches the history of ideas at the City University of New York. "I had a heart attack from this whole business." Richardson backs up the Gasmans' claims, saying that Arianna got away with using Lydia's dissertation as a "kind of dictionary." He says, "Throughout her book, Stassinopoulos Huffington systematically cannibalizes Gasman . . . and, almost as bad, cheapens Gasman's brilliant concepts."

When Gasman returned from Israel, she confronted Arianna. "I told her she was an intellectual kleptomaniac." Arianna then asked, "Don't you think I've added anything?" At one point, "she started to cry and said, 'I didn't mean it. I think like you.'" Then, says Gasman, "she proposed, '*Entre nous*, a secret arrangement if I can make it up to you.'" During dinner at a Manhattan hotel, Michael Huffington joined them. "How much money do you think your work is worth?" Gasman says he asked bluntly. She answered, "One million dollars. I worked all my life on it." The Huffingtons, she continues, rebuffed her. (According to the Huffingtons, it was Gasman who raised the money issue.)

When Lydia Gasman mentioned that Arianna's book *The Gods of Greece* owed a great deal to psychologist James Hillman, I called Hillman, who told me that he recognized many insights from his book *Re-Visioning Psychology*, presented by Arianna without attribution. Arianna cites Hillman eight times in her index, but "the basic ideas running through the book are mine," he said. "I'm happy people use ideas—that's what they're for. I just find her method not decent, not scholarly." Hillman added, "I praise her for her 'mercurial' gifts. As you know, Mercury was the god of thieves."

Before Arianna, Michael Huffington was so obscure that, despite his wealth, hardly anyone in his hometown of Houston knew of him. He once confessed to a California reporter that "before Arianna," whom he married when he was thirty-eight, maybe a dozen people had his phone number. "He was neurotic, tall, mournful, and in deep self-analysis, trying to figure out who he was," says a woman who was once fixed up with him. "You'd never mistake him for a good ol' Texas boy." As a teenager,

Huffington was sent to board at the Culver Military Academy in Indiana. Later, he got degrees from Stanford and the Harvard Business School.

Michael's father, Roy, a major donor to the Republican Party and George H. W. Bush's ambassador to Austria, is a Harvard-trained geologist and wildcatter who made a huge strike in natural gas and oil in Indonesia in 1968. He was apparently a master at maintaining good relations with the Suharto dictatorship, and by 1975, after $1.5 billion had been invested to build a plant, Roy M. Huffington, Inc., was shipping thirty thousand barrels of oil a day. Liquefied natural gas, however, was the greater treasure; by 1977, the equivalent of seventy thousand barrels a day was shipped to the Japanese. Privately owned, Huffco always guarded its books, but Bill Taylor, the company's former head of accounting in Indonesia, says that during the 1980s boom, Huffco's share of the joint operation (with its United States partners and the Indonesian government) was "$60 to $65 million a year in pure profit."

Huffington, who likes to tell voters that he grew up middle-class, has suggested that he earned his first million by the sweat of his brow. His first million actually came from a buyout by his partners in an investment-banking venture. He also portrays himself as a successful businessman who can stop the waste of federal money. In 1976, Michael joined Huffco at the financial end and sought to diversify the company. He spent years secretly buying up the equivalent of 11 blocks of real estate in downtown Houston and 419 acres near the airport. He also pushed for a multimillion-dollar drilling company, but by the end of the 1980s, both ventures were major busts. Huffco lost another $65 million on a California refinery project, which Huffington says he opposed. The company left unpaid both $6.7 million in taxes that the state of California claimed it was owed and a $6-million loan to a Texas bank, of which Huffington Sr. was a director. The bank later collapsed, and American taxpayers footed the bill.

"Michael didn't add any value to his father's company—it was all there," says George Berko, a vice president of Unimar, a Huffco partner in Indonesia. "There was always concern among the operators that Michael would take over. They weren't going to conscience that."

Given his wealth and tall, blond looks, Huffington would appear to be extremely eligible. But he was rarely seen out with women, and rumors have swirled about his sexual preference. "I'd be shocked to death if there were ever affairs with girls," says a Houston woman who grew up with him. "There were escorting situations—he never had date dates. He told me he thought it was terrible, the morality of young women today. He was appalled with a woman who put her hand on his leg after the third date."

When I asked Arianna about allegations that her husband is gay, she replied that no one had ever brought up the question to her, adding, "That's like saying that Michael is Chinese."

Michael Huffington has long had a spiritual bent and political aspirations. So it seemed perfect when Ann Getty got Arianna and Michael together at the San Francisco Opera in 1985. When he asked her what was the most important thing in her life, she answered, "God." Lightning struck. Getty offered to pay for the wedding reception, which she assumed would cost about $10,000. It ended up costing $100,000 more than that and is still being talked about, eight years later, for its ostentation. For several years afterward, Getty felt so violated that she would barely speak to Arianna.

Two years before the marriage, Michael had started lobbying hard for a job in Washington. He was first up for a job in the Commerce Department, but his name was suddenly withdrawn. The *Wall Street Journal* recently reported the probable reason: Huffco had been fined $250,000 by the Commerce Department for "repeated unlicensed shipments of shock batons, handcuffs, billy clubs, fingerprint materials and computer equipment" to Indonesia and Singapore, authoritarian governments with numerous human-rights violations.

Huffington finally landed a position in the Defense Department, as deputy assistant secretary for negotiations policy, but the job lasted only a year and, afterward, the Huffingtons abruptly left town and returned to Houston. "She was house hunting in River Oaks," says the doyenne of Texas gossip columnists, Maxine Mesinger, "and all of a sudden they went to California."

In fact, Huffington himself stayed in Texas. Following a three-day stay at an Episcopal retreat shortly after Arianna suffered a miscarriage, he persuaded his family to sell Huffco. In April 1990, Taiwan's Chinese Petroleum Corporation bought the holdings in Indonesia and the Houston real estate for an estimated $600 million.

Michael Huffington did not register to vote in California until September 1991. During the sale of his family's company, he avoided California state income taxes by keeping his residence in Texas. He thought for a while of starting a movie company and toyed with the idea of buying the *Santa Barbara News-Press*. Between 1988 and 1991, when her daughters were babies, Arianna was not stressing volunteerism. Then shortly before Christmas 1991, when Michael decided that he was entering politics, the Huffingtons gave nearly $100,000 to Santa Barbara charities and local initiatives. "Checks started flying all over town," says Blankenship. At first, the nine-term incumbent member of Congress, conservative Bob Lagomarsino, a well-to-do beer distributor who specialized in constituent services to placate his moderate district, appeared to be entrenched. But in 1992, California's congressional districts were redrawn, and Huffington stepped forward. "It turned into a civil war here," says Jim Youngson, who worked for Lagomarsino. "The whole Republican Party is still fractured and split to this day."

Lagomarsino was stunned by the money Huffington started throwing around and the viciousness of his attacks. "It was just awful. I was in Washington trying to do my job, which was probably a mistake, and he wouldn't debate—he'd send her," says Lagomarsino. "He's a PR consultant's dream and a congressman's nightmare," Norma Lagomarsino, the former representative's wife, explains. "I couldn't watch TV—his ads on all day long—direct mail almost every day, and videotapes to every registered Republican. . . . He'd make these allegations, and we couldn't answer the same way because he had *no record*." After the Huffingtons won the primary, Arianna approached Norma Lagomarsino at a Republican women's tea. "She backs me against the wall and asks, 'What can we do? We want his endorsement.' She kept saying, 'We're so sorry.' She started to cry big tears. . . . It was strange. *They're* strange. There is no shame." Arianna, who denies that she asked for the endorsement, says that Mrs. Lagomarsino "makes things up."

Only eight months after taking his congressional seat, Michael Huffington declared his candidacy for the Senate. By last July, his ambitions had escalated to becoming the running mate of Phil Gramm, the Texas senator who was seeking the GOP nomination for president. Since then, Huffington's supporters are talking openly about the White House, and Arianna has gotten herself seen in some journals as "Hillary's opposite." Blankenship says, "She's bought an election and she's won. Why should she not be measuring drapes in the White House?"

UPDATE: Arianna Huffington is the only person I've ever written about who sent a detective out after me—even before the piece was published! Clearly she had a lot to hide, as I found out. A day after the article was published, Bob Woodward called my husband to say that he had heard—"from an excellent source"—that Arianna had hired an investigator to dig up dirt on me. It didn't surprise me at all, but I was miffed that the veteran Republican political consultant Ed Rollins, whom I had considered a friend, was running Michael's campaign and must have known what Arianna was up to. In fact, Rollins did know, but he waited to unload the story in a book he later wrote, in which he called the Huffingtons "two of the most unprincipled people I have ever encountered." He proceeded to explain that he had threatened to resign if Arianna did not call off the dogs on me, but the book didn't make clear whether she had done so. I guess, in the end, she never found what she was looking for.

I was not at all surprised when the Huffingtons divorced and Michael came out of the closet—particularly considering his attempt to have me thrown out of the Capitol when I sought to question him about his sexuality and other matters. In Santa Barbara, Arianna had given me a curious nondenial denial when I inquired about the same subject. I was amused, however, to hear how weakly Arianna denied the rest of what I had written in the ten thousand–word piece: "[Maureen] says I have a lock on my refrigerator door. That's ridiculous. I have never locked my refrigerator."

Not long after the article ran, my then next-door neighbor in Washington, journalist Ellen Hume, gave a large cocktail party for an educational cause. Among those who came to the door was a woman with a girl in her arms and another whom she held by the hand. Since children were not invited, Ellen indicated to the woman that she might let them play with her four-year-old, who was with a babysitter in the family room. The woman, however, headed straight for the crowded, noisy living room. The hostess, thinking that the guest had not understood, reiterated her offer a little later. "Oh no," the woman answered. "Arianna wants them to be seen." Ellen learned that Arianna had been invited to the party but could not come. Instead, she sent her nanny to display her two daughters to the crowd. She apparently had hoped they would spark a conversation about her.

In her quest to become governor of California, Arianna, who proved to be quick with a quip, spent $700,000 during the bizarre Recall Campaign of 2003—much of it raised by celebrities. With her poll numbers crashing to .5 percent, she pulled out of the race six days before the election and ended up with a total of 44,000 votes. During the campaign she managed to trip herself up with her past inconsistencies, sometimes in more literal ways. (She knocked over microphones in her rush to be photographed with Arnold Schwarzenegger on the day he filed for his candidacy. The incident occurred after she had waited over an hour for the photo op of her going into the filing location with him.) To me, however, this latest reinvention of Arianna Huffington confirmed that, even in my beloved native state, and especially among the stars, there are new people to fool every minute.

Part III:

Political Theater

Notes from the Celebrity-Industrial Complex III

Laci Peterson's memorial was held at a church the family did not attend and was directed by a pastor they did not know. (He appeared on *Today* the next morning.) The Peterson family and entourage arrived in a fleet of white limousines. I had not seen vehicles like these in such profusion since I covered the funeral of Elvis in 1977 for *Newsweek*, although the Peterson family actually seemed to have more.

Elvis was, of course, one of the most famous people who ever breathed. He traveled around in a big old Convair 880 jet, the *Lisa Marie*, named for his daughter and purchased in 1975, two years before his death. Nicknamed *Hound Dog One*, it was used to tour and to take its restless owner on peanut-butter-sandwich runs to Denver. On board, the King slept in a blue crushed-velvet queen-size bed with a gold-plated seat belt strapped across him. He died on a Tuesday, but it took me until Thursday to convince the managing editor that the superstar's sudden demise was a big enough story to merit the attention of one of *Newsweek*'s own writers rather than a rewrite from wire copy. (Bill Murray, in his first season of *Saturday Night Live*, decided to come along because he—quirkily at the time—actually liked Elvis.)

On that hot, sweltering August day in Memphis, Elvis's manager, Colonel Tom Parker, a man usually not named without the adjective "legendary" attached, stood in front of Graceland himself. Wearing a short-sleeved shirt and baseball hat, with a cigar firmly clamped between his teeth, he directed the limousine traffic out of the gate. The place was a circus that paved the way for days to come. Frankly, I was amazed not just at Parker's appearance, but also by the salesmen peddling Elvis T-shirts who told me they had been called back by Parker from New York, where Elvis was supposed to have appeared the night before.

I did not mention in my story that the orders to bring the salesmen back were issued directly by the colonel, but my obituary differed from the accounts written in archrival *Time* and other mainstream media: I had interviewed groupies at Graceland's gates who had observed Elvis getting high and abusing drugs in Las Vegas, and my piece left the impression that the cause of death might have been more complicated than the official one given—heart attack. In those days one did not go out of one's way to tarnish famous reputations, and doing so was not my intent. But I thought the truth was important. I had covered rock 'n' roll— long before MTV's *Behind the Music*—and seen how drugs had ruined lives and broken up bands. Elvis overdosing was a billion-watt cautionary tale. Besides, cause of death, even gauged speculatively in an obituary, is a basic fact of journalism.

The editors were somewhat taken aback when *Newsweek* received hundreds of angry letters from fans upset not only because drugs were mentioned but because their hero hadn't merited a cover. (Bert Lance, President Jimmy Carter's portly budget director, was featured that week; the report revealed that, surprisingly, he *wasn't* being indicted.) It was inconceivable in those days that the death of a show business icon could bump off even a second-rate White House story. The *New York Times*, for example, gave Elvis's death a single paragraph. I would argue that today there is not a head of state alive, dead (of natural causes, at least), or imprisoned who would not be bumped for Elvis or his contemporary equivalent.

Today, if the country is not at war and/or if terrorists are not on the horizon, entertainment often trumps politics where coverage is concerned, although in the Age of Celebrity, superstars and presidents are increasingly part of the same entity: the world of the famous. Politics are going Hollywood, and vice versa, and the impact is showing more and more. Hillary Clinton's best-selling autobiography, *Living History*, is set to become a TV movie—a potential blockbuster of a vote getter if she runs for president, but an effort that may have only loose ties to reality.

We may see more and more crossover from Hollywood to Washington, as the lines between the venues of public life blur faster and further.

Having name recognition and deep pockets, particularly in states with big TV markets where it is extremely expensive to buy advertising time, means that you don't have to become a fund-raising slave or sell out to special interests to get noticed. The incessant fund-raising that former California governor Gray Davis was accused of—not to mention the charge that he was beholden to special interests—angered the electorate and paved the way for Arnold Schwarzenegger, following in Ronald Reagan's footsteps, who became the latest entertainer to cross the entertainment-politics divide. The TV movie based on his life, *See Arnold Run*, was announced by the Arts and Entertainment cable channel the day after he was elected. (No time would be wasted in waiting for the judgments of history.) But who knows what kind of truth about Arnold that film will present to would-be voters? Who will influence the final product? Will it serve to entertain or to inform? Will this documentary-like form of entertainment be made to boost Arnold's political career further? Who decides? Inside the giant media conglomerates, the boundaries between news and entertainment are becoming very hard to discern. Schwarzenegger announced his candidacy for governor on Jay Leno's *Tonight Show* and made a surprise appearance on Leno the day after his victory. Meanwhile, rival David Letterman hosted defeated Governor Davis, who read a top-ten list of advice for the new governor. Sample: "Listen to your constituents except Michael Jackson."

What struck me most in the aftermath of the Terminator's big win, however, was the on-target calculation on the part of his handlers that a star of Schwarzenegger's magnitude owed little more to his potential constituents than his presence. A postmortem shortly after the election by his campaign managers in the *Los Angeles Times* strikingly revealed how they took a candidate with no public record but huge celebrity and morphed him into everybody's favorite—left, right, and center. If interest groups wished to know where the candidate stood on the issues, Arnold's attitude was basically "I'll deal with that *after* the election." Schwarzenegger did not fill out their questionnaires or ask them for support—he just took it. "Our approach was 'We're going to win. We'd like to have you on board,'" explained one of his operatives. "I decided to use Arnold's time not asking, but thanking people, for endorsements. . . . When a star of Arnold Schwarzenegger's caliber is calling you and thanking you, people don't just hang up the phone—they come and help."

Ironically, it was Joe Kennedy, the grandfather of Schwarzenegger's wife, Maria Shriver, who went to Hollywood and brought back everything he learned to help his son Jack get elected president. Joe had cultivated JFK's celebrity for years. First Lady Jackie Kennedy, whose beauty rivaled many a star's and who behaved like a leading lady, ultimately became the biggest icon of her generation. So is it any wonder that, decades later, the now-deceased son of Jack and Jackie started a magazine (*George*) designed to treat politicians like movie stars? John Kennedy Jr. looked and acted like one himself.

Bill Clinton's weakness for all things Hollywood has been as amply documented as his weakness for women. Fittingly, it was his decision to provide a little help to one of his entertainment-industry friends, songwriter Denise Rich, that tainted his departure from office. Rich's fundraising efforts for Clinton and her contacts with the then-president's colleagues helped her obtain a presidential pardon for her fugitive, taxevading, and extremely wealthy ex-husband, Marc Rich. When the ensuing scandal broke, Denise Rich—who freely admits she talks to angels and has long desired to be famous—took all the attention as an opportunity for self-promotion. Because she couldn't resist a *Vanity Fair* photo shoot, she agreed to be interviewed by me, creating an opening for a fullscale investigation of herself, her ex-husband, and the Clinton pardon. Marc Rich was one of the first to do business with the old U.S.S.R., where he had practiced his particularly ruthless form of capitalism since the 1970s. After the Communists fell, he tutored the country's clueless new leaders in how to do business. Like Rich's unfettered capitalism, the American brand of campaign politics has also spread through the new Russia, making an impact.

Interestingly, one of the masterminds of Schwarzenegger's campaign, GOP consultant Mike Murphy, was working in the former Soviet republic of Georgia when he got the call to come help out in California. These days, I've found, you can tune in to just about any part of the globe to find, in some very surprising places, that the American way of selling candidates has taken hold: politicians are increasingly marketed like stars. And they, too, can be repackaged, with new acts and for new audiences. Again, the past can be made to disappear—right before our eyes.

Sinn Fein leader Gerry Adams, imprisoned by the British for seven years as an IRA terrorist, is a stunning example of this; the chapter of this book devoted to him shows the intensity of the effort to cleanse his bloody image to position him for a White House visit and an entry into the all-American prime time.

When covering the 2000 election of President Vladimir Putin in Russia, I tried to capture how his entrance onto the world stage was executed. I had traveled to Russia in the early 1990s to witness the alarming popularity of the demagogue nationalist Vladimir Zhirinovsky (who, for his part, loved the idea of being interviewed by *Vanity Fair*), so I already had a strong sense of how deeply ashamed the Russian people were about losing their power after the fall of Communism and how much they were suffering both economically and spiritually. In those early years of property grabs, with Mafiosi rampant and incomes slashed, the ordinary Russian, exposed to trash TV from the West, was beginning to equate capitalism with corruption.

Then came Putin, a slight, ordinary-looking retired KGB agent, who was cleverly packaged, by Yeltsin's own Russian spin doctors, as an incorruptible G-man secret service star who stood forcefully for Mother Russia against the Islamic uprising in Chechnya. Putin landed there during the campaign in flight gear, brandishing a knife and crudely telling the Muslim "terrorists" where he'd come get them. His image was patterned after a legendary KGB character named Stirlitz, from an old Russian movie, who embodied all things patriotic. Although positioned as a leader who could bring a sober order and firm authority to the wounded giant of a country, Putin was ideologically blank except for his undeniable sense of nationalism and love for his country. In what Gleb Pavlosky, the Kremlin's top political consultant, calls "a very deep mechanism," Putin's handlers cleverly managed to insinuate that, during his time as prime minister to the despised and corrupt Yeltsin, Putin (like the beloved Stirlitz) was working undercover but *for the people*. Thus Putin, handpicked as successor by Yeltsin's own regime, became the ultimate strong, silent leader admired for his enigmatic personality.

Politics aside, the desire to lead the lifestyle of the rich and famous seems to be spreading in Russia as well. I will never forget interviewing one of the leading real estate developers of Moscow during Putin's election campaign. The man had once been number two in the management of the subway system. In the middle of explaining his transformation through a translator, he suddenly blurted out in English, "I vant to be Donald Trump!" The fame disease is highly contagious. It crosses international borders with more ease than anything spread by dead cows.

In Argentina, Carlos Menem, campaigning from a bubble-top "Popemobile," exhorted the Argentines to rise up, like Lazarus. He, too, liked to rule by smoke and mirrors and made an auspicious entrance to fame and power. If he or Putin had a moment of self-doubt, neither one let you see it. Menem was the most outrageous, colorful political leader I have interviewed, certainly the most fun to observe, although his country was suffering. Argentina is so redolent of unfulfilled promise that I wanted to tell the story of the country as much as why Menem was able to become president, and here the Spanish I learned in the Peace Corps helped me, as it often has. After I described Menem in my lead as looking like a "lounge lizard from a tango bar in the provinces," I was introduced to the new press secretary of the Argentine embassy in Washington. "The president loved your article," he told me. "Just one question, though," he persisted. "What means *lounge lizard?*" Before I could reply, the outgoing press secretary, who had introduced us, interjected with an amazing spin: "I told him it was just like Humphrey Bogart in *Casablanca!*"

The Rich Is Different: Denise Rich and Pardongate

"All I thought at the time was, okay,
he's the father of my children."

June 2001

Denise Rich is finally getting the tidal wave of publicity she always craved, but there's a downside to it. Since she played a key role in persuading her friend Bill Clinton to pardon her fugitive billionaire former husband, Marc Rich, the songwriter and political party giver is blinded by flashbulbs at every event she attends; she is also bombarded with questions: *Did you buy Marc's pardon, Denise? Why are you taking the Fifth, Denise? Did you sleep with the president, Denise?* Rich, who adores the attention, eagerly wades right up to the lenses, flashing cleavage and major jewelry, and firmly stays on message as if no brash questions had been asked: "I'm just here to talk about my music. . . . Did you see my daughter's fabulous fashion show?"

Meanwhile, behind the scenes, her entire existence is "being turned upside down," according to Brad Boles, her "imagist," who acts as her dresser, makeup man, and confidant. "She has lawyers examining every inch of her life under a microscope," he says. In February she declined to appear before Congress, invoking the protection of the Fifth Amendment against self-incrimination. In mid-April her lawyer labored to work out a deal to have her cooperate with the office of the United States attorney for the Southern District of New York, which is investigating President Clinton's eleventh-hour pardons. In exchange for limited immunity, Rich is now expected to appear before the grand jury. She will also be called before the House Government Reform Committee.

Jews don't usually pray to angels, but Rich, who has endured more than her share of grief, fervently believes in calling on them for everything: "I got a whole angel chorus up there humming. I really believe angels are happiest when you're happy." After she petitions her angels, she claims, her song lyrics streak right through her. She also consults gurus and psychics, takes thirty vitamins a day, and believes in past-life regressions. "One great life I had, I was an Indian woman who ran around giving people herbs and lived in Native America." As her soulful lyrics for such rhythm-and-blues singers as Aretha Franklin, Natalie Cole, Patti LaBelle, and Mary J. Blige might indicate, Rich also believes "there is definitely a black person inside [me] waiting to get out. I'm sure I was once black." Cole, who is a close friend, told me one night in the living room of Rich's New York penthouse that before Denise's photo got published so often, "people thought she was black."

There is no denying that Rich is a real songwriter with a big career. "She's not afraid to be vulnerable," says Cole, who cowrote last year's "Livin' for Love," a number one dance hit, with Rich. "She speaks on behalf of women. Her lyrics are about what she imagines women have gone through, what she has gone through." Rich's duet for Franklin and Blige, "Don't Waste Your Time," was nominated for a Grammy, and she has written hits for Céline Dion and Marc Anthony, as well as the title song for the film *The First Wives Club.* After a recent radio-station appearance in Jersey City, Rich was on the phone in the backseat of a town car, chatting with Ricky Martin's manager in fluent Spanish. "This too shall pass," she said. "I want to write a song called 'Perdoname,'"—"Pardon Me." Although Rich may kid about her current situation, in the months ahead she'll need her angels more than ever.

According to Rich, her only sister, Monique, who died of cancer at forty-five in 1983, is the angel who gave her the gift of her first hit, "Frankie," a number one song in Britain recorded by Sister Sledge. Rich's mother also died of cancer, a few years after Monique, and in 1996, Rich's middle daughter, Gabrielle, died at twenty-seven of leukemia. Responding to Gabrielle's last wish, Rich formed a foundation to find a cure for cancer. Much of her severely scrutinized Democratic gift giving, in fact, began as a lure to get President Clinton to attend her biennial Angel Ball in New York. "She has to give a few hundred thousand in order to make sure Clinton shows up at the ball," says Kalman Sporn, the self-described "gay Republican businessman son of an Orthodox rabbi," who has helped

Rich organize the events. "It's a small price to pay to ensure he shows, and it means celebrities give more and all the corporations buy tables."

"Gabrielle is always with me," Rich says, and she often wears an old suede jacket of Gabrielle's for good luck. "I'd give anything—I'd die—to have my daughter back. But with her death I learned another strength inside me I didn't know I had." Rich is convinced it was Gabrielle whispering in her ear from on high that prompted her to forgive her former husband after a bitterly fought divorce and to intercede on his behalf for a pardon from Clinton, an action that has sullied her and stained Clinton's legacy forever. The fact that Marc Rich cheated on her after they fled to Switzerland seventeen years ago, that he participated in the biggest tax fraud in United States history, that he traded with Iran during the hostage crisis in the late 1970s and defiantly renounced his American citizenship rather than face a trial here—the entire record has been washed away with a mother's tears. As for her notorious list of gifts to the Clintons— $7,000 worth of furniture for their Chappaqua, New York, house; $450,000 for the Clinton Library; more than $100,000 for Hillary's Senate campaign; more than $1 million for the Democratic National Committee, in addition to the many millions raised at Democratic fund-raisers in her apartment—Rich dismisses her largesse airily. About the furniture for Chappaqua (two coffee tables and two chairs), she says, "Everybody gave furniture. There was a list going around from the decorator."

In her eyes there was no quid pro quo whatsoever. "The truth is, there are a lot more people who gave a lot more money. Of course it gave me access [to the Clintons]," she admits, "but it went beyond that. There was truly a friendship with both of them." Since the pardon, however, she has not heard from her good friends.

Rich has a staff of six maids, two butlers, a cook, and a secretary, as well as two drivers, two masseuses, a hairdresser, a trainer, a yoga instructor, and a personal photographer on call. Her imagist often travels with her, as does Jimmy Hester, the vice president of Denise Rich Songs, her music company. In Manhattan, four people work for the company, and two more are employed by her foundation. She also maintains staffs at her houses in Southampton and Aspen. Rich's mammoth two-story creamy-beige marbled apartment, said to be in the $40 million range, overlooks Fifth Avenue and Central Park, and is decorated with works by Picasso, Chagall, Miró, Léger, Braque, Warhol, Calder, and Lichtenstein, as well as a Julian Schnabel broken-crockery portrait of her. A recording studio, an office, a spa, and guest rooms are on the lower floor; there is also a rooftop garden. Two of New York's best-known publicists, Bobby Zarem and Howard Rubenstein, have her as a client. Even for someone with a nine-figure fortune, that is a big support team. Her eighty-eight-year-old father, Emil Eisenberg, a retired shoe manufacturer and art collector from Worcester, Massachusetts, where Rich says she grew up with "unconditional love," tries to keep tabs on her, but any effort to curb her spending is futile. She donates lavishly to countless charities and is a notorious soft touch.

Rarely idle, Rich is usually racing from one life to another—from the songwriter who shuts herself off in a studio every day to the party giver, the partygoer, and the New Age devotee. She is all about multiple use: each of her activities can be cross-pollinated with the others, and the goal is always to promote Denise, her two living daughters—Ilona, thirty-three, the married mother of three who in March launched her first fashion collection, and Daniella, twenty-six, an actress and writer—and her causes. "That's what I'm really about," says Rich. "Politics goes into music, which goes into social life, which goes into the arts, and everything connects."

After twenty-five years of being held down by a controlling husband, Rich likes to flaunt her freedom. If Brad Boles is called away to do makeup for a film, he calibrates her wardrobe for each scheduled event up to six weeks in advance, individually numbering the designer and custom-made outfits, often for as many as three changes a day. "What if she wants to wear something before the appointed day?" I ask. "She can't do it," he answers. "I won't let her."

Rich's appearance has also undergone a radical transformation since her married days. "Marc kept her in shirts buttoned up to her neck," says Boles. But now her curly hair has been straightened and highlighted, and her features have been altered. She still has a great figure, and she has elected to keep her own cleavage, which she is proud to display. With her big brown eyes and superglossed lips, Rich gives the illusion of being younger than her age, fifty-seven.

The striking physical changes over the years can be seen in dozens of neatly catalogued and dated photo albums of Denise Rich's parties, which show her with a mix of world leaders, rap stars, politicians, and B-minus tabloid celebrities—everyone from Foxy Brown and Dewi Sukarno to Luciano Pavarotti and Mike Wallace. Bill Clinton appears at one fund-raiser in a bright-blue shirt and yellow tie. "He's always very relaxed here," Rich says. "We are not judgmental." Noticeable in one photo of Patti LaBelle's birthday party in September 1998—a full year before his services were engaged by Marc Rich to handle his pardon petition—is former White House counsel Jack Quinn. "I've known Jack socially for a long time," Rich explains, but she says she did not recommend him to her former husband.

There are also videos of Rich's two Angel Balls to support the G&P Foundation, named for Gabrielle and her Lebanese husband, Philip Aouad. The biennial balls, given in 1998 and 2000, were among the few private events both President Clinton and the First Lady agreed to chair. According to the charity's tax returns, the first ball raised $2.3 million, but "fund-raising expenses" of $855,000 ate up thirty-seven percent of that (the rule of thumb for nonprofits is to stay below twenty-five percent). Nobody who was there has forgotten that evening. The seating plan was lost and celebrities had to scramble for tables, but the inconvenience (even hassle) was easily offset by Plácido Domingo singing "Granada," Dan Rather presenting an award to CBS president Les Moonves, Bill Cosby introducing President Clinton, Stevie Wonder singing "Happy Birthday" to Milton Berle, and the duchess of York making a speech.

In the Manhattan offices of the United States attorney for the Southern District, there are six hundred locked boxes of evidence prepared for the prosecution of Marc Rich and his partner, Pincus Green. In 1983 the two men fled to Switzerland rather than face a sixty-five-count indictment. Fifty witnesses, many of them granted immunity, were waiting to testify. Rich's saga, however, really begins in the 1970s, when oil trading was carried on mainly by a group of giant companies known as the Seven Sisters. Rich broke the market open when he persuaded Third World producers in countries such as Iran and Nigeria to sell to him. Rich invented the spot oil market, by trading oil both in units and in futures, just as he would any of the other commodities he dealt with—metals, coal, sugar, grain. Green managed their transportation all over the globe. One oil broker tells me, "Pinky knew how to move it. Marc knew how to trade it."

In the late 1970s and 1980s, the Department of Energy controlled the price of oil by age and provenance. The government learned that Rich was conspiring with two Texas companies, West Texas Marketing and Listo, to convert the certification on his barrels and sell them at a higher price. The illegal trades were meticulously recorded in two sets of books. Rich also had "pots" in which, in just six months, he hid $100 million in illicit profits. To "lose" the profits, as well as evade taxes and dodge the DOE, he laundered them in a series of phony transactions between Listo, West Texas, and his offshore companies.

The indictment charged Rich's companies with evading $48 million in taxes and lying about it. In October 1984 the firms pleaded guilty to seventy-eight felonies. The government also accused him of trading with Iran when Americans were being held hostage there and, under the Racketeer Influenced and Corrupt Organizations Act (RICO), charged him with two counts of wire and mail fraud. At the time of his pardon, Rich was still facing sixty-five felony counts.

From the beginning, Rich threw the best legal minds he could find at the government, beginning with the late Edward Bennett Williams, whose Washington firm now represents Bill Clinton. The seventeen motions the attorneys filed to delay the case took more than two years to resolve. Rich and Green fled before they were indicted, but Williams always insisted that they would show up. At one point, with contempt-of-court fines of $50,000 a day mounting, Rich's lawyers agreed to pay the fine and turn over disputed documents. Instead, prosecutors received a call from Rich's New York company saying two steamer trunks full of documents were being shipped to Switzerland that afternoon. Agents stopped the plane and hauled the trunks off the runway. Rich let the fine run for a year, until the government served restraining notices on his American banks and customers. Then he folded, after having accumulated $21 million in contempt fines alone.

To avoid extradition from Switzerland, Rich and Green eventually renounced their U.S. citizenship, which, according to Morris Weinberg, made Edward Bennett Williams very unhappy. Rich became a citizen first of Bolivia, then of Spain and Israel.

In June 1983, Rudolph Giuliani was appointed United States attorney for the Southern District. By then the case had been going on for eighteen months. Yet of all the people involved in the prosecution, it was the specter of Giuliani, the demon government lawyer who threatened to put Rich away for good, that would haunt Rich through the years. That image of Rich's fate became a powerful tool for Quinn to use in lobbying Clinton, when Giuliani was fresh in the president's mind as Hillary Clinton's fierce onetime opponent for the seat of junior senator from New York.

Denise Rich taught herself to play the guitar at Boston University, and she originally began writing songs to communicate with her husband, who constantly put her down. "I have a gentle soul," she tells me. "I have difficulty with confrontation. So it's much easier for me to communicate through writing."

Marc expected her to stay home and entertain his business associates. She claims he told her almost nothing about his business. "She was the perfect wife," says a longtime friend of theirs. "She did everything for him." But for years they did not get along. "She wanted to have a career in music, and Marc didn't take it seriously. She wanted to be an artist, creative—she's out there. He's not; he was born with a phone in his hand. But it was his way or the highway."

When Marc fled, it was not easy for Denise to move to Europe with three daughters and begin life anew as the wife of a man whose companies had pleaded guilty to seventy-eight counts of tax evasion, wire fraud, and making false statements, and who was one of America's most wanted fugitives. On top of that, Denise's sister was dying. But the Riches moved to the tax haven of Zug, Switzerland, and had a sumptuous villa in Marbella, Spain. Heavily guarded by former Israeli soldiers, Marc was not free to travel. But Denise was, and once she began taking trips to promote her music, he started appearing with a good-looking, six-foot blond German woman, Gisela Rossi, the widow of a German-Italian businessman and the mother of two young boys.

By 1991, Denise was spending more and more time in New York, and in 1992 she sued for divorce in Switzerland. With the aid of a well-known attorney, the late Max Lebedkin, she asked for a $1-billion settlement. Marc's first offer was about $3.6 million. In 1993, after Marc reportedly moved Rossi into the lakeside villa outside Lucerne that he and Denise had been constructing, Denise's fury spilled out in an interview she gave to a Swiss magazine: "For 25 years I was a loyal wife and dedicated mother. People gossiped, said he was a crook. But I stood by him. He shows his thanks by cheating on me with another woman and publicly humiliating me and my children."

As the fight wore on, all three daughters went through health crises. "Gabrielle had cancer, one was anorexic, one had a back operation," Denise says. By then she was ensconced in New York and independently wealthy. Her father had given Marc money to start his company, and in 1990, when Denise and several partners redeemed their shares in Marc Rich & Holding Company AG, Denise's 13.9 percent was worth, according to court documents, $165 million.

Aaron Richard Golub, who had delivered groceries to Denise's house in Worcester when his father owned a grocery store and her father owned the shoe factory, became her New York attorney. Golub knew that Marc was a master of assets subterfuge, and he drove Denise's legal team to work such long hours that one attorney quit because her hair began to fall out. Golub tells me he had no choice: "Marc Rich uses lawyers the way carpenters use nails. Lawyers and rabbis are his pawns."

The prominent Washington attorney Lloyd Cutler was hired by Denise to see how she might benefit from congressional hearings held by Democrats in 1991 and 1992. These hearings examined why a company owned in part by a fugitive had been able to sell $45.5 million worth of nickel to the Mint and why another Marc Rich company had managed to collect $55 million in grain subsidies. The embarrassed federal government ceased doing business with Rich.

After countless trips to Switzerland, Golub felt he could pinpoint assets of Marc Rich's totaling at least $1.4 billion; his strategy was to take up where the government's case had left off—particularly with regard to the valuation of his former company, Marc Rich International. On the eve of the day Rich was obliged to produce his financial records for the Swiss court, he retained a California lawyer to negotiate a settlement with Denise's father. The divorce became final in June 1996, while Gabrielle was living with Denise in New York and undergoing chemotherapy. The terms of the settlement remain confidential. In addition to the $165 million Denise had redeemed for her shares in Rich's company, informed sources estimate, she collected between $100 and $200 million in her divorce settlement.

Gabrielle Rich was twenty-three in 1993, when she felt a small lump under her jaw. Her sister Ilona remembers a doctor telling Gabrielle not to worry about it. Six months later, the lump had progressed to stage-four Hodgkin's lymphoma. In May 1996, Gabrielle moved from California to her mother's Fifth Avenue apartment for chemotherapy. That July she summoned Brad Boles to her room and said, "Brad, you're from Seattle. I have decided to go to the Fred Hutchison Cancer Research Center there for a bone-marrow transplant." Denise was going to give Gabrielle her bone marrow. "They tell you it's like being kicked by a horse, but it's really like being in a very bad car accident," Boles says of the procedure Denise endured for her daughter. "Mommy, I'm looking at your bone marrow—it's the color of red wine with gold specks," Gabrielle told her. "You're giving birth to me again!" Denise rejoiced and said it was a miracle.

But nine days later, Gabrielle developed a staph infection, and there were indications that her liver was failing. "Denise decided she needed all the help she could get," says Boles. The call went out, and soon the hospital corridor was full of "Orthodox rabbis, Buddhists praying on sacred mats, Hindus, Christians reading from Bibles."

Marc and Denise began to speak for the first time in years. "At one point he wanted to come, and Gabrielle just didn't want it. God forbid something should happen to him," Denise tells me. "His pain was so great, but I had no strength for that—to deal with his pain." Boles says, "There was so much speculation whether he was going to come into the country or not, disguised as a doctor or an orderly. In the end he didn't enter the country. He made that choice—he decided his freedom was worth more."

Marc was informed by phone when Gabrielle died. "We spoke, but he was so devastated," Denise says. "I didn't find comfort in speaking to him. My strength came from God. I had a vision of her when she died—she was walking with my mother and sister." But Gabrielle's death allowed Denise to come to terms with the man she hated. She explains, "After you've lost a child, you don't ask questions anymore. There's a forgiveness that goes on after you've lost a child."

Before Gabrielle left New York for Seattle, she had asked Boles to buy a safe she could keep in her room. After her death, Philip Aouad opened the safe to reveal a wedding ring and a note from her in a manila envelope informing her family that the two had secretly married in 1993.

The next time Denise Rich saw Bill and Hillary Clinton, in a receiving line at a 1996 White House Christmas party, they both hugged her and told her that they, too, believed that nothing compared to having a child die. That meant a great deal to her, she tells me.

For fourteen years, until he retired in 1997 at age fifty, Ken Hill was the United States marshal in charge of tracking down Marc Rich and bringing him to justice. He has never before spoken on the record to a reporter. In his first seven years on the case, Hill pursued more than fourteen hundred "investigative actions" and followed the activities of thirty-seven of Rich's close associates and important business contacts in thirty-three countries. Ivan Boesky, the jailed financier, told Hill something he never forgot: "Just remember, there are very few people in this world who can lend each other a billion dollars, no questions asked." Competitors who were "appalled by Rich's business practices" were more than happy to give Hill inside information. "I was shocked by the numbers of people who came forward," he says. "He screwed a lot of people to get where he was." Some of Hill's sources had code names—Concorde, Empire, Merlin, Trader. "I was the Riddler," Hill tells me, "because it was always a riddle or a puzzle trying to figure out what would or could happen next."

Rich flourished as a lender and a barterer with Third World and Eastern-bloc countries that, strapped for cash or in debt, had commodities for collateral that Rich could get hold of and sell for fat profits. When I inform Hill that British customs agents recently seized a briefcase containing $1.9 million in cash that Rich was sending to London, he replies without hesitation, "The first thing I'd do is check which head of state or oil minister was visiting London that week." Hill continues, "The smoking gun is greed. This is what Marc thrived on—the greed of those who had commodities and were in positions of influence and power." According to one of the world's top independent oil traders, "From Nigeria to Russia, everyone was on the payroll of Marc Rich. Dollar for dollar in his time, no one, including sheikhs, had more money than Marc Rich." He adds, "You have no idea the strength this man had in the world economy."

"He virtually hijacked Jamaica's economy," Hill says. "He involved himself with Venezuela, Angola, Romania, Yugoslavia, Bulgaria, and North Korea." Sources told Hill that Rich was trading with the North Koreans, for example, through the Russians, who by the mid-90s, Hill says, were "coming over here in droves, looking me up, looking to get revenge on him. He was just ripping them off, manipulating their ministers and politicians better than they were." Rich, however, has repeatedly refused to discuss his international business relations.

Rich once was the bauxite trader in Jamaica; he is rumored not only to have prepaid Jamaica's debt to the International Monetary Fund but also to have financed the country's 1988 Olympic bobsled team. Wherever Rich went, says Hill, he made his own rules. "I had a South African law-enforcement contact [during the time of the trading sanctions against South Africa]. I called and said, 'Is it true at least 6 percent of your oil is coming from Rich?' He said, 'We've been friends for a long time. Don't call me anymore.'"

Hill saw a pattern over and over again whereby "Rich through his department head would make a longtime offer for a country's commodity at the fair market value or higher. But there are two sides to the deal." The good side, Hill explains, was that the country would have its product contracted for at a decent price and in some cases have its debts paid off as well. In return, however, "Rich became the sole provider of energy needs, grain, gas, oil, coal at a higher-than-fair rate, and since he controls the commodity, he controls the country." Then the opportunity always existed to have inside cooperation in order to "get more of his commodity than he actually paid for. These practices drove U.S. businessmen up the wall. How could they compete?"

"No matter where I was in the world, he was always ahead of me," says Douglas Jaffe, who comes from a wealthy Democratic Texas oil family and outfits private jets. "In Romania in 1990–91, he was in control of all their resources, all their trades." Jaffe calls Rich a "mastermind," who dictates to any number of "heads of state. They like him because he gets things done, he's practical, he understands. A lot of these guys were thrust into their positions and have never dealt in the capitalistic world. They're used to the Communist Party, where orders came down from the top. He had to go in and explain things, explain how they work."

One thing Hill learned, he says, is that Rich never comes at anything directly. As Paul Klebnikov observes, Rich is "a man who makes his greatest profits in places where markets function badly, either because of corruption or ignorance or because a particular country is a pariah state or isolated by sanctions." Klebnikov, author of *Godfather of the Kremlin,* a biography of the Russian oligarch Boris Berezovsky, continues: "He came in and became Russia's largest single trading partner for commodities and helped pioneer a system of fraudulent foreign-trade deals involving setting up shell companies, double contracts with secret kickback clauses, bank accounts in Switzerland, and whole banks set up in the Cayman Islands and South America." Along with the KGB, Klebnikov says, Rich "served as the teacher of a new breed of corrupt Russian traders, who looted the country's natural resources, which ruined the economy and bankrupted the government."

Marc Rich's name popped up in connection with investigations of the notorious BCCI banking scandal in the 1990s. As a result, he was listed in the appendix of the official report, issued in December 1992 by the Senate Subcommittee on Terrorism, Narcotics, and International Operations, as one whose business with the discredited bank "requires further investigation." His name also popped up in the murky shadows of a $2.7-billion lawsuit between two Russian aluminum magnates filed in federal court in New York last December by Robert Abrams, former state attorney general. "The world of aluminum trading is filled with incredible acts of treachery, including murder, extortion, money laundering, bribery, and corruption of public officials," Abrams tells me. "Rich is a player in this whole milieu."

In many areas, Hill says, Rich "wore his fugitivity as a badge of honor: 'I'm not an ugly American—I'm a fugitive.'" In Israel, which receives more American aid than almost any other country and where money laundering is still relatively easy, Rich and Green were always afforded full protection. Rich, with his charitable donations totaling $100 million, is one of the biggest philanthropists in Israel.

"Other white-collar fugitives, like Eddie Antar [owner of the Crazy Eddie stores], fled to Israel, and the authorities there were fully cooperative [with us]," Hill says. "Why wouldn't they help us capture those two? With Israel, it was like staring into a black hole. The irony is, Israel was more than forthcoming in asking for a pardon."

As Marc Rich's chauffeur drives me up to the Villa Rose, the lakeside manse just outside Lucerne where Rich lives with his second wife, Gisela Rossi Rich, he phones ahead and the iron gates swing open.

Rich, who was born in Antwerp, Belgium, considers himself a European, even though he was raised in Kansas City and New York after his family, to escape Hitler, had crossed Vichy France and booked passage in 1941 on an ocean liner from Morocco. Like Denise's parents, they found success in America; his father owned a burlap-bag factory. Rich's view of Lake Lucerne with the Alps beyond is striking, and in the house's beige living room with red accents, two needlepoint pillows on leopard-print chairs announce, "It's expensive being rich" and "I don't think we're in Kansas anymore, Toto." Although there are paintings by Braque and van Gogh on the walls and the villa is luxurious, it is quieter, smaller, and less dramatic than Denise Rich's penthouse.

Rich, who is sixty-six, has clearly opted not to talk to me. He has made plans to go helicopter skiing, but he leaves his vivacious wife to deal with me in her rapid-fire English. She is loaded for bear, with a trim, wealthy air about her. While carefully casual in jeans and loafers, without makeup or rings, she is poised and attractive. Over a lunch that begins with Galician broth and ends with an apple tart, she keeps emphasizing that her husband is an honorable man, who was given "very bad legal advice" from Edward Bennett Williams to "stonewall" the United States government. "But that doesn't make him bad," she says. "He started working when he was seventeen, so he is in a business—very volatile, the commodities business—based on integrity, reliability, and also trust. Nobody ever had any lawsuit or anything with him."

She claims that the very idea that there was a calculated campaign for a presidential pardon is absurd: "That's the whole misconception. Marc basically gave up on the idea through proper channels—the Justice Department, whatever. Nothing ever worked." In fact, she says, he was very pessimistic when Avner Azulay, the former Mossad (Israeli intelligence) operative who runs the Rich Foundation in Israel, urged the pardon route. And the onetime White House counsel Jack Quinn, who presented the petition to the president, was at the very least cool to the idea. While visiting the Riches, he said, "I don't think this will ever work." Gisela insists no money for a pardon ever changed hands between Marc and Denise, especially any intended for the Clinton Library. "She has a life of her own in New York. She likes the Democrats, and she contributed for years and years and years, and that has nothing whatsoever to do with Marc. She has enough money of her own—everybody should know that. She doesn't need a couple hundred thousand from Marc."

Nor, she says, has Marc's generosity been in any way targeted to curry favor with the dozens of VIP Jews who wrote letters in support of his pardon petition both in Israel and the United States. "Do you think he made all the charitable donations in his life in the last thirty years because one day some American president is . . . going to give him a pardon? That's so far-fetched. And the money given by Denise came from him for the pardon? That's ridiculous!"

Gisela maintains that they were really stunned that he received the pardon. "I tell you frankly, when we heard it was done, we couldn't believe it! I said, 'No, Marc, there must be some mistake.'" Azulay called with the news very early on January 20. "We were in [our house] in Saint-Moritz, in bed. It was four o'clock in the morning."

There is a six-hour time difference between Switzerland and Washington. According to testimony given by the Justice Department pardon attorney Roger Adams to Congress, the Pardon Office was notified about Rich shortly after midnight. Therefore, Rich heard that he had been pardoned two hours before anyone in the White House told the Justice Department. It was already after six A.M. in Switzerland when someone in the White House counsel's office finally got around to asking Justice to obtain the FBI's criminal-record checks on Rich and Green, who also received a pardon. The White House said it would probably not find much, because "the two men had been living abroad for several years."

I believe that if a political decision was made at the highest level of this government that we go apprehend Marc Rich and Pincus Green and use all the tools that are available to the U.S. government, we would have Marc Rich and Pincus Green very quickly.
—Howard Safir, former director of the United States Marshals Service

Howard Safir was speaking in code when he made this statement in 1992 before a House committee, referring to an edict that had come down from "the highest level of the Justice Department" instructing law enforcement not to employ "extraterritorial renditions"—not to kidnap fugitives, because doing so was not worth the political fallout. Nevertheless, Ken Hill almost got Rich several times, including once when the United States marshal hid beside a runway near London's Biggin Hill Airport, holding an early satellite phone, with the knowledge that Rich was due to land any moment in a private plane. "Ken called me at four A.M.," says the prosecutor James Comey, now the United States attorney for the Southern District of New York, "to tell me, 'Damn, the fog hasn't lifted.'"

For years, Hill and Rich and Green played an elaborate cat-and-mouse game. At Rich's fiftieth-birthday party, according to Hill, a boxer representing Rich knocked down a boxer representing a New York police officer again and again. Hill once had a bottle of Rich's favorite scotch sent to his hotel in Saint-Moritz with a card saying, "Have a drink on me." One year Hill's Christmas was ruined when British authorities received information that two men dressed as women and resembling Rich and Green were about to land at Biggin Hill Airport.

Huge sums of money were offered to get the two men off. Morris Weinberg says that in the early days, Edward Bennett Williams promised $100 million to the government to resolve the case. Safir claims he was present at a spy exchange at Templehof Airfield in West Berlin in 1986 when an East German lawyer offered $250 million on behalf of Rich. During Clinton's first term, Douglas Jaffe was approached by the Egyptian financier and arms dealer Adnan Khashoggi to intercede for Rich. "He was prepared to pay a hell of a lot more," Jaffe says. "Adnan asked me, 'Is it something you could work on?' I said, 'No, it really isn't.'"

"Every year there was a new initiative," says Comey, who in 1992 joined Otto Obermaier, then United States attorney for the Southern District, at a meeting in Switzerland with Rich and Green and their lawyers. According to Comey, they had been led to believe that the two men were ready to plead: "Rich said, 'I don't want to spend a day in jail,' and we said, 'We won't make that promise.'" In 1992 the Russian Interior Ministry requested a meeting in Moscow to see if Russia might help capture Rich. American officials proposed that the Russians try to lure him to their country. "They were willing to explore the possibility," says a Justice Department attorney who was present, "but nothing ever came of it."

By then, Rich was represented by former Nixon White House counsel Leonard Garment and by Lewis ("Scooter") Libby, who would become Vice President Dick Cheney's chief of staff. Bradford Reynolds, head of civil rights at Justice under Ronald Reagan, also worked for Rich, and for a while Frank Mankiewicz, who had been Robert Kennedy's press secretary, handled Rich's PR. Libby has testified that over the eleven years he did work for Rich (at three law firms), he received more than $2 million.

Meanwhile, rabbis from Brooklyn, where the Orthodox Pincus Green grew up, also got involved. David Luchins, who oversaw Jewish affairs on the staff of former New York senator Daniel Patrick Moynihan, tells me about a warning he got from the late New York rabbi Morris Sherer. "Sherer said he was offered a million-dollar donation to charity if someone could get through to see Moynihan about Rich and Green." No one ever did. Luchins adds, "However much money Marc Rich was throwing around Israel, Pinky Green was throwing it around New York."

Although Rich's and Green's WANTED posters remained on the Internet until January 20, 2001, the Oklahoma City bombing in 1995 and threats of further violence had priority with United States marshals. Rich never let up, however. His lawyers even offered the United States his help, both in the drug war and in apprehending Tom Billman, another white-collar fugitive. The last and most sophisticated campaign on Rich's behalf, though, was launched from Israel.

Former Israeli intelligence officer Azulay laid meticulous groundwork for his patron's pardon. For nearly a year, as head of the Rich Foundation in Tel Aviv, he managed an ingenious campaign on two fronts, in Israel and in the United States. In fact, if the House Government Reform Committee had not obtained the e-mails of Jack Quinn—Rich's latest factotum in Washington—the whole thing might have gone off without a hitch. Instead, the intricate web of charities, diplomacy, credentials, connections, and cunning suddenly unraveled.

At the center of the web were Azulay's ties to Prime Minister Ehud Barak, whose One Israel Party had been fined $3.2 million in 2000 for illegal funding practices in Barak's 1999 campaign. A criminal investigation was also launched into the activities of Barak's cabinet secretary, Yitzhak ("Bojie") Herzog, the son of a former president of Israel, who was suspected of channeling money from two of Rich's foundations into two phony foundations set up to funnel funds into Barak's campaign. Recent reports in the Israeli press allege that at least $120,000 of Rich Foundation money went into Barak's coffers. Michal Herzog, Bojie's wife, works for the Rich Foundation. Bojie and his mother both wrote letters included in the pardon petition without mentioning Michal Herzog's connection to the foundation.

Also under investigation is a foundation begun by former Israeli foreign minister Shlomo Ben Ami, who received over $100,000 from the Rich Foundation. He wrote to Clinton on Rich's behalf and lobbied King Juan Carlos of Spain, who phoned Clinton to commend Rich.

The Rich Foundation donated $300,000 to former Prime Minister Shimon Peres's Peace Foundation—the equivalent of a presidential library—on whose board Azulay sat. Peres, too, phoned Clinton on Rich's behalf.

"It's time to move on the GOI [government of Israel] front," Quinn e-mailed Rich's longtime attorney in New York, Robert Fink, in March 2000, nine months before Quinn personally delivered a two-inch-thick pardon petition to the White House on December 11. The petition contained dozens of letters from "a Who's Who of Israeli society," says Luchins. It later came out that a number of charities solicited for letters had no idea they were for a pardon petition, and many of the letters were drafted within days of one another, in English, a language that Israeli journalist Mody Kreitman, who has reported extensively on the pardons, says some of the signatories can't write. "Azulay created an outer circle based on people who did not know the real purpose of his plan, and they wrote letters of courtesy," Kreitman tells me.

Simultaneously, Abraham Foxman, national director of the Anti-Defamation League of B'nai B'rith, persuaded Azulay to cultivate Denise Rich. After receiving a $100,000 contribution from the Rich Foundation, Foxman had dinner with Azulay in Paris in February 2000. On March 18, following the rebuff of another attempt to reach out to the court of the Southern District, Azulay e-mailed Bob Fink and sent a copy to Quinn: "We are reverting to the idea discussed with Abe—which is to send DR [Denise Rich] on a 'personal' mission to No. 1 with a well prepared script."

Contrary to what Azulay has said in published reports, Denise was first approached to consider supporting the pardon late in the spring of 2000. "Denise hesitated—her father was against getting involved—and she struggled until summer," says a close friend. "Meanwhile, several friends of Marc's kept pressuring her to use her relationship with the president." So did her daughters. "They did say, 'Please help,'" Denise tells me. When I suggest that some people feel she supported the pardon to ensure her daughters' full inheritance, she denies it. "All I thought at the time was, okay, he's the father of my children, and if that's what they've asked me to do, I'll do it." On December 6, 2000, she signed a letter to President Clinton that she had not written herself: "I support his application with all my heart."

Denise, the trump card, had further ingratiated herself when she threw a big fund-raising lunch for the Clintons and the Gores that brought in $3 million right after the release report by the independent counsel Kenneth Starr, detailing Clinton's affair with Monica Lewinsky. But Denise was not enough. Knowing Clinton's White House as intimately as he did, Quinn realized that he needed advocates deep inside the president's most trusted circle. He chose the Arkansas lawyer Bruce Lindsey, perhaps Clinton's closest confidant and a good friend of Cheryl Mills, Clinton's impeachment attorney, who was formerly on the staff of the White House counsel and is now a trustee of the Clinton Foundation. Although Mills was no longer employed at the White House, she, too, received the pardon petition.

Rather than approach Clinton's chief of staff, former law professor John Podesta, who would undoubtedly have sent the pardon petition immediately to the Justice Department Pardon Office for proper vetting, Quinn sought out Lindsey on December 13 during a sentimental farewell visit Clinton made to Northern Ireland. When Quinn realized that Lindsey had reservations because Rich and Green were fugitives—the pardon application neglected to mention that they had renounced their citizenship—Quinn followed up with a letter on December 19: "Their failure to return to New York was not a crime and no one has ever accused them of a crime for failing to come to the US for a trial." In an e-mail to Azulay, Quinn said he was working the White House counsel's office "pretty hard."

Meanwhile, at the Justice Department, according to Adams, the pardon attorney, "none of the regular procedures were followed." Quinn relied primarily on his friend Deputy Attorney General Eric Holder, who, at the time, was sending Quinn résumés of people on his staff and asking for his help in finding them jobs after Clinton left office. Between November 2000 and the night of January 19, Quinn wrote to and spoke with Holder several times. On January 19, Quinn told Holder he would be called by the White House counsel's office about the pardon. Holder later testified to Congress that the opinion he gave, "neutral, leaning toward favorable," was out of foreign-policy considerations, because it would help Barak. He now says he never thought a pardon would be seriously entertained. But at no time during this period did Holder attempt to notify anyone at the Justice Department's Pardon Office or the Southern District of New York about the application.

Quinn also turned to his friend and business associate Beth Dozoretz, a trustee of the Clinton Library who had proudly visited the White House ninety-six times in the preceding two years. The aggressively social, thrice-married Dozoretz—a former New York garment district executive—had come out of nowhere to become finance chair of the Democratic National Committee (she was later asked to resign). After pledging to raise $1 million for the library, she solicited $450,000 of the amount from her friend Denise Rich.

With her customary can-do attitude, Dozoretz, who is friendly with the Barak family and serves on the executive committee of the American Israel Public Affairs Committee, plunged into helping her friend Denise's wealthy former husband. She seems to have been the final arbiter on whether to enlist Hillary Rodham Clinton in the pardon effort. Denise said no to the lawyers after an e-mail from Bob Fink to Jack Quinn revealed that "Beth warned her not to raise the issue while HRC was in earshot." Then Quinn e-mailed Azulay on January 10: "DR called from Aspen. Her friend B—who is with her—got a call today from potus [president of the United States] who said he was impressed by JQ's last letter and that he wants to do it and is doing all possible to turn around the WH counsels. DR thinks he sounds very positive but 'that we have to keep praying.'" Although Denise Rich and Beth Dozoretz were both in Aspen, they were not staying together, and Dozoretz has claimed that the president did not mention the resistance of the White House counsels to her. Nevertheless, she definitely queried the president about the pardon, and, like Denise Rich, she has taken the Fifth Amendment before Congress, on "stuff Denise has told her," according to a friend. "The president on the phone to two girls in Aspen? Come on," a prominent Democratic senator said to me. "It has to be sex or the library."

Denise Rich brought the pardon up with President Clinton at least four times: in her letter, in a second copy of the letter sent with a cover note written by Marc Rich's attorneys for her signature, in a phone call, and in a brief conversation at a party at the White House on December 20.

The petitioners knew how seriously Clinton would take a major request made by Ehud Barak on behalf of Marc Rich. At the end of his administration, Clinton was pushing Barak—who was locked in a difficult election he would lose—to deliver a Middle East peace agreement, which would burnish the Clinton legacy. In addition, Hillary Clinton had recently been elected as a senator from New York, where the Jewish constituency has an outsize influence. Although Barak originally denied that he had petitioned Clinton, he now admits to having spoken three times on behalf of Rich.

On January 19, the White House was in chaos. Clinton, loath to leave, had not slept in days, and his primary concern was working out a deal with the independent counsel's office to stave off an indictment over his perjured testimony in the Monica Lewinsky affair. Although Podesta, Nolan, and Lindsey all later testified to Congress that they had opposed the Rich pardon, they certainly did not argue against it vigorously after the president received a final call from Barak, which Clinton belatedly spun as a deciding factor.

Late that night the White House heard from Justice, following an FBI criminal-record check, that there might be a problem for Rich with arms dealing. Once again the president turned to Quinn, who denied it. Clinton simply said, "Take Jack's word."

In congressional hearings, members queried Quinn about his representation of Rich to his old boss in a case that ultimately made the president look bad. Shouldn't Quinn have been more loyal? And wasn't Quinn stretching a "revolving-door" rule that he had helped write which barred former presidential-staff members from lobbying the White House for five years? Quinn, when pressed on this question, countered that he didn't believe he was violating his own rule—there was an exception for "criminal proceedings."

Martin Auerbach, who prosecuted the Rich case in the United States attorney's office, recognized the classic Marc Rich strategy: "An important piece of Rich's success comes from information arbitrage—knowing something the guy across the table doesn't know and getting the guy to betray his primary allegiance. In this case he gets Quinn to push the definition of lobbying, because it's in Marc's best interests instead of the president's best interests, with a package giving only one side of the story. And he's able to time it so precisely that it can't be checked. What Marc Rich finally figured out is, if you attack the pardon process the same way you attack your business, you will achieve the same result." Morris Weinberg adds, "It's really why [Rich and Green] ran—because they thought money would always resolve everything. Now, twenty years later, it appears they're right."

UPDATE: The pardon Marc Rich received from Bill Clinton on his last day in office did nothing to help the country's largest tax cheat in history return to the United States. Marc Rich still lives in Switzerland and has not risked coming home. Both the United States attorney's office and the State of New York have made it clear they are continuing to investigate the pardon and his tax situation and will question him as soon as he sets foot on American soil.

Subsequently, National Security Council records, released through a congressional inquiry and published in *Newsweek*, confirmed that in the three phone conversations with then-president Clinton that I mentioned above, former Israeli prime minister Ehud Barak pleaded the case for Marc Rich. (Barak described Rich as being very helpful to Mossad.) Clinton, who seemed fully briefed on the conversations, admitted to Barak that he knew Denise Rich wanted him to pardon Marc. ("If your ex-wife wants to help you, that's good," he apparently commented.) Clinton was obviously much more involved in the case than he or his former staffers had let on. At one point, the former president advised Barak, "It's best we not say much about that."

Later, in 2002, Clinton told *Newsweek* that he probably would not pardon Marc Rich again, but only because "it was terrible politics. It wasn't worth the damage to my reputation." In other words, giving Marc Rich a pardon wasn't wrong—it was just bad for Clinton's image.

Denise Rich, who threw the wedding shower for Liza Minnelli's ill-fated marriage to David Gest, has continued to make headlines instead of hit records. Last year a former employee sued her for wrongful dismissal, claiming she fired him the day she learned he was HIV-positive. He also revealed that she directed him to donate $2,000 (the limit) to Hillary Clinton's senate campaign, which Denise, as his boss, then reimbursed—a violation of federal campaign spending laws. The disclosure has prompted another criminal investigation. Denise Rich countersued, claiming that the employee broke a confidentiality agreement. Meanwhile, Hillary Clinton's campaign staff returned the money. In October 2003, the Federal Election Commission dismissed a complaint accusing Denise of violating campaign laws in connection with her own donations of money and furniture to Hillary Clinton, but investigations into other aspects of Pardongate continue.

Even more embarrassing, Herbert Black, a former business advisor and wealthy Canadian metals trader—and Denise Rich's date the night she lobbied for her former husband at the Clinton's White House Christmas party—launched another suit against her, for breach of contract in 2002. After he spurned her advances, Black says, she reneged on fees she owed him. She then countersued, saying there was no such deal for advice. He claimed that her fortune, once estimated at more than $200 million, had dwindled to $125 million. Apparently under Black's guidance Rich adopted some austerity measures. According to the *New York Times,* these included the dismissal of her Reiki therapist, whose duties for a mere $50,000 annually, included the rearrangement of Rich's scarf drawer while her employer slept in the morning. Perhaps the most arresting revelation, though, was Denise Rich's geriatric canine care: a dog walker was paid $52,000 a year "to dress up two old dogs like children and push them around Central Park in an $8,000-baby carriage" because they were too elderly to walk.

Revolutionary War: Gerry Adams

"I can only describe this as a killing zone."

January 1997

"Did you see the wee fox?" Gerry Adams inquires gently of two little "boggers" who live at the top of Black Mountain, a rural area above the West Belfast neighborhood where he grew up. Shyly they ask when the next march is: "Our granny takes us to all the marches." He asks, "What is your granny's name?" and recognizes it instantly. A key to the adoration of Adams is how close he keeps to his base, how—despite the fact that he strides the world's stage—he never forgets to high-five a kid such as eight-year-old Eamon in his dirty Lion King T-shirt, or to send regards to his granny. After observing Adams closely in Belfast, Dublin, and London—where he is by turns reviled as an apologist for terrorism and embraced as the great green hope—one begins to grasp the Sisyphean nature of his struggle and to see what a consummate juggler he is.

As president of the Sinn Fein party, the political arm of the Irish Republican Army, Adams has assumed a terrible responsibility: weaning the insular, ruthless, and unstoppable IRA away from more than two decades of violence. Without alienating the Republican "hard men," who see anything less than a united Ireland without Britain as unacceptable defeat, Adams must somehow help engineer a satisfactory political settlement with both the British government and the recalcitrant majority population of Protestant Unionists in Northern Ireland. With the help of

"Irish America" and direct White House intervention, Adams was instrumental in delivering the IRA cease-fire that lasted from August 1994 to February 1996.

Then, tragically, the peace was broken and since then, all hell has broken loose. After seventeen months of what the IRA considered British intransigence, it resumed bombing, and since February three bombs on British targets have killed three people. Within nineteen days of the first, the British suddenly called for talks, once again sending the message, Sinn Fein claimed, that they respond only to violence. Meanwhile the British said that Sinn Fein would be excluded from negotiations until the IRA restored the cease-fire. Then, last summer, British security forces fired more than five thousand plastic bullets at Catholics during and after a protest against a Unionist march through a Catholic neighborhood in Drumcree. In the aftermath, 2 died and 240 were wounded. The attack sent shock waves through Nationalist Ireland (i.e. Catholics and/or those who want a united country).

In the House of Commons today, the Conservative votes of its twelve unyielding Unionist members—virtual descendants of the Protestant King William of Orange, victorious over the Catholic King James II in 1690—hold the balance of power for John Major's precarious one-vote majority and ensure that Ireland will remain divided. The Unionists are joined by Tory backbenchers who believe that any give regarding Northern Ireland will make the natives in Scotland and Wales equally restless. Both groups view Gerry Adams, who is forty-eight years old now, if not as the Devil's adjutant, at least as his messenger boy. "John Major has said on a number of occasions that he will not be the British prime minister who will preside over the breakup of the United Kingdom," says Adams. "There's a certain mind in the British Tory party who thinks they still have an empire, and we're it."

As recently as three years ago Adams was considered so subversive that he was not allowed to be seen on Irish television; in Britain until 1994, he could be seen on TV if his voice was dubbed by actors. Subject to an "exclusion order," he was forbidden to travel to England (even though he is a citizen of the United Kingdom and was an elected member of Parliament for ten years). In 1994, under former prime minister Albert Reynolds, the Irish changed their rules on broadcasting, and—seven months after Adams had received a tumultuous reception in New York in February—the British rescinded their restrictions. Still, the first time Adams appeared on one of Ireland's most popular TV shows, *The Late Late Show* with Gay Byrne, two years ago, Byrne was told that his program would be canceled if he shook Adams's hand. Last September, however, the line in Dublin waiting for Adams to sign his autobiography, the number one best-seller, *Before the Dawn,* stretched for blocks, and he signed copies for seven hours.

Perhaps his star power, fueled by his dangerous reputation, is the most subversive thing about Gerry Adams. On Black Mountain, Adams—who is six feet one, with penetrating dark eyes and undeniable charisma— seems less the controversial pol-cum-celebrity author and more the earnest instructor who has written five books of nonfiction and two volumes of sentimental stories about life here. From the high vantage where we are standing, he points out various sights of Belfast below: we see the shipyards where the *Titanic* was built and the rusted-out factories where few Catholics could obtain even the most menial jobs. "West Belfast grew up where it did," Adams says, "because Catholics were forbidden to live within the city walls."

Currently there are seventeen thousand British troops stationed in Northern Ireland, and they show no signs of retrenchment. A local man strolls over and hands Adams a pair of binoculars to give him a closer view of the new British barracks being constructed nearby. "Look, Gerry, it's all ground-level, and they're planting grass. That means the bunkers are underneath."

I ask the man, "Have you been in prison?" "Aye," he says, glancing at Adams, who smiles ever so slightly. It is probably a superfluous question around here. "These people don't worry about a lot of things you and I worry about," Niall O'Dowd, publisher of the *Irish Voice* and *Irish America Magazine*, has told me. "Life is lived at a much different pitch. Day-to-day decisions are all about putting your life in danger or not."

Below us, snaking through dilapidated West Belfast, are the oxymoronic "peace lines," walls built to keep Catholic Republicans and Protestant Loyalists from tearing at each other's throats. Along them are the guard towers of the British special forces, which look like sets from World War II movies. Only they're real, and "the Troubles"—which began in 1969, when Catholics, who had been gerrymandered out of fair representation and had organized civil rights marches based on those led by Martin Luther King Jr., were attacked by Protestant gangs—have now gone on for twenty-seven years. More than three thousand Catholics and Protestants have been killed, and many thousands more wounded.

"What we've had here for a long time is an apartheid statehood," says Adams. "You have Ireland, a small island, partitioned. You have the British maintaining control over this part of the island. And in order to maintain that control, they give a section of our people—the Unionists—a position of privilege, or perhaps a perception of privilege. Because at the working-class level, they got whatever jobs there are, but in terms of living conditions, they weren't much better off than their Catholic neighbors."

Adams has spent a total of four and a half years in jail, and has been beaten senseless and interrogated for days at a time. In 1984 he was wounded with four bullets by a would-be assassin. His wife, Colette, and his twenty-three-year-old son, Gearoid, a Gaelic hurler, have had a grenade thrown into their house. For more than twenty years he has not slept in the same place in Belfast two nights in a row. For appointments and interviews, you do not go to him—you are taken to him. When I arrive, he shows me the patch of grass on a narrow street in Ballymurphy, at the north end of the Catholic Falls Road, where his boyhood home, part of a housing project, once stood.

In a little house here at 11 Divismore Park, Adams lived with his parents and nine brothers and sisters until he came to be seen by the British military and the local police—the Royal Ulster Constabulary (RUC)—as a native menace. "We had a community uprising, a very popular uprising, and the British army were obviously targeting those whom they wanted to take out of circulation, and I was one of those," Adams says. Before that, after dropping out of Saint Mary's School, he had worked as a bartender and led demonstrations for better housing. "Almost the best part of the struggle was '68 to '72-ish, because the *armed* struggle was very much the lesser part of it. More people were involved."

In August 1971, when he was twenty-two, the British began rounding up suspected IRA members to be "interned," or held indefinitely without charge, trial, or due process. (Despite the fact that the Unionists had begun the killing, only a handful of Unionists were interned. The British were censured by both the European Court of Human Rights and Amnesty International for their brutal treatment of Republican prisoners.) Adams's father, "Big Gerry," had been jailed for IRA activities from the time he was sixteen until he was twenty-one, although Adams says he was not particularly aware of growing up with "a Republican acoustic." Nevertheless, the Adams family, associated with Republican activism on both sides for generations, was singled out. Big Gerry was arrested the night before internment was instituted, on August 9, 1971. That morning Gerry's mother fled with the younger children. Thus began twenty-five years of one or another of Gerry Adams's relatives—or himself—being imprisoned by the British.

By Adams's account, special-forces members threw canisters of tear gas in the windows of his family's house, repeatedly rammed the facade with an armored vehicle, and ended up smashing sinks and defecating on the furniture. "My mother never came back," he says as we lean on the wire fence enclosing the lot and he points out the space where his father, a frequently unemployed construction laborer, built a shed in the backyard. Gesturing around the neighborhood, he says, "I can only describe this as a killing zone."

Adams shows me the cul-de-sac not far away where one day, while lying on the floor of one of the houses to hide from British soldiers, he proposed to Colette McArdle, neighborhood activist. "If we get out of this, I'm going to marry you," he whispered to her.

The hunger strikes declared by Republican inmates in Maze Prison in 1980 and 1981 provided Adams's most wrenching and dramatic involvement with life and death. Ten men, ranging in age from twenty-three to thirty, led by one just as young named Bobby Sands, died after Prime Minister Margaret Thatcher ordered British authorities not to yield to the prisoners' demands to be treated as political prisoners instead of common criminals.

Adams, who got to know Sands in jail, acted as go-between for the prisoners, their families, and the British authorities. Ironically, it was the idea of putting Sands up as a candidate that ultimately galvanized Sinn Fein into electoral politics—its unofficial motto became "The armalite [rifle] *and* the ballot box"—beginning a process that eventually got Adams himself elected to Parliament twice, although he would not take his seat. "I won't take an oath of allegiance to an English queen," he states flatly. Previously the IRA and Sinn Fein had followed an abstentionist policy, but the worldwide tidal wave of sympathy for Sands in the wake of his death, Adams writes in his autobiography, "had a greater international impact than any other event in Ireland in my lifetime."

Despite such a catalyst for transformation, the Unionists and Nationalists continued their strife. In 1984, Adams was shot in the neck, shoulders, and chest while riding in a car with four others after leaving a Belfast courthouse. Within minutes of the incident, British security officers in an unmarked car that had been following Adams apprehended two Loyalist paramilitary gunmen, who were sentenced to eighteen years in prison for the crime. According to *Big Boys' Rules*, by Mark Urban, former defense correspondent for *The Independent* in London, army intelligence had been tipped off about the murder plot but had waited until Adams was shot before intervening. The British army insisted that its presence in the area was a "complete coincidence." Sinn Fein spokesman Richard McAuley says his people took Adams from the hospital as soon as they could. "We had to keep an eye on the RUC not to let someone come in to finish him off."

"We are born in separate hospitals, we attend separate schools, we register at separate unemployment exchanges, and, to add insult to injury, we are buried in separate graveyards," the Protestant ex-paramilitary leader David Ervine, head of the small Progressive Unionist Party, tells me in his hole-in-the-wall office on Shankill Road, the main Loyalist thoroughfare in Belfast. Like many of his counterparts in Sinn Fein, he has spent several years in jail—for possession of explosives and arms—and he recently received his tenth death threat. "I really don't do anything anymore that could be familiar. I can't go watch my son play football or go shopping with my wife." He has never met Gerry Adams, although they passed each other once in a corridor in Washington.

"We fight for two grand dreams," Ervine explains. "I'm a British Nationalist, and he's an Irish Nationalist. The backdrop of all those dreams is that everything else is lost. A pathetic education system, bad infrastructure within Loyalist and Republican working-class areas, lack of employment, destruction of family life: all are on the back burner because of the adherence to the grand ideals of dreams." Yet, he says, "the one thing that won't allow us to have anything in common is the tendency of both sides to have a sense of domination."

During my time in Belfast, the news broke that the British had foiled a potentially huge IRA plot in London; they discovered ten tons of explosives and killed a suspect, twenty-seven-year-old Diarmuid O'Neill, in a shootout and arrested five others. (It later turned out that O'Neill, who was shot six to ten times—reports varied—was unarmed.) That morning, September 23, Adams was at a neighborhood meeting to decry the inadequacies of local housing. He told the media that he "regretted" the death and that circumstances such as these were the result of the "dangerous vacuum" the British had created by not allowing the peace process with Sinn Fein to go forward.

Once the reporters had their sound bites, I was instructed by Big Eamonn, Adams's brother-in-law and driver, not to ride in the car to our next stop, at the Belfast BBC, but to get into a car driven by another former prisoner, Cleeky Clarke. I soon realized that the precaution was for my own protection.

Why are the British still after Adams, and why have they pursued him so doggedly since the 1970s? Why did he spend so much time in jail even though he has never been convicted of any crime—except an attempted prison escape—including being a member of the IRA? And why was

Adams suddenly yanked out of jail in 1972 to participate in hastily called high-level peace talks with the British, only to be rearrested and beaten up a short time later?

According to the British, there is only one answer. They believe that Adams was part of the leadership of the IRA and that when he joined it, at sixteen, the difference between Sinn Fein and the IRA was nonexistent. "You don't become the president of Sinn Fein for standing in the dark," says Belfast reporter Eamonn Mallie, who has cowritten a book on the Provisional IRA. In the book he states flatly that by the time Adams was twenty-three he was the Belfast Brigade second-in-command of the Provisional IRA. Other sources confirm Adams's high status in the terrorist organization, but Adams's consistent denial absolutely infuriates the British. "He looks you straight in the face and gives you barefaced lies," says Conservative MP Michael Mates, the former minister responsible for security in 1992–93. "Of course, that's what terrorists do." Yet the British, who invest heavily in "psych ops"—psychological warfare, media manipulation, and disinformation—in Northern Ireland and have been attempting to track Adams's every move for a quarter of a century, have never offered conclusive proof that he is a terrorist.

In our first interview, Adams categorically denies any association with the IRA. And so begins a Kabuki scenario that every chronicler of Adams is forced to participate in, knowing that the truth is somewhere deep behind the fan that conceals him. "I've never seen myself as an apologist for violence or even for the IRA. The IRA have their own spokespersons, and they make their own case," says Adams. "At all times I have made it clear that I have not been involved with the IRA."

"Ever?"

"Ever. I've also made it clear that I won't distance myself from the IRA, both because I think it would be wrong and, second, it would mean my influence in the situation would be diminished."

In the foreword to his autobiography, Adams explains that he is concealing certain circumstances to protect individuals, but he frequently leaves the reader hanging as to what exactly *he* was doing in those situations. At one point he writes that killing is wrong but sometimes "there was no choice." Adams is not easy to pin down. When I inquire why he was taken out of prison to negotiate with British authorities, he answers, "Because the Republicans asked. I think it may have been a convenience for the British. They would have taken whomever out of jail they were asked to."

"They must have thought you were terribly important, or the Republicans thought you were important."

"Yeah. Whether they thought I was important or not, they obviously thought I could make a contribution."

"Do you deny you were an IRA battalion commander?"

"Yes, I do."

"You never pulled the trigger or planted a bomb?"

"No."

"You never checked out the route for a killing?"

"No. My position—and we could talk about it forever—is that I have not been involved with the IRA."

In *Phoenix: Policing the Shadows,* the story of Ian Phoenix, the head of the Northern Ireland police countersurveillance unit, Jack Holland and Susan Phoenix (the detective's widow) claim that by 1993, sophisticated detection equipment used by the police and Britain's domestic intelligence branch, MI5, "had built up a detailed picture of the republican movement's structure—financial, political and military. It showed considerable overlap between the leadership of Sinn Fein and the Provisional IRA." Gerry Adams, onetime "Northern Command Number 2," according to the book, was one of four people on the IRA's governing Army Council of seven who also "held high positions in the political party."

Only in October 1995, says Holland, did Adams leave the Army Council. Mates, the former security minister, told me that Adams left for "tactical reasons." Sinn Fein spokesman McAuley scoffed: "It's rubbish. Gerry would need forty-eight hours every day to do all these things people claim he's done."

I contacted Holland, a native of West Belfast who writes for the *Irish Echo* in New York, to ask if he had seen hard copies of transcripts of surveilled conversations kept by Ian Phoenix, who died in a helicopter crash in 1994. "I saw concrete evidence that Adams was involved in meetings with high-ranking members of the IRA as late as November 1993." He added, "I've seen names, dates, and places."

According to Holland, the data have been deliberately suppressed by the British. "Because of Adams's political value and his influence over the IRA, they realized he might be the guy who could deliver a cease-fire, and why jeopardize it by proving he's in the IRA?" McAuley counters that Holland should produce the physical evidence.

Ironically, Adams's most potent weapon has always been words. In his autobiography he recounts that when he was stopped by British soldiers, who could have arrested him, he always managed to talk his way out of it. Adams's main technique to keep from breaking under interrogation was to lie away his very existence, to refuse "to admit that I was Gerry Adams." In Long Kesh Prison, where Adams debated and instructed endlessly, he was considered "ultra-leftist." (One of the people he thanked in his prison book, *Cage Eleven,* was Ho Chi Minh.)

For most Unionists, Adams's gift with language makes him deeply suspect. "The Protestant view of the Catholic Irish stereotype is that he is a mendacious fellow handy with words, and if you get into an argument with him, you can only lose with words," a former official of the Northern Ireland government told me. "Unionists find it easier to respond to force."

Adams acknowledges that his power derives from his "ability to bring Republicans to the negotiating table and keep them there." To be effective, however, he must bring them *all* in. "What would be the point if he brought half into the cease-fire and half continued to wage war?" asks the reporter Eamonn Mallie. "He can't condemn. This is like asking Nelson Mandela to condemn the African National Congress during the struggle for independence. The only power revolutionary leaders have is to stay with the foot soldiers."

"Adams has privately said that they'd kill him if he distanced himself publicly from them—the hard men," a former high-ranking British official told me. The British, of course, have negotiated secretly with Adams for years, even though John Major got up on the floor of Parliament and said it would "turn my stomach" to talk to Adams.

"If the politics of condemnation could have resolved this problem, it would have been resolved thirty years ago," says Adams. "I would disempower myself if I slipped into that type of nonsense where moral denunciation becomes a code for political advancement." I tell Adams that when innocent civilians are blown up and all he says is that he "regrets the mistake," people don't feel his language is strong enough. "I have never attempted to condone or justify or explain any action in which civilians have been either injured or killed," he responds. "Second, even in terms of this interview, I no longer see it as my role to answer questions like this. I wouldn't answer questions like this with local journalists." He clearly is annoyed. "We have moved beyond all that. Sinn Fein has a credibility because people know we're taking risks for peace."

By the next day Adams, who is extremely courteous, is more relaxed. I bring up an item in a British paper. Adams used to write a column for a Republican newspaper under the pseudonym Brownie, and the London *Sunday Times* has printed an excerpt: "Rightly or wrongly I am an IRA volunteer. The course I take involves the use of physical force. . . . Maybe I won't fight again . . . but I will move aside for the fighter."

"Are those your words?" I ask him.

"We've been through a sort of trying moment—back to our discussions yesterday about all these questions," Adams replies. "All I can tell you is that if I had written that, it would be worth at least ten years in jail. So I wouldn't like you to write anything that's going to put me in jail."

"A nondenial denial?"

"That's a judgment you have to make, you know."

"I'm really cheesed off I have to go do this book tour in London," Gerry Adams said. Without telling him, his London publisher had obtained a room in Parliament for Adams to launch his autobiography. As a former member of Parliament, he was entitled to the space, but with the headlines screaming about IRA terrorism and Diarmuid O'Neill's being killed, Adams was reluctant to go. For two days the London papers raged.

Adams decided not to force the issue. Instead, he held a press conference at the London Irish Centre in nearby Camden, entering like a rock star, with an entourage wearing green ribbons for the IRA "prisoners of war." Adams is ultracool under fire; questions about his book profits' being blood money didn't seem to faze him. Even while responding to questions, he often doesn't answer them.

On BBC radio, interviewers opened up on Adams with both barrels. For example: "You're asking us to believe *they*, your friends and colleagues, were going out there, joining the IRA, killing people, but *you*— even though you felt as strongly as they about the injustice of it all, in your terms—decided not to join them. *Really?*"

On a call-in show, Adams's first opportunity to talk with ordinary Britons, one man snapped, "When you talk of Hitler, Idi Amin, and Saddam Hussein, then mention in the same breath Gerry Adams, for he is an evil man and disgusting coward." The Unionist member of Parliament Ken Maginnis, who followed Adams on the show, said that Adams "personifies all that is evil in the terrorist campaign that we've had for twenty-five years."

Outwardly, there was little to indicate that any of this was getting to Adams, but it was. In a van leaving the morning press conference, Adams said to his aides, "Do ye not know that I also need time not to be talking to anyone for a while, just to be by myself, alone?" Later, as he was being crammed into a crowded elevator to go before another barrage, he said plaintively to his press aide, McAuley, "Richard, I need a hug."

On the night after Saint Patrick's Day 1995, I was present in the State Dining Room at the White House to witness John Hume, the leader of the Social Democratic and Labour Party, the Martin Luther King Jr. of Irish

Nationalists, sing a duet of the Derry song "The Town I Love So Well" with his political archrival and peace partner, Gerry Adams, Ireland's Black Panther. Although no one knew it then, that spontaneous moment between the two pivotal figures of contemporary Irish nationalism was the highlight of the Northern Ireland peace process.

It was the result of a dialogue begun by the two nearly a decade earlier. And it was fueled by the trust between then–Irish prime minister Albert Reynolds and John Major, which had allowed them to issue the Downing Street Declaration of December 1993, stating that Britain had no selfish strategic or economic interest in Ireland and that Irish unity would not be imposed without the consent of the governed. Major also said that Britain would begin all-party peace talks within three months of a cessation of violence.

Hume and Adams's attempt at harmony was brought about by a remarkable Redemptorist priest, Father Alec Reid of West Belfast's Clonard Monastery, who had grown close to Adams, a practicing Catholic, and understood his increasing desire to break out of the political isolationism in which he found himself. "He is the real catalyst, the facilitator," Adams told me. "I would now consider him to be a dear friend. . . . I think he has redeemed the Catholic Church in Ireland on this whole issue of conflict resolution. There isn't an Archbishop Tutu here."

Reid has been described as a "Christian electrician" for trying to wire together Republicans and the Irish government. The image of him weeping over the body of a British soldier set upon by a Catholic mob and executed by the IRA in 1988 has become an icon of "the Troubles." That same year, according to Eamonn Mallie and David McKittrick's absorbing book, *The Fight for Peace: The Secret Story behind the Irish Peace Process*, Reid secretly arranged for delegations from Hume and from Adams to meet at the monastery. "[We asked] them to state their reasons [for violence]," Hume told me. "Their reasons were that the British were in Ireland defending their own interests by force—economic and strategic interests—and preventing the Irish people from recognizing their right to self-determination. My response to that was that was true in the past but not today. . . . We are all together in the new Europe. Secondly, the Irish people have the right of self-determination, but the Irish people are divided on whether the right is to be exercised."

Hume, who is fifty-nine and has represented Foyle, which includes Londonderry, in Parliament since 1983, has been criticized harshly for consorting with Adams. "The attacks were relentless and regular," he told me, but he persevered. "If as a political leader I could save a single life by dialogue, then it was my duty to do so."

In Hume's book, *A New Ireland*, he says that fifty-five percent of the people "who died in the Troubles in the North were innocent civilians—people killed 'by mistake' or in tit-for-tat revenge killings by Loyalist paramilitaries." Also, "of 279 Nationalist paramilitaries who lost their lives, 117 were killed by the security forces, 20 by Loyalists and 142 by themselves, either in 'accidents' [usually with explosives] or [punishment] 'executions.' " These numbers alone had to indicate to Sinn Fein that it was clinging to a failing strategy.

"I do give John Hume great credit for the part he played in the process," says Adams. "He knows that you cannot marginalize people."

But the peace process might never have moved forward if it had not been for a group of Irish Americans who were able to win over President Clinton and who, for a time, severely strained United States relations with Britain. All because of Gerry Adams.

In the White House that night in 1995 were gathered an extraordinary cast of characters: national security advisor Tony Lake and his deputy Nancy Soderberg; Senators Ted Kennedy and Chris Dodd; billionaire Charles ("Chuck") Feeney, Robert Miller's estranged partner in the duty-free-shopping empire; Bill Flynn, CEO of Mutual of America Life Insurance; publisher Niall O'Dowd; former member of Congress from Connecticut Bruce Morrison, a Clinton classmate at Yale and a Lutheran; and ambassador to Ireland Jean Kennedy Smith.

It was the sixth month of a total cessation of violence by the IRA and its counterparts, the Loyalist paramilitaries, who were represented that night by Gary McMichael of the Ulster Democratic Party. The mood was hopeful. Irish prime minister Albert Reynolds had put Northern Ireland at the top of his agenda and had, in effect, led Adams in from the cold. John Hume, who was a favorite of the Kennedys and had wide contacts in the States, had gone to Reynolds shortly after the latter's election in 1992. "He believed that there was a window of opportunity to be exploited, and he couldn't take it any farther if the two governments weren't prepared to take up the initiative and run with it," Reynolds told me. "Hume brought me in and said, 'You bring in Major,' and I also brought in Clinton. I told them it was my view that [Adams's] morals had changed and he was traveling a very different road."

In fact, Adams was working both sides of the street. On one side were the Irish government, the British government, and the secret dialogues he was carrying on to attempt a breakthrough in the stalemate. On the other were the Republicans, whose reliance on violence, Sinn Fein spokesman McAuley told me, was so strong that it "was like a comfort blanket, something they're used to that leads to people getting killed." Adams, says McAuley, got them to accept a different attitude. "Gerry took us through a painful barrier of having to assess who we are, what we are, where we want to go, and how are we going to go there."

In 1986, Adams led the Sinn Fein convention to abandon abstention-ism and enter into electoral politics on the national level. Encouraged by Father Reid, he also began to hold secret talks with a small group of Protestants at the Clonard Monastery. "We asked him, 'Are you willing to do more than just talk about making peace and pursue the peace process?'" says Presbyterian minister Ken Newell. "In private he has been very critical of the armed struggle. I know from things he's said in private that he regrets every British soldier brought back in a coffin."

For his leadership Adams was rewarded at the White House party. It was not lost on Clinton, of course, that in the 1990 census, 38 million Americans described themselves as Irish American or that in the most recent *Forbes* magazine list of the four hundred wealthiest Americans, one out of four had an Irish name. The day before the party, Clinton had met Adams for the first time, at the traditional Saint Patrick's Day Speakers Lunch on Capitol Hill, begun by the late speaker of the House Tip O'Neill and continued by Newt Gingrich. The *Irish Times* correspondent Conor O'Clery reports in his engrossing book, *Daring Diplomacy: Clinton's Secret Search for Peace in Ireland*, that Adams was still considered so radioactive that their handshake was not allowed to be photographed. For added protection, as Clinton shook Adams's hand, his other arm was draped around the apostle of nonviolence John Hume. A beaming Clinton toasted, "Those who take a risk for peace are welcome in this house."

But across town in the British Embassy and at 10 Downing Street in London, the British were so outraged at Adams's having been allowed into the United States that they became, in no small part, responsible for turning him from an outcast into a celebrity. As Adams says, "If the British had never opposed me getting a visa to the States, whoever would have noticed me going to the States?"

The visa was the centerpiece of a package deal. John Hume told Albert Reynolds that the hard men needed to be convinced by concrete actions on a government level that laying down their arms would result in funda-mental changes. Before they gave up violence, they wanted proof. A big battle was the visa.

As it happened, during the hotly contested New York Democratic pri-mary in 1992, a group of "concerned Irish Americans" had extracted from candidate Clinton the promise that, if elected, he would grant a visitor's visa to Adams. (After Clinton's election, a coalition of politically active Irish in America believed that they now had sufficient clout to build their version of the Jewish lobby that so effectively fights for the interests of Israel.) Clinton also never forgot that, in 1992, Major's Conservative Party had sent two operatives to work for the reelection of George Bush.

Seven times in the past, the State Department and the Justice Department had denied Adams's request to visit the United States, basically to raise money for the Nationalist cause. In 1988, former deputy secretary of state John Whitehead said in an affidavit that he had considered Adams a terrorist since 1983. Then, shortly after Clinton's election, Niall O'Dowd went to Dublin to make contact with Sinn Fein and see if the IRA would call a temporary cease-fire so that he could bring a delegation of Americans over to talk. On his next trip, he met with Adams. "My main objective was to get in high enough to the IRA so I could put a serious proposal at number one about how to reach out to America," says O'Dowd. "The State Department and the British never even saw us coming."

O'Dowd preached the "box theory" to a Sinn Fein representative: "They had to come forward. All the players were locked into this little box. Each move has a countermove, and nothing ever gets done. So you pitch in an outside force—the U.S.—whose dynamic changes it forever. That's what happened." Finally, in September 1993, O'Dowd, Flynn, Feeney, and Morrison went to Ireland for talks with a variety of people, including Reynolds, who was helping to put the Downing Street Declaration together, and the IRA granted them an unprecedented seven-day cease-fire. The Americans now looked at Adams with fresh eyes. Feeney told me, "Right from the first time we met, I felt a certain charisma in this man." Flynn adds, "He's a man of honor. He means every word he says."

The Americans kept the National Security Council advisors at the White House informed of their every move. All through 1993 and 1994, Reynolds, in visits or phone calls to Washington, was allowed to bypass the heads of much larger countries and was "getting lots of time with the president," Bruce Morrison told me. "To the untrained eye, nothing much was happening. But there was a conscious attempt to raise his stature."

O'Dowd's contact inside the White House was NSC staff director Nancy Soderberg. But she did not talk to him directly; she wasn't even sympathetic to him, because he had written articles critical of her former boss Ted Kennedy and his stance on Northern Ireland. Kennedy was totally opposed to those who use violence. Moreover, Soderberg needed deniability if anything went wrong. Their device was to talk through Trina Vargo, who works on foreign-policy issues for Senator Kennedy.

Meanwhile, Hume was also speaking to Soderberg and discussing Adams with the new American ambassador to Ireland, Jean Kennedy Smith, as was Reynolds. In an interview I had with the former prime minister, he said, "I also called John Major and told him straight up what I was doing. He told me he would be opposed." O'Clery writes in his book that Smith's first reaction to a change in United States policy was also negative. She reportedly said, "These are the kind of people who killed my brothers." By December 1993, however, when Ted Kennedy went to Ireland for a visit, she was convinced, and at a private dinner at Reynold's apartment she helped convince the senator.

At Tip O'Neill's funeral in Cambridge, Massachusetts, in January 1994, Ted Kennedy asked John Hume if he wanted Adams to have a visa. Hume said yes. That did it. The Irish then had Kennedy's enormously influential support. "Teddy was the rainmaker," says Niall O'Dowd. "He gave Clinton the space to act."

Meanwhile, the private-sector wheeler-dealers were getting impatient. To force the issue, Bill Flynn came up with the idea of inviting Adams to a one-day peace conference in New York, set for February 1, 1994, and sponsored by Flynn's privately backed group, the National Committee on American Foreign Policy. Morrison says, "It was, give the White House a proposal they couldn't say no to."

The visa issue now started to become public. Smith went against the wishes of two of her top deputies and recommended that Adams be granted a visa. The way she handled their opposition caused her to be reprimanded later by Secretary of State Warren Christopher. Ted Kennedy got Senators Daniel Patrick Moynihan, John Kerry, and Dodd to sign a letter to the president in Adams's behalf. Then the *New York Times* weighed in with a favorable editorial, and influential members of Irish America started a lobbying effort.

The State Department and the British Embassy, who usually saw eye to eye on Northern Ireland, were appalled. "We said to the White House he shouldn't be given a visa until the IRA declared a cease-fire or at least he had called on them to," said Sir Robin Renwick, the British ambassador to Washington at the time. John Major's foreign secretary, Douglas Hurd, even visited the White House to voice strong disapproval.

Finally, in the latter part of January 1994, the White House tried to get Adams to renounce violence unilaterally by answering questions posed by a United States consul. But he couldn't do so to the satisfaction of the White House or State Department. In the end, after more semantic jockeying and with only a few hours to spare before his flight was to take off for Kennedy Airport, Adams got the visa anyway. It was the president's decision, and a total gamble.

When Adams arrived at Kennedy, "it was an absolute mob scene," says the Republican member of Congress Peter King of New York, a longtime friend. Adams registered as Schlomo Brezhnev at the Waldorf and began a whirl of appearances, starting as a guest on *Larry King Live.* "It was just a huge helter-skelter," says Adams. "People here think I've seen the States. I haven't. I've seen escalators, elevators, TV studios." The British were so icy in their revulsion that saturation coverage was guaranteed. On CNN, Robin Renwick said, "When I listen to Gerry Adams, I think, as we all do, it's reminiscent of Dr. Goebbels. It's an extraordinary propaganda line. The line is 'I want peace, but only after we've won.'" The British press went after Clinton, calling him "guilty of shamefaced deceit."

Seven months after getting his visa, Adams was able to arrange what so many had been counting on him for: the cease-fire. But before it could be announced, Adams had one more amazing request: a visa for Joe Cahill, a longtime IRA member who had been caught on a boat in 1973 with five tons of weapons from Libya. Cahill had to go to New York to explain the cease-fire to the hard-core supporters of the IRA, some of whom had allegedly bankrolled the terrorists. Forget it, Soderberg said. But the "Irish Mafia" came out in full force, badgering the White House. "Jean Kennedy Smith was wonderful," says O'Dowd. The president gave in one more time, although, O'Clery reports, he seemed taken aback by Cahill's résumé. The cease-fire was actually announced shortly before Representative King accompanied Cahill to the upstairs of a bar on Second Avenue in Manhattan, where, he told me, a group of "lawyers and contractors and businessmen" were waiting. On August 31, 1994, a total IRA cessation of the armed struggle was a done deal. Six weeks later, the Loyalist paramilitaries also announced a cease-fire.

But the euphoria was short-lived. "It was like, okay, you made a giant step," says the writer McKittrick of the British attitude toward the cease-fire. "Now take another one." Giving Republicans almost no credit for what they had done, the British immediately started imposing conditions. Then, three months later, Albert Reynolds's government fell. Adams lost not only a skilled protagonist who worked well with John Major but also someone willing to take risks. (The current prime minister, John Bruton, has compared the IRA to Nazis and has not shown dynamic leadership regarding the peace process.)

The British were further incensed when Adams was granted another visa to the States, to fund-raise for Sinn Fein. They believed the money would go directly into buying weapons for the IRA. But the Kennedys started lobbying again, and Chris Dodd asked Bill Clinton, on the seventeenth green during a golf game, whether he was going to give Adams another visa or not. It turned out that he would. John Major was so furious that for five days he refused to take calls from Clinton.

With justification, the British, as well as the State and Justice Departments, felt that the president was granting Adams's every wish without asking for anything in return. Meanwhile, Adams was continuing to wow Washington. "He's very disarming," says the former director of White House communications Mark Gearan, who is now Peace Corps director. "What I did not know was how effective he would be as a public personality. You have to put a face on policy. He's been helpful for Americans to better understand 'the Troubles.'" At a reception on the Hill, "congressmen were lined up like kids getting their picture taken with Santa Claus," says Peter King. "Suddenly he was their hero, a media star." In New York, Bianca Jagger and Donald Trump attended a $200-a-plate lunch for Sinn Fein. At a $1,000-a-plate dinner at the Plaza, four hundred people showed up.

As Adams's popularity soared and he went to parties in Beverly Hills with the likes of Anjelica Huston and Oliver Stone, the British dug their heels in even further. To Washington's astonishment, on a lobbying visit in March 1995, Northern Ireland secretary Sir Patrick Mayhew set forth the most stringent precondition of all: decommissioning. The IRA would have to give up some of its weapons before Britain could sit down at the table for peace talks. To the IRA, decommissioning means surrender, and Republicans point out that never before in history has an undefeated army had to give up its weapons before it could negotiate.

Gerry Adams realized that the peace process was crumbling. The major Unionist parties, which would lose power in any settlement, were vetoing Sinn Fein's presence at the table. Adams began to feel the strain. "You don't know how many times I wake up in the middle of the night wondering if I am doing the right thing," King remembers Adams telling him shortly after the Reynolds government collapsed.

Certainly everyone's worst fears were realized on February 9, 1996, when the IRA broke the cease-fire and set off a bomb at Canary Wharf in London, killing two. Adams insists he had no advance warning. "It was a trauma to me." Yet if that is true, what does it say about his power and influence? "If he did know, that's terrible, but if he didn't, it's worse still," says an Irish government official. The White House was stunned. Adams was able to warn the National Security Council about the collapse of the cease-fire only a few minutes before the bomb went off. Senator Kennedy, who was particularly angry, cut off communication. One White House staffer said, "Adams clearly understands that when the cease-fire ended, he would not be welcome here."

Ironically, within two and a half weeks of the bomb's exploding, the Irish government got Britain to agree to come to the bargaining table for peace talks headed by George Mitchell, former senator from Maine. Negotiators would discuss an interim government for Northern Ireland, the structuring of relations between Northern Ireland and the Republic of Ireland in sharing "cross-border institutions," and relations between Britain and Ireland. But in June, a second IRA bomb went off in Manchester, injuring 206, and a third killed a British soldier at the Lisburn army barracks outside Belfast in October—the first to go off in Northern Ireland in two years. Martin McGuiness, one of Adams's chief deputies, who is known for his close contacts with the militants, told me, "Many believe the British don't come to the table unless you bomb them there."

"The Protestants should cut a deal," says Tim Pat Coogan, the Dublin author of *The Troubles*. "The tides of history are overwhelming them." Catholics now make up forty-three percent of the population of the North. Catholic schoolchildren have a pass rate on university-track exams that is four times higher than that of Protestant children. The Nationalists are moving up, while young, middle-class Unionists are emigrating at a higher rate. "If Gerry Adams and John Hume ever cut an electoral deal between their two Nationalist parties, they would win all the seats," says Coogan.

"We're in the endgame," Gerry Adams tells me one morning in a crowded van in London. It is a favorite line of his, and given the events he has helped to shape in recent Northern Irish history, perhaps he can see the outlines of a future not yet visible to the foreign eye. "It could take one year, six months, or a number of years. Making peace is more difficult than making war." He adds, "The British say that politics is the art of the possible. I think it has to be that politics is the art of the impossible."

UPDATE: Gerry Adams now has offices inside the British Parliament building and is a doting grandfather. He still receives death threats and sleeps in safe houses and he still maintains what many consider to be the fiction that Sinn Fein and the IRA are totally separate.

In a gesture of hospitable neutrality, George W. Bush's administration has continued Clinton's tradition of inviting representatives from both sides of the conflict in Northern Ireland to the White House for St.

Patrick's Day. The Bush administration has also maintained a presence in the difficult peace process. Gerry Adams still counts on the U.S. to raise money for Sinn Fein and continues his amazing juggling act: In some circles Adams is hailed as a latter day Nelson Mandela, highly praised for taking an armed revolutionary movement and putting it on a more peaceful political path. But to many who oppose unification in both the north and south of Ireland as well as in Britain, he remains a dangerous, silver-tongued devil.

In 1998, the historic Good Friday Accords were signed, creating a power-sharing formula for governing Northern Ireland. As President of Sinn Fein, Gerry Adams became part of the twelve-member governing Assembly and former IRA official Martin McGuiness even became the Minister of Education. But the peace process that Adams has labored so many years to achieve has proved extremely fragile and has broken down several times. The sticking point for Protestant Unionists is whether or not the IRA, which insists on secrecy, has given up its arms. In the fall of 2003—to speed the process for new Assembly elections after the Protestants had walked out a year before—Adams issued his strongest statement ever that Sinn Fein is "opposed to any use or threat of force for any political purpose." The IRA concurred, effectively putting itself out of the business of armed aggression. Whether diehard Unionists would ever believe that is quite a different story. In elections held in November of 2003, prospects for peace were dealt another serious blow when Ian Paisley's militant Democratic Unionist party became the majority for unionists in Ireland. Meanwhile, Sinn Fein also increased its numbers in the British Parliament where it elected four (although, like Adams, they don't take their seats because they refuse to pledge allegiance to the Queen) and five in the South.

What is undeniable and was really unthinkable a decade ago is that both Catholic and Protestant young people can go to clubs in downtown Belfast today without worrying they might be shot. There is a new police force that is split 50-50 among Catholics and Protestants. Sectarian killings are viewed as a thing of the past and The Troubles are over. Gerry Adams, who recently published his memoirs of the peace process, has also become an avid gardener.

The Secret Agent: Vladimir Putin

"Of course, power should be, in a way,
mysterious and magic."

October 2000

The muddy lot in a working-class section of Saint Petersburg is filled with debris and gives no hint of the city's shabby grandeur. But housed there in a beat-up building behind a turbine factory is the sports club that helped form so much of Russian president Vladimir Putin's discipline and character. For fifteen years Anatoly Rakhlin, a slight, tautly muscled man with Bozo the Clown white hair and penetrating blue eyes, trained Volodya to become a champion in sombo and judo. Putin and his team traveled all over the Soviet Union. On one wall of the sports club, Putin's sad teenage face stares out from a picture of an old lineup of the club's Masters of Sport, the Russian equivalent of all-stars.

Sombo, a Russian acronym for "self-defense without weapons," is a mix of judo and wrestling that caught on when Putin was growing up in the mid-1960s. It places a premium on quick moves, calm demeanor, and the ability to keep from showing emotion or uttering a sound, no matter how intense the struggle or the pain. A laconic, inscrutable introvert to the world and a wry charmer to his intimates, Putin seems to have learned sombo's lessons well.

Clearly, Putin, then as now, was not only calculating but also willing to take a risk. Although he was barely five feet seven and competed in the lightweight, 135-pound category, he was Leningrad's judo champion in

1976, and he would take on teammates twice his size. "He could throw me," says 316-pound Slava Okumen. "His will to win was superstrong." (Okumen was only 246 pounds back then.) Coach Rakhlin explains, "Volodya was not a wrestler of physicality, but more of intellect—a smart wrestler. He always did the unexpected, because he was versatile, very strong, so the speed of the fight was intense."

During Putin's first four years of training, Rakhlin had to change the club's location five times in the sprawling city. Other kids dropped out, but not Volodya, who traveled long distances on the trolley. The only child of what Rakhlin calls poor working-class parents, Putin stuck with the coach, even when he was studying at Leningrad State University, where he was pressured to be on the teams, and later as a young KGB officer, when he was practically ordered by university authorities to join the police club. According to Rakhlin, "The best wrestlers come not from talent but from dedication to sport. Volodya was dedicated to sport and loyal to his coach."

And loyalty is what has catapulted Vladimir Putin through the ranks, from an obscure, disillusioned KGB lieutenant colonel home from Germany in 1990 to deputy mayor of Saint Petersburg, to a series of increasingly powerful posts in the corrupt Kremlin of Boris Yeltsin. (Think Robert Duvall as the consigliere in *The Godfather*.)

On December 31, 1999, Boris Yeltsin—in a brilliant tactical move—resigned as Russia's president unexpectedly and made Putin, then prime minister, his successor, thereby forcing early elections, in March. Putin, one of whose first decrees was to absolve the vulnerable Yeltsin of any prosecution after he left office, got fifty-two percent of the vote. The campaign was designed as a clever series of macho photo ops in which Putin said almost nothing but proclaimed a "dictatorship of the law," while the state-owned media mercilessly slandered his opponents.

On May 7, the day of Putin's inauguration, Rakhlin was outside Moscow at a tournament, but the next day the Kremlin tracked him down the moment he registered at a hotel in the capital. Picked up in an official car, Rakhlin was whisked in his sweats to the inner sanctum of the Kremlin, to have lunch alone with the exhausted Putin in his private dining room. "I was with him fifteen years. His mother died, his father died. I am a second father."

Rakhlin tried to relax Putin by "speaking of nothing. I told him how to take care of his knees." The president confided to him that the hardest part of his job was meeting so many "simple" people during his travels outside Moscow. "He told me they just complain or cry because they live so badly," Rakhlin says during my interview with him. "They can't believe they are seeing the president, and they hope he can make their lives better, because they are so miserable. It's getting to him."

At the G8 summit in Okinawa in July, Putin capped an impressive first appearance with the heads of state of the world's leading industrial nations—one of his suggestions was that they should start e-mailing one another—by visiting a Japanese judo club and pinning a young opponent, whom he then invited to throw him. He told reporters that his favorite judo move is the deashibari, a swift attack that knocks the opponent off his feet.

Putin's instant popularity took Kremlin image makers totally by surprise last fall, when, as the third prime minister Yeltsin had appointed in two years, he accepted full responsibility for waging a bloody, brutal war on Chechnya, which has leveled Grozny, the capital, and left untold thousands of civilian casualties. Putin considers the conflict in Chechnya a terrorist civil insurrection and says that "Chechen bandits" are the shock troops of a fundamentalist Muslim drive to deprive the Russian Federation of vast stretches of territory. His efforts to demonize Chechens were aided by the fact that many Muscovites believe downtown Moscow is controlled by the Chechen Mob. After highly suspicious "Chechen terrorist" apartment bombings in three Russian cities last fall, in which about three hundred civilians were killed, Putin's ratings soared, although there's little evidence that Chechen terrorists actually carried out the bombings.

During the struggles over Chechnya, Putin, who was being "tested by Yeltsin" according to the Kremlin's top political consultant, Gleb Pavlovsky, was a revelation. His performance garnered admiration. Yeltsin's "Family," or inner circle (intent on managing the succession and maintaining its tainted power), had been plotting the post-Yeltsin era almost from the day of Yeltsin's 1996 election (Pavlovsky calls the strategizing "a sort of Manhattan Project"). They secretly polled to find out what kind of person the Russian people considered heroic. Suddenly, right under their noses, they realized that in Putin they had a Stirlitz, the dashing KGB officer who is the hero of a popular old film, an undercover agent in the SS in Germany in World War II who embodies Russian ideals. They immediately launched a campaign to turn Putin into another Stirlitz, complete with an ideology-free political party called Unity.

The Stirlitz image was used by Pavlovsky to help Putin overcome the dual handicaps of coming from the KGB (not exactly consonant with democratic reform) and being handpicked by the despised Yeltsin. "For an intelligence officer it was easy," says Pavlovsky. "He had the alibi: he's hiding and in secrecy awaiting orders. . . . Did he take part in reforms? Yes, but he was Stirlitz, working undercover. . . . Was he seen at demonstrations? Of course not! He is Stirlitz and not supposed to be seen there. And here we are reaching the paradox," Pavlovsky continues. "But Yeltsin named him as successor, and Yeltsin was hated by the whole country. Yes, but he is Stirlitz, and he earned Yeltsin's trust so well that even Yeltsin counts on him! That was a very deep mechanism." Pavlovsky adds, "Of course, power should be, in a way, mysterious and magic. Especially in Russia. Putin answers that need perfectly."

The opposition did its part. According to Pavlovsky, "They were conducting an anti-Yeltsin campaign only. . . . Our hope was that they would be thinking of Putin as another fatal mistake of Yeltsin." They were. "When Putin was superpopular, they called themselves his enemy—total stupidity!" The strategy played out perfectly. "When we understood everyone was thinking the way we wanted them to, psychologically we began to drink champagne," Pavlovsky crows.

After the parliamentary elections on December 19, 1999, "we understood we couldn't hide him anymore. People came to vote for Putin," Pavlovsky says, explaining that the citizens realized that they were really voting for who would succeed Yeltsin. But timing was crucial if Putin was actually to ascend. Had Yeltsin not taken himself out early, "that would have forced Putin to position himself regarding Yeltsin and Yeltsin's past." But after Yeltsin resigned on December 31, "we understood that we had one or two months [before the elections] for Putin to become stronger and stronger as the head of executive power."

The image makers poured it on: Russians saw Putin distributing hunting knives to Russian troops at the Chechen front on New Year's Day, Putin using crude prison slang to say how he'd deal with Chechen guerrillas ("We'll ice them while they're shitting in the outhouse"), Putin flying a two-seat military jet. "Putin demonstrated all the time he can do things," says Pavlovsky. "He showed that as a secret intelligence officer, he is able to handle weapons, the jet." The Russian populace, humiliated by the loss of the first Chechen war in 1996 and the loss of their status as a superpower, and weary of the ubiquitous corruption in the government and the downturn of their economy, yearned for a young, vigorous leader they could be proud of—someone who would restore law and order and show who was boss. By March, when Putin officially became Yeltsin's successor, democracy was almost a secondary concern.

Until the tragic sinking of the *Kursk* nuclear submarine in August 2000, when 118 men perished and Putin failed to come home from his Black Sea vacation to provide leadership in the crisis, the new president had been consolidating his power at a dizzying rate. He had managed to scare and offend many of the elite while keeping his approval ratings high. He had cut a deal with the Communists in the Duma, the Parliament's lower house, to share power with his Unity Party, and he seemed to be getting almost everything he wanted. Even now he is moving toward a two-party system of Unity and the Communists.

More important, he has divided Russia into seven federal zones, each with its own administrator, a move designed to rein in Russia's eighty-nine elected regional governors, many of whom are corrupt in forging deals that bypass the national government. What is alarming to many observers, both inside and outside Russia, is that five of the seven administrators are former generals from the military or security forces. Echoing fears that the security forces are in the ascendant, human-rights activist Yelena Bonner, widow of the famed dissident Andrei Sakharov, says, "I believe [the KGB] would never allow anyone to leave the zone of its influence. Physically you can resign from this organization, but mentally and professionally Putin will never get out from under their influence."

Putin has gotten legislation passed to expel the governors from automatic membership in the upper house of Parliament and to strip them of their offices if they have been found to break the law. They now have to return much more tax revenue to the federal government. The Parliament will be further weakened by the establishment of a new state council, predicted to take over many of the key powers traditionally held by the upper house.

With a team of liberal economists, Putin has also introduced a supply-side economic plan for Russia, featuring a radical tax-reform package to attract Western investment, the cornerstone of which is a simplified flat tax of thirteen percent to encourage the wealthy to pay at least something. But there are also more punishing tax hikes on gas, vodka, and cigarettes, and the worst is supposedly yet to come this fall when the government reduces utility and housing subsidies. But with the sinking of the *Kursk,* and the explosion of a bomb in a crowded Moscow underground passageway a week earlier, the perilous nature of Russia's security and military preparedness was brought into stark relief.

The Russian press responded with more vigor than it ever had, and public opinion suddenly demanded to be taken into account. But Putin—instead of displaying the reflexive instincts of an experienced politician rallying his country at a crucial moment—behaved like a timid, secretive Soviet bureaucrat out of the past: distancing himself, refusing foreign aid for four days, allowing disinformation fed by the Russian navy about the fate of the submarine to flourish. The long-term effect of the *Kursk* on Putin's ability to govern will take months to assess.

Before the *Kursk* crisis, Putin's most controversial move had been a clampdown on the opposition media with the arrest of one of New Russia's powerful oligarchs, Vladimir Gusinsky, chairman of the Media-Most empire, which includes NTV, the influential television network, for alleged fraud. Gusinsky says the charges are baseless, although the analyst Dimitri Simes cautioned, on the *NewsHour with Jim Lehrer*, that Gusinsky is "closer to Meyer Lansky than a real democrat." The government says he acquired a controlling stake in a lucrative TV station for $5,000 after the official in charge of the sale allegedly received a payment of $1 million.

In July, after strong negative reaction at home and abroad, the charges were suddenly dropped. Rumors abound that a deal was struck to have Media-Most sold and put under state supervision, but NTV officials deny it. Igor Malashenko, the number-two man at Media-Most, warns, "Putin's consolidation of power is very simple: it's to put everything under his control. He doesn't believe in a system of checks and balances. Any checks and balances are a nuisance." Putin's government appears to be serving notice that rogue elements will be forced into compliance.

Gusinsky's case was extreme but not isolated. Freedom of the press remains a very sensitive issue. Last winter, Putin was widely criticized for defending the Russian troops who kidnapped Radio Liberty correspondent Andrei Babitsky, a vocal opponent of the Chechen war. Pavel Felgenhauer, *Moscow Times* columnist and Radio Moscow commentator, says, "I know from the inside there is no free press. The press here is either distorted, not published, or told what to write."

The Russian press and Internet thrive on *kompromat*, "compromised material," which is usually bought from underpaid government security-force employees or former security agents who wiretap, intercept e-mail, and tail. Phone tapping is believed to be more widespread today than in Soviet times. In fact, Gusinsky was accused of having a private security force—all the oligarchs do—that engaged in massive wiretapping, and indeed a former KGB general, Philip Bobkov, now gathers and analyzes information for Media-Most.

But beyond the press, the corrupt economics of the New Russia is where Putin must show some zeal. Most oligarchs don't even bother to deny how ill-gotten their fabulous fortunes are, and Putin has begun to move against several of them, declaring, "All should be equally distanced from power." Whether he will carry out his threats, merely use them as leverage, or is staging a PR stunt for the benefit of the masses remains to be seen. In July, Putin assured a group of nervous big-business executives that he was not going to overturn their unscrupulous privatizations of state-owned companies. "You built this state yourself to a great degree through political or semipolitical structures under your control," Putin said bluntly, "so there's no point in blaming the reflection in the mirror."

"Imagine a prison," Alexander Starkov, one of the major real-estate developers in Moscow, tells me. "You cannot live in prison with the laws of a free life—you have to live with the laws of the prison. We in Russia all live in one big prison."

Putin has also launched into a frenzy of diplomacy with the Vatican, China, and North Korea, and his highly publicized visits with Tony Blair in Britain and Gerhard Schroeder in Germany pointedly indicate that he is seeking to ally Russia with Europe rather than with the United States. But since his inauguration, Putin has met twice with President Clinton, at the United States–Russia summit in Moscow in June, and in Okinawa at the G8 meeting in July. This month the two men will meet again for the United Nations Millennium Summit in New York.

I was sitting in the front row during the signing ceremony at the Moscow summit, watching Putin, whose skin is yellowy beige, slump in his seat in the newly restored Saint George's Hall in the Kremlin and absently drum his fingers on the table while a tired-looking Clinton read from his notes about the summit's "successful" conclusion, with a joint agreement for each to destroy thirty-four tons of plutonium intended for nuclear warheads. Several hundred journalists present were confined to four questions and sat like props at a photo op. Putin had spoken without notes, yet unlike Clinton or Yeltsin or Mikhail Gorbachev, with their obvious charisma, he would never have been the one picked out by an observer as the group's natural leader.

A few hours earlier, I had witnessed Putin greet the United States delegation before sitting down to negotiate—he presented a bouquet to ambassador James Collins for his birthday and greeted Clinton in English. Deputy Secretary of State Strobe Talbott, who was a Rhodes scholar at the same time as Clinton and has had wide latitude over United States–Russian relations since his friend's election, hobbled in with a cane, a result of knee surgery. Clinton playfully pointed to three little monkeys Secretary of State Madeleine Albright had pinned to her lapel, and said, "'See no evil, hear no evil, speak no evil'—that's Madeleine's entire foreign policy." Putin smiled politely. But this was definitely not Boris and Bill poking each other in the ribs to share yet another joke.

Saint Catherine's Hall, where the meeting took place, was a vision of imperial opulence. These luxurious rooms were also a testament to the Mabetex scandal, named for the Swiss contractor responsible for the restoration, who stands accused of bribing Yeltsin's Family with, among other things, credit cards. During the investigation of the matter by Switzerland, Yuri Skuratov, Russia's general prosecutor (attorney general) from 1995 to 1999 and later one of Putin's opponents for the presidency, had urged Swiss authorities to search the contractor's office. For that, he told me, he was removed from office. The Family panicked, fearing that the Swiss—who were building a substantial case—would uncover their secret bank accounts. Soon after, a videotape of a cavorting threesome alleged to be Skuratov and two prostitutes was aired on state television. Skuratov denied it was he.

Putin, then head of the Federal Security Service (FSB), successor to the KGB, had already crossed swords with Skuratov in 1996. (Skuratov had gone after Putin's former boss Anatoly Sobchak, then Saint Petersburg's mayor, for corruption.) Skuratov says Putin was present in the hospital room when an ailing Yeltsin demanded Skuratov's resignation, which he at first refused to give. Skuratov tells me, "I am very pessimistic for the rule of law in Russia—because I know the real situation. Respect for the law was never a requisite for Russia." Skuratov found it "a very powerful symbol" that one of the first presidential decrees Putin signed, to pardon Yeltsin, "contradicted existing federal laws and the constitution."

At the Moscow summit, Putin declared that "the United States is one of our main partners." He said, "One would hope that the very worst of our relations is far, far behind us." Nevertheless, Putin is currently exploiting a wedge issue—the proposed recasting by the United States of the failed Star Wars project to build a nuclear shield to guard against missiles from so-called rogue states. Doing so would violate the 1972 Anti-Ballistic Missile Treaty, but George W. Bush, the GOP candidate for president, favors such a plan. Clinton said he would decide this fall if testing to construct such a system should continue. After being ignored by the United States, following his proposal that the two countries join forces to develop the system, Putin (who pleased American officials by finally getting the Start II Treaty ratified in the Duma) is now the leader of the opposition. His analysis at the G8 of his visit to North Korea's leader, Kim Jong-il (in which Kim told him he would give up his plans to build missiles with warheads if others would help North Korea launch its satellites), was pronounced "brilliant" and "impressive" by several heads of state. These same leaders believe that if the American plan goes forward, a new arms race will start. A month later, however, the mercurial Kim told South Korean media that the idea was "a joke."

Ordinary Russians, who aren't used to a sober leader who works out every day and drinks Diet Coke, much less one who gets heady praise from other world leaders, have mostly applauded Putin. Nevertheless, with his swift, unexpected moves, the president has been keeping friend and foe alike guessing as to what his real motives are. Will the mysterious Mr. Putin ultimately save a weak Russian state by becoming a latter-day Pinochet? To what extent will he remain the captive of the evil Kremlin Family, which put him in power, the very people who had made a Faustian pact with the oligarchs, handing them vast parts of the country's resources in exchange for the means to reelect Yeltsin in 1996? Will he wake up all of Stalin's ghosts with the siren call of the newly energized state security services?

If Putin doesn't succeed, Russia—already off its feet ethically, economically, and demographically—will be in danger of being decisively knocked out. "The real threat to Russia is to implode," Malashenko, of Media-Most, told me. "The government cannot collect taxes or maintain the armed forces—it's all falling apart." At the same time, nationalistic fervor is being reasserted. According to Malashenko, "They want to restore Russian grandeur militarily; they don't understand how bad the situation is. They don't understand that Russia may be disappearing as a viable nation."

To save her, Putin will need more than judo. He'll need voodoo.

Two out of three Russian men die drunk. It doesn't matter if they die of a heart attack or in an accident or as a murder victim or a suicide; they are drunk when they die, mostly on a Monday after a binge weekend. The life expectancy for Russian men is 58.8; for women, it's 71.7. (In the United States, it's 72.9 for men and 79.6 for women.) Only ten to fifteen percent of Russian babies are born healthy. Approximately two-thirds of Russian pregnancies end in abortion; at least seventy-five percent of pregnant women have serious pathologies. "It's horrendous," says Murray Feshbach, emeritus research professor at Georgetown University, who is the leading American authority on Russian demography. "Anemia during pregnancy has quintupled during the last decade. The syphilis rate among young females from ten to fourteen has gone up roughly forty times since 1990—that really means ten- to fourteen-year-olds who are doing drugs and having intercourse. Among fifteen- to seventeen-year-old males, only ten to thirty percent are healthy." Feshbach also has shocking statistics on the environment in Russia today. One recent health minister, he says, "issued a list of thirteen Russian cities where he advised the population, 'It doesn't pay to go outside.'" Meanwhile, in May, Putin abolished the State Committee on the Environment.

Heroin addiction has exploded in Russia in the last two years. Heroin from Afghanistan is cheaper than marijuana. As a result, Russia has one of the fastest growth rates of HIV infection in the world, up more than 350 percent between 1998 and 1999, spread mostly by dirty needles. An estimated 300,000 to 500,000 individuals are infected with HIV, and there is no way the collapsed health-care system can provide for them. In England, *The Guardian* reported in May that only 13 percent of the youths conscripted annually for the Russian army actually show up; of those, according to the Committee of Soldiers' Mothers of Russia, an advocacy group, about one thousand commit suicide. Their pay is less than $2 a month. More than half of the Russian people live below the poverty line, with incomes that are 40 percent lower than in 1991. "For Russia, to restore a sense of national pride, you must think about things as mundane as living like a human being," former prime minister Sergei Stepashin, who is now head of the State Audit Chamber, told me. "The average Russian pension is $25 a month."

"We are in danger of becoming a senile nation," Putin told the country in a forceful first State of the Nation speech in July. "It is difficult to live. Year by year, we, the citizens of Russia, are getting fewer and fewer. If this continues, the very survival of the nation will be under threat." That was the first time a top Russian leader had spoken publicly about these truths. The fact is, some 800,000 more Russians are dying per year than are being born. One member of the Duma's Parliamentary Committee on Health glumly predicted that by 2025, the population, currently at 146 million, will be down to 100 million. "The situation is apocalyptic," says Feshbach.

Meanwhile, filthy-rich Russians have replaced Arabs as the most conspicuous consumers in the chic watering holes of Europe. In the last decade, an estimated $300 to $500 billion has been siphoned out of Russia into offshore companies and foreign banks. In the summer of 1999, for example, Vladimir Posner, the Russian broadcaster, witnessed the "baby billionaire" Vladimir Potanin, who was thirty-six, sailing a 250-foot yacht into Nice "with a bevy of Russia's most stunning models, and the money flowed like the champagne." He added, "The Russian people would love people to go after these guys." And the oligarchs know it. After Putin's tax police arrested Gusinsky, eighteen of the country's top tycoons wrote an open letter to the president: "We have no doubts that the law-enforcement authorities could have serious questions concerning his activities, as can be applied to any substantial and successful business-man in Russia."

"How shall I explain to my readers," I asked a leading Russian oli-garch, billionaire Mikhail Khodorkovsky, thirty-six, the chairman of Rus-sia's second-largest oil company, Yukos, "how a handful of men in your country ended up with thirty percent of one-seventh of the entire world's resources?" (Khodorkovsky is also the former chairman of a failed bank, Menatep, whose depositors lost hundreds of millions of dollars when the ruble crashed in August 1998. In 1995 the CIA claimed that he was "con-trolled by one of the most powerful crime clans in Moscow" and that Menatep "had set up an illegal banking operation in Washington," a vast money-laundering scheme connected to offshore companies in the Caribbean. Khodorkovsky denies the charges.)

With a straight face, Khodorkovsky likens the situation in Russia to the need in Silicon Valley to import skilled managers from India. "Chances are you will not find personnel for a justifiable wage. It's a seller's market." He explains that in Russia "there's a total absence of managers, so somebody who was a skilled manager could pick and choose his company." He makes it sound as if he had done the govern-ment a favor by taking a two-million-barrels-a-day oil enterprise off its hands. Yet it has been reported that the state accounting chamber charged Menatep with using government money being held for other purposes, such as paying workers' salaries, to make a sweetheart bid for Yukos in a less-than-transparent auction.

Such auctions were part of the infamous loans-for-shares scheme designed to help the cash-strapped Russian government pay its debts and speed privatization. In the mid-1990s, private Russian banks were given shares in state enterprises in return for loans. These shares were to be held in trust, and if and when they were turned into equity, the banks could bid for them at auction. Many of the auctions were outrageously rigged.

Last February, while Putin was acting president, three Family-friendly oligarchs—Roman Abramovich, a principal owner of Sibneft Oil; media mogul Boris Berezovsky, acting through his company Logovaz; and a Siberian magnate—ended up with more than sixty percent of Russia's multibillion-dollar aluminum reserve in a questionable takeover that was found not to violate antimonopoly laws. Berezovsky has been the pet Tyrannosaurus rex oligarch of the Yeltsin Family. Dark, voluble, and cunning, he is a thoroughly political animal who takes credit for getting Yeltsin elected in 1996 (by rallying other oligarchs to pony up millions to keep the Communist candidate, Gennady Zyuganov, from winning) and also for getting Putin elected in 2000 (by discrediting Putin's opponents on the state channel ORT, of which he owns a minority share). His rival, Igor Malashenko, claims Berezovsky has a very simple principle: "If we have complete control of TV and unlimited financial resources, we can elect anybody president."

Swiss prosecutors have frozen Berezovsky's assets in Swiss banks, and accuse him of having misappropriated an estimated $700 million from Aeroflot, Russia's national airline. At first, few believed that Russian prosecutors would pursue him, but lately things have soured. Putin thinks Berezovsky talks too much, and Berezovsky split with Putin over the president's plan to strengthen the federal government's grip on the governors, some of whom, according to Posner, "sit deep in his pocket."

"We oligarchs believe in Russia," Berezovsky, fifty-four, a onetime mathematician, assures me in his "club," a heavily guarded town house in Moscow, where he is surrounded by a white grand piano, faux French furniture, a bar, and surveillance cameras. "Then how come so many billions have gone out of Russia?" I ask. "Because in Russia today there are no laws to protect capital."

In many ways Berezovsky echoes Khodorkovsky in declaring that he deserves his riches because, unlike his colleagues during the early perestroika days, he was willing to take a risk. "The Russian people have a slave mentality," Berezovsky declares. "They didn't believe in new developments. We [oligarchs] are rational to spend less energy and get more profit, and if the state would have formulated other rules, we'd fulfill those. . . . [But] the legal system is inadequate and incomplete for business reality."

I am curious to know to what extent Berezovsky understands how he is viewed. "In the West you are perceived as a caricature of an oligarch, a crook, and a clown," I inform him. "Why would you want that reputation for yourself?"

"There are two reasons why not only me but Russian business has a bad reputation," Berezovsky replies. "First, the revolutionary transition Russian business has undergone gave birth to colossal corruption, and the cause is the historically unprecedented redistribution of wealth. In 1990 everything belonged to the state. By 1997 almost seventy-five percent of the property was held privately. The redistribution of property was in the hands of bureaucrats who made salaries of $100, $200 a month. And with a single signature . . ." He trails off, then adds, "I am sure there are no corrupt American bureaucrats. There wouldn't be many bureaucrats who in the same situation would refuse bribes."

"So many millions of people have suffered because of policies you've perpetrated," I say. "Don't you feel bad about that?"

"I don't feel bad about it, though I can't say I feel comfortable," Berezovsky replies. "Russia was grappling with the problem of transforming itself into a new economic and political system. By any measure, this would be called a revolution, and the basis of such a transformation is always the redistribution of property. . . . This was done without a civil war. The way to judge whether a transformation was successful or not was that there was no civil war."

Obviously, there is no love lost between Berezovsky and the second-most-hated man in Russia, the Saint Petersburg economist Anatoly Chubais, the chief architect of the loans-for-shares program. Before I met Chubais in Washington, I spoke in Moscow to one of his top aides, Leonid Gozman, who told me that massive privatization had been the only way to rescue a floundering state that was in danger of going back to Communism. "Certainly, we're a fantastically corruptible system—but America in its early capitalist days had its robber barons, too—Carnegie, the first Mayor Daley."

Whenever I hear that argument, I think of the testimony that former CIA Russia chief of station Richard Palmer, who after retiring served as a consultant to Russian banks, gave to the House Committee on Banking and Financial Services in 1999. Palmer has spent a decade studying Russian financial and organized crime. This is his chilling analysis of what Putin faces in attempts to impose a "dictatorship of the law":

> For the United States to be like Russia is today, it would be necessary to have massive corruption by the majority of the members of Congress as well as by the Departments of Justice and Treasury, and agents of the FBI, CIA, DEA, IRS, Marshal Service, Border Patrol, state and local police officers, the Federal Reserve Bank, Supreme Court justices, United States District court judges, with the support of the various organized-crime families, the leadership of the Fortune 500 companies, at least half the banks in the nation, and the New York Stock Exchange. This cabal would then have to seize the gold at Fort Knox and the federal assets deposited in the entire banking system. It would have to take control of the key industries—such as oil, natural gas, mining, precious and semiprecious metals, forestry,

cotton, construction, insurance, and banking—and then claim the products and services to be their private property. The legal system would have to nullify most of the major provisions against corruption, conflict of interest, criminal conspiracy, money laundering, and economic fraud, and weaken tax evasion laws. This unholy alliance would then have to spend about fifty percent of its billions in profits to bribe officials that remained in government and be the primary supporters of all the political candidates. Then, most of the stolen funds, excess profits, and money from bribes would have to be sent to offshore banks for safekeeping.

Yet even today, as Russia suffers with a mostly barter economy, where the average wage has recently risen to $82 a month, Anatoly Chubais remains Washington's and Harvard's golden boy. Chubais, who accrued oligarchic status if not wealth in Russia for becoming synonymous with the manipulation of United States aid and billions from the International Monetary Fund, is husky and genial and speaks good English. He is now head of United Energy System of Russia; this vast electrical utility, with more than 700,000 employees, is thirty-four percent owned by foreign shareholders, who have recently challenged his leadership.

Chubais, along with economist and former prime minister Yegor Gaidar, Harvard professors Jeffrey Sachs and Andrei Schleifer, and Sachs's aide Anders Aslund, is known for being the driving force behind the Russian-American aid program that advocated "shock therapy" to push a market economy in Russia. Chubais had the run of both the Kremlin and the Clinton White House, where Vice President Al Gore, a Harvard graduate, was the point man on Russian policy. The group's mentor was Treasury secretary Larry Summers, who had been an economics professor at Harvard and chief economist of the World Bank. "The whole ideology for the privatization of Russia was worked on American calculations," Yuri Skuratov, the former prosecutor, informed me. And there was much to be questioned. In June 1997, the U.S. agency for International Development suspended funding to the chief funnel for U.S. assistance, the Harvard Institute for Internation Development, because two of its chief executives, Jonathan Hays and Andrei Schleifer were accused of inside knowledge and speculating in the Russian stock market through Hays's girlfriend and Schleifer's wife.

"I know the common understanding here in the U.S. of what Russia is," Chubais told me. "Russia is corruption, bribes, oligarchs, Mafia, murder. I disagree with that completely. This is an extremely superficial understanding of the forces of change which are fundamental to the revolution. If you go deeper, you need to see that the absolutely fundamental institutions, which never existed previously in my country, are now accepted." He listed freedom of speech, division of power, democratic elections, private property, and the Russian constitution. In Putin's pre-election manifesto, Russia at the Turn of the Millennium, he said that if the Russian economy grew eight percent a year (a fairly utopian notion) for the next fifteen years, it would reach the per capita gross domestic product of Portugal.

When Volodya Putin was studying chemistry in a technical high school in Leningrad in 1970, he already knew that he wanted to be a spy. He set his sights on the law school of Leningrad State University, which would put him on the path to the KGB, and he took extra courses in Communist ideology. When one of his teachers announced that a pure Communist state would be achieved by 1980, Volodya jumped up. "It's not possible. This is a lie. Nobody believes this. Let's vote, guys. Who believes this?" "No one put his hand up," says Raisa Sergeevna, one of his teachers, who recalls that Volodya came in second in the school paper drive for being "the hardest-working person."

"Volodya's father was very tough on him, but Volodya never challenged him," says Sergei Roldugin, Putin's close friend. A cellist with the Maryinsky Theater Symphony Orchestra, Roldugin taught Putin about classical music and got his two daughters started on the piano and violin. Putin's father, a factory worker and the son of one of Stalin's cooks, had gone through a tough time in the war and was, says Roldugin, "a member of the party, a strong believer. He hated democracy." Volodya came to his parents late in life, after two other young sons died, and so, says a classmate, Aleksandr Matveev, "he was like a light in the window to them." When they won a car in a state lottery, they could have sold it and lived off the proceeds for several years. Instead, Putin became the only student at the university with a car.

At Leningrad State University, Putin, at eighteen, was younger than many of his classmates, who had served in the army. Sports occupied a lot of his time, and he passed up privileges by sticking with Coach Rakhlin and not joining the university team. He was focused on his goals, disciplined, quiet, but with a good sense of humor. His friend Leonid Polokhov, the outspoken, piano-playing son of a Soviet general, recalls, "He told me he wanted to be a spy, and of course I tried to talk him out of it." But Putin was determined. "We had a pretty closed society," says Nikolai Egorov, of the law firm Egorov, Pughinsky, Afanasiev & Marks, another close friend and former deputy prime minister, "so in the opinion of many

Russian people at that time, the KGB was seen as a highly respected organization, very difficult to get into, an honor." Pavel Koschelev, a classmate and later a colleague, says, "We came to the KGB to serve the state."

According to his KGB officemate, Valery Golubev, Putin's work in Leningrad was "gathering information from Russians with contact with foreigners." "We were taught to be secretive," says Koschelev. "You could not show your real emotion." Sergei Roldugin once asked Putin what he actually did. "I'm a specialist in human relations—people, that's my profession," Putin told him. "He never spoke of the KGB," says Roldugin. "The goal is to establish connections with people when they come to Russian cities," says Golubev, who told me Putin's KGB class studied Dale Carnegie's *How to Win Friends and Influence People.*

After a few years in the KGB, according to Polokhov, Putin became restless and wanted to go abroad. By 1985, when he was assigned to Dresden, East Germany, where he recruited Stasi (East German secret police) and kept tabs on German Communist political figures, Putin had spent considerable time in training in Moscow. He had also married Lyudmila Aleksandrovna, a flight attendant from Kaliningrad, Russia's westernmost city. In 1985 they had their first child, Masha, and in 1986 Katya was born in Dresden. German is the daughters' first language.

Lyudmila would fly to their dates in Leningrad. Outspoken and energetic, she has devoted herself to providing a comfortable home for a husband who often appears oblivious to time and place. Putin has always worked long hours. Egorov told me he was once in their home when Putin came in and Lyudmila asked him, "Did you eat lunch?" "I can't remember," he said. "Do you want food?" "I don't know." "Do you need food?" "Yes, probably I do."

"Women like him," says Roldugin. "He has some kind of mystery. He knows how to treat and take care of women."

When the Berlin Wall fell in 1989 and Russia did nothing to stop it, Putin, like many of his colleagues, was stunned to see everything they had worked so diligently for come crashing down around them. "Every morning, to go to work and hear yourself be described as traitors," says Pavel Koschelev. "It was worse than the collapse of your ideas and values. We had the feeling we had been betrayed personally." Putin had been relatively nondescript in his job, but the European press reports that shortly after Putin returned to Leningrad, one of his recruits, a former Stasi police detective, gave information to German domestic intelligence unmasking fifteen East German spies, thereby nullifying much of Putin's work and casting a shadow over him. Putin says in his book *First Person,* a campaign biography, that he turned down a more prestigious position in Moscow and opted to go to Leningrad, where, as a KGB lieutenant colonel on "active reserve," he took a job as an assistant to the president of the university, responsible for international liaison. He also pursued a doctorate in international law.

Through Egorov, Putin became reacquainted with Anatoly Sobchak, his flamboyant former law professor at Leningrad State University, an early conspicuous democrat, and the leader of the Leningrad City Council. Sobchak became the city's first mayor of the post-Communist era. When Sobchak asked Putin to work for him in 1990, Putin disclosed that he was in the KGB. "At first my husband was taken aback," says Sobchak's widow, Lyudmila. But intelligence officers were considered "very reliable. So he said, 'Damn it, it's okay.'"

The risk more than paid off. As head of the Committee for Foreign Economic Relations for the city, Putin soon made himself indispensable as a shrewd detail man. According to former City Council chairman Alexei Belyaev, "He became a real shadow mayor, because he signed all the decrees when Sobchak was absent, and Sobchak was gone a lot." Although Putin shunned the media, he soon became known as the Gray Cardinal. Nothing got done without his knowledge. "Saint Petersburg was very open to American business entrepreneurs who came to visit," says Philadelphia lawyer Jerome Shestack, who once held the account for the city of Leningrad. "Basically they were all screened by Putin in advance. His KGB training came in handy." Other visitors greeted by Putin ranged from Queen Elizabeth II to Ted Turner and Jane Fonda, and more than once he translated when Boris Yeltsin met high-ranking Germans in Saint Petersburg. In 1996 he campaigned for Yeltsin.

One of Putin's duties was to look after Sobchak's feisty wife, whom he accompanied to the United States twice. Once, they were in a small elevator in Monaco with an elderly relative of Prince Rainier's. Sobchak was shivering in her backless gown. "'I know the points of the body to touch to make it warm,'" the randy old nobleman said. "Then he bit me on my neck," Sobchak recalls. In Russian, Putin whispered, "You know, Lyudmila, I'm lost. I have to defend your honor, but I can't take him and beat him up, because he's the prince's relative." Just then, Sobchak says, "the elevator door opened, thank God."

Putin got into politics at an auspicious moment. People were giddy over the idea of democracy and capitalism, but most Russians were dancing in the dark. According to Roldugin, Putin at one point wanted to bring Augusto Pinochet to Saint Petersburg for questioning about how he had achieved the "economic miracle" in Chile, but the plan was dropped. Sobchak and Putin had to feed a hungry city without the backup of the old Soviet Union, which collapsed in 1991. "Sometimes he made mistakes about judgments of people," says Vatanyar Yagya, a chief advisor to Sobchak and a deputy in the Saint Petersburg legislative assembly who admires Putin. "Along with honest, talented, and creative people came people with low, immoral interests. . . . There were newfound opportunities to take bribes and be corrupt."

The most publicized scandal Putin was involved in was a barter deal to sell oil, wood, and metals for food in early 1992. Some $92 million worth of materials left Saint Petersburg, and just a few bottles of cooking oil came back. Not only that, the contracts were made out for a fraction of what the resources would bring on the world market—a scam used earlier by the KGB to spirit money out of the country for Communist Party chieftains in the early days of perestroika. Putin became a target of investigation. Marina Salye, the city councilwoman investigating him at the time, has documents showing that Putin signed two irregular contracts. He was called as a witness before the Council and charged, according to the investigative report, with "complete incompetence," but he was not accused of benefiting personally. The Council wanted him fired, but Sobchak refused.

Russian reporters have come up with other scandals that appear to have involved Putin, but they are ignored by the presidential press office. Misdeeds that are not aired on TV don't count. The most intriguing alleged illegality had Putin giving money for the restoration of an Orthodox nunnery in Israel from the mayor of Saint Petersburg's "unforeseen expenses fund." The journalist Vladimir Ivanidze, who, with his wife, Agathe Duparc, uncovered the Mabetex scandal, was vilified in a local Saint Petersburg paper for merely asking standard questions about a bank he found operating out of the mayor's office and a real-estate development company to which Putin was attached.

At one point, Roldugin asked Putin point-blank, "Don't you have a little candle factory somewhere?" Putin answered, "You know I don't have anything." Roldugin pressed again. "Bureaucrats exist to take bribes, and it cannot be that you don't take anything." Then Roldugin says, Putin responded more firmly. "'You know, Sergei, I can survive without that.' But he knows the prices, the amounts being taken around him. He told me, 'If I would take bribes, I'd be extremely rich by now. . . . I could do nothing but pass information, and people would offer me good money for that. But I didn't take that, and that's why I'm worth a lot now.'"

In the Kremlin, Putin worked for Pavel Borodin, the property manager who has been indicted by the Swiss for his role in the Mabetex scandal. Each year from 1996 on, Putin was promoted, from overseeing the regions to heading the FSB, to being secretary of the Security Council and, in August 1999, to prime minister. The question naturally arises: How can you work for so many people directly implicated in scandal and not be implicated yourself?

"There are no clean politicians in Russia," political analyst Vyacheslav Nikonov informs me. Putin may not have become rich, but he got ahead. "Yeltsin used him as an enforcer," Nikonov says, and time and again he proved his loyalty, especially in 1998 and 1999, when the Duma wanted to impeach Yeltsin. An American who is a close observer in Moscow told me, "Every time Yeltsin had serious trouble in the Duma, Putin and the FSB intervened. They made sure the FSB had information on [Yeltsin's enemies] and would use it."

Now that he's in power himself, Putin supposedly feels different. Explaining what Putin meant by "dictatorship of the law," Egorov says his friend is convinced that "officials never have the right to spin the law in their own favor." "He is extremely intelligent, part of a new breed we hadn't seen before," says James Wolfensohn, head of the World Bank, who at the time of Putin's election spent nine hours with him in his Kremlin apartment. "For a Russian leader, he's as clean as you're going to get. . . . Everybody I've met feels he's the best chance we're going to have."

"Spies must be charming," Ednan Agaev, a former arms negotiator for the Soviet Union, tells me. But even more important than wooing Western investors and negotiating for debt relief, Putin must convince Russians that they can once again believe in the motherland. They have to obey the law, pay taxes, and trust the state. "The historic mission of Yeltsin was to destroy Communism without violence, to put Russia on a new track and then open a door to the future," says Agaev. "Putin's mission is to go through the door."

"Lots of people surrounding Putin are very anti-American, maybe as a result of [the NATO bombing of] Kosovo. It looks like a very different moment between Russia and the U.S.," says the *Kommersant Daily* correspondent Nataliya Gevorkyan. "It's not nice at all."

"Democracy in Russia has become a dirty word," Vladimir Posner told me. "If you write 'dermocrat,' that's a play on words in Russia. 'Dermo' means 'crap'—it's a crapocracy. Over the last ten years, because of what's happened, for a lot of people democracy has become crap, because it has destroyed their livelihood, their culture. Also, that specific anti-Western, particularly anti-American sentiment, that's where the real problem lies. At first, democracy dazzled them. What it's turned out to be for many

Russian people is misery." As the Moscow-based Swedish journalist Jan Blomgren said to me, "I'm sure Putin's not good for democracy, but he might be good for Russia. Democracy is not the highest ideal now."

"Even the most anti-Russia Washington administration cannot inflict more harm on our country than the true 'friends of Russia' of Clinton's team," says one Russian political commentator. "An increase of isolationist tendencies in the U.S. would be a boon."

"The real issue is, can you establish law and order and respect the constitution as written?" says Posner. "Putin has the majority support of the population, who support the idea: let's curtail democracy and then we'll come back [to it]." Moreover, Posner says, "Putin is under a lot of pressure from different groups. He feels a moral obligation to the oligarchs who put him in. I don't think he feels pressure from liberals—they don't have any power. I do think he's under pressure from the military and the more nationalistic elements of the country—those who believe Russia . . . has to be a superpower again." In the words of Constantin Borovoy, an early business tycoon, "Russia is only important if it's scary. If you can't solve old problems, you create new ones."

Now Putin's dreams of reviving his country as a superpower will most certainly have to be curtailed. After the *Kursk* sank, Kursk's regional governor, Aleksandr Rutskoy, said that Russia was "losing not a submarine—it was losing a national idea." Vladimir Putin's formidable challenge is to keep hope alive not just for the motherland but for himself.

UPDATE: At *Vanity Fair* there is a small window of time when a finished story is at the printer but has not yet hit the newsstands, about ten days to two weeks. It was during just such a period in early September 2000—before the October *VF*, with the Putin piece, was out—that Tom Brokaw invited me to a dinner for journalists that he hosted for Putin at the 21 Club in New York. I dined at a back table, one seat over from Putin's press secretary Alexei Gromov. Putin answered questions from us after dinner.

Naturally, at that point, I was minutely briefed on all the current events in Russia, and when Putin put his particular spin on the events surrounding the sinking of the *Kursk* submarine, I challenged him. The give-and-take between us was tedious for some, since it had to go through translation. "Who *are* you?" Putin wanted to know. "What is your name?" I told him that my *VF* piece about him would appear soon. He said, "Why have you not come to me personally to ask me these questions?" What irony. Putin usually gave one interview per country and had granted his sole interview in the United States to my friend Tom Brokaw. I turned toward his press secretary and answered, "I have been sending him faxes asking to speak to you for months!"

Afterward, Putin was cordial, and a number of my colleagues congratulated me for having taken him on, but I just had to wonder at my bad luck in not being able to include the exchange in my story. Putin has proved himself a shrewd performer on the world's stage. After meeting the Gray Cardinal (but before Putin opposed the war in Iraq), George W. Bush enthused that he had looked into Putin's eyes and "gotten a sense of his soul." All three tycoons interviewed and discussed in this article have since been arrested or forced to flee Russia: Berezovsky, Gusinsky, and Khodorkovsky—who appeared to have political ambitions himself—and failed to understand sufficiently just who was in charge at the same time.

In Putin's first term of office, robust oil prices fueled the improving Russian economy: Life expectancy has inched upward and poverty has declined, but HIV continues its shocking ascent and the birthrate has not increased.

As he approaches a second term, Putin appears to many to be fulfilling the prediction that the old KGB way of governing is working against the country's growth into a freer, more democratic society. In January 2004, Secretary of State Colin Powell published an essay in the Russian newspaper *Izrestia* criticizing Putin's regime and saying that "Key aspects of a civil society—free media and political party development, for example—have not yet sustained an independent presence."

¿Quien Es Más Macho?
Carlos Menem

"It's really the country that needs the ambulance."

November 1989

Carlos Saúl Menem looks like an aging lounge lizard from
a nightclub in the provinces. He is tiny and dark, with a high forehead,
watery eyes, a major nose, a protruding lower lip, and strange skunk-
striped sideburns. But, as his wife well knows, women adore all five feet
four virile inches of him. His reputation as night crawler makes Gary
Hart look like the pope.

Menem is not a habitué of some remote tango bar, of course. He is the
president of Argentina, at the moment engaged in the greatest campaign
of seduction in his life. Menem has to convince the despairing citizens
that if they do what he says, their once rich but now economically hem-
orrhaging land can be rescued from the brink of abyss. And as with all
seductions, this one requires a certain bravado. So for several months
now, ever since he assumed office in the summer, Menem has engaged all
Argentina in a calculated game of *¿Quien es más macho?*—Who is the
machoest in the land? He has taken to the soccer field, playing respectably
for ninety televised minutes with the Argentinean national team. He even
scored thirteen points in an all-star charity basketball game. He played
tennis with Gabriela Sabatini.

Thus it is not strange to find the fifty-nine-year-old president (his official bio claims he's fifty-four) in full test-pilot regalia one chilly morning
in the military sector of the Buenos Aires airport, his little feet encased in

brown combat boots, a white crash helmet cradled in his arm. It is Air Force Day, and five TV crews and a dozen reporters and still photographers are waiting to greet him as he walks toward the *Pampa*, a spiffy black-and-red jet.

Waiting to greet their elated leader as he scrambles down from his cockpit bubble on the windswept runway are two improbable crimson-coated waiters, each balancing a tray, one with a champagne bottle, the other with glasses. Before making his toasts, Menem accepts a souvenir cap and sky-blue silk Red Baron scarf from the test pilot who sat behind him in the cockpit. He dashingly knots the scarf, the exact color of the Argentinean flag, and then, with a flourish, accepts his champagne from the head of the air force. A few minutes later, having changed into a blue business suit, the president, who is also, naturally, a Formula One race car driver, gets behind the wheel of his red Renault, bodyguards in back, to plunge into the winner-take-all Buenos Aires traffic, an ambulance trailing behind.

"You know, it's really the country that needs the ambulance," cracks a bystander.

Since he took office on July 8 (an astrologer pointed out that the ninth, Argentinean Independence Day, was not propitious), Menem—the son of a Syrian merchant who immigrated to La Rioja, a poor province in the far northwestern end of the country—has been cast as the savior of Argentina. Not a great deal in his past suggests he can fulfill this role, although he himself cultivates it by adopting as his administration's theme Christ's words to Lazarus: "Get up and walk!"—advice even his most enthusiastic subjects are finding a little difficult to follow. In the last year Argentina, which has always prided itself on being more European than Latin American, experienced galloping inflation that had soared to nearly two hundred percent the month Menem was inaugurated and has caused the once vast middle class to vanish in a twisted tango of capital flight and endemic corruption.

Menem, governor of La Rioja since 1973 (with a hiatus of seven years, for five of which he was jailed by the repressive right-wing generals who were running the country), won the presidency as an outsider, first defying his own party's favorite in the primary and then rolling over the Radical Party opposition in May. And, so far, he has taken the exhausted country by storm, practicing a "politics of surprise" and suggesting the unthinkable: rapprochement with Britain (an enemy since the 1982 Falkland Islands War) and the possibility of pardons not only for the imprisoned generals who caused thousands of citizens to "disappear" in the "dirty war" of the late 1970s, but for some of the jailed left-wing guerrillas they pursued. As a first step, Menem announced in September that he would pardon about twenty generals and admirals still facing trial or not yet sentenced.

Perhaps most stunning of all for someone who represents the party of Juan Perón—the party of the labor unions, founded on hatred of the rich and dedicated to maintaining inefficient state-run enterprises—is Menem's embrace of an economic plan espoused by a team from Argentina's only multinational corporation, Bunge & Born, an ultracapitalist conglomerate. The plan, using strict wage-and-price restraints, has so far lowered the inflation rate dramatically. It calls for the privatization of money-losing state-owned industries, and will have serious consequences for the heavily featherbedded unions that have dominated Argentina's economic policies for the last forty years. Menem's free-market approach also calls for a revolution in the Argentinean (non)work ethic. His aides call it Menemstroika.

Certainly Menem is no longer a traditional Peronist, but he doesn't fit in with members of the Buenos Aires elite, either. They seem astounded that this earthy primitive has landed in their midst, this *turco* (as Arab immigrants and their descendants are referred to) with his corny mutton-chop whiskers and his messy and outrageous (even for them) sex life. A man with a history of contradictions and lies. The word used most frequently to describe him is *insólito*, "eccentric."

"He's charming, absolutely charming," says Máximo Gainza, the aristocratic right-wing publisher of the Buenos Aires daily *La Prensa*. "But I've never met a con man who wasn't charming."

"There is the most beautiful Sargent right over the mantelpiece. It is such a pity that you cannot see it." All is dark inside one of Buenos Aires's great mansions, which has been converted into a museum of decorative arts. My guide is a reigning Buenos Aires beauty from the 1940s who used to dance in the elaborate, three-story-high ballroom seen now only in the dimmest of shadow. One can barely make out an intricate parquet floor and enclosed overhead balconies, a Hollywood set for a Napoleonic masquerade. The three attendants with holes in their cashmere sweaters deeply apologize to the elegant señora who has offered to show me the Barrio Norte, the exclusive residential part of this city, with its once manicured parks and chic shops that still prompt the comparison of Buenos Aires with Paris.

Not so much anymore, of course.

Because of energy shortages caused, everyone says, by the failure of the government to maintain the equipment in the hydroelectric plants supplying the capital, vast sections of the city have been without power for three to five hours a day. Television used to go on in the early morning; now it doesn't broadcast steadily until six P.M. There is no change to be had. Foreigners and the rich who live off hidden dollars (it is estimated the Argentineans have $46 billion in foreign banks) can only obtain bills of fifty thousand australes. In September there were 560 australes to the dollar; two years ago there were fewer than 10.

"We used to have such wonderful parties here," my guide reminisces. "Everything was imported. The architect for this house was French. In those days when families traveled to Europe by boat, they would bring their own cow along for milk. Oh, they'd be gone for months at a time—six months here, six months there."

"And the wealth was from cattle?" I ask.

"Always from cattle," she replies.

Today, as Menem attempts to juggle the demands of a restless military—the sword of Damocles hanging over any democratically elected civilian president—an unproductive and intransigent labor force, and entrepreneurs not used to competition but merely living off sweetheart deals with the government, one can only imagine how very rich Argentina once was, with its thousands of acres of fertile pampa yielding wheat and cattle, its Andean mineral resources and Patagonian oil.

"Oh, God," goes a Chilean joke. "It's not fair. We have nothing—no resources, no agricultural land. The Argentineans have everything, all those resources, oil, and millions of acres of the richest soil. . . . It's not fair, God." Then God answers, "Ah, but I also gave Argentina the Argentineans."

In 1934, Argentina had a GNP greater than that of Canada. In 1946, when Perón, who was a great admirer of Mussolini, staged his revolution of the *descamisados* (the shirtless ones), there was so much gold bullion stacked inside the national bank that Perón could not make his way down the corridors.

Today the country lies in virtual ruin, like a great ravaged beauty who never bothered to take care of herself. Yet even today there are fifty million head of cattle in Argentina and an official literacy rate of ninety-four percent. But the government also estimates that 9 million people live at the poverty level ($30 a month) and that many go hungry. The external debt alone is $60 billion. Tax evasion is a way of life. Because of a scam at the federal mint, forty percent of all the currency in the country is probably counterfeit. The system of government rots from within, and the result is paralysis and cynicism, plus an almost childlike hope among both rich and poor that somehow Carlos Saúl Menem will save them.

Politically, yes, Menem seems to have changed. Personally, it's another story.

According to all of Buenos Aires, the First Lady is depressed. For the moment, Zulema Fátima Yoma de Menem is receiving no one. Amalia Lacroze de Fortabat, the vivacious billionairess "cement queen" who serves as Menem's ambassador-at-large, explains that the president's wife "is depressed first about her biopsy and then about her son. Two depressions at the same time are too much." The biopsy—for breast cancer, it is said—took three hours, according to Fortabat. On top of that, her son, Carlitos, twenty-one, was injured in a motorcycle accident, and his mother was leaving any day to accompany him to the Mayo Clinic, where a nerve on his leg would be operated on.

She is undoubtedly depressed also about her husband. All of Buenos Aires knows that Menem and his fifty-year-old bottle-blond wife have a beyond-soap-opera marriage that has included two major separations and many public, mutual recriminations. It is said that they aren't even living together in the president's official residence, Olivos. Menem denies this, but the very night his wife left for the United States, he showed up at my hotel in a flurry of security to claim his regular suite. "We attend him well here," a waiter said with a wink.

According to those who know her, Zulema is domineering, tempestuous, ambitious—a storm cloud waiting to burst. One report places her and Menem at dinner with another couple in a Buenos Aires restaurant shortly before the election. At around eleven P.M. a white Volvo pulls up with a luscious blond at the wheel. The blond gets out and beckons Menem. Without much adieu he follows her into the night. Infuriated, Zulema says she is sick of his "exhibitionism" and vows that someday she will put a knife in his back. Is that story merely gossip? Most people found it plausible. And it's certainly true that she would not go, nor even let the children go, to their father's birthday celebration in La Rioja a few days before his inauguration. "I had a Lear waiting," says Fortabat, "but she would not allow them to leave."

Everyone in their hometown of La Rioja, where her family did well selling textiles and remained firmly Muslim, while his family had the children baptized Catholic, is convinced Menem had to pay Zulema a million dollars to come back to him during his second campaign for governor.

She denied that, but shows off the sapphire-and-diamond pin he gave her to commemorate their latest reconciliation—just in time for the presidential campaign.

Interestingly, the Argentinean constitution has a special clause, article 19, which stipulates that the private actions of people that do not cause hurt (to society, not necessarily to wives) are outside the law and are to be judged by God alone. In Menem's case, God intervened. A high-ranking Catholic priest let it be known that the church would not look kindly on a candidate with an "irregular" relationship. Although formal separation proceedings had begun in 1987, Menem got the message. He even went to the trouble of personally demonstrating for the repeal of the Argentinean divorce law.

Menem and Zulema met in 1964 in Damascus, where Zulema's father had returned to live out his last years in the land of his birth. Since then, it appears, Menem has said "I divorce you" about three thousand times. Their son, Carlitos, was born in 1968. When he was about a year old, Zulema returned to Syria with him. Menem's previous girlfriend, Ana María Luján, seems still to have been in the picture. "He continued to see her many times," Zulema claimed in 1984. After her husband pleaded that she come back, she did; their daughter, Zulema María Eva (named for Eva Perón), was born in 1970. Zulema says she suffered three miscarriages during the early years of marriage—"probably my marital insecurity had a lot to do with it."

Now Zulema wants an official job at the Ministry of Social Welfare, in imitation of the still-mystical Eva Perón. But Menem won't let her. He doesn't want her to be Evita II. "She is a woman of very strong character, very sweet, who is not very happy. . . . She's been told that she is going to work at the ministry but that because she is the wife of the president, she doesn't need a title," says Amalia Fortabat. "He treats her officially much nicer than she treats him."

No wonder. During his five-year arrest by the military, Menem was sometimes only under house arrest. According to Zulema, he began living with the daughter of a lieutenant-colonel cellmate while she and the children were in the same small town. Later, Menem was transferred to a village near the Paraguayan border. He was reminded of that stay last year. At one of his campaign stops, a provincial deputy representing his opponent turned out to be the mother of a son fathered by Menem during the last months of his house arrest. But nothing seems to mortify Menem. During his recent trip to the United States, for example, the *Today* show brought up his reputation as a playboy. "Why should I change?" he countered. "Maybe I couldn't be reelected."

When Zulema reconciled with Menem for the first time, it was just days before his election as governor of La Rioja for his second term, in 1983. But their donnybrooks continued, occasionally spilling over into public fits, like the one during which Zulema threw an ashtray at an eighty-year-old official who had called her a "shit busybody." Meanwhile, Menem was linked to a number of actresses who passed through La Rioja and a number in Buenos Aires as well. "He is famous for denying no one," a man in La Rioja told me. "He is always ready to be the conquistador. Actually, women like him for being macho like that." The man's wife nodded in agreement.

Zulema herself did not remain idle. Rumors swirled about her and the police chief of La Rioja, Héctor García Rey. Menem wanted the chief and his family off the premises of the governor's residence, where they had been living in the guesthouse. But Zulema took umbrage and gave the chief a room in the governor's mansion in which to hold a press conference denouncing Menem for the "leftists" in his government. (Zulema held her own press conference under the covers in her bedroom.) Menem then said if García Rey wasn't out by the following morning at nine A.M., he'd send the police in after him.

Zulema countered, Martha Mitchell–style, with the charge that "there is a conspiracy to declare me insane." She hotly denied the rumors about her and the police chief. "I swear it as a Muslim on my own Koran. . . . This is infamy." In fact, she went on the radio, declaring: "Even if it costs my husband the governorship, I'm going to keep talking."

Within a month Zulema was in another magazine, asserting that she would go back to her husband only "if he cleans up La Rioja's government." She would not accept "the lack of respect even if it costs me the position of First Lady." But she was already figuring the odds. "If a marriage doesn't work as a couple, perhaps it can work politically." Yet as late as February 1988, Menem still considered the marriage off, telling a magazine, "The reason I do not remarry is that I'm trying to become president." That prompted his children to take out a newspaper ad declaring that their parents *did* live together and that gossip about a separation was harming the family.

By the summer of 1988, it was more or less the best of times, the worst of times. In July, Zulema went to visit a famous Brazilian plastic surgeon. During the tummy tuck, she lost a lot of blood but refused a transfusion for fear of contracting AIDS; she remained very weak. The month before, she and Carlos had been sailing happily down the Luján River. "Actually, Carlos and I were never separated," Zulema declared. "If we had fights, we weren't different from other couples. We knew how to solve our problems and our differences. I think our problems were motivated by capricious circumstances."

The governor's mansion in the dusty little provincial capital of La Rioja, where temperatures often soar to 110 degrees, operated as if it were an apparition out of Gabriel García Márquez: late into the night an incredible circus of humanity entertained the governor and competed for his ear. At dinner there would be all manner of schemers and inventors, diplomats from exotic, obscure locales, women of indeterminate virtue. It drove his ambitious wife to distraction as she tried to be the gatekeeper—Zulema once complained that his major fault was that he was "too easily influenced." Perhaps. But if so, then how much substance actually lurks behind the colorful facade?

"Nobody has real influence over Menem," proffers Julio Aiub Morales, political editor of the scrappy La Rioja daily, *El Independiente*. "He'll listen to people, spend the night with them, and then do what his intuition tells him." Menem, who came up through politics as a lawyer defending out-of-favor Peronists, is impatient with protocol. "He's the most intuitive man I've ever known," says his top aide and alter ego, Alberto Kohan, a half-Jewish, half-Catholic agnostic who is currently the secretary-general of the presidency.

Very little is straight-ahead in Argentinean politics, but what is clear is that in the last two years, Menem, accompanied by Kohan and a small band of others, simply outhustled the opposition. He barnstormed every forgotten little corner of the country, making ten complete trips around Argentina, which is roughly the size of India. Since the Radical Party government controlled the television stations and there was almost no TV coverage on Menem until very late in the primary, few of the movers and shakers in the capital had any idea of his popularity. Menem profited by not being taken seriously.

Ironically, and not without consequence, Kohan says he considers Jerzy Kosinski's *Being There* as pertinent politically as Machiavelli's *The Prince*. Kosinski's hero, Chauncey Gardiner, a simpleton who wins national acclaim by spouting ridiculous platitudes, had nothing on Menem as he toured the countryside in his Menemmobile, making pronouncements about Argentina's "greatness," blessing the multitudes from a converted bus à la John Paul II in his Popemobile.

Even the Prince, however, might have been taken aback. First, Menem got caught sending good-luck telegrams to both sides in the Chilean plebiscite on General Pinochet. He lied about his age, of course, and late in the campaign he called for Argentina to win back the Falklands, even if it meant "the spillage of blood." That statement was immediately retracted after another garbled denial that he'd ever said it. "It got so we'd wonder, What mistake will he make today?" says a journalist who covered the presidential campaign. Even after the election, Kohan took a sudden vacation out of the country when Menem announced that he would nationalize the banks. Menem's brother Eduardo, the leader of the Senate, who is friendly with big business, reportedly went ballistic on that one.

Menem remains ever calm amid the turbulence. After all, he grew up hearing that, at his birth, the Virgin appeared to his mother. Menem's parents were humble. His father, Saúl, owned a general store in La Rioja and later went into the wine business. Both he and his wife, Mohibe, were Syrian immigrants who had come halfway around the world to settle in exactly the same kind of godforsaken arid land they had left behind. Mohibe fell into delirium minutes after the birth of her firstborn. "Don't you see her, Saúl?" she reportedly babbled of the Virgin to her uncomprehending husband. "Look how pretty she is." Neither of Menem's parents was particularly religious. They were lapsed Muslims, part of a great wave of Arab immigration to Argentina in the early part of the century. Although Menem's parents never fully embraced Catholicism themselves, their children received the sacraments. The Koran, magic, and mysticism were all a part of the ether of their childhoods as well. To his parents, "Carlitos" was like a little Dalai Lama—marked by miracle.

Carlitos was "a born politician," according to his half brother, Amado. "He could enter a strange house and feel completely at ease immediately. He was very easy to be friends with." "He was always very attentive, especially to the girls," recalls a high-school friend. The family was not political. Only when Carlos went off to the University of Córdoba to study law at a time when Peronism was in full flower did he begin to take an interest in a political career.

Menem won the governor's seat in 1973 and quickly developed a flair for the dramatic. In 1974, for example, he made a trip across the Andes to Chile on a mule to demonstrate La Rioja's need for a road to give it access to Chilean ports. In those days he was a fairly orthodox Peronist championing an insular corporate state. It was only after his years in jail, where some nights he could hear the screams of those being tortured, that Menem became a defender of democracy. When Raúl Alfonsín was elected president in 1983, Menem formed part of the loyal opposition, quickly defending the primacy of constitutional government over the military whenever a crisis arose. Once he started running hard for the presidency, however, he started to hedge his bets somewhat. For example, after asking to be received by Jimmy Carter, whose administration did much to promote human rights, Menem canceled Carter three times to visit his old friend General Alfredo Stroessner in Paraguay, hardly a champion of human rights but certainly in a position to contribute heavily to Menem's campaign. After flirting with "privatization" and foreign investment, Menem reverted to a standard Peronist stump speech promising business as usual with higher wages.

Above all, Menem is a pragmatist. Says his brother Amado, "He's very open in his politics. He's not ideological." Another explanation is heard frequently in Buenos Aires. "He's an Arab, don't forget," people say. "He has a very Oriental way of thinking." And "He's not an Arab of the mosque, he's an Arab of the bazaar." This Middle Eastern mysteriousness seems to serve Menem very well among his racially sensitive countrymen. They long for him to cast a spell so they can forget their terrible reality and go back to the old dream that Argentina is a rich country.

One afternoon I drive south for a half hour through the bleak working-class neighborhoods of Buenos Aires to see a shantytown with raw sewage running in the muddy street—a typical vista in any poor Latin American barrio. The cabdriver offers to wait—for no extra charge, it is understood; fares are scarce enough. In a dingy day-care center, with a dozen filthy mattresses on the floor, more than seventy toddlers are being attended to while their parents work or look for work. The center exists on charity alone—there are no government programs to help it. For many, the lunch of rice and carrots is the only meal of the day. A short distance away two men are hauling a cart, coolie-style, picking up cardboard to sell. I encounter a woman in tattered clothes in the muddy path. She tells me she, too, likes Menem. "He has soft eyes. I like him very much. I view him as sincere."

Ironically, there are many *porteños,* as the denizens of Buenos Aires are called, who refuse to believe that such poverty exists—they certainly won't go to see it—and it's also hard for them to comprehend that life in the middle class as they experienced it no longer exists. "You cannot treat me like I am in a Third World country," charges the forty-seven-year-old owner of a fleet of rental cars, who has seen his savings vanish and has not bought new clothes in three years. (Naturally, he wears only cashmere.) "I'm not some Bolivian who'll obediently go back into my little hut. This is not Paraguay or even Peru. We are Argentineans!"

Indeed, the lines to see the Marc Chagall exhibition at the National Museum of Fine Arts on a weekend stretch for at least five city blocks.

The theater goes on—Noël Coward's *Hay Fever* plays alongside *Social Security*, although both "hits" fill only a few rows of seats. Directing and starring in *Hay Fever* is one of the country's most distinguished actresses, the Uruguayan-born China Zorrilla. She has always been politically active—championing human rights and conspicuously supporting the Radical Party. But she, too, has been received by Menem in his first month in office. "I'm one of the Argentineans whom he's buying little by little," she confesses. At a large dinner they both attended, Menem summoned Zorrilla to his side. "He embraced me warmly and said, 'We need you. I want everyone to be near us.' I told him the line from Borges, when somebody asked, 'Do you think we have the right to be hopeful?' He answered, 'No, we have the obligation to be hopeful.' Menem loved that."

The following Sunday, Zorrilla takes me to Patio Bullrich, a sparkling mall that rivals any American galleria, where scores of shoppers, far better dressed than one sees at home, crowd to drink their coffees in the central café, out of habit perhaps, for the fashionable shops are nearly devoid of customers. "It's as if I say to you I want to buy that telephone for a hundred dollars," Zorrilla explains in a shop offering exquisite, inexpensive hand-embroidered baby clothes. "Then I come back two months later and they tell me, sorry, it now costs $3,500. That is the reality we have been living with."

Et tu, Amalia? "Everyone has to lower their standard of living—yes, even me," sighs Amalia Fortabat, the richest woman in Argentina, perhaps in South America, a woman who buys $7-million paintings and, in her lavish Buenos Aires apartment, curiously mixes them with portraits, in the wide-eyed style of Alice Keane's subjects, of her grandchildren. Fortabat rises from her chair in the chandeliered library, its hand-carved wood paneling acquired from San Simeon—"one of those times when Hearst was poor"—and goes over to switch off the lights. "Ah, but it's too dark," she says. The lights go back on immediately.

But why have things come to such a sorry pass? I ask. "We are a nation of immigrants," Fortabat answers, "and there are many people who have made their fortunes who don't feel they are Argentine. They don't make any efforts to better the country, and they don't have any sense of community."

In lieu of jewels, both of Fortabat's wrists are tied with bright-red ribbons—undoubtedly, she is about the biggest present Menem has ever received. Amalia Fortabat is his entrée to the international rich and famous, the most influential hostess of his administration. But, most important, Fortabat is Menem's personal link to Argentina's ruling elite—who have not, in recent times, gone out front to take responsibility for whether the country rises or falls, and certainly *never* for a Peronist. Fortabat, who freely admits she is one of "four or five upper-class Peronists, but of course now *everyone* is Peronist," was recruited to the cause by Menem's brother Eduardo.

With Fortabat, Menem organized a secret team of four rich industrialists to advise him before the election, even while he said nothing in public about his plans for the Argentinean economy, when everyone assumed he'd just throw the traditional freeloader Peronist program out there. "One could never believe that he had the four of us meeting with him; we never thought he would say, 'Well, I must go to Bunge & Born now,'" says Fortabat. "Suddenly, we were playing politics. We were not politicians, but we were playing politics. We had meetings with union leaders—I never felt anything so fantastic."

What got Fortabat about Menem was the courtly "old Spanish way" he treated her, the widow with the billion-dollar fortune, an extraordinary woman who has continued paying the salaries of thousands of workers when there is no work for them to do. How did Menem get Amalia? Audaciously. He never asked for money.

"Finally, one day during the primary I said, 'But Carlos, I think maybe you will need some help. Can I give any help to you?' And then his eyes became literally wet. 'Please, between you and me, *never* a question of money. Talk with my brother, who admires you and is a very good friend of yours'—but he never asked me."

On Sunday evening I am summoned to the headquarters of the president, Casa Rosada (the Pink House), to wait for Menem. The entrance to Casa Rosada is impossibly ornate—the ostentatiousness of much of the Argentinean capital, in fact, is almost overwhelming. Here in the grand entry room the ceiling is of gilded-and-white hexagons, supported by two wedding-cake soldiers, red plumes on their silver helmets.

Suddenly the familiar red Renault pulls up and the impeccably groomed little president alights on the burnished-gold carpet. He briskly walks to where I stand on a marble step, seizes my hand, and leans forward on tiptoe. I instinctively draw back. "*¿Señora, cómo anda, bien?*" asks Carlos Saúl Menem. And then he disappears down a dark corridor.

"The president leaned up to kiss you," admonishes the press secretary. "When you leave, you will correct your mistake."

Inside Menem's outer office there are at least thirty people, including a chubby nine-year-old girl, an aide-de-camp dripping gold braid, a huge bodyguard, and a miniskirted blond about forty, legs crossed, her brown Emba mink thrown on the back of her chair. She is holding a bright red cigarette in one hand and dangling expensive worry beads in the other. While sections of the capital may be without power for five hours a day, at least the president understands that ideology is no substitute for electricity. Two huge banks of spots have been set up inside his office, generating enough light to shoot a major motion picture.

A big thirty-five-millimeter Arriflex camera is mounted just outside the door. "Is there going to be a press conference?" I ask. "No," I'm told. "Just a filming." Menem's office is outsize and lavish. The carved mahogany walls have areas of padded white leather encased in wood frames that are themselves embellished with jewel shapes. Three crystal chandeliers also blaze—the gilt is nearly blinding. By far the largest piece of furniture in the room is the glass-topped Cabinet table with its matching high-backed, overstuffed white leather chairs, which are embossed with the presidential seal—in gold, of course.

Galloping around the office, his shoulder-length hair flying, is Eduardo Scuderi, one of Argentina's best-known directors of commercials. Waiting for the president, should the need arise, are a dozen shirts and ties to try on, four producers, each with a production assistant, functionaries, functionaries of functionaries—a crew of dozens milling around, as well as the entourage. Fewer than ten are actually needed.

"What exactly is going on?" I ask Scuderi's still photographer. "Oh, this is an insert of the president we're shooting for a commercial about working." How ironic. But hey, even in the president's very office, revolutions aren't made in a day. So far the crowd has withstood two attempts to clear it out. The press secretary tells the blond she can forget about getting an interview tonight. She hikes up her skirt a little bit higher and stays.

Carlos Menem looks very small and very *árabe* behind the glass table, seemingly oblivious to all around him, pretending to read a sheaf of papers for a long shot. "*Un té,*" he says softly. Several people break into a dead run. Within seconds the waiters appear with hot tea. Finally Scuderi is ready for the close-up. He whispers in Menem's ear and races back behind the camera. "*¡Acción!*" Scuderi yells. Menem leans forward. Everyone else in the room leans forward, too. Will he speak? Apparently not. Now he moves, tugging on his immaculate shirt cuffs, then ever so slightly pushing his sleeves up. The gesture takes perhaps four seconds. "*¡Excelente!*" screams Scuderi. Then he makes Menem roll his shirts sleeves up seven more times. "Do the shirt sleeves faster, Presidente." One can just imagine all of Argentina rising up and grabbing work tools. About the fourth take in, Menem, who clearly enjoys this time in the limelight, begins to crack a little smile. Scuderi acts thrilled. "*¡Excelente! eso es!*" Each take the smile gets a little broader and a little more studied.

Now, in one magic moment, the shirt sleeves fly up and a smile positively bursts across Menem's face. Scuderi is in ecstasy. The entire room breaks into applause.

The theatrics over, the press secretary makes one last attempt to extricate the blond as I am ushered to a small reception room to wait for Menem so we can talk one-on-one. Given all I've heard about his warmth, charisma, and intuition—"He can know you completely in five minutes," his brother Amado assured me—I am ready to be charmed. But Menem isn't wasting a drop of charisma on me. Still in those shirt sleeves, he is unsmiling as we greet each other again, all business, certainly not the "very tender, very sweet, very calm" man Amalia Fortabat described. He paces back and forth to a corner of the room. "There are three essential steps to being successful," he tells me in Spanish. "One, the information. Two, the secrecy of the information. And three, the element of surprise. When you think the right moment has arrived, you put your plan out there and wait to see the reaction of the people. If you've done your homework, the people will approve. But you must have the confidence to know the plan will be approved when you launch it in this unexpected way. I have always operated like that, and here I am, president of Argentina."

And so he is. A few days before, he stunned the country, not just because he proposed absolution for both sides in the "dirty war" of 1976–81 but because he did so in a way that was pure Menem. At first, the form of forgiveness was unspecified. Menem told me it could range from outright amnesty, which, it turns out, only Congress could grant, to a suspension of sentences. (The generals do not wish to be pardoned, just released, since, they argue, they have done nothing wrong.) At the same time, Menem trotted out Jorge Born, a Bunge & Born heir kidnapped by the Montonero guerrillas in 1974. Born reputedly paid $60 million in ransom, yet he declared to the press he was willing to forgive everything. (The public, however, was not. A poll taken later showed that a large majority were against releasing or forgiving the guerrillas; Menem has since modified his stand.)

But that night, when I contrast his position on amnesty with that of the previous government, Menem grows testy, arguing that the last government also passed two laws to limit further trials and to absolve over a thousand of the military who claimed to have merely been following orders.

"But aren't you afraid, Presidente," I ask, "to let those generals and guerrillas who committed brutal and cruel acts back out on the street, to take the risk of things like that happening again?"

"That won't happen again," Menem pronounces impatiently. "Argentina needs peace. Anyway, I don't understand why the foreign press is so worried about those things which concern only the Argentinean people."

"Because human rights are universal."

Now Menem, who sat down briefly, jumps up and locks me with a cold stare. "Really, if they are universal, they should be respected all over the world. I can bring up a lot of things which have happened in this world that occurred as a result of the interventionist politics of certain powers. Do you think that providing the contras in Nicaragua with armaments is respecting human rights? Let's not talk about it anymore, okay?

"In my trips I realized the country yearned for drastic political change," Menem says. "They wanted to finish with the corruption; they were tired of the inefficient and oversize government. . . . When someone storms the government as we did, it is because you are sure of being successful. . . . I think I'm doing what the country is clamoring for. . . . Argentina has changed. We have established credibility. We will implement a drastic program that will make Argentina a worthwhile country to live in." (Menem's self-confidence reminds me of a García Márquez joke: "The human ego is the little Argentine inside all of us.")

"But, Presidente," I say, "it is generally understood that to be a politician here is to have your own means of robbing the country. What are you going to do to change that?"

Menem accepts the premise, but counters, "It doesn't mean that if in past governments they stole, they are going to keep stealing."

"But how?" I ask. "How do you change the mentality?"

Menem reverts to the quick fix, skewing his answer toward public relations. "We will send out constant messages saying what's best for the country. These things require a lot of time, but it is the best way to govern, with examples, with concrete facts."

I ask him how that approach meshes with what I heard in La Rioja, where another message altogether had been sent, because the president's plane has landed there numerous times, "filled with friends of yours."

Menem explodes. "Who said that?" he challenges. "The presidential plane went twice. I can't believe it! I assume a Radical gave you that. Did you ask a Radical?"

A good source, the editor of *El Independiente* in La Rioja—on the record. "Was he lying?" I inquire.

"Of course he was lying."

(After the interview, I called Leandro López Alcaraz, the editor, back. He confirmed the story and pointed out that his paper had written about it.)

As if on cue, the press secretary starts warning me about time. "Tell me, Señor Presidente," I say, "if you were not a politician, what would you be?"

Menem's whole demeanor suddenly changes. His shoulders relax and he smiles. "If I wasn't a politician? A politician! I love politics. It is my passion. I've assumed it as my cause—I was born to work for my country."

"I hear that many years ago, an astrologer told you that you would be president. Is that right?"

"Many years ago I had the desire to be president and someone said that a man from the north of Argentina would govern the country—that happened thirty or forty years ago. It was more like a prophecy, and, well, I am from the north of Argentina and I am president of the Argentinean Republic."

"You are so sure you will be a success, aren't you?"

Menem gives a little laugh of dismissal. "I am totally convinced of it."

A month later, after snagging a confidence-boosting $1.5-billion loan from the International Monetary Fund on his trip to the United States, Menem declared, "In seventy days of government, we have done more than forty years of anyone else."

There is this hole. A vast, dry, empty dust-bowl hole stretching almost as far as the eye can see. It has cost millions, this hole, only a stone's throw from the Menem-family land about sixty miles outside La Rioja, in a place where rain does not fall nine months of the year. Into the unyielding earth the backhoes have been scooping and the bulldozers shoving dust for nearly five years now, in an attempt to transform this parched desert country into a garden spot for trout and tourism—it's to become an expensive dam and lake fed from hidden springs in the mountains, all for the benefit of the people who reside in the tiny Menem-family village of Anillaco, as well as the president himself, who is having a new home built here.

This public-works project of the government of La Rioja Province, which was originally estimated at $2 million, has soared in cost over the years, inflation aside. But who's counting? The contract for the dam had been conveniently let to Maciel Construction, the company that is building Menem's new house and that is owned by Menem's former secretary of public works, who also runs the local gas company and owns a major newspaper in the province. The hole is nowhere near finished, but do the people of La Rioja know how much it is costing them? Certainly not. Nowhere has the phrase "throwing money down a hole" been so strikingly illustrated.

In Carlos Menem's fiefdom, nobody ever knows where the money goes. Not once after his reelection as governor in 1983 did he present a budget to the state legislature for discussion before approval was rubber-stamped. Never was the one elected representative from the opposition Radical Party consulted, nor was he included in any budget meetings. (The Radical Party usually manages to get thirty percent of the vote but somehow only one representative.) When the journalist Patricia Gómez Aguirre was working on an article last year for *Gente* magazine about Menem's performance as governor, different agencies gave her completely contradictory versions about how money was being used.

What kind of president will Carlos Menem make? What kind of a governor was he? In La Rioja, opinion is divided. "In Argentina there is no politician who transmits confidence except Carlos Menem," says Agustín de la Vega, a provincial deputy who has known him since childhood. "If he doesn't do it, nobody else will." Leandro López says, "I have fundamental doubts about his ability. As head of state here, he was a good politician, not a good governor." Even Amalia Fortabat acknowledges that as governor, Menem was only "*comme ci, comme ça.*"

The governor lived well in La Rioja—there are two spacious residences, one for summer and one for winter, both with swimming pools. But La Rioja is one of the poorest provinces in Argentina, the kind of place that might not have developed at all if there hadn't been wandering Arab immigrants looking for some new dust to kick up. The landscape is sparse, sprinkled with donkeys and cactus. Interestingly, however, La Rioja seems to have more new houses under construction than Buenos Aires. When I mention this, my guide, a twenty-eight-year-old secretary, Alicia, from the local transport-company office, laughs derisively. "You know how it goes. People go to work for the government and then within two or three years they get new cars, they build a house, they start to travel to the 'exterior.' How? Well, how is the question. These people were robbing the country. There's no other explanation."

But the real story of Menem's tenure in La Rioja is the way he bloated the public sector and bankrupted the state. Although La Rioja's population of 200,000 increased by only ten percent during his administration, government employment rose fifty-four percent. Forty percent of the employed of La Rioja work for the state. "Every family has at least one," says Alicia. "If I wanted a job from him, I'm sure I could get one."

To pay for these unneeded workers, Menem, with no money left in the treasury, began to pay the salaries with special La Rioja bonds, good only inside the province. In 1983 the provincial bank of La Rioja was solvent;

by 1988, loans to the bankrupt government made up forty percent of the assets of the bank, which had been excluded from the national currency system. Checks drawn on La Rioja's bank could be deposited nowhere else. "During the campaign he'd say, 'Come to the paradise of La Rioja,'" recalls Alicia. At the same time, the state was a month behind in paying salaries even with the bonds.

Most of the time he was governor, Menem was away campaigning. He left La Rioja in the hands of squabbling officials. Nevertheless, they were rewarded. "On New Year's of 1986 he threw a dinner for his Cabinet," remembers the journalist Julio Aiub Morales. "He gave them all vacations in Buenos Aires in expensive hotels, including whores. How do I know? They all came home and bragged about it."

Whenever questions have arisen about the impropriety of any of his people, Menem has the same response: "Until someone is judged guilty by the court," they are allowed to go about their business as usual.

On the long drive back in the dark, Alicia brings up the question of amnesty. "I don't believe Menem should give it." She begins to talk about how hard it was for her generation to come of age during the military regime, when families in fear spent years whispering to one another inside their homes. I tell her of the defiance toward Menem's plan I saw a few days before, in the Plaza de Mayo in Buenos Aires, from the mothers of the disappeared, who have marched for twelve long years demanding to know what happened to their sons. Some of the sons' own children are marching now, too. "You have to understand. Everyone knows somebody who disappeared. I still have a hard time opening up to people, because I was made to be so afraid as a teenager. It was prohibited to discuss ideas in school. We would be at a party dancing and the police would come, cut off the lights, and throw everyone out. There was no freedom of expression. I spit on them. If the military comes again, I will cross the Río de la Plata and live in Uruguay, no matter what."

Sometimes the politics of surprise backfires.

The day after I return from La Rioja, I make an excursion to the annual cattle-and-livestock exhibition, where Menem is to announce a reduction of cumbersome export taxes on Argentinean agriculture. The show—with its parade of colorful gauchos from every part of the nation, with its dashing young polo stars and attractive women who barrel-race atop Arabian stallions, and entire families outfitted in nineteenth-century British finery command ponies pulling wicker carriages—makes one realize what a spirited and beautiful country this is.

Menem is preceded into the exposition plaza by a mounted guard, red plumes flashing atop chin-strapped patent-leather caps. The mounted marching band of the "army"—led by a conductor on a prancing white stallion who guides the musicians by brandishing a sword—includes dozens of drummers, a pair of large red-and-gold felt-covered kettle-drums slung over each side of their saddles, followed by trumpeters and tuba players; in the middle of it all, Carlos Menem stands up and blows kisses to the crowd from a 1954 black convertible once owned by Juan Perón.

"I come to wake up a sleeping Argentina!" Menem announces to the attentive crowd at the exhibition, fully aware that one year ago President Raúl Alfonsín was booed on this very platform, drowned in catcalls and whistles. "Argentina, I say to your men and women, get up and walk!" The audience of gentry, diplomats, socialites, and the hoi polloi loves it. "It's easy to talk about the blame of yesterday instead of talking about the chal-lenges of today and tomorrow. My government won't do that. I'm not going to deal with the Argentina of the past . . . disunion is the principal illness of the democracy. I want a contemporary society not ashamed of itself. . . . Money is not God. The economy is not God. The dollar is not God. Only God is God. I don't want us to spend half our lives saying what we want to do and the other half explaining why we couldn't do it!" The crowd roars. The livestock show has become a revival, and the yearning to believe that Carlos Menem can save Argentina has become almost palpable.

But still, Argentina is always ready to break your heart. Menem had to wait almost an hour before he gave that speech, impatiently twisting the large onyx ring on his left hand while other politicians droned on. Mem-bers of the crowd were not so constrained. They had been diverted. For right in the middle of the speeches calling for the dawning of a new era, Perón's black Cadillac convertible had stalled. No one could get it off the field. As the inspirational rhetoric was beamed live on national TV, a mechanic in overalls walked across the plaza, lifted the hood of the car, and—practically under Menem's nose—started to tinker with the engine. The Cadillac sputtered to life after a while, and lurched off.

Sometimes you can't help wanting to cry for Argentina.

UPDATE: Even after my surprise at being told that Menem really liked my article (except for asking, "What means lounge lizard?"), I still had trepidations about the way it would play with sophisticated Argen-tineans. Then I was invited to the Argentine embassy for dinner and the charming ambassador just laughed and laughed about the piece—he told me he'd really enjoyed it.

Menem began with such a bang. He privatized moribund state enterprises, and his brilliant finance minister, Domingo Cavallo, took runaway inflation—which stood at 200 percent a month when Menem was elected president in 1989—to 3.9 percent. This figure was the best in Latin America in 1995, when Menem was overwhelmingly reelected after changing the constitution to allow a second four-year term. At times, his statesmanship was even compared to that of Nelson Mandela. (But in his turbulent private life, Menem, who had divorced Zulema in 1991, also suffered the death of his twenty-six-year-old son in a helicopter crash in 1995.)

Then the endemic tax evasion and the corruption of his government, rampant even by Argentinean standards, began to undermine the boom that did not trickle down; Mexico and Brazil also had economic crises that hurt Argentina; Cavallo departed and when Menem left office, in 1999, only twenty percent of the public supported him. By the time he ran for the presidency for the third time, in 2003, at age seventy-two, the economy was in complete collapse, the country in chaos once again, and Menem had served 167 days of house arrest for his involvement in illegal arms sales to Croatia and Ecuador. True to his flamboyant self, however, Menem had remarried, in 2001; his bride was a thirty-six-year-old former Miss Universe from Chile, Cecilia Bolocco, who promptly got pregnant for the campaign. Alas, Menem's virility (and his ego) seemed to be the sum of his platform. He was also accused, on page one of the *New York Times*, of taking a $10-million payment from Iran to cover up the 1994 terrorist bombing of a Buenos Aires Jewish community center, which he denied. I happened to be in Santiago, Chile, at the time of the election in May 2003, and one newspaper columnist there opined that the entire election turned "on the uterus of a former Miss Universe from Chile." But this time the old razzle-dazzle didn't work. In the face of his first electoral loss, Menem dropped out of the race a few days before the election. Carlos Menem was no longer the más macho.

Part IV:

Little Gods

Notes from the
Celebrity-Industrial
Complex IV

"You can tell a lot about a person by the kind of plane he has," Donald Trump told me when I interviewed him for a story on private jets. At the time he was flying a Boeing 727 equipped with a movie theater and a bedroom. Fellow casino owner Steve Wynn had two Gulfstream G IVs in Las Vegas, one for himself and one for high rollers. The international arms dealer Adnan Khashoggi's leased 707 had a master bedroom separated from a second bedroom by means of a mirrored wall with a concealed door. Some wags in the business refer to these big-boy toys as "ego containers."

In the course of reporting the story on private jets—the ultimate status symbol of privilege and power (the kind that go for, say, $30 million and up)—I found myself on a Boeing 737 that had been sparklingly refurbished for the Orlando Magic basketball team by the team's owner, Amway founder Richard DeVos, whose personal fortune then stood at around $4.3 billion. The forty-two-seater—painted blue, black, white, and silver with a burst of stars on the tail—had previously belonged to the heiress Doris Duke. (Although the plane was built to hold 150, she never flew more than 12, preferring to use the remaining space for futons for guests or dogs.)

At the time of my visit, the Magic—starring seven-foot-one-inch Shaquille ("Shaq") O'Neal, Anfernee ("Penny") Hardaway, and some of the NBA's hottest young talent—were crusing from Memphis to Orlando after an exhibition game. The 610-mile, 1.5-hour flight was charted on a twenty-seven-inch video screen framed in stained burl wood and partitioned from the players by a panel of frosted glass designed with the team's name coming out of fluffy clouds. In the players' section, Hardaway and three teammates unwound in special oversize chairs playing dominoes. Across the aisle, over plates of barbecue, roast chicken, cole slaw, and beans, former Chicago Bulls forward Horace Grant and three other team members played cards. In the rear, Nick Anderson was watching *Batman Returns*. Meanwhile, in the third section, Coach Brian Hill was conducting a meeting with his assistants. "This plane is a statement that this organization treats its players as well as humanly possible," Coach Hill told me. Assistant Coach Tree Rollins added: "This plane is about the best thing since grits."

In the aft section, sprawled across an eight-foot built-in seat that converts into a bed, was Shaq himself, a rhyming dictionary on his lap, listening to beats on his boom box, trying to come up with lyrics for his third rap album. Across from him on the other convertible sofa bed was teammate Dennis Scott, who produces Shaq's videos and concerts. Being in the NBA today, Scott says, "means so much more than basketball." Shaq, who endorses products ranging from Reeboks to Pepsi, had finished his second movie, *Kazaam*. "This is my section," said Shaq somewhat devilishly, tapping his size-22 foot. "I can make it into a bed, close the curtain, take off all my clothes, and relax." The plane saved not only time but wear and tear on the body, especially for Shaq. With his notoriety, trying to hide out in airports is impossible. This plane was just like being home. In jet high life, the height of the cabin ceiling is a definite status point, and on this plane the ceiling was seven feet tall. The carpet was specially woven so thick that the players can sleep on it. But during our flight, no one seemed in need of rest. As we approached our destination, Shaq, the team's captain, was roaming the aisle, sporting a huge gold belt buckle with the letters TWISM.

"What do they stand for?" I asked.

"This world is mine," said the then-twenty-three-year-old wonder.

Those words encapsulate the feeling of fame for those whose ability to make billions, or sometimes mere millions, for their companies or teams has put them in a position so privileged that anything is possible. If you have reached the pinnacle, everything around you serves to confirm your specialness, your power. But the air gets thin up there, and it is easy to forget that all people do not necessarily bend to your will. Like Shaquille

O'Neal, Kobe Bryant—who now faces rape charges—also moves in that strange, heady atmosphere.

If anything, Kobe was even more isolated than most superstars: He grew up in Italy, where his father played pro basketball until Kobe was fourteen. The black street culture, home to many of his fellow pro players, is foreign to him. If he had gone to college, he might have had a better chance to develop as a person and function as a member of a team. Instead, his doting family—with their eyes on the millions he could reap—decided to have him skip college, where he might be injured; they put him right into the NBA, so that he could start earning the big bucks.

To many, Kobe Bryant seemed a spoiled, hothouse flower, indulged by family members (in a way that recalls Scott Peterson, Laci's husband) who treated him with such deference that he later had adjustment problems—particularly with teammates. *Newsweek* reported that he and Shaq (both men now play for the Los Angeles Lakers) once got into a fistfight because Kobe was such a ball hog. When he married a half-Latina, half-white high school girl, his family became estranged. When rape charges were first lodged against him by a nineteen-year-old blond concierge in a posh Colorado hotel, he denied having sex with the woman, but then switched his story, saying that the sex had been consensual.

Kobe's travails have given Laci's reality soap opera a run for its money as television drama. But one feature the two dramas have in common is the attempted shredding of the reputations of the primary female witnesses involved: Amber Frey (Peterson's former mistress) and the unnamed woman who is Bryant's accuser. The harsh scrutiny and ugly treatment of these women—quite apart from the truth or falsity of their stories—appear to justify the fears of the alleged victims of Michael Jackson, who were scared to go public with their accusations against the superstar. (In Jackson's latest case of sexual abuse of a thirteen-year-old boy, the boy's *mother* is the target.) Mia Farrow was similiarly reluctant to put her then eight-year-old daughter, Dylan, on the stand to testify against her father, Woody Allen, whom Farrow had charged with sexually abusing her.

The machines built up by big-name attorneys are fierce. No less so are the arsenals of supporting players available to superstars like Jackson or Allen. When the handlers gear up to smear the victims who take the high and mighty to court, we witness the fate of those who dare to attack the rich and famous. I cannot imagine a sane person coming forward into such an environment with false charges. For those who have the guts to stand up to men (or other women, for that matter) who believe that the world—and all it offers—is theirs, the consequences are just too painful.

"He's treated like a little god," the late Leonard Gershe, a longtime friend of Farrow's, told me about Woody Allen, "and little gods don't have to do what everybody else does." In fact, the ultimate power that celebrity provides is media access that allows the famous to slant the truth and put forward their own version of reality, which many Americans accept.

So many today seem to forget that Allen seduced Soon-Yi Previn—the adopted daughter of his longtime love Mia Farrow—a girl who had been raised to think of him as a father figure. Mia discovered the affair when she came across pornographic pictures of Soon-Yi on the mantel of Allen's living room fireplace. (Soon-Yi was either nineteen or twenty-one at the time; her exact age is impossible to identify because she was a battered Korean orphan when adopted by Mia.) Yet despite this incident, Allen is still treated as a cultural treasure. Nor does anyone seem to recall that, in a separate incident, he was barred by the court from contact with Dylan, his adopted daughter, because of the seriousness of Mia's charges that he sexually fondled the little girl. Woody Allen remains a celebrated polymorph, although his films no longer make any money. And amazingly, he and Soon-Yi, whom he married, have been allowed to adopt two children themselves.

Having done the research and reporting on the Woody and Mia saga, I remember this disturbing situation only too well. The case of Allen showed me that the innocent victims of fame suffer hugely when the little gods of the world—aided by well-paid PR staffs, by the stars' psychologists, and impressionable judges—are elevated so high as to be removed from reality, not to mention culpability.

Sometimes it is tempting to believe that the victims of fame are the famous. The desire for recognition can drive some people so far off the track they can wind up deeply unhappy, in jail, or dead. For some, the pursuit of attention and acclaim becomes a kind of addiction or illness—and its effects are all too clear in the pages of this book. A Time Warner executive I spoke to about Madonna was not the first to observe that people can become as dependent on bigger and bigger bursts of fame as they can on hair chemicals of choice. ("More just feeds on itself. It's like an addiction, he noted.") But he was unusually candid about what is demanded from stars. ("Sometimes in business, you like people to give up everything.")

Today there is a psychological term for celebrity meltdown—acquired situational narcissism—and a glance at magazines or television can reveal its pervasiveness. Yet many people persist in thinking that fame blasts all troubles away. Liz Taylor once remarked that there is "no deodorant like success." Yet fame and success are strange, alienating things—as Taylor knows better than anyone else. Maybe it's no wonder that so many tough-as-nails celebrities portray themselves as victims: Madonna obsesses over losing her mother, Michael Jackson forever mourns his terrible childhood, Mohamed Fayed will never forgive being denied British citizenship. Rarely do they realize that the people they should fear most are themselves. (One can even make the case that it might be healthier for all concerned not to become famous at all. Rosie O'Donnell and Roseanne Barr spring to mind.)

Beyond the problems of the famous, however, obsession with star power is producing more and more ordinary people who have inordinate desires to identify with celebrity. Along with acquired situational narcissism, there is now a phenomenon, seriously discussed, called celebrity worship syndrome. A scale has been developed to measure the intensity with which the syndrome's victims overidentify with celebrities. The thwarted ambitions of these celebrity junkies can backfire on all of us, as the frenzied race to be powerful or famous drives some people into dysfunction.

"I do so enjoy those case histories you write on borderline personality disorders," a psychologist mother of one of my son's classmates once told me after reading about the quest of Fayed (the owner of London's luxurious Harrods, he would have become Princess Diana's father-in-law had she lived to marry his son, Dodi Fayed) to be accepted by the British establishment, particularly the royals. Were the questionable behaviors that fueled Fayed's rise prompted more by greed or by his fixation on being knighted and becoming known and, finally, accepted? He certainly obsessed about his station and hired loquacious mouthpieces to make his case. After my story appeared, the British press substantially changed its view of Fayed, and the article was widely quoted. As is his wont, Fayed sued *Vanity Fair* over my reporting and the magazine, which stood by the story 100 percent, prepared a vigorous defense. But following Dodi Fayed's death in 1997, the suit was settled, and the following statement is what I may comment: "Mohamed Al Fayed and Condé Nast Publications announced the conclusion of Mr. Al Fayed's libel suit against the international publishing firm, which was based upon an article published in *Vanity Fair* in September 1995.

"In the aftermath of the tragic events involving the deaths of his son Dodi and Diana, Princess of Wales, Mr. Al Fayed caused discussions to occur between representatives of Condé Nast and himself. Discussions took place amicably, and the proceedings were satisfactorily concluded.

No payments were made by either side and each side will bear its own costs. Mr. Al Fayed notes that he had received a personal letter of condolence for his son's death from the chairman of Condé Nast International, for which he was deeply appreciative.

"No further statement will be made by either party."

Dana Giacchetto was a bright young money manager with an amazing ability to persuade the hottest young stars in Hollywood—Leonardo diCaprio, Ben Affleck, Tobey Maguire—to allow him to invest their money. Then he got so caught up in the experience of being part of "Leo's posse" and in the reflected glory of his star clients that he forgot what his assigned role was. Because of his power and proximity, he seemed to believe that he was a star, too. He began spending a lot more time in clubs with a white cockatoo perched on his shoulder than he did poring over stock quotes at the office.

You don't have to be famous yourself to get drunk on glory; there is definitely the danger of a contact high. Eventually, Giacchetto was indicted and convicted for secreting funds from his less famous accounts—the A-minus or B-plus list—so as not to lose face with the A–plusers. In his eyes, his status depended on his clients' stardom and on their admiration of him.

Some of the people I chronicle here actually gave their lives for fame or style. Some died as fame's victims and others were willing to kill for it. (Death or a near-death experience, of course, is the surest way to move up, by giant steps, on the fame-o-meter.)

My own experience of death as the ultimate high dive into fame came when the obscure serial killer Andrew Cunanan shot Gianni Versace on the steps of the flamboyant designer's Miami mansion in 1997—one of the more challenging episodes I have covered. Interestingly, when the Miami Beach police called the Italian consulate in Miami to notify the authorities of Versace's death, the vice consulate had to ask police who the famous Italian designer was. Not so a week later, when Cunanan committed suicide on a Miami houseboat after the then-largest manhunt in United States history. By that time, not only Versace but Cunanan was assured name recognition for the ages.

No Laughing Matter: Woody Allen and Mia Farrow

"Little gods don't have to do what everybody else does."

November 1992

There was an unwritten rule at Mia Farrow's apartment on the West Side of Manhattan: her longtime boyfriend, Woody Allen, was never supposed to be left alone with their seven-year-old adopted daughter, Dylan. Over the last two years, sources close to Farrow say, the eccentric director has been discussing, in sessions with child psychologist Dr. Susan Coates, his alleged "inappropriate" fatherly behavior toward Dylan. In more than two dozen interviews conducted for this article, Allen was described again and again as being obsessed with the bright little blond girl. He would monopolize her time, spending hours whispering to her. She was fond of her daddy, but if she tried to go off and play, he would follow her from room to room, or he would sit and stare at her.

During the school year, Allen (who maintained a separate residence in Manhattan) would arrive early at Farrow's apartment, sit on Dylan's bed, watch her wake up, and take her to school. Last July, at Farrow's country house in Bridgewater, Connecticut, he promised to keep away from the children's table so that Dylan could enjoy her birthday party with her friends, but he seemed unable to do so. Allen, who was a feared figure to many in Farrow's household, was so needy where Dylan was concerned that he hovered over her. When the cake arrived, he was right behind her, helping to blow out the candles.

Calling attention to someone's birthday-party behavior may seem trivial at best. But on another occasion Coates—who was at Mia's apartment to work with one of her other children—had only to witness a brief greeting between Woody and Dylan before the therapist initiated a discussion with Mia that resulted in Woody's agreeing to counseling. At that point, Coates didn't know that, according to several sources, Woody, wearing just underwear, would take Dylan to bed with him and entwine his body around hers. Or that he would have her suck his thumb. Or that he liked to play with Dylan in bed. He called Mia a "spoilsport" when she objected to what she referred to as "wooing." According to Mia, Woody said her concerns about the situation stemmed from her own sickness and that he was just being warm. For a long time, Mia backed down. Her love for Woody had always been mixed with fear. He could reduce her to a pulp when he gave vent to his temper, but she was also in awe of him, because he presented himself as "a morally superior person."

One summer day in Connecticut, when Dylan was four and Woody was applying suntan lotion to her nude body, he alarmed Mia's mother, the actress Maureen O'Sullivan, and her sister Tisa Farrow when he began rubbing his finger in the crack between her buttocks. Mia grabbed the lotion out of his hand, and O'Sullivan asked, "How do you want to be remembered by your children?" Woody answered, "As a good father." O'Sullivan replied, "Well, that's interesting,"

Says Tisa: "It only lasted a few seconds, but it was definitely weird."

Woody's own mother was also heard to remark on his fawning behavior with Dylan when Woody and Mia would take the children over for visits. Undoubtedly, this added tension to Allen's legendarily complex relationship with his mom. ("She's the Wicked Witch of the West, Dylan," Woody once said to the little girl. "Twist her nose off.")

No such favoritism was shown toward four-and-a-half-year-old Satchel, Woody's own son by Mia. From the start, father and son seemed to have been allergic to each other. Mia told friends that Woody referred to the baby, who cried a lot, as "the little bastard" and that once, when Satchel kicked Woody, the father twisted Satchel's leg until he screamed, and said, "Do that again and I'll break your legs." On another occasion, Satchel poked Dylan in the eye in Woody's presence. Woody scooped up the little girl, cradled her in his arms, and railed obscenely at Satchel.

"I just don't buy it when a parent becomes so constantly angry at such a little boy," says Casey Pascal, who witnessed the scene. (Pascal, Mia's friend since boarding-school days in England, also has a seven-year-old, plus twins Satchel's age, and often visits Mia.) "Woody clearly said he wanted a girl. Satchel was wrong from the beginning for him."

Dylan, who has just begun second grade, tests in the upper-ninetieth percentile. Contrary to recent reports, family members say she has never been in therapy for an inability to distinguish fantasy from reality. She *has* been in therapy for separation anxiety (she didn't want to be left by her parents at nursery school) and for her shyness. Several times last summer, while Woody was visiting in Connecticut, Dylan locked herself in the bathroom, refusing to come out for hours. Once, one of the babysitters had to use a coat hanger to pick the lock. Dylan often complained of stomachaches and headaches when Woody visited, but the symptoms would disappear when he left. At times, Dylan became so withdrawn when her father was around that she would not speak normally but would pretend to be an animal.

On August 4, Woody was visiting in Connecticut. When Mia and Casey went shopping, they took Mia's two most recently adopted children—a blind Vietnamese girl named Tam, eleven, and Isaiah, a seven-month-old black boy born to a crack-addicted mother. While they were gone, there was a brief period, perhaps fifteen minutes, when Woody and Dylan vanished from sight. The babysitter who was inside searched high and low through the cluttered old farmhouse, but she couldn't find them. The outside babysitter, after a look at the grounds around the house, concluded the two must be inside somewhere. When Mia got home a short time later, Dylan and Woody were outside, and Dylan didn't have any underpants on. (Allen later said that he had not been alone with Dylan. He refused to submit hair and fingerprint samples to the Connecticut state police or to cooperate unless he was assured that nothing he said would be used against him.) Woody, who hates the country and reportedly brings his own bath mat to avoid germs, spent the night in a guest room off the laundry, next to the garage, and left the next morning.

That day, August 5, Casey Pascal called Mia to report something her babysitter had told her. The day before, Casey's babysitter had been in the house looking for one of the three Pascal children and had been startled when she walked into the TV room. Dylan was on the sofa, wearing a dress, and Woody was kneeling on the floor holding her, with his face in her lap. The babysitter did not consider it "a fatherly pose," but more like something you'd say, "Oops, excuse me" to if both had been adults. Later she told the police that she had been shocked. "It just seemed very intimate. He seemed very comfortable."

As soon as Mia asked Dylan about it, Dylan began a harrowing story, in dribs and drabs but in excruciating detail. According to her account, she and Daddy went to the "attic" (a small crawl space off the closet in Mia's bedroom), where Daddy told her that if she stayed very still, he would put her in his movie and take her to Paris. He then touched her "private part." Dylan said she told him, "It hurts. I'm just a little kid." Trying to explain, she told Mia, "Kids have to do what grown-ups say." Mia, who has a small Beta video camera, made a tape of Dylan for the child's psychologist, who was in France at the time. "I don't want to be in a movie with my daddy," Dylan later said, and asked Mia, "Did your daddy ever do that to you?"

According to people close to the situation, Mia called her lawyer, who told her to take Dylan to her pediatrician. When the doctor asked where her private part was, Dylan pointed to her shoulder. A few minutes later, over ice cream, she told Mia that she had been embarrassed when talking to the doctor. Mia asked which story was true, saying it was important that they know. The next day, back at the doctor's, Dylan repeated her original story, which has remained consistent through many tellings to authorities. After examining Dylan and finding her intact, the doctor called his lawyer. He told Mia he was bound by law to report Dylan's story to the police.

Mia, who never sought to make allegations public, also told Coates, who is one of three therapists Woody Allen has seen on a regular basis. Coates, too, said that she would have to report Dylan's account to the New York authorities but that she would also tell Woody. Mia burst out crying, she was so afraid. Ironically, the next day, August 6, Woody and Mia were supposed to sign an elaborate child-support-and-custody agreement, months in the negotiating, giving Mia $6,000 a month for the care of Satchel, Dylan, and fifteen-year-old Moses, the other child of Mia's whom Woody had adopted on December 17, 1991.

One of Mia's lawyers, Paul Martin Weltz, notified Woody's lawyer J. Martin Obten of the incident by hand-delivered letter. On August 13, Allen's lawyers responded with a jolting preemptive strike. They filed a custody suit against Farrow, charging that she was an unfit mother. They have also denied any suggestion of child abuse or therapy for it.

In Houston, the week Mia and Woody's problems surfaced publicly, the Republicans at their national convention were unsheathing rhetorical swords to do battle over family values. But the war between Mia Farrow and Woody Allen knocked George Bush and Dan Quayle off the covers of both *Time* and *Newsweek*.

Woody told *Time*, "Suddenly I got a memo from her lawyers saying no more visits at all. Something had taken place. When I called Mia, she just slammed down the phone. And then I was told by my lawyers she was accusing me of child molestation. I thought this was so crazy and so sick that I cannot in all conscience leave those kids in that atmosphere. So I said, I realize this is going to be rough, but I'm going to sue for custody of the children."

The stage was set for a gripping morality play starring two people so famous that they are routinely referred to by their first names the world over. Their reputations and careers were suddenly at stake, along with the lives of innocent children. Shockingly, however, there was another revelation. The relationship between Allen and Farrow had begun to unravel seven months earlier, when Farrow discovered that Allen was having an affair with her nineteen- or twenty-one-year-old adopted Korean daughter, Soon-Yi. Was it incest? Farrow believed Allen to be a father figure to nine of her eleven children, not just to Satchel and the two he had adopted. She felt that his behavior could not be excused or rationalized.

Farrow had made the discovery of Allen's affair with Soon-Yi when she found a stack of Polaroids he had taken of her daughter, her legs spread in full frontal nudity. Woody would later say publicly that the pictures had been taken because Soon-Yi was interested in modeling. Mia came across the pictures while she was in Woody's apartment waiting for one of the children to complete a play-therapy session with a psychologist. (Until recently, Allen paid for all these shrinks; therapy was considered a family tradition.) The pictures were under a box of tissues on Allen's mantel. Each shot managed to contain both her daughter's face and vagina, and when Mia saw them, she later told others, "I felt I was looking straight into the face of pure evil."

"The charges will never go forward. Woody will be cleared of all that, he'll see his kids, they'll come to some settlement," says Letty Aronson, Woody Allen's sister. She categorically denies that Woody was ever in therapy for inappropriate behavior toward Dylan or that he ever favored Dylan over Satchel. "He'll be the giant in the industry he is," she continues, "and she'll be exactly what she is—in my opinion, Woody notwithstanding— a second-rate actress, a bad mother, a completely dishonest person, and someone who is operating completely out of vindictiveness."

Those close to Allen have insisted that the alleged incident with Dylan in Connecticut never occurred. They maintain that the longest period of time unaccounted for on the afternoon of August 4 was less than five minutes. (A principal involved has given an affidavit to Connecticut police stating clearly that the time was at least twice that.) Woody's lawyers say that he has passed a lie-detector test, and Woody's side charges that the videotape is suspect because it was made in a series of stops and starts. They also maintain that Dylan's story is either a fabrication of Dylan's or of Mia's. Mia, they point out, wrote a glowing letter to the judge in favor

of Woody's adopting Dylan and Moses, only a short time before she discovered that he was "taking Soon-Yi out." (According to Paul Weltz, who
handled the adoptions, "There was no glowing letter. It was an affirmative
affidavit consenting to the adoption, but at all times reserving her right as
a custodial parent.")

"I didn't find any moral dilemmas whatsoever," Woody told *Time* about
his relationship with Soon-Yi. "I didn't feel that just because she was
Mia's daughter, there was any great moral dilemma. It was a fact, but not
one with any great import. It wasn't like she was my daughter."

But nothing could have hurt Mia Farrow more. Having been born to
privilege in old Hollywood, she was carrying on a family tradition by acting, but she had also grown up one of seven children in a Catholic, peri-
patetic household. The ideal family, in theory at least, was sacred to her.
Farrow's mother, Maureen O'Sullivan, was a beautiful movie star, most
famous for playing Jane to Johnny Weissmuller's Tarzan. Her late father,
John Farrow, whom Mia adored, had been a screenwriter and director
whose greatest success was as the author of the best-selling inspirational
book *Damien the Leper*, which went through thirty-three printings. Along
with being celebrated for his way with women, he was knighted by the
pope for his erudite history of the papacy, *Pageant of the Popes*. The
family lived on an enormous lot in an exclusive Beverly Hills neighborhood, and they had a beach house in Malibu and later an apartment in
Manhattan. The children also resided with their parents on location in
Spain and England, and Mia was educated in a convent boarding school
in London. Her brother John recalls that as a child, Mia identified with
Wendy in *Peter Pan*, who mothers a gang of lost boys. "We lived in a tall
row house in London, which made it seem very real." At nine, Mia was
stricken with polio; her toys had to be burned, and the little girl in the
iron lung next to hers in the hospital died. Every Christmas after she
recovered, she put on a play starring her brothers and sisters and the
neighborhood children—the sons and daughters of the producer Hal
Roach and the actor MacDonald Carey—and charged a one-dollar admission. The money was donated to a polio fund. "Mia was mother figure in
the family. She tended to be in charge," says her oldest friend, Maria
Roach. "With *her* family she's tried to achieve more of a Norman Rockwell
experience, with her kids around her all the time. Deep down, we all just
wanted to be more normal."

"There was nothing fragile about Mia," her mother says. And nothing
remotely conventional. By the time she was eighteen, she was a porcelain
beauty eating butterflies at the Saint Regis Hotel with her dear friend
Salvador Dalí. At nineteen, as a budding flower child and ingenue star of

the most popular prime-time soap of the mid-1960s, *Peyton Place*, she made sure she caught the eye of forty-nine-year-old Frank Sinatra on the Fox lot one day and promptly flew on his jet to Palm Springs for a weekend. About a year later, her mother got a frantic phone call from one of her neighbors in New York: Mrs. Basil Rathbone. "She said, 'Something terrible has happened to Mia.' I said," recalls O'Sullivan, "'tell me what. Is she dead?' 'No, she's married to Frank Sinatra.' 'Oh,' I said, 'is *that* all.'"

The marriage started falling apart when Mia landed the starring role in *Rosemary's Baby*, made by the hot new director Roman Polanski. When they divorced, in 1968, Mia astounded Sinatra by not asking for a penny of alimony. (After hearing of her recent troubles, the crooner, who still has a soft spot for Mia, offered help and money.) In 1969, Mia herself was the younger woman who broke up a marriage; she became pregnant with twins by André Previn when he was married to the lyricist Dory Previn and was principal conductor of the London Symphony Orchestra. With their marriage and the arrival of the twins, Mia found what gave her the greatest joy: mothering. The marriage lasted ten years, during which the couple produced another biological child and adopted three others. Previn pays child support and half the tuition for their children.

Previn, who has also been supportive of Mia, has told friends, "If Mia is not a good mother, then Jascha Heifetz didn't know how to play the violin." Ironically, Woody Allen in the recent past praised Mia specifically as a mother. He told Eric Lax, the author of the 1991 biography of Allen, "She has raised nine children now with no trauma, and has never owned a thermometer. I take my temperature every two hours in the course of the day."

Little Allan Konigsberg (Woody's real name) didn't grow up surrounded by stars, the way Maria de Lourdes Villiers Farrow did. But for twelve years they shared a life—she starred in thirteen of his films—and he credited their time together with opening him up to an understanding of fatherly love. "Mia's been a completely different kind of experience for me, because the predominant thing has been family," Woody told Lax. "She's introduced me to a whole other world. I've had a child with her, and we've adopted one. She's brought a completely different, meaningful dimension to my life." Two years later, Woody Allen and Mia Farrow are locked in ugly and hurtful conflict and Lax now says, "I find it baffling. Up to the time I finished the book, the relations between them seemed very solid, and the relations with the children seemed perfectly normal. I'm crushed for all of them."

The crisis has been shattering for Mia, who after the discovery of the photographs, would rant on the phone at all hours to Woody. (Her friends insist he kept begging her to take him back.) In August the endless back and forth came to an end. Allen and his friends mounted an aggressive campaign of damage control, painting Farrow as filled with rage and out for revenge, hysterical, and a compulsive adopter of damaged children. Chaos reigned at Mia's house, according to Woody's side; several teenage children were hinted to be seriously out of control. Woody's supporters, many of whom have depended upon him for their living, claimed that Mia had turned her older Asian daughters into housemaids, favored her biological children, and beaten Soon-Yi, even breaking a chair on her.

Particularly vicious were the tabloid Hamill brothers, Pete in the *New York Post* and Denis in the New York *Daily News*. (Their brother Brian has worked for Woody as a still photographer on seventeen movies.) In a single column, Denis incorrectly charged that Mia "breast-fed Satchel until he was 3½ and even had a special harness constructed to do so over Woody's objections." He quoted Woody minions who said that Mia washed down tranquilizers and antidepressants with abundant red wine. Hamill went on to say that, according to those sources, she had staged a fake suicide attempt in April in Woody's apartment after a quarrel over Soon-Yi. What had Woody done, was the leitmotif, to deserve all this?

"It's a classic case of a woman scorned," says Jane Martin, a close friend of Woody's who worked as his assistant in the 1980s. "I've never been chewed out like I was twice by Mia. She can go from zero to one hundred miles an hour in one second. She went berserk screaming crazy at me for two situations I had nothing to do with." Martin, who is convinced Mia favors her natural boys over her adopted girls, likens her presence to "having a huge cobra coiled up in the corner of the room and having to watch it every day so it wouldn't come out." Martin also thinks that Mia's "revenge" has been successful. "She's put an indelible black question mark at the end of Woody's name forever."

Ultimately, the usually reclusive director called his first press conference in years at the Plaza Hotel to deal with the situation. He told the world of his love for Soon-Yi, a sophomore at Drew University in New Jersey, "who continues to turn around my life in a wonderfully positive way." Revenge for his being attracted to the "lovely, intelligent, sensitive" Soon-Yi was the reason, Allen implied, for Farrow's claims that he had abused his beloved kids Dylan and Satchel. (If rumors existed about Satchel, he had never been publicly mentioned by the authorities or by Farrow.)

In December 1991, less than a month before Mia discovered the photos, Woody had formally adopted Dylan and Moses, but at the press conference he spoke of their romantic relationship as if it had ended long ago—shocking old friends in the process. "I had dinner with them on October 28. Everything was just the same. Woody spent the whole night talking about the adoption—that he was willing to move hell and high water to get it through," says the playwright and lyricist Leonard Gershe, one of Mia's closest friends and confidants. "Would you be so anxious to adopt a child with a woman you're not going to see anymore? And would she have allowed it? Maybe it was over in his mind. It certainly wasn't in hers," Gershe adds. "But if it were over, then it makes his eagerness to adopt Dylan even more sinister."

As the media battle intensified, Soon-Yi issued her own statement to *Newsweek*, asserting her independence, savaging Mia, and declaring, "I'm not a retarded little underage flower who was raped, molested and spoiled by some evil stepfather—not by a long shot. I'm a psychology major at college who fell for a man who happens to be the ex-boyfriend of Mia." Soon-Yi declared in writing exactly what Woody had said, that Mia would have been just as upset if he had slept with "another actress or his secretary."

Audrey Sieger, who has a doctorate in learning and reading disabilities and tutored Soon-Yi from the sixth grade through high school, was concerned after Soon-Yi spoke out. She says that when Soon-Yi was in the third grade, her IQ tested below 100. She came to Sieger with "very deprived early language development, which carried throughout the years." Sieger and Soon-Yi became close, and Soon-Yi worked very hard. "She's a very typical [learning-disabled] kid, very socially inappropriate, very, very naive," says Sieger. "She's very, very literal and flat in how she interprets what she sees and how she interprets things socially. She misinterprets situations." Sieger doubts that Soon-Yi could have written the statement to the press.

"The words were often exactly the same as Woody Allen's, if you compare the two," says Priscilla Gilman (the longtime girlfriend of Mia's son Matthew Previn) of Soon-Yi's statement.

After Woody's press conference, Mia declined all offers of interviews giving her equal time, although she did speak briefly to *Newsweek* about her family. Diane Sawyer was willing to give her a whole show; Barbara Walters was ready to hop a plane back from Italy; Maury Povich even sent flowers to one of the babysitters. That several of Mia's children, however, elected to give statements of support for her led Woody to charge that she was "parading" her children to the press in an unseemly fashion. It didn't help that Maria Roach read a letter from Mia—with Mia's permission, she said—to an Associated Press reporter in Los Angeles. In the letter Mia confessed that she had come to a "genuine meltdown." Says Gilman: "Mia was sobbing when that letter was released. I spoke to her, and she said, 'I'm so humiliated, I can't believe this—and she's saying I authorized this.'"

"I just read it to show she has all her faculties and that she had been dealt a terrible blow," says Roach. "I read the letter thinking he would paraphrase it. In the end it was misquoted."

Not only did Mia Farrow feel massively betrayed; she was also terrified that Woody Allen was deliberately tearing her family apart. She was dependent on him both emotionally and financially. "One of the things that happened to Mia," says Gilman's mother, Lynn Nesbit, "is that she got cut off, too." Although *Variety* recently reported that "Woody Allen makes expensive pictures and demands a rich deal," all Farrow reportedly earned from Allen was a modest $200,000 per film.

Over the years Mia had turned down other directors' offers to act—including the role in *Father of the Bride* played by Diane Keaton, Woody's former girlfriend—in order to stay in New York with her family and appear only in films by Woody, who attacked her confidence. "Mia told me he was always telling her she had no talent at all," says Gershe. "She was only good in his pictures, not anybody else's. Nobody would ever hire her again." Mia, who throughout their relationship had endured blistering putdowns by Woody—she told friends he once lit into her in front of the Russian Tea Room because she was off four degrees on the weather, and another time because she was unable to tell him how many kinds of pasta there were in the world—now so feared Woody that some of her behavior was classic textbook "female victim." For example, when the Connecticut police asked her for Woody's home phone number, she refused to give it to them. The police just laughed at her.

To close the nightmare down, a few days before the *Newsweek* and *Time* cover stories came out, Mia told friends that Woody had agreed to drop the custody case and sign the original agreement if Mia would say she was dropping the abuse charges. "I think Woody's big thrust is: You poisoned the atmosphere so much that Dylan's making this thing up," says Lynn Nesbit. But an eyewitness who has given an affidavit to police says that Mia asked Dylan if she wanted to recant. (Mia said, "Dylan, you know, we all make up stories. Everybody does that. Sometimes we know we made it up, and it's perfectly okay to say you made it up." But the little girl would not back down.) "If he says he didn't," Dylan answered, "he's lying."

Since the incident, Dylan has burst out, even in the middle of playing games, with statements like "I don't want him to be my daddy," and Mia's friends say she is making every effort to support her child. "The thing that people have to understand in this case is that it is not Mia versus Woody; it's just a plain simple fact that a seven-year-old child has told her mother something and that her mother has to choose to believe her," says a member of the household. "If her mother doesn't believe her, who is going to believe her?" Nesbit observes, "Mia says, 'How can you turn your back on a seven-year-old?' Believe me, her life would be a heck of a lot easier if she dropped it."

To those on the inside who have watched the departure of Soon-Yi from the family and who have heard Dylan on the videotape and seen her changes of behavior, who have read the lurid headlines about Mia, who wonder if their phones are being tapped, Woody Allen is a chilling figure of power, a potentate of reel life who doesn't seem to have to play by the rules. "The man is so exalted in the business," says Gershe. "Regular morals, conscience, ethics—that's for slobs like you and me." The effect, says Gershe, "spills over into real life. He's treated like a little god, and little gods don't have to do what everybody else does." A member of the household adds, "He just scares me. I think he scares everyone who knows all the things he has done. And anybody who is close to him—that he has any possibility of destroying—I think is scared of him."

In various interviews, Woody or his supporters have mentioned shoplifting, truancy, turnstile jumping, and check forgery as the dirty secrets of Mia's kids. These are the facts behind those stories. According to those close to the family, two years ago Lark, nineteen, and Daisy, eighteen, and two of their friends were picked up for shoplifting some underwear from a Connecticut mall. Around four years ago, Lark got caught jumping a subway turnstile on the way home from a party that she had sneaked out to. Last year, Daisy—who hadn't yet received her monthly allowance from André Previn—forged Soon-Yi's signature on a check while Soon-Yi was away at school. She was immediately made to pay the money back. Daisy also skipped five days of school last year when Mia was in Vietnam to arrange for an adoption.

"Most of my students are New York City kids. Many have parents who are glamorous and famous, and most of these kids are very neglected and troubled and grow up very fast," says Audrey Sieger, who has been tutoring the children in the Previn-Farrow-Allen households for the last twelve years. "Mia's family is very unusual. She—at any time in these twelve years—has been able to tell me in detail about every one of her kids. These kids travel on buses with bus passes. They cook dinner for each other. They do their own laundry. Different kids over the years have been assigned the job of going to the supermarket. They have not been raised by nannies."

"I couldn't get over how much the biological children weren't favored. They all viewed each other as equal," says Lorrie Pierce, who has gone to the house to teach the children piano for the last seven or eight years. "Mia passes down family heirlooms to each one, without regard to who is adopted." The piano teacher echoes Sieger: "Mia's the one the kids threw up on. She gets right in the arena and does all the dirty work. She doesn't push them off onto the help."

Creating a large family "is not the act of a compulsive. It's too much hard work," says Mia's friend Rose Styron, the human-rights-activist wife of the novelist William Styron and Soon-Yi's godmother. "I've never known anyone who cared so selflessly about children and who put so much of herself into them. . . . They always came first."

Leonard Gershe remembers, "Mia told me long ago, when she was adopting the fifth or sixth child, 'Lenny, I was so lucky to find out fairly young that pink palazzos and swimming pools were never going to fulfill me. They don't do it for me. I'm not interested in fashion, I'm not interested in jewelry. I'm interested in giving a life to someone whose life would not exist if it weren't for me.' What's so terrible about this? It's absolutely sincere."

Throughout the ordeal, Mia's other children have been loyal to their mother; none of her older children speaks to Woody any longer. They appear to be furious over the things Woody has said. "The insensitivity of someone who could say that brothers and sisters would not care that their mother's boyfriend was having an affair with their sister . . . devastated the entire family," says Priscilla Gilman. "She wasn't jealous; it wasn't that at all. It was a sense of moral outrage."

Soon-Yi has reportedly told her mother that she doesn't need her anymore and, for the time being, she is out of the family. Woody pays her tuition at school, where his limousine has been seen picking her up on Fridays. The empty space at the dinner table at Mia's where Soon-Yi used to sit has been taken up by Isaiah's high chair, although all in the family insist they still love Soon-Yi and want her to come back.

Both Woody Allen and Mia Farrow had to make strenuous efforts to get these children: a New York adoption law had to be stretched for Woody to adopt Dylan and Moses, but it required an act of Congress for Mia to have Soon-Yi.

For the first three years Mia cared for her, Soon-Yi referred to her as "Good Mama," as opposed to her biological mother, "Naughty Mama." Naughty Mama was reportedly a prostitute; for punishment, she would force Soon-Yi to kneel in a doorway, and she would slam the door against the girl's head. One day she left the child on a street in Seoul and said she would be back in five minutes. Then she disappeared forever. When the orphanage found Soon-Yi, she spoke no known language, just gibberish.

Mia waited almost a year to get her, and finally had to request that Congress change the law that limited the number of alien children an American family could adopt. (Altogether she has adopted nine children.) She then stayed at the orphanage in Seoul washing dishes for ten days until Soon-Yi's papers came through. To get to know the child, Mia brought her a doll and a pretty new dress. The doll frightened Soon-Yi; she had never seen one before. Later, when Mia dressed her up and stood her before a mirror, Soon-Yi hated what she saw and tried to kick the mirror in. She despised men more, and hissed whenever one came near.

Nobody knows how old Soon-Yi really is. Without ever seeing her, Korean officials put her age down as seven on her passport. A bone scan Mia had done on her in the United States put her age between five and seven. In the family, Soon-Yi is considered to have turned twenty this year, on October 8. Prior to Tam, she was the oldest child Mia had adopted; she was also the most learning deprived, the quietest, and the least socialized of all the children. She has always worked extraordinarily hard, spending hours on homework it took others half an hour to complete. Because of her learning disabilities, she took her SATs untimed.

At Mia's, Soon-Yi shared a room with Lark and Daisy, both of whom were far hipper and more outgoing than she. Soon-Yi seemed to live in a world of fairy-tale romance, dreaming of boyfriends who never called. She had a picture of Fred Astaire next to her bed. "My personal opinion is that she's basking in the sunlight of the attention," says Sieger, "kind of like she's in a romance."

The family sensed that Soon-Yi had a crush on Woody, which he seemed to delight in. But they thought nothing of it, since Soon-Yi had yet to receive her first phone call from a boy. When Woody started taking her to basketball games, Mia reportedly told her to stop dressing up for them as if she were going to a disco. During the summer of 1991, Soon-Yi stayed in the city to work, living in Mia's apartment with her big brother Matthew, whom she idolized, while Mia and the younger children were in the country. At night she would get dressed up and go out, never telling Matthew or Priscilla where she was going. "All of a sudden she started wearing these incredibly sexy clothes, and putting on these black, really slinky shirts and little skirts and these pumps and stuff," says Gilman. "She would say, 'Don't tell Mom. I'm going to a friend's house.' And I said to Matthew, 'I think she has a secret boyfriend, and I think we should find out who this is.' And Matthew said, 'Oh, no, just let her do her own thing.' Matthew is very into respecting people's privacy."

Around last Thanksgiving, a few weeks before Woody's formal adoption of Moses and Dylan was to become final, Woody began to take a special interest in the teenage Daisy. Four different times, according to several sources, he tried to engage her in intimate conversation, asking her to tell him all her secrets, things she wouldn't tell her mom about a boyfriend: Where do you go at night—do you sneak out? Daisy, those close to her say, couldn't figure out if he wanted to become more of a father figure or "some cool friend or what." "But she didn't tell Mia at the time, because Mia would be hurt," says Gershe. When Woody saw Daisy defend her mother in the media, he reportedly called her "a lying little twit" and threatened that he'd see her in court.

From the beginning, Woody Allen has seemed curiously numb to the implications of his relationship with Soon-Yi. "To this day I don't think he really understands what everybody's so excited about," says Leonard Gershe. "He does not understand the morality of it. He's deflecting things with 'She's over eighteen.' Nobody ever questioned that he did anything *illegal*. He did something *immoral*, and that's what he can't understand."

It was Gershe whom Mia called when she discovered the photos. "Her voice was shaking, and I knew something god-awful had happened. . . . She said, 'I can't believe this. I have nude pictures of Soon-Yi.'" After Mia phoned Woody and told him she had found the pictures and "to get away from us," she went back to her apartment, where Soon-Yi was and a donnybrook ensued. Mia slapped her daughter four or five times over a few days. Woody said that Mia locked Soon-Yi in her room and also smashed her with a chair, but one eyewitness denies it. "I was over there the next day," says Casey Pascal. "The room wasn't locked, and I never saw any bruises or anything [on Soon-Yi]."

Woody came over immediately. He first told Mia that he loved Soon-Yi and would marry her. "Fine," Mia said. "She's in her room. Take her and go. Get out of here, both of you." Then, Mia told friends, Woody dropped to his knees and started to cry. He begged Mia's forgiveness and asked her to marry him. "Put this behind us," he said, "Use it as a springboard to a better relationship." He called what had happened with Soon-Yi "a tepid little affair that wouldn't have lasted more than a few weeks anyway." He also told Mia that the affair was "probably good for Soon-Yi's self-esteem."

The next day Mia asked Casey Pascal to go to Soon-Yi. "'I'm too angry to talk to her, but go in and make sure she knows that I still love her.' And I went in carrying that message," Pascal recalls. "Soon-Yi just cried and said, 'I didn't mean to hurt my mother.' And I said, 'What did you think was going to happen?' And she said, 'I never thought she'd find out.'"

Soon-Yi would not accept the idea that Woody was at fault. "He's not to blame for this," she told Pascal, and admitted that their affair had begun in the fall. "She was saying things like 'My mother didn't understand him—she didn't have time for him and all his needs.' The child was absolutely tortured, and she was totally loyal to him."

Soon-Yi's big confrontation with her family came the following weekend. Most of the children had been in the apartment the previous tense days, witnessing tears and fights, yet Woody blamed Mia for telling them anything at all. "It was *her* fault they were mad at him," says Leonard Gershe. That Sunday in Connecticut, while Dylan and Satchel watched *The Little Mermaid* in the TV room, the older children and Priscilla Gilman and Mia had a family meeting with Soon-Yi. "The whole notion that Mia kicked her out of the house is completely a lie," says Gilman. "It was a choice. She said, 'Soon-Yi, we want you in this family. We love you. But you are going to have to choose whether you want to be in this family or to be with Woody. And that you can promise me that you will never do anything like this again.'" Then the brothers and sisters spoke, trying to understand what had happened. "All I remember Soon-Yi saying was 'It's my fault, it's my fault, it's just as much my fault as Woody's,'" says Gilman. Soon-Yi refused to explain anything. "She just ran out."

Not long after, Mia finished her last two days of shooting on Woody's film *Husbands and Wives*. "She was in denial, obviously. Her whole life was tied up with this man," says her sister Tisa. "He made her feel like she couldn't live without him. She took a long time to get pissed off. But she is angry now; her feelings are strong and raw." On Valentine's Day, Mia sent Woody a picture of her and her children, with a toothpick stuck in each person's chest. The message: "This is how many hearts you've broken in this family."

UPDATE: When the news first hit about the break-up of Woody Allen and Mia Farrow and the charges flew about the sexual abuse of seven-year-old Dylan and the seduction of Soon-Yi, Woody Allen was able to rally most of the media to write the story from his point of view. After all, he was one of New York's most beloved cultural figures and Mia had to be kooky for adopting all those kids. But I had also heard stories that made me believe there might be another side to this shocking tale. And indeed there was.

It was not until the fall of 2002, however, that I finally met Mia Farrow and then seventeen-year-old Dylan—now called Malone—when Mia appeared in a play in Washington, D.C. Malone, who has been through years of therapy connected to her ordeal, has not seen her adopted father, Woody Allen, since Mia Farrow won custody of her after a bruising, month-long trial in 1993. (Allen also was ordered to pay over a million dollars in Mia's attorney's fees.)

The legal fallout took several years: First, a Yale–New Haven team of medical experts cleared Woody of charges that he molested Dylan. But the Connecticut state attorney disagreed, saying he found probable cause to bring the celebrated director to trial, but did not want to inflict the trauma of that on the little girl. Judge Elliott Wilk said he was not sure if he shared the medical experts' opinion, either. He used his custody decision as a way to take Woody to task and he also chastised Woody's affair with Soon-Yi. He criticized Woody "for demonstrating no parenting skills that would qualify him as an adequate custodian for Moses, Dylan and Satchel." He forbade Woody from seeing Dylan/Malone for six months and his decision was upheld on appeal with an even more scathing decision handed down from the appellate court. From that time forward, Dylan's psychiatrists were able to argue successfully that contact with Woody Allen would injure her.

Today, Dylan is Malone, a shy, sweet brunette in her first year of college, who fights serious depression and displays tentativeness around others that I found similar to other victims of abuse whom I had previously interviewed. Mia Farrow says Malone is haunted by the fact that she did not stand trial as a little girl because had she done so, "perhaps Woody would not have been able to adopt those two little girls with Soon-Yi." Woody Allen and Soon-Yi married in 1997, and subsequently were able to adopt.

In 1998, Allen revealed his bitterness over everything that had happened, telling writer Erica Jong that Farrow kept her children "in a cultish compound in Connecticut where going out has always been discouraged."

Satchel, now called Seamus, the biological child of Woody and Mia, is the image of Mia, slight with porcelain skin and wide blue eyes. A genius, he entered college at age eleven and will graduate from Bard College in New York as he is turning sixteen. In Washington during the summer of 2003, I also met Seamus for the first time. He wants to study law to work for "social justice." He has not seen his father since he was eleven years old and was unable to breathe in a courtroom when faced with the prospect of having to continue supervised visitation with Woody.

"You know I never read your piece that you wrote about my family," Seamus told me. I explained that was not at all necessary but asked if he had ever had any contact with his father—the answer was no. I expressed regret that it had turned out that way. "I know," Seamus answered, "but he married my sister."

Interestingly enough, Moses—the oldest of the three children that Woody and Mia adopted—now works as a marriage counselor.

Show Me the Money: Dana Giacchetto

"What Dana turned into was a nightclub-crawling, Prada-suit-wearing boy."

April 2000

Not long ago, to be young, gifted, and financially secure in Hollywood meant that Dana Giacchetto was managing your money. While a few skeptics never could grasp how the foppish, thirty-seven-year-old money manager gained the trust of such A-list stars as Leonardo DiCaprio, Cameron Diaz, Matt Damon, Ben Affleck, and Tobey Maguire, Giacchetto himself rarely displayed any self-doubt. Exuberant, generous, part court jester, part shrewd operator, he often partied in the hottest nightspots until five A.M., and even dined out with a cockatoo perched on his shoulder. He bragged that his company, the Cassandra Group Inc., controlled $400 million or $500 million or even $1 billion belonging to hundreds of top-drawer clients on both coasts—major artists in SoHo (David Salle, Ross Bleckner), rock stars such as REM's Michael Stipe, and a constellation of leading figures in the film industry, ranging from actress Courteney Cox Arquette to former Creative Artists Agency (CAA) head Michael Ovitz. To add to his cachet, Giacchetto had formed a separate, $100-million venture-capital partnership with Chase Manhattan Bank, a Wall Street credential guaranteed to impress his glittering investors.

But the glitter is quickly being ground to dust. Giacchetto is the subject of inquiries by the Securities and Exchange Commission as well as investigations by United States attorneys in New York and Los Angeles, and the FBI has been contacting potential witnesses. Authorities are attempting to ascertain whether Cassandra was involved in an elaborate Ponzi scheme: taking the money new clients gave Giacchetto and putting it into deals gone bad, to bail out earlier investors. In addition, the investigators want to know if Giacchetto lied to his clients about the amount of money in their accounts. Both charges are considered fraud. Giacchetto and his lawyer deny having any knowledge of such an investigation and say they have not been approached by any United States attorney.

Until the fall of 1999, when the news broke that some seventeen of Giacchetto's highest-profile clients had deserted him, he was throwing wild bashes with DiCaprio and the rapper Q-Tip, jetting to Paris with Cameron Diaz, or squiring around the sons and daughters of the rich and powerful. Christopher Cuomo, a son of the former New York governor Mario Cuomo, was on the payroll of Cassandra; art dealer Arne Glimcher's son Marc was one of Giacchetto's best friends; literary agent Mort Janklow's daughter, Angela Janklow Harrington, and financier Ivan Boesky's daughter, Marianne, invested money with him; and he elevated Bob Dylan's son Jesse, thirty-three, to be the chairman of a publicly traded entertainment company. Many of Giacchetto's clients were thrilled with the amount of money he made for them, and they raved about him as a financial genius.

Giacchetto basked in the heat emanating from DiCaprio's *Titanic* celebrity—DiCaprio often stayed in the money man's SoHo loft, and Giacchetto once proposed a deal to offer shares in the star's future earnings, an enterprise called Leo Inc. Swept away in reflected glory, Giachetto even granted press interviews, and in the presence of a reporter from the *New York Times Magazine*, called out, "Get me Leo!" At the time, there was no one else in the room. Hollywood was not amused. "'Get me Leo' was the death knell," says Janklow Harrington. "Believe me, it doesn't take a lot to disengage the folks out here."

At first, "he seemed harmless," says Bryan Lourd, a managing partner of CAA, who is not a Giacchetto admirer. (Lourd's brother, Blaine, who is also a money manager, has recently acquired some of Giacchetto's former clients.) "He was charming in his geekiness," adds Lourd. But soon Giacchetto began popping up in the gossip columns and in magazines such as *Interview*. "What he turned into was a nightclub-crawling, Prada-suit-wearing boy," Lourd explains. "It's all the better if you can hang out with your money manager, but he shouldn't be getting more women than you or living in nicer places than you. They're supposed to be sitting behind a desk."

In December 1999, the *New York Observer* caught Giacchetto in several flagrant lies. Although he claimed to have dropped out of Harvard "two credits shy" of an MBA, he had, in fact, taken only extension courses at Harvard. As it happened, he had also failed a trader's exam administered by the National Association of Securities Dealers. He did not have $400 million to manage, as he had often stated in the press—it was only $100 million. According to veteran CAA agent Bob Bookman, "This is a business where people make a lot of money not because of business skills but because of creative skills. There's a long history of people who made a lot of money in Hollywood and entrusted it to the wrong people. It's part of an ongoing saga."

Also in December, the *Los Angeles Times* and *Daily Variety* reported that Giacchetto's partnership with Chase Manhattan had ended abruptly and that big-name clients, including DiCaprio, Diaz, Affleck, and Damon, had taken their money out of Cassandra. Rumors of an impending scandal swirled, but nobody seemed to know what it might entail. "I have not heard one person come out publicly to say what he has done wrong," says Michael Ovitz, who supports Giacchetto "unless he has done something illegal." Nevertheless, last summer he removed the $300,000 he had invested with Giacchetto for trading options, not because there was anything amiss—Giacchetto had done well for him—but because Ovitz's accountant couldn't decipher his statements. Bookkeeping for option trading can be a nightmare, and Ovitz felt that Giacchetto had to get his accounting squared away.

On December 13, 1999, Giacchetto struck back. He sued his former Chase partners—Jeffrey A. Sachs, Samuel Holdsworth, and Robert L. Egan—for $300 million. He charged that Sachs had spread "untrue statements and grossly exaggerated slander, rumor, and innuendo" and that the other two partners (based on what they had heard from Sachs) joined with Sachs to force Giacchetto out of Cassandra–Chase Entertainment Partners (referred to hereafter as the Fund). He further alleged that Sachs had contacted numerous people Giacchetto did business with to warn them that Giacchetto would become a target of investigation by authorities and was "going to get arrested." Moreover, the suit asserted that Sachs's call to Steve Warren, one of DiCaprio's lawyers, had resulted in the star's pulling out of a major merchandising deal to market DiCaprio overseas. (Giacchetto was to receive $100,000 a month in compensation.)

Sachs admits to advising clients to have their accountants scrutinize their monthly statements but claims, "There were no untruths. There were definitely not any defamations." After hiring Mario Cuomo to defend them, he and Holdsworth denied all of Giacchetto's charges and asked that the suit be dismissed. They also sued for the $950,000 they had lent to Giacchetto.

The sizzling backstory is that two insiders have alleged that Sachs, relying on information that he had paid a young Cassandra employee to obtain for him, called certain key Cassandra clients to warn them to get out. "No one has ever been paid by me for information," says Sachs. "That is a pure fabrication." Giacchetto, however, admits that he was warned about the alleged payments over a year ago. He says that he had a number of calls from clients about Sachs. "They said, 'This guy is not working on your team. He is basically abandoning you. You had better be careful.'"

Dana Giacchetto was putting up a brave front when I spoke to him in his spacious loft on lower Broadway in early February, a week before his former senior vice president, Soledad Bastiancich, was called in to the office of the United States attorney in New York to answer questions about how Cassandra's bookkeeping was done and whether Giacchetto provided clients with an accurate accounting of their funds. Giacchetto was dressed nattily in black. His cockatoo was on a perch nearby. Peter Brown, his impeccable British PR representative, was at the ready, and an attractive young blond woman was making tea for us.

"After all this crap in the press, all my clients will come back," Giacchetto tells me confidently. "I'll continue to build value for people, and the people will realize that." He is quite charming, short and energetic, with a shock of straight blond hair falling over his forehead. He wears wire-rimmed glasses and gestures flamboyantly. His skin is so pale that it is easy to see when he becomes emotional or nervous, because his face flushes bright red. From time to time the facade collapses, and he nearly cries when he mentions the recent betrayals and losses. "I'm an optimist. I love people. I've always felt since I was a little kid I was here to do good things. I have to be more careful. I didn't realize so many people would be working against me to create damage."

Giacchetto, a onetime rock keyboard player who grew up in a middle-class home in Medford, Massachusetts, staked his business on creating "value" (money) for artists. His first boss, Ellyn McColgan, fondly recalls him as part of a small team hired to install and support a computerized account system for the Boston Safe Deposit & Trust Company. "He was twenty-four. A delight. So much fun, very smart, and he worked so hard. Dana was already managing his own portfolio—he owned Disney, even back then." She adds, "He was on the fashion edge. He dressed in black long before Boston understood that as a color."

Giacchetto started the Cassandra Group in 1987, and it became his mantra that the firm would deal in conservative, blue-chip stocks and corporate bonds. He emphasized low-risk securities and usually shunned popular technology stocks. "I always felt artists—visual, musical, creative minds—were not comfortable talking about money or hard economics, or were kept in the dark. My dream was to create an entity in which [creative] people would feel comfortable that they were dealing with people who could understand both the left brain and right brain." Giacchetto also fought for artists to own pieces of "equity" in companies they were attached to. He once even tried—unsuccessfully—to get Madonna to give up a piece of her record label when she signed Alanis Morissette, a close friend of his. "People who create content have to understand the value of their content. You've seen the power that emerges around these artists."

Giacchetto's most successful deal was to sell a forty-nine percent share in the small, independent, Seattle-based Sub Pop Records—the original label of Nirvana—to the Warner Music Group for an astounding $20 million in 1994. "When we sold Sub Pop to Time Warner," he says, "a lot of it had to do with the success of Kurt Cobain [who was already dead]. These deals are driven by content providers, and a lot of these people want to know, How do we access capital markets? That's the puzzle I'm trying to get at."

Others would disagree. "Dana's love is to be in a room with Leonardo," says a close associate. "He loves the feeling he can walk up to the door and walk right in. He loves that feeling much more than money." Friends say that Giacchetto's ultimate dream is to be sought after by everyone: Get me Dana!

"You just made $10,000 in Nike options," Giacchetto would coo on the phone. "Do you want to keep going?" His financial seduction was silky, and many people made a lot of money with him. "When Alan Greenspan described the market as having 'irrational exuberance,'" says Ross Bleckner, "I thought of Dana. That's how I would describe him."

Giacchetto would show up on studio lots, asking young executives he had just met to provide him with introductions. Always emphasizing that he specialized in blue chips, he was also conscientious about such things as the rain forests, and he steered clear of tobacco stocks. Film producer Bill Robinson, Diane Keaton's business partner, remembers meeting Giacchetto at the Chateau Marmont in Hollywood about three years ago. According to Robinson, Giacchetto boasted that he was part owner of the venerable star hangout. Giacchetto says he was referring to the Standard, the other Los Angeles hotel owned by his client André Balazs. In fact, through Giacchetto, Balazs got DiCaprio, Diaz, and Benicio Del Toro to put money in the Standard.

Several of the big-star names, it should be noted, invested relatively small amounts with Giacchetto, as if they were reserving membership in an exclusive private club or the coolest high-school clique. Robinson continues: "Dana and his friends were holding forth about how he represents Leo, Cameron, Matt Damon, Ovitz—how Mike Ovitz called him every week for financial advice. He had this boyish charm, like a laid-back Silicon Valley boy-wonder star, and 'Oh yeah,' he said, he once happened to be in a punk band in Boston. 'And, oh, by the way, I'm a financial genius.' He told me he controlled $1 billion in assets and I could have an incredible return on investments."

Robinson recalls that Giacchetto whipped out his laptop and punched up several portfolios in which Robinson could invest. Ordinarily, he told Robinson, he didn't take anyone with less than a million. "He created this sense that you would be in this elite club and you were missing the boat if you didn't buy in. . . . Plus he'd say, 'Here are the keys to my loft, and, oh, Leo might be staying there.' In a way, he exploited the incredibly sheeplike nature of all of us out here."

To those who were market challenged, Giacchetto would patiently explain that once they had signed his management agreement, he would have absolute discretion to make trades using the money in their accounts and would receive a fee of 1.5 percent of their total assets. Unlike most money managers, however, he included moneys borrowed on the margin to buy stocks as part of that total—hardly a conservative procedure—and he chose not to disclose his performance to such standard money-management reports as Mobius and Russell. Monthly statements from Brown & Company, a Boston-based discount brokerage house owned by Chase, brought clients up-to-date on their stock holdings. But it was harder for them to find out how money placed in private deals was faring. Any questions along those lines, according to former employees, were answered only by Giacchetto.

Moreover, there appeared to be no rhyme or reason to the private deals Giacchetto favored. Katie Ford, the wife of André Balazs and president of Ford Models Inc., sought a few investors for her business, as did the publishers of the downtown Manhattan publication *Paper*. Giacchetto put his clients' money into both, and *Paper* ran a prominent interview with him without disclosing that he was an investor. He also promised Tom Pickens, the son of the legendary corporate raider T. Boone Pickens Jr., that he would raise $50 million for the Pickens Capital Fund, a project to buy up water utilities in southern towns and privatize them. He managed to raise only $5 million, and when it became apparent that the fund was not really liquid, Giacchetto's clients' moneys were converted into bonds, which were not paid when they were due, on December 31, 1999, but were extended to January 31, 2000. By late February they had still not been paid.

One of those waiting for his money from Pickens Capital is the artist David Salle. A person close to the situation says that shortly before the bonds defaulted, Salle gave Giacchetto approximately half a million dollars realized from the sale of his loft to invest, and Giacchetto put the money into Pickens Capital. Did Giacchetto put Salle's money into a deal he knew was failing? He insists that he did not. Today, Giacchetto distances himself from the project and says, "It concerns me that technically it is in default." After seeing the latest figures from Pickens, however, he adds that "it gives me confidence that there are considerable assets here."

The largest Cassandra loss was in Iridium, a now bankrupt global satellite phone network backed by Motorola, which many other money managers also took a bath on. Together with Soledad Bastiancich (the ambitious, thirty-four-year-old former investment broker at Allen & Company who became a Cassandra senior vice president), Giacchetto bought millions of dollars' worth of Iridium shares when they were selling at nearly $100. Today they are almost worthless. One longtime Hollywood client said it was "unconscionable" that he was not consulted before Giacchetto bought him $40,000 worth. Other well-known clients lost much more—hundreds of thousands of dollars—in Iridium. "I bought Iridium in part because it was backed by Motorola and was underwritten by Chase Bank, and it turned out to be a disaster," Giacchetto says. "Like five hundred other money managers in America, I believed it to be a good value. That was not in any way outside of what I would have bought for these clients. So I wouldn't have talked to them."

Perhaps the most controversial deal of all, though, was Giacchetto's rescue of Paradise Music & Entertainment, which ended up involving one of the most complicated figures in his life, Jay Moloney, the former CAA agent and Ovitz protégé who committed suicide in November 1999 at the age of thirty-five. According to Bryan Lourd, "Jay was a Pied Piper," whose approval and contacts were invaluable to Giacchetto. After the two met through Marc Glimcher, Moloney took an instant liking to Giacchetto, gave him his money to manage, and introduced him to Ovitz and to the talent manager Rick Yorn, who had inherited Moloney's former client Leonardo DiCaprio. At the time, Yorn was living with *Pulp Fiction* executive producer Stacey Sher (now a partner in Double Feature Films), and they, too, became Giacchetto's clients. Along with the producer Michael Besman and the casting director Margery Simkin, this group recommended him around. He was clearly in good company. "In those days," says the entertainment reporter Josh Young, "if you were hot, you wanted Yorn to baby-sit, Moloney to make your deals, and Dana to manage your money."

Meanwhile, Moloney started to fall apart from manic depression, which he attempted to erase with cocaine. In 1996, he spent more time in rehab than he ever had doing drugs, and during this time, Giacchetto continued to hold his money. In November 1997, while Moloney was staying at the Hazelden rehab center's halfway house in New York, he called Giacchetto with an urgent plea: a drug dealer was threatening him and he needed $6,000 immediately. Without calling anyone else first, Giacchetto personally delivered the money. Moloney took it and went on a four-day drug binge, ending up in a hospital on Long Island after a suicide attempt. Those closest to Moloney have never forgiven Giacchetto. "To me he tried to kill Jay. In fact, he almost killed him," says Moloney's mother, Carole Johnson.

Giacchetto's explanation is that he had no power to deny Moloney's request; Moloney had the right to demand his money, which came from his account with Cassandra. "I didn't have the legal ability to say no at that time. . . . I felt horrible about it, but I don't feel I did anything that I wouldn't have done for someone I loved and cared about. I don't think I was an enabler with Jay. I tried everything to help Jay."

As a result of this episode, Moloney's family and friends moved to put his money into a trust, which he could not get at without permission. Moloney agreed and wrote Giacchetto a formal letter asking for an accounting of his funds, which he wanted transferred to the trust. His holdings were both in art and in funds held by Cassandra. No one knew exactly how much Cassandra held, but it was thought to be between $2 million and $3 million. According to the trustees and their accountant, months went by without their receiving the paperwork. Jerry Chapnick, Moloney's business manager and also a client of Giacchetto's, was enlisted in the cause, but to no avail, according to the trustees. They claim Chapnick stalled; Chapnick, however, maintains that he complied with all their requests promptly.

"Irregularities came up in the beginning, figuring out what resources Jay had left besides art," says Moloney's mother, who administers her son's estate. "The trustees said, 'Where's the money?' And Dana said, 'I don't know. It's here, it's there.' It was a battle back and forth until they got to settle and Dana gave them a check, not on Brown & Company for stock—instead, it was a Cassandra check Dana wrote."

The trustees discovered several private deals that, Giacchetto insists,

Moloney knew about—among them, $25,000 to Ford Models and a contribution to Pickens Capital that originally appeared to be $100,000, then $300,000, then, according to a Cassandra document the trustees saw, $669,000. (When they double-checked with Tom Pickens, they learned that he was reading the total off the same document that the Cassandra Group had provided.) Furthermore, say those involved, a Pickens employee, Rusty Muñoz, told them that the delay of payment resulted from a request from Giacchetto that Moloney's original investment in Pickens Capital be backdated—a request Muñoz told them he had refused. Today, Muñoz says he does not recall any backdating request, and Giacchetto denies it. (Muñoz does recall Giacchetto's promising to raise $50 million for the fund, however, and raising only $5 million.) Finally an accord was reached—Giacchetto gave the trustees a check for $600,000. "Dana made a settlement," says Carole Johnson, "and then calls back and says, 'I think I overpaid. The whole thing is a mistake.'"

Johnson continues, "I don't know how anyone can be that sloppy—it sounds peculiar to me—in that business. If it was a movie producer, I'd say fine, but a stockbroker? No. If an accountant can't tell me how much I spent the last month, and can't tell me how much I have in my account, something's wrong." Giacchetto pleads total ignorance of Johnson's misgivings about the $600,000 payment: "I don't think that's accurate. I think there's some confusion. I think it was settled." Moreover, he says, he had very little to do with his clients' investments in such projects as Pickens Capital. "They were basically deals that were done between the principals but facilitated by our firm." Yet several clients say that they never would have known about or invested in Pickens without Giacchetto's enthusiastic endorsement. (Tom Pickens did not return calls for comment.)

Moloney was never apprised of the difficulties his trustees say they had with Giacchetto. He and Giacchetto continued to remain close, and Giacchetto said he wanted to help his old friend get back to work. In short order, he thought he had found the perfect vehicle for him.

When Giacchetto became involved with Paradise Music & Entertainment, it was a fledgling company consisting of several previously existing small businesses—a creator of advertising jingles and TV and radio scores, a production house that did music videos, and a musical-artist management company. Begun in October 1996, it had gone public three months later, raising about $5.5 million. But the cash had quickly disappeared; much of it was spent on a new music label called Push.

Paradise's savior arrived in December 1998 in the form of Dana Giacchetto. He tried to interest his partners in the Fund in an investment in Paradise, but they turned him down. In addition, he tapped his other major source of capital, the portfolios of Cassandra's largest investors. In mid-December, he invested $2 million of his clients' money in Paradise stock, buying at $1 per share.

Many Cassandra clients bought in: Ben Affleck and Matt Damon each bought 75,000 shares and became known as Giacchetto's clients. Also buying in at $1 a share were Cameron Diaz, Benicio Del Toro, and Lauren Holly; David Salle; Stacey Sher, Margery Simkin, the CAA executive Michelle Kydd, and the screenwriters Akiva Goldsman and Richard LaGravenese; musicians Jakob Dylan and members of Phish; and David Kuhn, the former editor in chief of *Brill's Content* magazine, who bought 25,000 shares. Soledad Bastiancich, who played a role in lining up investors, herself bought 15,000 shares.

Paradise was dramatically transformed in the months following the Cassandra investment. Giacchetto signed on as a consultant to the company, to be paid with 200,000 shares and warrants to buy another 800,000 at varying prices. Since Giacchetto also had the right to vote his clients' stock, he was by far the most important investor in the company and therefore had enormous influence over its stock.

Jesse Dylan, one of the three new members installed by Cassandra on the Paradise board, was named chairman of Paradise in April 1999. Well thought of as a TV advertising director, Dylan sold his two video-commercial businesses to Paradise for a million shares of Paradise stock. (A major reason Dylan entered the deal, says a Paradise board member, was that Giacchetto promised him $40 million of the $100 million in the Chase Fund—an amount Giacchetto's Chase partners said it would have been inconceivable to put in any one place.)

Most dramatic was the announcement of who would become president of the new Paradise: Jay Moloney, who had not held a job in more than two years. Although he was clean, Moloney was still extremely fragile and his original mentor, Michael Ovitz, was dead set against the move. But Giacchetto thought it would be good for Moloney to go to work someplace "under the radar." Within four weeks, Ovitz later told friends, Moloney was so far down he couldn't get out of bed.

In May, in order to lure new investors, Paradise announced that it was going to raise $8 million. By then the stock had begun to rise, trading at between $4 and $5 a share. The famous names involved were clearly part of the draw, and some of the prominent names even popped up in *Daily Variety*. Affleck and Damon, among others, were upset to be used in this way. But Giacchetto failed to see that he was alienating his base. Furthermore, he once again asked the Fund to back Paradise.

In the back of his mind, it seems, Giacchetto envisioned Paradise as evolving into a studio of sorts, where his biggest clients, especially DiCaprio, could make movies or videos and create the kind of equity and value that Giacchetto had always talked about. "It could grow, be aggressive," he says, "grow into a big entertainment company."

Cassandra arranged for all its clients who were interested to buy new Paradise stock at $4.25 a share. New investors included the actors Ben Stiller and Tobey Maguire as well as the artists George Condo and Ross Bleckner. According to Bleckner, "they were going to develop entertainment properties both new and old: films, music, video—whatever." DiCaprio bought 50,000 shares. But even with DiCaprio in, Giacchetto was not able to raise the $8 million. It took him about three months, until July, to raise just over $4 million. Some Cassandra clients who had paid $1 a share the previous December did extremely well by selling out at a profit later in the year. Other clients were not so happy: they told Cassandra that they had not wanted any Paradise stock but found it in their accounts anyway.

One entertainment attorney, who said he had a specific agreement with Giacchetto not to make trades for him without consultation, was irate. "In August, I saw out of nowhere he bought me a load of Paradise Music. That made me crazy. He had sent me the prospectus. It was not a stock I wanted in my portfolio." The lawyer suspected that Giacchetto was desperate. "He really was looking to get rid of the stock."

Another money manager, who had reviewed the offering for some Cassandra clients, had the same experience with someone who ignored his advice and bought the stock. "All this stock was accumulating, and he was selling them a company with absolutely nothing in it." He concluded, "The only way I avoided a legal battle is the stock ramped up one day to seven and they were able to get [my clients] out."

When news spread on the Internet that one of Paradise's founders had composed the Pokémon CD, the stock traded heavily for two days and shot up to $9. At that point, a third client told me, Giacchetto called him to say that he was going to sell half the client's holdings in Paradise. But he never did. "Then I heard he had sold for someone else at nine. He told me and my bookkeeper he couldn't sell the stock because he didn't have the certificates." But it was unclear why the certificates were needed in making a trade. Giacchetto claims that, in this instance, as in all his eleven years as a money manager, "I did everything by the book."

He tells me, "If you're suggesting that there were famous people in the stock [and] that's why it ran up and those people benefited, it's just not true. A lot of my clients are famous, and some made money in the stock and some would lose money in the stock. It was not being manipulated. We bought the stock. We disclosed who the clients were. We sold it when the clients wanted to sell it. I still believe in the stock. Everything I did was copacetic."

At times, Giacchetto's favored clients did not even have to worry about losses. "If you call and say, 'You should have called me on that,'" says commercials producer Mark Hankey, a longtime friend and satisfied client of Giacchetto's from Boston, Cassandra would "make it right." Generous to a fault, Giacchetto gave a client of modest means, the photographer Nubar Alexanian, an outright gift of $20,000 when he had to care for his oldest sister, who was dying of cancer. Giacchetto liked introducing his clients to one another; if they got together on projects, he said, he had more money to invest. For example, he introduced Hankey and Alexanian to the rock band Phish. As a result, Hankey was able to produce a documentary film, and Phish appeared in a book Alexanian published about music. Explaining his approach to me, Giacchetto says, "How can I help you meet people you want to meet in that community? My job is to make you as much money as possible."

Even some of Giacchetto's severest critics concede that he did not set out to line his own pockets at the expense of his clients. In fact, for his most spectacular networking coup, he received absolutely nothing.

In 1998, when Michael Ovitz was reeling from his short, unhappy turn as president of Disney, Giacchetto helped bring him together with the young elite of Hollywood, including Rick Yorn and his sister-in-law Julie. Ovitz wasted no time in luring the Yorns, along with DiCaprio, Diaz, and Minnie Driver, to his latest venture, a move that caused enormous resentment both in Ovitz's former agency, CAA, and in the Yorns' former employer, Industry Entertainment. Although today both Rick Yorn and Ovitz scoff at the idea that Giacchetto was anything more than "a cheerleader" in the formation of their company, AMG, those observing the courtship—from SoHo dinners to cruises on Ovitz's yacht—believe otherwise.

"Would Leo get along with Mike? Everyone was worried," says one close observer. Giacchetto had enormous influence over the sensual young actor—he even read scripts for him. "Being with Dana the last half of '98 and most of '99, you were at the center of power. If you wanted to get Leonardo DiCaprio in a movie, you'd have to go through Dana. If you wanted to talk to Leo, call Dana's house—he lived there. All those people—Tobey Maguire, Q-Tip, Alanis [Morissette]—stayed there. And Dana would have kept them if he'd just invested in blue-chip stocks and never mentioned them in the press."

Last year, Ovitz declared in *Manhattan File* magazine that Giacchetto was not only a financial advisor; he was "a life advisor." Last July, Yorn said to CNN, "He's an incredible money manager and a savvy assessor of artistic talent." Recently, Yorn has acknowledged only that Giacchetto was friendly with DiCaprio for a time but has said that he had no involvement in the actor's career.

It was in October 1998 that Giacchetto became partners with Jeffrey Sachs and Sam Holdsworth in Cassandra–Chase Entertainment Partners (the Fund), a $100 million venture. Sachs, who served in the administrations of New York governors Hugh Carey and Mario Cuomo, had been a financial consultant and lobbyist and gravitated toward glamorous individuals. Rooted in New York Democratic circles, he coached Billy Baldwin on politics and befriended both John Kennedy Jr. and Christopher Cuomo. His PR man, Ken Sunshine, soon replaced DiCaprio's longtime representative, Baker, Winokur, Ryder (BWR).

Sam Holdsworth, forty-six, was the former publisher of *Billboard* magazine and a freelance investor. He had worked with Giacchetto on the deal to sell the Sub Pop music label. Lately, he had been intensely involved in promoting Global Source, a troubled financial-information service with no Internet capability, which became obsolete and lost more than $3 million, much of it coming from Giacchetto's clients.

Sachs had made the original contact to create the Fund with his friend Mitchell Blutt, the second-in-command at Chase Capital Partners. Giacchetto and his partners had no authority to use money independently—all investments had to be approved by Blutt and the bank.

Giacchetto and Sachs soon became close friends. Almost immediately, one observer says, Sachs shed his Dockers for Prada and Blutt, his Wall Street wear for tight jeans as they went out on the town with Giacchetto in New York and Hollywood. Soledad Bastiancich, who remained a Cassandra vice president, quickly became alarmed at what she considered Giacchetto's wild spending, slipshod office administration, and careless bookkeeping in the Cassandra Group.

For example, Jerry Chapnick not only handled Affleck and Damon with Giacchetto but was a client of Cassandra's. Chapnick received a $100,000 loan from Giacchetto against the collateral of his portfolio. When I brought the subject up with Chapnick, he denied that he had ever received such a loan. After a moment's pause he suddenly was able to recall the transaction, insisting, however, "I paid it back in full."

Giacchetto was often out of the office, working on the Fund or out late at night "maintaining Leo," in the words of one executive, and he frequently picked up checks for expensive dinners for fifteen or twenty guests. During the end-of-year holidays in 1997, he and Sachs led a group of thirty—including DiCaprio, Morissette, Jesse Dylan, and Christopher Cuomo—to Havana. "I really think in this community the lines between business and social are blurred—it's delicate," says Giacchetto. In the entertainment world, he adds, business "is not done in a boardroom; it's done at 11:30 after a rock show, or in an airplane, or in the subway, or in an art gallery. . . . I needed to become part of the fabric of the community."

In a letter Bastiancich wrote to Giacchetto in March 1999, she alleged that his travel and entertainment expenses for the previous year had been more than $550,000 and that the Cassandra Group "has had several hundred thousand dollars' worth of trade errors during the past couple of years." Other problems arose when Giacchetto, always seeking to ingratiate himself, allegedly told clients that they had made more money than their monthly statements eventually showed. Clients started to complain. Giacchetto insists nothing untoward was going on. "There is absolutely no hanky-panky, and there never has been." But at times these situations got heated. The British movie director Brian Gibson, for example, threatened legal action; a settlement was reached, but he left Giacchetto.

Blissfully unaware, Giacchetto had spent two weeks in January 1999 visiting DiCaprio on the set of *The Beach* in Thailand. He had big plans for yet another worldwide merchandising deal featuring DiCaprio and other young stars, which he would run. "I do not want to steal your business from you nor do I want to subvert your power in any way," Bastiancich, the girlfriend of a wealthy investor friend of Sachs, said in her letter. Then she suggested that Giacchetto might not really want to "actively trade anymore," and proposed that she become president of the Cassandra Group and that Giacchetto move up to CEO. She also proposed that if her salary was reduced, she might be granted a small share of the profits or equity in Cassandra. "When I was away in Thailand," says Giacchetto, "I thought everyone was working on my cause in the office. When I came back, I realized they didn't feel that way."

In the third week of January, to allay her fears, Bastiancich got Giacchetto's permission to have a securities attorney and forensic accountants come into the office and look at the Cassandra Group's books. In the words of a close observer, "Soledad was having her Al Haig moment: 'I'm in charge here.'" She called a meeting and, according to one participant, brought up the possibility that, after this accounting, Giacchetto might be forced to leave the securities business. (Bastiancich declines to comment on the meeting.) When the expensive accounting was finished two months later, however, no fraud or other criminal wrongdoing was found.

But Giacchetto was advised that he needed to streamline his procedures, to stick to blue-chip investments, and to be careful not to commingle his clients' funds—that is, not to mix clients' assets with the firm's assets or with other clients' assets.

Sachs and Holdsworth claim that since Giacchetto was having cash-flow problems, they lent him $500,000 and $450,000, respectively, to rectify any mistakes uncovered by the audit. Bastiancich left the Cassandra Group after pressuring Giacchetto to give her a six-figure bonus, which she never received.

According to the defamation lawsuit Giacchetto filed against Sachs, Holdsworth, and Egan, he was supposed to give only twenty-five percent of his time to the Fund; Sachs was supposed to give fifty percent of his time, and Holdsworth, seventy-five percent. There was no question that Giacchetto's contacts had fueled the creation of the Fund; but, almost from the beginning, everything that could go wrong did.

The one big investment the Fund took the lead on, Digital Entertainment Network (DEN)—which Giacchetto had had little to do with—quickly became an embarrassment, resulting in a $6.5 million loss for the Fund. The salaries of the company's top eight executives, excluding the three founders, totaled $5 million. In the fall of 1999, on the eve of the launch of their initial public offering, on which investors, including executives at Microsoft and Lazard Frères, hoped to raise $75 million, news leaked to the press that its president, Marc Collins-Rector, had been forced to settle a lawsuit in which he was accused of sexually molesting an underage boy.

Meanwhile, Giacchetto got more and more frustrated as his partners kept nixing deals he came up with. The bank also brought in another partner, Egan, now thirty-seven, an investment banker with no entertainment experience. According to Giacchetto, Egan told him, "You're just trying to help your clients." Giacchetto says he was astounded. "Of course I am! That's why I created the Fund." He was turned down cold by his partners and the bank after bringing Ovitz in for a preliminary discussion on a movie-distribution deal and after proposing a Danny DeVito Internet project. "And I was like, 'What the hell are you doing?'" Giacchetto recounts. "'So you use my client base, in my name, to get this access to everyone in the entertainment business. I don't understand—this is why you [created the Fund].'" He concedes, "So we were going in different paths. We were diametrically opposed."

By the summer of 1999, Giacchetto's partners say, they were getting fed up, scared that his antics would undermine the Fund. Giacchetto couldn't stop talking—to the press, to one client about the business of another, to his colleagues in terms many of them thought were wildly exaggerated. How many plates could he keep spinning before they and he both crashed? Colleagues became concerned about his manic behavior. "I would say the press is his drug. He could not resist it," says Jeffrey Sachs. "It was a combination of Leo and going to work with Chase—the biggest, most respected bank in the world and the biggest movie star in the world."

According to Giacchetto's lawsuit, in August 1999 he was given a talking-to at the Royalton Hotel in New York by Chase honcho Mitchell Blutt, who informed him that his partners wanted to distance the Fund from the Cassandra Group because clients were finding it difficult to distinguish between the two. In September, Giacchetto's partners moved to a space two blocks from the Cassandra offices, taking all the files with them. Within a week Sachs demanded that Giacchetto resign from the Fund, which he refused to do. At the end of October, Sachs and Holdsworth sent a letter to Giacchetto, according to his suit, removing him from the Fund and eventually making him eligible for only eight percent of the business.

Giacchetto has a hard-core group of supporters who feel that the negative publicity that has befallen him was the result of an orchestrated hit. Several days before a December 6, 1999, story appeared in *Daily Variety* announcing that as many as seventeen of Giacchetto's high-profile clients were defecting, there were whispers in the entertainment community that this would be a "career-ending story" for Giacchetto.

Wanting to remain loyal yet ready to be quoted only anonymously, Giacchetto's friends say they are willing to overlook his failings. "There is a whole group of people who feel very, very supportive of Dana," says a prominent New York figure. "All of us acknowledge his shortcomings, his lack of finesse, lack of discretion, and the name-dropping thing. With Dana I never found it obnoxious. He was so out there you don't hold it against him." Another Giacchetto loyalist adds, "Dana is going to pay for everybody's sins."

UPDATE: Less than three weeks after the article appeared, Dana Giacchetto was indicted for securities fraud by the United States attorney's office in Manhattan, for misappropriating $6 million worth of his clients' money, mostly to finance his high-flying life. He was also sued in a civil case by the Securities and Exchange Commission, for diverting $20 million from his clients' accounts and misappropriating more than $4 million of it. His parents mortgaged their house to put up bail, which was revoked. The revocation occurred, about a week after his indictment, when—following a trip to Las Vegas—he was rearrested at Newark Airport with two tickets to Rome in his possession. (He had proposed to his ever-loyal girlfriend and thought that Italy might be a fun place to get married.) At the time, however, he was also carrying $44,000 worth of first-class airline tickets to other destinations, such as Singapore, $4,000 in cash, and a doctored passport. He ended up pleading guilty to one count of securities fraud and was sentenced to nearly five years in jail— but not before sobbing in the courtroom, "I was living in a world of fantasy" and pleading for mercy from the judge, who received a thirty-one-stanza poem from him, entitled "Vive, Vive, Goblum":

Stanza 16

Remember, understand
That a soul is never
Truly responsible, only tempered
By some higher form of
Reason, and to clot,
And to clot.

The judge was not impressed and sentenced Dana Giacchetto to fifty-seven months in an upstate New York prison, where he later charged that he was abused. In August 2001, the SEC announced it had settled its civil suit against him. He agreed to a lifetime ban on working in the securities industry and promised to pay back $14.37 million of misappropriated funds. He also had to pay a fine of $100,000.

The SEC also said that Giacchetto had not been forthcoming about where his clients' missing money went as he dipped into one till to put into another. In fact, the bankruptcy trustee of Giacchetto's Cassandra Company was forced to sue those favored ones to whom Giacchetto had improperly transferred funds. Hardest hit were those that the SEC suspected of being aware they were getting funny money in the first place. *Variety* reported that Rick Yorn settled with the SEC for $610,000, and Richard Lovett, the head of CAA, Jay Moloney's old agency, for $75,000. The SEC was seeking $800,000 from the Maloney estate. Meanwhile, the Web site smokinggun.com said that Cameron Diaz had paid back $100,000 and Alanis Morrisette a mere $1,800. The rock band Phish, which reportedly lost nearly $5 million, took a number of paintings from Giacchetto's valuable art collection.

After six months in a drug rehabilitation halfway house, Giacchetto was released from prison in July 2003, getting time off for good behavior. From now on the federal government will take twenty-five percent of the gross of any money Giacchetto earns outside prison. He continues to say he wants to help artists and is planning a gourmet food business called Taste. Naturally he hopes the debt might be paid off from an authorized biography, now in the works and if a movie deal happens, perhaps all his old clients and former friends can play themselves. Get me Leo!

King Harrod: Mohamed Fayed

"They think I'm a wog."

September 1995

One day in May 1995, Harrods chairman Mohamed Al Fayed, flashing a megawatt smile, was gleefully throwing his dough around. The flamboyant Egyptian owner of the London retail landmark and the fabled Ritz Hotel in Paris, had put on chef's toque to toss pizzas for the cameras. Journalists had been invited to sample the wares in the new pizzeria in Harrods' famous Food Halls. At the time, Fayed was celebrating a victory in his ongoing battle with John Major's government to obtain British citizenship for himself and his brother Ali: he had just gained the right to appeal the government's refusal to allow them to become citizens. A few days later, Fayed was in media heaven again—photographed with the queen herself at the Royal Windsor Horseshow, which Harrods sponsors. One can only imagine what officials in Major's scandal-rocked administration were thinking as they watched the antics from the man who has accused them of accepting his payoffs in return for favors rendered and has now announced his plans to overthrow them because they have spurned him.

The previous October, in a fury over the stalled citizenship applications, Fayed disclosed the names of three ministers in Major's administration who, he alleged, had taken cash from him (or had stayed free at the Ritz) in exchange for asking questions on his behalf in Parliament. According to Andrew Neil, a former London *Sunday Times* editor, who is pro-Fayed, "He feels very bitter. The younger Tories were happy to take his largesse, to take his suites at the Ritz, but this government has stayed in power so long. . . . They decided, we don't need Mohamed Al Fayed anymore." Neil adds that he thinks England needs "another hundred Al Fayeds. So he comes from the wrong side of the tracks; so does Mrs. Thatcher."

The film producer David Putnam, who got half of the $6 million to produce his Academy Award winner *Chariots of Fire* from Fayed, agrees. "Mohamed is somebody who works on an old-fashioned system: favors done, favors received. . . . For ten or twelve years the government said, 'Anything goes.' . . . What I find unfair is that what Mohamed's accused of is an everyday occurrence in London."

Fayed's life story is right out of Aladdin or Ali Baba. The characters include global fixers and dealers who think nothing of trying to destabilize countries, seduce the world's wealthiest man, sue whomever whenever, buy the press, and wage private wars. This tale takes place in the habitat of the offshore superrich, complete with yachts and jets, where friends become enemies, enemies become friends, and the enemy of my enemy is my friend. Truth here is rather like a Platonic ideal—it must remain an abstraction.

I met Fayed last fall, in his heavily scented office in Harrods, which he bought ten years ago, with the help of Thatcher and the Tories, in a coup of incredible audacity. Peeking around a giant teddy bear, he told me, "The more good you give, the more angels guide you, protect you. The more terrible, the more dishonor for you." Since then, the angels have been playing hard to get. The government's rejection of the Fayed brothers' petition for citizenship (without explanation) was a stunning rebuff, and it appears that the establishment has made up its mind: those he most wants to impress—the British upper class—have decided to give him the cold shoulder. "Nobody quite accepts him," admits a friend of his, former *Daily Express* executive editor Alan Frame. "We're still a class-ridden society. He sponsors lots of things involving the royal family, and he's still not accepted."

As the aggrieved merchant prince himself told me later, Fayed sees himself as the victim of the worst British snobbery: "The devastating thing is the class system, created by people who think they are above the rest of the human race," he says. "They think they can shit just on anyone. They think I'm a wog."

For two-plus decades, Mohamed Al Fayed, who is sixty-six but says he's sixty-two, has lived in London as an unabashed Anglophile guided by a simple Middle Eastern motto: To give is to receive—whether it be presents, favors, or influence. Charming in public, he is privately phobic about germs and fanatical about loyalty. Surrounded by bodyguards, he often conducts business on a cellular phone in a tent pitched on the lawn of his country estate in Oxted, Surrey. His fervent love for Britannia goes hand in hand with his strings-attached mode of generosity: political pay-offs, Parisian junkets for journalists, toys for their children, and Harrods Christmas baskets to half of *Debrett's Peerage*.

On the Continent, his long-sought-for status is assured. On display in his office is a citation from the Italian government, and France gave him the Légion d'Honneur after he restored not only the Ritz but also the for-mer home, in the Bois de Boulogne, of the duke and duchess of Windsor. On the far wall of the office are four "warrants" to supply boots and sad-dles, housewares, linens, and other goods to the British royal family. Har-rods, after all, is the second-greatest tourist attraction in London, after Big Ben, and Fayed has announced that when he dies, he wants to be mummified and entombed on the roof.

Although Fayed lives luxuriously, he carries a staggering amount of debt and spends prodigiously. The losses on the Ritz through 1993, for example, totaled 1.2 billion francs ($212 million). Nevertheless, Fayed prides himself on owning world-class status symbols and maintaining the highest level of service. Generations of English schoolboys have gotten their hair cut at Harrods, which will order anything, from a castle to a Learjet, for grown-ups. But before Fayed bought the vast Knightsbridge store—the largest department store in Europe—it was a fading institu-tion, where toilet paper was sold on the first floor. Fayed has poured many millions into restoration, installing the Room of Luxury and the Egyptian Hall, with his own face carved on the sphinxes around the molding. He has upgraded the toy department, opened restaurants, and recently, as the British retail market has sagged, introduced a more affordable line of Harrods private-label apparel.

At the Ritz—which was founded by the master hotel manager César Ritz in 1898 and which has catered to Garbo and Hemingway, Rocke-fellers and royalty—no expense has been spared; indeed, the red ink has flowed to keep up the 187-room establishment as the finest hotel in the world. Leaky pipes were torn out, the antiquated heating system was replaced, every room was redecorated. Today, guests can luxuriate in theme suites—the Cocteau, the Chopin, the Chanel. The Imperial Suite, overlooking the Place Vendôme, costs more than $10,000 a night. Fayed has also added an underground swimming pool, a culinary school, and a nightclub for the Ritz clientele: "people who care for nothing but the best."

Just in case a foreign visitor might not intuit the level of aspiration that seeks to become reality here in the heart of the Empire of Fayed, Harrods' dashing director of public affairs, Michael Cole—his master's voice—is superb at interpreting. Tall, silver-haired, and silver-tongued, the onetime BBC-TV royal reporter (who lost his post after leaking the queen's 1987 Christmas message during a festive holiday lunch) is quite a contrast to the short, balding Fayed, who, for all his ambition, struggles to read and write the language of his adopted land. Theirs is a symbiotic relationship: one knows how to parse and one holds the purse.

Cole is a magician of royal spin. The first day I spoke with him, he introduced me to Harrods' most beloved veteran, an elderly green-suited messenger who delivers, to all the little royals, gifts from "Uncle Mohamed." Cole declared, "If it weren't for Rodney, the princes might not even know there was a Father Christmas!" Another time, Cole called me from his car phone and began speaking as if he were back filing a BBC report: "At a £200,000- [$312,000-] party at Spencer House given by Lord Rothschild but paid for by Gulfstream, the Princess of Wales arrived, stunning in a beaded dress. She ignored everyone else and went straight up to Mohamed and said, 'I didn't know you were rich enough to have one of those planes!' Mohamed said, 'At your disposal, whenever you wish.' Diana is so easygoing with Mohamed. . . . Mohamed is not one of those who's overwhelmed by her. They spark off each other very well."

Cole encouraged me to call other friends of Fayed's, naming General Norman Schwarzkopf, *New York Times* publisher Arthur ("Punch") Sulzberger, financier Ted Forstmann, and cosmetics mogul Estée Lauder, who, Cole claims, Mohamed bounces on his knee. Many believe Fayed would like someday to be Lord Al Fayed. "I don't want that," Fayed protested when I spoke with him. "But they didn't also say thank you for everything I have done. It's the opposite. They just could shit on me, everyone."

Fayed was perched restlessly on the edge of his seat, wearing ankle boots with zippers on the sides and a plaid sports coat. "I did it to take my revenge, to show people who really runs this country, what quality they are. . . . These days it's only the trash people." He was referring to his disclosure last October of the names of ministers who, he claimed, had received favors from him. When Fayed made these charges, British newspapers reported that he might bring down the government. Several weeks before the scandal broke, Major had received a warning—via a newspaper editor—of Fayed's allegations and was told that Fayed wanted a meeting to discuss withdrawing or revising a report released in 1990 by the Department of Trade and Industry (known as the DTI report) that accused Fayed of lying about his past and making fraudulent claims about his fortune.

When a member of Parliament asked Major if Fayed was attempting to blackmail the government, Major appeared to give credence to the charge by saying that the matter had been referred to the director of public prosecutions for investigation. Fayed was later cleared of any wrongdoing and demanded an apology, which has not been forthcoming. Today, Fayed continues to insist that the British government was indeed for sale—"like selling me ice cream," he told me. Michael Cole quickly rushed in: "Mohamed said, 'I'm a merchant. They came to me. I sell ice cream, I sell sausages. They came selling MP's.'"

Fayed's fury was stoked, he says, because he was given assurances that his and his brother's citizenship applications would pass. The government calls that claim "rubbish." The British petition for citizenship requires, among other things, that the applicant be eighteen or over, have up to five years' residence, and be of sound mind and "good character." Regarding character, the British civil service is bound to respect the conclusions of the DTI report, which was written by two prominent "inspectors," Sir Henry Brooke, who is now a High Court judge, and Hugh Aldous, who is now the managing partner of a prestigious accounting firm.

"The Fayeds dishonestly misrepresented their origins, their wealth, their business interests and their resources," the DTI report states early on. More than seven hundred pages later, it ends, "Mohamed Fayed and his success in 'gagging' the Press created . . . a new fact: that lies were the truth and that the truth was a lie." A vehement denial issued by Fayed at the time said that the report was "worthless" and "shocking." The fact that no action was ever taken against him by the British government, he asserts, proves that there was no wrongdoing. His enemies, on the other hand, charge the government with a massive cover-up to protect him.

When Fayed and his two brothers, Ali and Salah, suddenly burst onto the scene in 1984 to buy Harrods, they said they came from an old, rich Egyptian cotton-growing family. The DTI report later documented that Fayed was actually the firstborn son of a humble schoolteacher and grew up in the slums of Alexandria. The report also claimed that the Fayeds were not remotely wealthy enough to have used their own money to put up the $700-million cash bid to buy House of Fraser, Harrods' parent company, a vast department-store chain extending from Scotland to Scandinavia. The report suggested that the money had come from the sultan of Brunei, without his knowledge. Fayed maintains that the money was his.

.   .   .

Lord McAlpine, a longtime confidant of Margaret Thatcher's who was Conservative Party treasurer, used to visit Fayed regularly. Fayed says that McAlpine accepted £250,000 ($367,000) in political contributions from him between 1985 and the election year of 1987, when it was announced that the DTI was going to investigate Fayed. (British law does not require disclosure of political contributions from individuals.) Lord McAlpine acknowledges several Fayed donations to Conservative causes but not specific amounts, adding, "He would have been sent a thank-you note and a receipt from me. Ask him to show you the receipts."

Alistair McAlpine responds to the Fayed brothers' charges of snobbery and racism by saying, "Then why do they want to live here? I feel very sympathetic towards Al Fayed. I feel he's been very badly treated, but it's largely their own fault. They get misunderstood; they try too hard. I can't fathom why they *want* British citizenship."

"Do you know what 'wog' stands for?" asks Lord Wyatt, another Thatcher confidant who has attacked Fayed in print. "Wily Oriental gentleman." Woodrow Wyatt calls the whole business "absolute nonsense." He says that Fayed's attacks are a result of his losing his case in a unanimous decision in September 1994 at the European Court of Human Rights, in Strasbourg—the final stage in a futile attempt to have the DTI report erased. "The government said no, and it sort of drives them dotty. It remains a slur on their character."

The DTI investigation was ordered in 1987, a full two years after Fayed's petition to buy Harrods was hastily waved through the Thatcher government in just ten days, without careful scrutiny. Fayed believes the probe came about through the ceaseless, vengeful efforts of the man he had outwitted to win the store, the equally eccentric Roland W. ("Tiny") Rowland, then chairman of the conglomerate Lonrho, which is based on mining and agricultural interests in Africa.

After the face-off, Rowland hired private detectives to comb the world to uncover whatever incriminating facts they could about Fayed. Using the best investigative reporting that his money could buy, including the resources of his own newspaper, *The Observer*, he flooded the establishment with a series of detailed reports depicting his rival as a liar who had bought off the government and a con artist who had used the sultan of Brunei's money to buy Harrods.

Michael Cole, however, continues to define his boss as a wronged and selfless hero who has been consistently victimized. "He thinks he did the right thing for this country. He has a *very* developed sense of morality. Of course, he wouldn't call it that," Cole says. "He's so used to being slapped in the face he doesn't even think about it. . . . All he's interested in is his good family name and reputation, his children, and his own health and happiness. He doesn't look for praise. He has his own foundation to relieve real suffering—he thinks it's his *sacred* duty. He has a very personal relationship with his God." Cole sighs. "I sometimes think this is a charity with a business attached."

"Enter a different world," Harrods' longtime slogan beckoned. With Mohamed Al Fayed (the "Al" was added in the 1970s) at the helm, it is a darkly suspicious world with laws unto itself. Fayed, who spent hundreds of millions of dollars refurbishing Harrods, has visibly tightened security and has had five managing directors. He is embroiled in numerous cases brought for unfair dismissal, and he is accused of enforcing HIV tests, bugging employees' phones, and making unwanted advances toward a fleet of comely assistants, according to a former employee. It is, says former Harrods deputy chairman Christoph Bettermann, "management by fear."

Fayed has a personal security staff of thirty-eight—two teams that alternate, one week on, one week off, at his residence at 60 Park Lane, at his castle in Scotland, and at his country house in Oxted, where his family lives. (Mohamed is married to a Finnish woman named Heini, whom he met in the 1970s. They have four children, aged eight to fourteen, but are rarely seen in public together. The union is considered volatile.) His "close-protection team" consists of eight or ten. One assumes that the millions of dollars this security costs and the level of his apparent paranoia, which extends to wearing only clip-on ties so that he cannot be strangled, must mean that Fayed's life is under constant threat. Not so, according to half a dozen former guards I interviewed, who say that his security is mainly for show.

"He modeled himself after whatever the prime minister of the day used," says Bill Dunt, a guard for three and a half years, who says he was fired after being accused of speaking to a female guest and who accepted an out-of-court settlement of his unfair-dismissal suit. "If the prime minister used a Rover fastback, he would. If they changed to a Ford Scorpio, he'd change. It's part of trying to get into the establishment." Like the president of the United States, who has a military aide to carry nuclear-launch codes in a soft black leather bag, Fayed had guards travel back and forth between Switzerland and England with his hard silver box, which contained unspecified floppy disks.

Fayed's building at 60 Park Lane contains fifty apartments, which he uses for his family, staff, and guests. He also owns the adjoining number 55, consisting of apartments for rent, as well as a building around the corner on South Street. All three buildings are connected to the Dorchester Hotel—which Fayed purchased for the sultan of Brunei—by a series of secret passageways and an elaborate alarm system. One man who was being interviewed for a job at Park Lane was ushered into a waiting room and heard the click of a lock as the secretary left the room and closed the door. After about twenty minutes, the man looked up to see some bookcases that he had thought were built into the wall suddenly swing open and Fayed walk through them, hand outstretched.

Guards say that bugging equipment is kept in a basement room on the corner of South Street and Park Lane. In addition, says Dunt, "everybody who calls Fayed at 60 Park Lane is recorded, and all telephone calls in and out of the building are logged on a computer." Harrods' management offices are regularly swept for bugs and wiretaps. Another former guard, Russ Conway, told me that he personally bugged meetings at Harrods. Employees' phones were also tapped. A former Harrods executive, newly hired, watched a guard come into his office every afternoon, open a panel in the wall, and take out what looked like a videotape and replace it with another one. Curious, he discovered a tiny video camera trained on his desk.

In 1990, Christoph Bettermann became Fayed's number two, the deputy chairman of Harrods. He had worked for Fayed in Dubai since 1984. In April 1991, Bettermann was approached by an American headhunter to work in the Arab emirate of Sharjah, and almost immediately, he tells me, Fayed said to him, "I hear you are leaving me." In June, says Bettermann, "he showed me a written transcript of a phone conversation between the headhunter and me. He accused me of breaking our trust by talking to these people. I told him, 'If you don't trust me, I resign. I cannot trust you if you bugged my phone.'" Bettermann quit Harrods and took the oil-company job in Sharjah.

Fayed promptly wrote the ruler of Sharjah, accusing Bettermann of stealing large sums of money. Bettermann was cleared by three courts in which Fayed had pressed charges, but Bettermann's defense cost him $160,000. "Fayed has every law firm in London sewed up. It was intimidating," Bettermann says. "Fayed charms you at first. Once you do not turn out the way he wants, you're the bad guy, and he tries to get rid of you, sometimes in appalling ways."

Bettermann's wife, Francesca, who was Harrods' legal counsel, resigned when her husband did. "The most common thing at Harrods was unfair dismissal," she says. "We had a huge amount." Last year Harrods was facing thirty-two such cases, compared with two at Selfridge's department store, which has a similar number of employees. "The law says you can't fire people without cause. Mohamed says, 'I can, as long as I pay for it.'" Francesca Bettermann adds, "He settles them all. He has never gotten into the witness box. I think he'd be very frightened to go to court." Yet even when his lawyers told him that he couldn't win, she claims, he'd say, "Sue. Sue anyway."

When Francesca Bettermann was hired, she had to take an HIV test— a number of women working close to the chairman had to undergo full internal exams and be grilled on their entire gynecological histories—and her handwriting was analyzed. (In 1994, three former employees of Harrods claimed that they were given HIV tests although they had specifically withheld permission to be screened. Michael Cole says it was the doctor's fault. The doctor has blamed the medical lab.) Fayed has a phobia about germs. He does not eat out except on rare occasions, and eats only what his personal cook prepares for him. Each plate he eats from must be boiled and rimmed with a cut lime to disinfect it. When he helicopters from his country house to London, he wears a gas mask so that he won't inhale fumes. He also keeps a supply of wet wipes available so that after shaking hands he can wipe his own.

He does not abide smoking. Revlon chairman Ronald Perelman showed up to meet Fayed in his office several years ago with his trademark cigar stuck between his teeth. According to an observer, before Fayed shook hands or said a word to Perelman, he yanked the cigar out of his mouth and threw it against a wall.

The boss's strong likes and dislikes quickly become apparent to those who work closely with him. "He likes a pretty face. He wouldn't hire someone who was ugly. He likes them light skinned, well educated, English, and young," says Francesca Bettermann. "I remember there was something on the application that said, 'Your color, race . . .' I said, 'You're not allowed to put that on the form,' and he said, 'Well, make sure they put the proper photos in, then.'" Meanwhile, *The Guardian* reported that a Harrods spokesman said, "Mohamed Al Fayed is very aware of the evils of racism. He hates racial discrimination in all its forms, and he would not entertain anybody working for him who might decide they should start acting this way."

According to former employees, Fayed regularly walked the store on the lookout for young, attractive women to work in his office. Some were asked to go to Paris with him. Good-looking women were given gifts and cash bonuses almost before they understood that they were being compromised. "Come to Papa," he would say. "Give Papa a hug." Those who rebuffed him would often be subjected to crude, humiliating comments about their appearance or dress. A dozen former employees I spoke with said that Fayed would chase secretaries around the office and sometimes try to stuff money down women's blouses. A succession of women were offered the use of a free apartment in Park Lane or a luxury car.

Former Harrods workers can tell Fayed stories late into the night. He would brandish sex toys at male visitors and ask them about their health. He bought several of Liberace's pianos and ordered a painting of Harrods on Waikiki Beach, by the actor Tony Curtis, to be reproduced for sale. Then there is Salah Fayed, the peculiar third brother, code-named by security guards "the fruit bat" because he came out only at night. Salah, who lives in Egypt, has not applied for British citizenship; indeed, he is no longer even a director of Harrods. Salah once bought two eighteen-inch miniature horses, one for one of Mohamed's daughters and one for himself, which he would walk on a leash down Park Lane. When Mohamed found out, he ordered Salah's horse to be removed.

There's an old Arab saying, "Find out what a man wants and give it to him." Mohamed Al Fayed never forgot it. From his early boyhood in the Gomrok slum in Alexandria—not far from the exclusive yacht club—he has tracked the rich. After a flamboyant, checkered early career, he ended up as a commissions agent and middleman for one of the world's wealthiest men, Mahdi Al Tajir—the right hand of Sheikh Rashid of Dubai. But they had a falling-out. "He was a bagman. Your role as a bagman is exactly that. You owe ninety percent of the money to those who bag what you're carrying," says the financial journalist Michael Gillard, who professionally has been both a friend and a foe of Fayed's. "If you do enough deals and the deals are big enough, you can make hundreds of millions of dollars."

In 1979, Fayed renewed an acquaintance with the chairman of Lonrho, Tiny Rowland, whom he met in the early 1970s. He began to feed business reporters from Rowland's *Observer* leads for stories on bribes and corruption among his enemies in the Persian Gulf. He and Rowland used to breakfast together, and Terry Robinson, Lonrho's former director responsible for its House of Fraser holdings, remembers that Fayed always seemed obsessed with sex. "He'd thrust on Tiny all these sex toys. He'd come back from breakfast laden with devices."

Born Roland Walter Fuhrhop in a German internment camp in India during World War I, Tiny had made a fortune in Africa by 1979 and held a 29.9 percent stake in the House of Fraser department stores, which owns Harrods. Lonrho frequently expressed interest in buying all of

Fraser, but had been ruled against by the British Monopolies and Mergers Commission. When Fayed, whom Rowland nicknamed Tootsie, offered to buy Lonrho's shares in House of Fraser, Rowland believed he had found a perfect place to park the stock until he could find a way to acquire the whole company himself.

Like Fayed, Rowland was a self-invented outsider who sought to be more English than the English. Elegant, amoral, charismatic, and six feet two, he was condemned in Africa for bringing to that continent a way of doing business that depended on payoffs and the granting of favors. In Britain, where he was educated (as well as detained and jailed during World War II as a German sympathizer), he was adored by Lonrho shareholders but scorned by the establishment.

Rowland had a vast network of contacts and close personal relationships with African leaders. He knew things before anyone else. "Rowland could never be prosecuted in this country," Michael Cole claims. "Within a half hour he could say enough to destroy the British Commonwealth. He's the man who knows too much." I asked Cole if Rowland's information was correct. "Yes. He knows everything." (Ironically, Cole denies most of what Rowland alleges about Fayed.) But for all his savvy, Rowland underestimated the wily Egyptian.

The purchase of Harrods came at a propitious moment in Fayed's life. He had ingratiated himself with the richest man on earth, His Majesty Sultan Haji Hassanal Bolkiah Mu'Izzaddin Waddaulah, the sultan of Brunei. Fayed told me that he had known the sultan as a little boy and his father before him. He also said they got to know each other over a discussion about building a trade center in Brunei. Tiny Rowland gave the DTI another explanation. Fayed had told him that he negotiated an introduction to the sultan for $500,000 plus a piece of the action of any resulting business with a hustling, globe-trotting Indian holy man, Shri Chandra Swamiji Maharaj, known as the Swami.

The Swami, a heavyset former scrap-metal dealer once detained in jail on fraud charges, is today a power broker in New Delhi with close ties to Indian prime minister P. V. Mrasimha Rao; he has numbered Imelda Marcos and Elizabeth Taylor among his followers. He was especially sought-after once he became "spiritual advisor" to the sultan's second wife, Mariam, a former flight attendant, in the course of predicting (incorrectly) that she would give birth to a son. When I asked Fayed about his association with the Swami, he laughed and said that they had met only once.

Beginning in the summer of 1984, Fayed received several powers of attorney and written authorizations from the sultan to carry out certain tasks, which gave him legal access to large sums of the sultan's cash. Two mandates to act on the sultan's behalf were given on August 20, 1984, and were to be used to cancel two previous contracts for the construction of a luxury yacht. Another, dispensed three days later and naming Fayed "our personal and official Financial Advisor," was issued to retrieve nearly $100 million the sultan had advanced to a Swiss businessman, Carl Hirschmann. Hirschmann was to have customized for the sultan a stretch 747 jet with several bedrooms and stalls so that the sultan could fly nonstop from Brunei to London with his polo ponies. They were trying to find out what to do about the horses' urine when Fayed reportedly persuaded the sultan to dump Hirschmann. Hirschmann's son was detained in Brunei until $86 million of the sultan's money was returned to a bank account Fayed would have control over. In addition, according to the DTI report, another $200 million of the sultan's on deposit for the design of the yacht was transferred away from the marine designer's control by Fayed "once he had himself been granted appropriate authority by the Sultan."

In June 1984, say the inspectors, the Fayed brothers had £50.5 million ($69 million) on deposit, "whatever its original source," in the Royal Bank of Scotland. But in the next two months, Mohamed was also busy incorporating two holding companies as receptacles for the brothers' assets in Liechtenstein and traveling between Brunei and London acquiring the powers of attorney from the sultan. During that same period, according to the DTI report, the three Fayed brothers' bank, the Royal Bank of Scotland, received a sudden transfer of hundreds of millions of dollars from Switzerland into the Fayeds' accounts. Fayed has never really explained where this money came from; the bank assumed it belonged to the sultan. However, Fayed told the bank that his portfolio was separate from the sultan's. It may be no more than a coincidence that this vast increase in disposable wealth followed quickly on the admission of Mohamed to the sultan's confidence.

By November, Fayed had struck a deal with Rowland to buy his House of Fraser shares for £138 million ($171 million). Rowland incorrectly assumed that the shares would be safely parked if he let Fayed have them, because he was sure that Tootsie didn't have the capital to acquire more. "I sold because I wanted him to keep the stock," Rowland told me. "I've made many mistakes in my life, but the worst was I trusted him!"

Almost immediately, Fayed demanded that Rowland leave the House of Fraser board and went behind Rowland's back to court the House of Fraser chairman, Professor Roland Smith, who received a handsome retroactive bonus from Fayed once the latter obtained ownership.

Rowland also wrongly believed that if Fayed made a bid to buy a controlling interest in House of Fraser, it would never get past government investigation. "We were in the right place at the right time," says Michael Cole. "They'd let *anybody* buy it who wasn't Rowland."

Next, the little-known Fayeds and their new advisors had to convince the government and the public that they controlled enough assets to be able to hand over $700 million for controlling interest in the company. It required the family to invent a history of old money; overnight they became "fabulous pharaohs." The Fayeds were represented by the investment bankers Kleinwort Benson and the law offices of Herbert Smith, two old-line British firms that basically accepted at face value what the Fayeds told them. "Remember," said Kleinwort's John MacArthur, "Kohlberg Kravis Roberts was buying out RJR Nabisco on bus tickets. It was go-go time."

The Fayeds' bankers submitted a now discredited one-and-a-half-page summary of their assets, which the British government accepted. On November 2, Kleinwort issued a press release about its new clients: the Fayeds were an "old established Egyptian family who for more than 100 years were ship owners, land owners and industrialists in Egypt." To this day, the brothers are said to have been "raised by British nannies, educated in British schools and unabashed admirers of British history, traditions and ethics." With a couple of notable exceptions, the press swallowed the story whole.

"Statements about the sources of their great wealth and about the scale of their businesses formed part of their central story," wrote the DTI inspectors later. "If people had known, for instance, that they only owned one luxury hotel; that their interests in oil exploration consortia were of no current value; that their banking interests consisted of less than 5 percent of the issues share capital of a bank and were worth less than $10 million; that they had no current interests in construction projects; that far from being 'leading shipowners in the liner trade' they only owned two roll-on roll-off 1600 ton cargo ferries; if all these facts had been known people would have been less disposed to believe that the Fayed really owned the money they were using to buy HOF."

Fayed entertained the wowed House of Fraser board at the opulent 60 Park Lane and flew the Harrods manager over to the Ritz. American public relations advisors were hired—never knowing whether they were being paid by the sultan or Fayed—to broadcast the sultan's good works. Sir Gordon Reece, one of Margaret Thatcher's kitchen Cabinet and her TV-image advisor, who was also advising Fayed, was provided with a Park Lane apartment.

In January 1985, Fayed received another power of attorney to quietly purchase the Dorchester Hotel for the sultan. On January 29, Fayed accompanied the sultan to 10 Downing Street to visit Thatcher. The pound at that time was in drastic decline, threatening the economy, and the sultan, who had moved £5 billion ($5.6 billion) of assets out of sterling, did Britain a grand favor. He moved it back in. Fayed has taken credit for the assist and also for persuading the sultan to give British defense industries a half a billion pounds ($560 million) in contracts.

On March 4, 1985, the Fayeds announced a formal cash offer for House of Fraser of £615 million ($689 million), which Kleinwort claimed was untethered by any borrowings. The financing of the Fayeds' bid has been the source of intense scrutiny, and while no one, including Fayed, has supplied a comprehensive account, some numbers have emerged. According to the DTI report, by October 1984 the Fayeds had at their disposal at least $600 million in the Royal Bank of Scotland and in a Swiss bank.

"We were not told the source of any of these funds or given a credible story as to how and where they were obtained," said the inspectors. Tiny Rowland claimed that the architect behind the sultan's 1,788-room palace, Enrique Zobel, had said that Fayed controlled $1.2 billion in yet another joint account with His Royal Highness. Whatever the amount, the huge pile of cash the Fayeds claimed as their own was apparently used as collateral in order to guarantee more than £400 million ($480 million) to buy House of Fraser.

"If you have a company with tremendous assets like Harrods," Fayed told me, "you have no problem. You don't need to use cash." That first loan, drawn on a Swiss bank, was then quickly replaced with another loan, secured by House of Fraser shares. Thus, within a short period of time, it seems, the Fayeds owned House of Fraser and didn't have any of their own money in it.

"Nobody's been able to find out whose money is behind the purchase, because of secrecy laws of Swiss banking codes," asserts Terry Robinson, who spent nearly two months researching the Fayeds' accounts for Lonrho. "The DTI inspectors tried, and sought British-government assistance. The Swiss will cooperate, but it has to be on a government-to-government basis. The British government refused the inspectors' request. That, to me, is the fishy side of things." The inspectors were thus denied definitive proof, but said they were left to conclude "that this was somebody else's money." Further, "the conclusion that the money was derived from [Fayed's] association with the sultan looks not only possible but probable."

Tiny Rowland wrote Thatcher's trade minister, Norman Tebbit, a seven-plus-page letter repudiating the Fayeds' story, according to Tom Bower, who wrote an unauthorized biography of Rowland. A full-scale press battle began. Brian Basham, a slick PR advisor whom Kleinwort brought in for the Fayeds, was spinning pro-Fayed pieces while Tiny Rowland sought to influence his newspaper, *The Observer*. On Sunday night, March 10, on national television, John MacArthur of Kleinwort blithely reiterated that the Fayeds were worth "several billion dollars." Yet he also admitted, "I have got no statement of their consolidated financial position." The next morning the Fayeds bought more than fifty percent of House of Fraser.

Fayed issued what was later referred to in the DTI report as a "gagging" writ, a libel suit against *The Observer* for a story it ran on March 10. Whenever any newspaper deviated from the Fayed version, similar writs were threatened or issued. Virtually all critical reporting outside *The Observer* stopped.

On March 14 the government issued a press release announcing that it would not refer the Fayeds' bid to the Monopolies and Mergers Commission. The bloody battle was over. The Fayeds owned Harrods. But the war had just begun.

Between 1985 and 1993, Tiny Rowland relentlessly pursued Mohamed Al Fayed. "Anyone who fell out with Mohamed knew where to go," says the journalist Michael Gillard.

Rowland's suspicions had been further aroused when, just a few hours before the House of Fraser announcement on March 14, 1985, Fayed showed up at 10 Downing Street for a reception in honor of President Hosni Mubarak of Egypt, whom he had never met. According to Bower's biography, the invitation had been arranged by Mubarak's and Mrs. Thatcher's mutual advisor, Gordon Reece, who, several people told me, kept his free Park Lane apartment courtesy of Fayed from the spring of 1985 until the summer of 1994. (Reece denies both claims.) Since then, according to former Harrods employees, the Egyptian president's family has enjoyed Fayed's hospitality at Harrods, and while Mubarak's son was living in London, his apartment was decorated by Fayed.

After the controversy generated by the House of Fraser affair, business relations between Fayed and the sultan suddenly ceased. On April 25, 1985, the sultan and Fayed terminated, by mutual agreement, all powers of attorney given to Fayed since 1984. Publicly the sultan has always denied that his money was used for the House of Fraser purchase. "What the sultan says . . . is that if any of his money was used in the purchase of the House of Fraser, it was without his knowledge and consent," explained the sultan's public relations advisor Lord Chalfont in 1989.

In a 1988 article in *Forbes* by Pranay Gupte, it was first reported that the Swami and the sultan had met in Singapore in 1985 to discuss ways of getting back part of the $900 million the sultan had "entrusted" to Fayed. Acting on behalf of the sultan, the Swami persuaded Fayed to meet with him on June 6 and 7, 1985, in a rented apartment at 1 Carlos Place in Mayfair, and the meetings were secretly tape-recorded. On these infamous "Carlos Place tapes"—partly in Hindi, partly in broken English, but mostly gibberish—which the DTI subsequently had authenticated by an audio lab, Fayed brags to the Swami about his influence with both Mrs. Thatcher and the sultan. Gupte, who speaks Hindi, and Gillard, both of whom have interviewed Fayed, told me that the voice on the tapes is unmistakably Fayed's. Fayed once swore in an affidavit—and still avers today—that the tapes are not authentic.

To Rowland, however, the tapes were just the smoking gun he had been looking for. Once he found out about them from Fayed's old enemy, Adnan Khashoggi, he flew to New York, where he met the Swami in Khashoggi's forty-fifth-floor duplex, and then to Canada, where the tapes were stashed, to listen to them. Later, a delegation from Lonrho met the Swami aboard Khashoggi's yacht in Antibes and paid $2 million for the tapes. The transcript of the tapes yielded Rowland a 185-page peccadillo-laden biography of Fayed, printed privately and sent "to anybody who was qualified"—eighty thousand copies. The work was called "A Hero from Zero," which is how the Swami described Fayed at Carlos Place, and it caused a sensation.

When I visited Rowland at his posh town house on Chester Square last November, the silver-haired titan casually picked up a phone and promptly got through to "His Holiness," the Swami, at his ashram in India. His Holiness would be interviewed only in person. Then Rowland made another call and handed me the phone. I was talking to Khashoggi— on the record.

"The tapes are authentic. The Swami taped him on the sultan's orders," Khashoggi said. "In my mind he definitely, officially bought Harrods with the sultan's money. I saw the agreement. He gave the sultan £300 million [$390 million] back." Did the sultan show you the agreement? I asked. "No. The sultan showed it to the Swami, and the Swami showed it to me."

Khashoggi and Fayed have a long history. They got to know each other in the early 1950s, when Fayed was married to Samir Khashoggi's sister, whom he had met on the beach in Alexandria. She gave birth to a son,

Dodi. Today, Dodi Fayed, who had a producer's credit on *Chariots of Fire*, continues to function in the film business. Khashoggi claims that at the time of their meeting, Fayed was a Singer sewing machine salesman who had previously sold Coca-Cola. Khashoggi gave him a job coordinating furniture deliveries for a company he owned. "He started making side deals to put fees in his hands," Khashoggi claims. Fayed says that Khashoggi worked for him, and that he couldn't take Khashoggi's stealing and gambling away his money. "It was such a dirty family."

In fact, Khashoggi's father was the doctor of the late Saudi Arabian king Abdul-Aziz. According to Fayed and Michael Cole, however, Khashoggi's father was merely "a nurse orderly" who injected the old king so that he could perform sexually with the virgins who were brought to him nightly. When I repeated this to Khashoggi, he said, "It makes the story more fairy tale. My father is a surgeon, who studied with Madame Curie." Khashoggi added, "Mohamed always had the image of lying and making up stories—it's a sickness."

To this day, the British government has chosen never to explain fully why, although the DTI report was completed in July 1988, it was not officially released until March 1990 and why, since it was full of damaging findings, it was never acted upon. To most Americans, the failure would indicate a clear cover-up. The report might never have been published at all if Rowland hadn't gotten hold of it and printed its findings in March 1989, in an extraordinary midweek edition of *The Observer*, which usually comes out only on Sundays. Fayed and the government obtained an injunction that forced the paper off the newsstands within a few hours.

Only recently has it become possible to piece together how desperately Fayed was trying to curry favor with the Conservative Party while he was under investigation. Between 1985 and 1987, he not only gave the Tories £250,000 ($367,000) for the 1987 election but also met dozens of times with Tim Smith and Neil Hamilton—the two ministers whose resignations he would later force—sometimes alone and sometimes with the lobbyist Ian Greer, whose firm acted as Fayed's go-between. (Hamilton, who stayed free at the Ritz, admits to attending meetings but denies receiving payment. He and Greer sued, but their action was recently struck down.) The meetings stopped six months after the DTI report was published in *The Observer*.

During the late 1980s, while Rowland continued to flood the establishment with reports detailing the Fayeds' background, Mohamed, according to two former security guards, kept wooing high-ranking officials in the Thatcher government. He played host in Surrey, for example, to then home secretary Douglas Hurd, who resigned this June as Major's foreign secretary.

Since the scandal Fayed has continued to invite politicians of all parties up to his offices, where he plies them with drink and bags full of Harrods goodies. "He has loads of politicians up there, and they all get the red-carpet treatment," says the former security guard Russ Conway, who describes himself as having been dismissed on a whim in March. "There's liquor all over the place. Half of them can't walk because they're stone drunk. Then you're dispatched to go down and bring up big teddy bears in bags, and if they hadn't got a car, you'd drive 'em to Commons."

"Among all the boys, we called him Fayed the Liar," says Ibrahim El Araby Abou Hamed, a former classmate who says he has known Fayed since they were seven in the Gomrok. "All the time he was dreaming to be rich. He wanted to dress and walk around with the rich people. He is one week older than I am," says El Araby, who was born in 1929. Fayed claims he was born in 1933. The DTI report flatly says he lied.

Perhaps Fayed's greatest caper before Harrods was the brief time he spent in Haiti. "He introduced himself as Sheikh Mohamed Fayed," Luckner Camronne, Papa Doc Duvalier's former right-hand man, says today. Fayed arrived in Haiti in late 1964, when Papa Doc, the brutal dictator, was increasingly isolated. Fayed told people that he could bring Middle Eastern riches to the wretchedly poor island if they would allow him the concessions to build an oil refinery and develop the wharf at Port-au-Prince. Fayed was being driven around in a limousine with Tonton Macoute bodyguards and given a diplomatic passport. According to Raymond Joseph, editor of the *Haiti Observateur* newspaper in New York and one of the organizers of the opposition to Papa Doc at the time, Fayed became engaged to one of Papa Doc's daughters, and whenever he made a trip to Miami, he would send flowers to Madame Duvalier. "It was like giving Indians trinkets, and you steal the whole thing."

Although Fayed claimed that he had invested $4 million in Haiti and that the government owed *him* money, the DTI inspectors found his signature on an account for the harbor authority in October 1964, when the account held just over $160,000. By the end of the year, both he and $150,000 were gone. "We have no doubt at all that Mohamed Fayed perpetrated a substantial deceit on the government and people of Haiti in 1964."

After Haiti, Fayed landed in London and moved into a flat at 60 Park Lane, which he would later acquire. He began traveling frequently to Dubai, and today takes credit for building its harbor and trade center, although those claims are widely disputed in Dubai, where he has effectively been banned.

In 1979 the brothers bought the Ritz Hotel in Paris. Their accumulated losses on the opulent establishment have been enormous. The hotel's debts at the end of 1993 were 678 million francs ($42 million). "The only thing 'pharaonic' about the Fayeds is the size of their debt," says Gillard. The Fayeds are very highly leveraged, but the brothers explain away their vast borrowings as a tax advantage: under British law, interest on debt can offset tax on profits.

According to figures obtained from Companies House, the official British register of corporations, between fiscal 1990 and 1994, House of Fraser Holdings paid an astonishing £458.9 million ($785.6 million) *in interest* to the banks—hardly the business procedure to be expected of entrepreneurs with billions at their disposal.

By the spring of 1993, the Fayed-controlled House of Fraser had spent £616.3 million ($925 million) of a £668.2 million ($1 billion) credit line, and the banks wanted their money back. In what appeared to be a quick bid to raise cash, House of Fraser took a whopping £68 million ($105 million) loss on its sale of 10.37 percent of Sears, the British retailing company, to raise £156 million ($240 million) in April 1993. The Fayeds were also strapped by numerous Lonrho lawsuits challenging their ownership. Imagine the surprise, then, when in October 1993, Tiny Rowland decided to end the feud.

The news was so startling to those in the trenches that a forty-one-year-old lawyer, whose whole career had been made on keeping track of all the suits for Lonrho, suddenly dropped dead of heart failure.

Bassam Abu Sharif, a Palestinian advisor to Yasir Arafat, played the go-between. "I told Tiny if the Arabs and the Israelis could make peace, so could he and Fayed." The feud was ended amid lights, cameras, and a very public lowering of a large stuffed shark—which Fayed had dubbed Tiny—from the ceiling of Harrods' Food Halls. Both men insist that no money changed hands, and Fayed takes great pleasure in remembering shark day. "[Tiny] say he's sorry. Kiss my hand. He says, I am crazy to do this to you.'"

I asked Fayed why Tiny had ended the feud. As usual, Michael Cole had the answer. "Two things. One, it cost him £40 million [$61 million]. And the second one, if he was going to pursue his case against Mohamed, he would have had to go into the witness box. He would never have done it."

"He's a lovely man," Fayed jokes when I ask him what he thinks of Tiny today. Then his real feelings come out. "He's a criminal. He is the worst person this country has from Germany. He has—how do you call it?—Nazi background. . . . He's bullshit, and he's a liar." Only two weeks earlier, Fayed had secretly taped Rowland at a lunch at Harrods, although he insists Tiny knew he was in front of a camera. "I interview him like David Frost," Fayed claimed.

"Do you think I would have gone there for lunch to be videotaped? I was stunned," Rowland tells me. Rowland asked the press whether the tape also revealed the part of their conversation in which Mohamed urged Tiny to accompany him to the Mayo Clinic, where Mohamed would undergo a penile transplant. "I love the man," Rowland continues. "He's a pathological liar—he can't help it. He began sitting on the back of a truck carrying crates of Coca-Cola, and he only just started paying his taxes." (Cole claims that Fayed has paid more than £200 million [$320 million] in taxes in the last decade.)

For whatever absurd reason, the Fates have bound these two larger-than-life megalomaniacs together. Within a few days last March, tabloid headlines proclaimed that Tiny Rowland had been kicked out of Lonrho by Dieter Bock (a German businessman whom Rowland had brought in to succeed him someday) and that Mohamed Al Fayed had been denied British citizenship. Now Rowland vows to derail his new enemy, Dieter Bock, and Fayed hopes he can bring John Major's divided and struggling government to its knees. The two outsiders, who thrive on conflict and enmity, exchange condolences frequently.

UPDATE: Mohamed Fayed no longer even lives in London. The highly controversial merchant prince has been denied British citizenship and, despite many appeals, has lost his special tax status. In the aftermath of 9/11, with tourism down, Harrods—which continues its constant turnover of top executives—is far from the cash cow it once was.

This article, the stories it generated in the British press, and the way Vanity Fair stood up to the suit Fayed filed against us after it was published, were credited with having an effect on how Fayed was perceived in Britain. Subsequent articles and books were far less reverent toward him. But Fayed finally got his revenge when his son, Dodi, began a very public romancing of Diana on a yacht in the south of France in the summer of 1997. Before this, Fayed himself had constantly sought the princess's attention and approval, showering her and her sons with presents from Harrods. Dodi's short-lived romance with Diana, and the huge onslaught of global headlines and photographs, provided a glorious moment of comeuppance for those Fayed felt had wronged him.

His whole world turned upside down, however, when in September

1997, just after the yacht trip, Dodi and the princess were killed in a car crash in Paris after a high-speed chase to evade paparazzi. Ironically, the tragedy at last brought Mohamed Fayed the worldwide recognition he so craved and also a measure of sympathy. He was quick to erect a memorial to his son and Diana in Harrod's basement.

Yet almost immediately, Fayed once again enraged the establishment. He charged that a conspiracy of British and French security forces and the CIA, masterminded by Prince Philip himself, had murdered Diana, "taking Dodi with her." Fayed offered a $20 million reward for information substantiating his beliefs. His reasoning, according to news accounts, is that "the murder was to prevent her from marrying a man with brown skin and a Muslim to boot." A French government inquiry that called more than two hundred witnesses and produced six thousand pages of evidence and found Dodi's chauffeur that night, Henri Paul, had lost control of the car while speeding and was under the influence of alcohol and drugs, failed to dissuade him. Fayed claims Paul was affiliated with British intelligence.

In December of 2003, in the wake of a book that Diana's butler published stating she feared someone (later purported to be Prince Charles) might try to kill her and make it look like a car accident, the British authorities announced a public inquiry of both Dodi's and Diana's deaths that would take at least a year to complete. Fayed was elated. Emerging from the inquest on Dodi's death, the *Irish Times* reported that Fayed "threw his arms wide and his head back, rolled his eyes to heaven and accused Prince Charles and Prince Philip of 'horrendous murder.'"

Full-Dress Homicide:
Andrew Cunanan

"Thank you for remembering, Signor Versace."

September 1997

In Miami's pagan, over-the-top South Beach, particularly among the large gay contingent, Gianni Versace had been a tanned, adored idol. Now the emperor lay dead, gunned down almost Mob style on the steps of his lavish Mediterranean villa, shot in the head and face in broad daylight. The prime suspect, dressed in nondescript shorts and a baseball cap, came in close for the kill and then coolly walked away along Ocean Drive. He knew very well that the act of murdering Versace, the Calabrian-born designer whose flamboyant clothes virtually defined "hot," who tarted up the likes of Princess Diana and Elizabeth Hurley but whose gowns also made Madonna and Courtney Love more elegant, would instantly catapult him to where he had long fantasized about being: at the center of worldwide attention.

Until recently, Andrew Cunanan, twenty-seven, was just a gay gigolo down on his luck in San Diego. A voracious reader with a reported genius-level IQ, he coveted the lifestyles of the rich and famous, tracked possible sugar daddies with care, and would say with a pout that he didn't know whether to fly to New York or Paris for dinner. He could describe the texture and delicacy of the blowfish he claimed to have eaten at an $850-Japanese lunch. Or he could say of a work of art what year it had been painted, who had owned it through the centuries, what churches it had hung in. His wit was biting, his memory photographic. Cunanan's story is a singular study in promise crushed.

Wherever he went, he craved the limelight and aspired to the top, whether through charm or falsehood. In the end, he reached an exclusive pinnacle that provided him with the celebrity he had always sought: he became America's most-wanted fugitive. By the time it was over, the whole country was on alert and more than a dozen law-enforcement bodies, including the FBI, were seeking to question Cunanan.

Two of Cunanan's alleged victims, Jeffrey Trail, twenty-eight, and David Madson, thirty-three, looked as if they had walked off a Kellogg's corn flakes box. From upright, loving, midwestern families, they were intelligent, handsome, and well liked. Cunanan considered Trail, a graduate of the Naval Academy at Annapolis, to be his best friend, and referred to him as "my brother." Madson, a rising architect, was the great unrequited love of Cunanan's life. Although they had broken up in the spring of 1996, Cunanan still kept Madson's picture taped to his refrigerator door.

The third victim, esteemed in Chicago political and social circles, was much older and very rich, a type Cunanan was known to research carefully. Real-estate tycoon Lee Miglin, seventy-five, also professed to have been happily married for thirty-eight years. The Miglin family has vociferously denied that Lee or his twenty-five-year-old son, Duke, a fledgling actor in Hollywood, ever met Cunanan.

The fourth dead man, William Reese, a forty-five-year-old cemetery caretaker with a wife and son, is considered a "functional homicide," murdered simply for his 1995 red Chevrolet pickup truck. Trail, Madson, and Miglin, however, carried the personal signature of what criminologists call a "pathological, sadistic sexual offender."

The killer's trail ended on July 23, when a caretaker checking on an unoccupied houseboat anchored off Collins Avenue, less than three miles north of Versace's mansion, discovered someone inside and heard a shot. He immediately notified the police, who moved in a SWAT team and lobbed tear gas into the houseboat. It took more than twelve hours for the police to announce that they had found the body of Andrew Cunanan in a second-floor bedroom. They said that he had shot himself in the mouth and left no suicide note.

For nearly two months before Versace's murder, I had crisscrossed the country, from San Diego and San Francisco to Minneapolis and Washington, D.C., to learn the real story of Andrew Cunanan, a chronic liar and consumer of status. The weekend before he left California for Minnesota, where he probably murdered both Madson and Trail, signs were mounting that he was spiraling out of control. On April 18, Cunanan ran into his old friend John Semerau at the Midnight Sun, a gay bar in San Francisco, where he showed him a flyer for an S&M party he was planning to attend the next night. The two later argued. "He grabbed me around the neck so hard he was choking me by his grip," recalls Semerau, who angrily told Cunanan, "'Andrew, you're really hurting me—stop it!' Something had snapped in him. Now I realize the guy was hunting—he was getting the thrill of the hunt, the thrill of the kill. I saw it in his eyes. I saw it in his body. He had stepped over the edge."

Friends remember that Cunanan often dropped Versace's name, and during my investigation I learned that the two had come in contact in a San Francisco nightclub, Colossus, in 1990. Versace was in town because he had designed costumes for the San Francisco Opera. That night, October 21, an eyewitness recalls, Cunanan was smugly pleased that Versace seemed to recognize him. "I know you," Versace said, wagging a finger in the then twenty-one-year-old's direction. "Lago di Como, no?" And Cunanan replied, "Thank you for remembering, Signor Versace." It is not clear that there really was anything to remember, but Cunanan gushed over the encounter.

Doug Stubblefield, a research analyst and close friend of Cunanan's, recalls walking on Market Street around this time when a big white chauffeured car pulled up alongside him. Inside, he claims, were Cunanan, Versace, and the San Francisco socialite Harry de Wildt. "Andrew called out, and we had a conversation," Stubblefield says. "It was very Andrew to do that—have the car pull over." Although Stubblefield is certain he saw three, de Wildt told me the day before Cunanan's suicide, "I categorically deny Mr. Versace, Mr. Cunanan, and I were in the same car. I have never had the pleasure or displeasure of meeting Mr. Cunanan."

After Versace's murder, the words of Chicago police captain Tom Cronin, a serial-killer expert I had interviewed, rang in my ears: "Down deep inside, the publicity is more sexual to him than anything else. . . . He probably goes to a gay bar in the afternoon when the news comes on and his face is on TV, and he's sitting there drinking a beer and loving it. You hide in plain view."

Antonio D'Amico, Versace's longtime companion, who raced to the door of the Miami mansion within seconds of hearing the gunshots, about 8:45 A.M. on July 15, said he could identify Cunanan as the killer who walked left down Ocean Drive. Other witnesses say the killer then cut left into an alley, then right down another alley, where he was captured on a hotel's security camera. That alley was directly across Thirteenth Street from a four-dollar-a-day municipal parking lot, where witnesses reported seeing the killer enter and apparently change clothes beside a 1995 red

Chevy pickup truck, which proved to be the one that had been stolen from William Reese. It carried stolen South Carolina license plates. A garage attendant told me she had found the ticket for the truck, which showed that it had been parked on the third level since June 10. Drivers pay as they leave, and only after about six weeks does the garage begin to question whether the driver is ever coming back.

That morning, investigators say, Cunanan's discarded clothes were found beside the truck. Among the things found inside were his passport, a personal check, and a pawnshop ticket, which was traced to a gold coin stolen from Lee Miglin's house. Cunanan had pawned it in Miami, using his own name and passport for verification. The pawnshop, as required by law, had submitted the ticket with a thumbprint of Cunanan's to the Miami police a week before Versace was shot. The police's slowness in following up on the lead was just one of many errors made by diverse authorities in the course of the investigation.

Soon details of Cunanan's whereabouts for the two months following Reese's murder, on May 9, began to emerge. Since May 12 he had been living under an assumed name in a low-rent, pink stucco north-beach-front residence hotel, the Normandy Plaza, where he paid about $36 a day for a series of rooms. He left the hotel the Saturday before Versace was killed, skipping out on his last day's rent. The night manager, Ramon Gomez, told me that Cunanan had paid in cash and had brought no one to his room. Gomez also said that Cunanan frequently changed his appearance—sometimes his hair would be jet-black, other times almost white, sometimes curly, sometimes straight. "I think he wore wigs."

He still went out every night, all night, "dressed to the nines," however, and a bartender at the Boardwalk, a north-beach gay hustler bar told me that he had definitely seen Cunanan there. Cunanan also patronized Twist, a more upscale gay bar a few blocks from Versace's mansion. When Versace arrived in town on Thursday, July 10, Cunanan was waiting.

"I've seen him two or three times in the last week," Twist manager Frank Scottolini told me on Thursday, July 17, two days after Versace's murder. Scottolini says he doesn't know why, but for a fleeting second the previous Saturday night, as he glimpsed Cunanan leaving the bar, he was overwhelmed by a sickening feeling in his stomach. "I turned to the bartender and said, 'There goes the gay serial killer.' Then I dismissed it, like it couldn't be true." Scottolini and other Twist employees now say they are able to identify Cunanan on the bar's surveillance tapes.

What is striking in tracing Cunanan's life as a fugitive in South Beach is how easily he adapted. He was not unfamiliar with the territory. In 1992, according to a former member of a gay-escort service based in

Miami Beach, Cunanan, calling himself Tony, worked for the service in both Florida and California. "He told me in a letter that he was tired of California," says the former hustler, who claims he met Cunanan in the company of an older doctor from San Bernardino at a Beverly Hills show-business party in 1989. "He said there were too many other young guys there trying to do what he was trying to do."

On a Monday night in early June, I visited Hillcrest, the primarily gay area in San Diego, which, until late April, Cunanan called home. It was a busy evening for the middle-aged Mexican American drag queen Nicole Ramirez-Murray. Wearing a red ponytail wig and a green chiffon cocktail dress, Nicole first appeared at the Brass Rail, to introduce the Dream-girls, then raced down to the Hole, an outdoor bar with a shower, stage left, to hold forth at the Wet-n-Wild underwear contest. The Hole, across the street from a former Marine Corps recruiting station, gets a raucous crowd of closeted military men, openly "out" muscle-flexing gym rats, and a few staid elderly gentlemen from the wealthy enclave of La Jolla. They all roared when Nicole said to one shivering contestant, "You look like Andrew." After all, this is the community in which Andrew Cunanan, the big spender with the loud, look-at-me laugh who called himself Andrew DeSilva, cut a wide swath.

"I remember the first time I ever saw Andrew, sitting on that stool," said a tattooed waiter with spiky platinum-dyed hair. "He was holding a paper bag stuffed with a big wad of cash, saying, 'I'm going to buy me some drugs and sell me some drugs.'" That would be a typically flamboy-ant gesture for the young poseur who constantly claimed center stage for himself. "He was like Julie, the cruise director on *The Love Boat*," said Erik Greenman, a waiter who met Cunanan a few years ago. He targeted people he wanted to meet. "Andrew did his homework," said San Diego restaurateur Michael Williams. "He would investigate older, wealthy gay men who didn't have families, and he would place himself in those circles. And that was his living."

Ramirez-Murray, who also writes a social column, said his mouth had dropped open to hear Andrew discussing Henry Kissinger's role in poli-tics with some big shots at a closeted private party during the 1996 Republican National Convention in San Diego. "He was very knowledge-able. Most young men his age I call 'S and M'—stand and model. . . . He was visible at some parties he certainly shouldn't have been at."

Cunanan was last kept with lavish indulgence—in a seaside con-dominium and a hillside house in La Jolla—by Norman Blachford, a conservative retired millionaire in his sixties who made his fortune on sound-abatement equipment. Blachford allowed Cunanan time with his friends, reportedly gave him $2,000 a month, and provided him with a 1996 Infiniti 130T to tool around in. They went to Paris and Saint-Jean-Cap-Ferrat, in the south of France, in June 1996, and they would fly to New York to see Broadway shows.

Blachford is a member of Gamma Mu, the extremely private fraternity of about seven hundred very rich, mostly Republican, and often closeted gay men, which twice a year sponsors posh fly-ins to cities around the world. Two years ago, at Gamma Mu's last Washington, D.C., fly-in, members were treated to a private party in the Capitol Rotunda and a brunch on the roof of the Kennedy Center. According to one member, "The annual Starlight Ball in D.C. attracts 250 of the highest echelon of closeted Washington." Through Blachford, Cunanan—as Andrew DeSilva—briefly became a Gamma Mu member, and his contacts in the group afforded him access to a storehouse of privileged information. There are reports that certain members were alerted by the FBI this past June and July to be on the lookout for Cunanan, who was in a position, it was feared, to blackmail them.

In the summer of 1996, Blachford and Cunanan shared a house in Saint-Jean-Cap-Ferrat with Larry Chrysler, a Gamma Mu member from Los Angeles. Cunanan, Chrysler reports, said he was descended from Sephardic Jews and spent his time lying by the pool underlining passages in books, dining at the finest restaurants, and soaking up information "like a sponge." He had an opinion on everything. One night they were discussing the Mamounia, the old landmark hotel in Marrakech. Chrysler recalls, "Andrew said, 'Oh, nobody stays at the Mamounia anymore. It's been redone.' Two weeks later I pick up a magazine in the house, and there in it was the same direct quote about the Mamounia from [Yves Saint Laurent's business partner] Pierre Bergé."

Chrysler found Cunanan "fascinating," if full of "BS." Once, Cunanan came back from the village of Beaulieu with a tiny jar of jam that cost $20. "I never look at any price," he said. "My family never looked at any price."

On their way back from France, Blachford and Cunanan continued the swell life, spending several days that July in East Hampton, on Long Island, as the guests of a wealthy gay couple. They attended parties and dined at the trendy restaurant Nick & Toni's. Once again, Cunanan charmed his older companions, but he told stories that made them raise their eyebrows: he said that he had been married to a Jewish woman and that his father-in-law was the head of Mossad, the Israeli intelligence agency. "He was young and attractive, entertaining, good company—what's not to like?" said one, who also found him "sad on two levels. He's got a lot going for him, I thought. He was also a young man ultimately with no career ambitions in any direction. He pretty much said he was interested in older men for their financial situations. He made no bones about that, and he would do it in front of Norman."

Blachford, however, apparently *did* look at prices, and when Cunanan left him soon after and moved in with Erik Greenman and Tom Eads, he complained that Norman was "too cheap." The least Norman could have done, he said, was give him a Mercedes 500SL, fly first class, and repaint all the rooms in the La Jolla house. According to Eads, "Andrew said he got tired of all Norman's nickel-and-diming."

Cunanan was astonished that Blachford would let him go.

It immediately becomes apparent that Andrew Cunanan rarely told—or faced—the truth about himself. To friends in San Francisco's Bay Area in the early 1990s, for example, Cunanan, then barely twenty, said that he had gone to Choate, dropped out of Yale, and transferred to Bennington. In fact, he graduated from La Jolla's private Bishop's School and eventually spent two years at the University of California at San Diego. In Berkeley, Cunanan cultivated a "messy professor look" older than his years. "He hung around very intelligent, talented people, because he wanted these people to be responsible for *him*," says a close friend from those days, Doug Stubblefield. Cunanan was then writing a book about his experiences in the Philippines, his father's native country, which Stubblefield describes as "subtle, poetic, and filled with metaphors."

Even then Cunanan was beginning to set his pattern as a con artist and court jester—to lie, to be glibly authoritative on art, to be witty and entertaining enough to live well without working. His first "patrons" were a young couple with a baby daughter who took him into their beautiful hillside house. Cunanan enjoyed taking their child—his goddaughter—out, and he had a passion for building dollhouses. He subscribed to a magazine on the subject and created a ruined French château complete with blackened windows.

Cunanan had known his patroness, Elizabeth Cote, since junior high school, and he would later spin a tale that he had been married to a Jewish princess and had fathered a daughter, whose pictures he liked to show. He had other stories as well. His father, he said, was a Filipino general close to ousted dictator Ferdinand Marcos, as well as a bisexual with a young lover, whom Andrew resented. "He has a car and I don't," he would tell friends. Cunanan boasted that he had a pilot's license and that a Filipino senator engaged him occasionally to fly him around in an old rattletrap Cunanan called the "Buddy Holly death plane."

Cunanan was always known as DeSilva in San Diego, and there he said at times that his father was an Israeli millionaire or a Fifth Avenue aristocrat. He never told the truth: that his father was a navy veteran and stockbroker from nearby Rancho Bernardo who—as a lawsuit filed by his wife alleges—had been accused of embezzling more than $100,000 and who abandoned his wife and their four children in 1988.

Did Andrew's Italian mother, who lives on public assistance, ever really "spa with Deborah Harry," as her son liked to relate? Hardly. Yet to San Diego friends, Andrew portrayed her as the ultimate spoiled Jewish mother, who stayed with his father in an unhappy marriage so that the children would not lose their vast inheritance. In reality, MaryAnn Cunanan is a devout Catholic, a bright but emotionally fragile woman. Cunanan never acknowledged to her, his sisters, or his brother what they all knew—that he was gay and lived in a world apart.

That was perhaps because he had so much to hide. I learned that in certain circles Cunanan apparently became a supplier of pharmaceuticals. "I once asked Jeff Trail, 'How does Andrew get by?'" says Michael Williams. "Jeff said, 'Oh, he's up to his old profession: he sells drugs.'" Anthony Dabiere, a waiter at California Cuisine, one of Cunanan's favorite San Diego restaurants, says, "I was witness to Andrew doling out drugs in bars—Percodan, Vicodin, Darvocet. He'd say, 'This will give you an overall sense of well-being.' We were given to understand he was using. We were also reminded that he had access to coke and high-grade marijuana as well." Tim Barthel, co-owner of Flicks, a video bar Cunanan frequented most nights, says, "I heard he started getting into drugs himself before he left—even heroin. The last couple of weeks he was more disheveled."

"Yes, he started dealing drugs again," says Greenman, who tells me that Cunanan had two phone listings, one under DeSilva and another, for "business deals," under his real name. "He'd do that if he needed money. He'd never get his friends involved. . . . He'd come in with a suitcase, dressed up very nice. He was a deliverer. The whole thing would take a half an hour. . . . He knew shady characters in New York." There wasn't much mystery to it, Greenman implies, despite the fact that some police claimed they had no knowledge that Cunanan dealt drugs. "We all knew he did it, and he knew we all knew."

There might even have been other criminal activities. A month before Jeff Trail was murdered, he confided to Rick Allen, a friend in Minneapolis, that Cunanan had approached him to help him in his illegal business.

Trail said he had refused. Cunanan, police assume, killed David Madson with Trail's .40-caliber handgun, which he may have stolen from Trail's Minneapolis apartment. "I never understood why they were best friends," says Tom Eads. "But they were thick as thieves for so long."

When Trail lived in San Diego, he and Cunanan would go target-shooting together. "Andrew knew calibers, sizes, weights of guns," says Eads. Trail, who was from De Kalb, Illinois, was an excellent marksman. He had been a small-arms instructor in the navy and had served in the Persian Gulf on a guided-missile cruiser. He left the navy as a lieutenant in 1996 and joined a training program for the California Highway Patrol. He was ambitious but responsible, always willing to help people out. He loved listening to Sinatra, dated very young men, and was attracted to cops. Later in 1996 he rather abruptly resigned from the highway patrol; eventually he found a job as a district manager for Ferrellgas, a propane retailer in a suburb of Minneapolis. According to his family and friends, Trail, the son of a mathematics professor at Northern Illinois University, was politically conservative and deeply opposed to drugs.

"What Jeff told me," says Allen, "was 'Andrew talked to me about doing security work for his "import-export" business.'"

"I don't even know what you're talking about," Allen says he told Trail.

"'Drugs, Rick, drugs,'" Trail told Allen. "Jeff was very hesitant to talk about it at all," Allen continues. "He told me, 'It's not something I tell any-body about.' I said, 'What did you tell him?' Jeff said, 'I said, "Fuck you."'"

For all his sociability, Cunanan often griped to Tim Barthel and others that he had a hard time picking up people for sex. "My impression was that he was always going for people out of his league physically," says Barthel. Erik Greenman agrees: "Andrew was not one to get dates. He had to flash money. A good-looking guy wouldn't look at him." In the months they lived together, Greenman says, Cunanan never brought any-one home, which was "unheard of."

Greenman concedes that Cunanan "had such extreme taste in sex—S&M-wise—he'd need privacy." Meaning? "It was way past normal. Whether it'd be whips or make him walk around in shackles—who knows? He always had bondage videos. . . . He was a dominator." In the early-morning hours of his last months in San Diego, the restless, noc-turnal Cunanan, who usually slept from six A.M. to two P.M., was also, according to Greenman, using crack and injecting himself with drugs. But when the sex fantasies and the crack wore off, he would feel terrible. Ever the snob, he told Greenman, "Never do crack. It's a ghetto drug."

In the first week of April, Cunanan went to San Francisco, where he met twenty-six-year-old Tim Schweger, an assistant manager in a local Denny's, at a gay dance club. Cunanan offered to get him drugs—ecstasy or cocaine—but Schweger refused. "He said he was associated with people who dealt in San Diego," said Schweger. "He was kind of like a middleman." Cunanan also bragged about knowing various celebrities— Lisa Kudrow, Elizabeth Hurley, Madonna. "He said he had lunch with Kudrow the previous weekend."

Cunanan eventually took Schweger back to the Mandarin Oriental Hotel, where Cunanan liked to stay in San Francisco when he was feeling flush. After that, Schweger's memory of what took place is hazy. "I think I was drugged that night, or I had too much to drink," he said. "But lately I've had these memory flashbacks of trying to fight him off during the night. I wasn't attracted to him sexually. I woke up with three hickeys on me." Schweger said he went to sleep in his underwear. "When I woke up, I had nothing on. After that night, I knew he had a rough side to him."

The one person who allowed Cunanan to live out his fantasies, if only partially, was David Madson. Madson, a former ski instructor, was so charismatic that he "blew people away" both personally and professionally. He worked for the John Ryan Company in Minneapolis, designing "retail financial centers" for large banks, a $70,000-a-year position that took him all over the country. "David was an absolute joy to be around and an immensely talented person, on the precipice of becoming a leading designer in the world in his field," says Ryan. His friends describe him as a "peacemaker" who avoided confrontation and could talk his way out of anything.

Madson and Cunanan met in San Francisco in December 1995. "It was pretty sparky," says a friend of Cunanan's who witnessed their first encounter. Cunanan spotted Madson at a bar and sent him a drink. That night they had a nonsexual "sleepover" in Cunanan's luxe room in the Mandarin Oriental. Soon they were dating long-distance, and their sex became rough.

"In the late spring of '96, I had a conversation with Andrew about exploring the S&M thing with David," says Doug Stubblefield. "He said he had wrist restraints, and they'd been trying it. David wouldn't let him go as far as he wanted, but he thought it was a lot of fun." Erik Greenman adds, "Andrew talked to me about it many times. David enjoyed it just as much as Andrew did."

About that time, however, at the urging of friends, Madson began to distance himself from Cunanan. He had become uneasy, because Andrew would often disappear or be unreachable. Presumably the reason for this secrecy was that Cunanan was living in La Jolla with Norman Blachford.

By September 1996, Cunanan and Blachford had broken up. But Cunanan told Greenman and Tom Eads that he felt he had been rejected by Madson.

Meanwhile, Jeff Trail was also cooling toward him, telling Michael Williams, a good friend in San Diego, that he had had "a big fallout with Andrew and never wished to see him again." Trail told Jerry Davis, a friend at Ferrellgas, that although he didn't want Andrew to stay with him in Minneapolis anymore, "he was like a relative you didn't like—you had to let them stay."

By April, Cunanan, who had uncharacteristically begun drinking— $36-bottles of Stonestreet Merlot "like there was no tomorrow," in the words of San Diego maître d' Rick Rinaldi—was confiding to select friends that he was broke. He had stopped going into the humidor at the cigar store Bad Habits for $8 cigars, and he said that he might actually have to go to work. About the only legitimate job he had ever held was as a Thrifty drugstore cashier, when he lived with his mother in a small, $750-a-month condominium in Rancho Bernardo in the early 1990s.

Cunanan next decided to relocate to San Francisco, and he was successful in convincing David Madson that Madson had been responsible for his moral turnaround, which included the decision to find honest work. Madson proudly told friends that Andrew was going to give up his shady business and his materialistic ways. But the evolution was slow starting.

Over the Easter weekend, Cunanan went to Los Angeles with Madson and a young engaged couple, Karen Lapinski and Evan Wallit, who were friends of Madson's from San Francisco. Cunanan insisted on taking two $395 rooms at the Chateau Marmont and persuaded Madson and the couple to stay there with him. He and Madson had supposedly not had a sexual relationship for almost a year, and Madson later claimed that they had argued when he refused Andrew's advances.

A few days after Easter, Cunanan was in San Francisco, staying with Lapinski and Wallit. Cunanan told the future bride, who had asked Madson to give her away, that he would pay for the wedding reception. He told her, the police say, that he had $15,000 he had to spend before tax day, April 15, and he gave her and Madson expensive leather jackets. He also gave Madson a suit.

Before moving to San Francisco permanently, Cunanan told friends, he had some unfinished business to take care of with Jeff Trail. According to the Minnesota police, Lapinski later told the FBI that Cunanan had also said he was going to start a business making prefabricated movie sets with a friend named Duke Miglin.

On April 24, at Cunanan's farewell dinner in San Diego, at California Cuisine, his favorite waiter, Anthony Dabiere, wrote in raspberry puree around the edge of his plate, "Goodbye to You." In his toast, a somewhat somber "DeSilva" said he was feeling bittersweet about leaving. What he was going to miss most, he said, was Barklee, Greenman's dog.

Nobody would have guessed, to hear him, that he had bought a one-way ticket to Minneapolis.

The last thing in the world Jeff Trail or David Madson wanted was a visit from Andrew Cunanan. Nevertheless, neither appeared capable of confronting him directly. Trail had made it clear that he wouldn't be around much the weekend of Andrew's visit. His boyfriend, Jon Hackett, a student at the University of Minnesota, was celebrating his twenty-first birthday, and Trail was taking him out of town Saturday night. Trail was known to have warned Madson that Cunanan was a liar. "You can't believe a word he says," Trail declared. "He'll say anything to get a reaction." Meanwhile, Cunanan had told a friend that he was uncomfortable having the two people he cared most about living in the same faraway city without him.

"David was apprehensive about Andrew's visit," says Cedric Rucker, a college administrator who was one of Madson's last boyfriends. "He held suspicions that Andrew was involved in the international drug trade, bringing drugs into the country from across the Mexican border. He probably had ties to organized crime. I said, 'Why would you want to be affiliated with this?' He said, 'Because he's trying to make a change in his life. Andrew just needs help.'"

Cunanan may have been jealous, or suspicious that Madson and Trail were gossiping about him behind his back. He may also have been angry at Trail for refusing to work with him. In any event, Cunanan told Madson that Trail was mixed up in the drug trade with him. "J.T." had been forced to flee California, he said, because of an impending investigation. Madson had no idea what to believe, he told friends. The police say they know of no such investigation.

Rob Davis, a handsome black businessman who succeeded Cunanan as Madson's boyfriend, heard the story at a Christmas party. "Andrew told David that he and Jeff had gotten mixed up in some cocaine deal that had caused Jeff to resign from the California Highway Patrol, because Andrew had gotten Jeff to transport cocaine across the border."

People who knew Trail—who rarely drank, never smoked, and was staunchly opposed even to pot—say the scenario is preposterous. One of Trail's closest friends, Jon Wainwright, a real-estate-development executive in San Diego, called the accusation inconceivable but acknowledges "some strange bond" between Andrew and Jeff. "Andrew would hook up people for J.T. It was kind of strange, actually. My belief is that Andrew was very infatuated with Jeff."

On Friday, April 25, David Madson dutifully picked Cunanan up at the Minneapolis airport. Yet at dinner with several friends from work that night, Madson appeared uncomfortable. "Show them what I got you," Cunanan urged. He had brought Madson a gold Cartier watch. It was "not new," Madson told them, just a thank you from Andrew for helping turn his life around.

During dinner Cunanan, who mentioned that he planned to return to California Monday morning, was up to his old tricks to impress new people. He mentioned the Rolls-Royce he had driven around as a kid. He informed one woman he had a company (as Norman Blachford had once had) that made sound-abatement equipment for movie sets. Later, at a camp polka palace, Nye's Polonaise, he and Madson met Monique Salvetti, Madson's best friend, for a drink. Cunanan told her that he was setting up a factory in Mexico to make prefab movie sets, a profession similar to that of a friend of his in San Diego. This time, however, he did not mention the name Duke Miglin.

Cunanan presumably spent Friday night at Madson's apartment. Monique Salvetti talked to Madson around 10 A.M. on Sunday, and he said he and Andrew had gone out to dinner again the previous night. "Is everything going okay?" Salvetti asked. "Yeah," he said. They made plans to meet later that day, but she couldn't reach him. That was Madson's last known conversation.

Cunanan apparently spent Saturday night in Trail's apartment, in nearby Bloomington, entering with a key left for him under the doormat. At 10 A.M. on Sunday, he politely took a phone message for Trail from Trail's friend Jerry Davis about a softball game. He left it on a yellow pad and signed it, "Love, Andrew." Trail went to the three o'clock game but left early to bake a cake, because, he said, friends were coming over to celebrate Jon Hackett's birthday. He did not mention that he had seen Cunanan.

That afternoon Trail told Hackett that he needed to talk to Andrew about something "pretty important," which would take only about half an hour. "Jeff didn't say he knew what it was about," Hackett told me.

When Hackett joined Trail at his apartment at six P.M., there was no sign of Cunanan or his bags. About eight o'clock, though, Cunanan left a voice message without identifying himself, just giving Madson's number and saying, "Give me a call, because I'd like to see you."

Trail thought of blowing Cunanan off entirely and suggested to Hackett that they go to a movie, but Hackett said he wanted to dance on his birthday. Trail said he would meet Andrew in a coffee shop and then rendezvous with Hackett between 10 and 10:30 at the Gay Nineties nightclub nearby. Trail left in his car between 9 and 9:15.

The caller ID on Madson's telephone, connected to his loft's intercom, shows that someone—presumably Trail—was admitted to Madson's apartment at 9:45 P.M. A neighbor recalled hearing shouting and somebody saying, "Get the fuck out," then shaking and thumping against the wall lasting from thirty to forty-five seconds. He looked out his door but saw no one. On Monday, another neighbor saw Madson in the elevator with a man matching Cunanan's description. On Tuesday, yet another neighbor saw the two men walking Prints, Madson's dalmatian.

Meanwhile, since Trail had not shown up at the Gay Nineties, Hackett was beside himself with worry. When Jeff did not return to his apartment Monday morning, he says, "I immediately started calling hospitals and the jail." He was hesitant to call Trail's parents, because Trail had never told them he was gay.

Monday night, about eight, Hackett returned to Trail's apartment to find it just as he had left it. Unbeknownst to him, the police say, an upstairs neighbor had seen a man matching the description of Cunanan in front of the apartment and, according to friends of Trail's, heard voices talking inside between 7 and 7:45 P.M.

About 1:45 on Tuesday afternoon, April 29, two women who worked with Madson went to his loft, because he had not shown up for work for two days and clients were clamoring to talk to him. When Laura Booher knocked, she thought she heard whispering behind the door. Although the dog was pawing and scratching, no one answered. "We said in a very loud voice that we better call the police—I'm sure they heard me," says Booher. When the police arrived, they said that in the event of a forced entry, if the dog became aggressive, they would have to shoot it.

At that the women backed down, and instead left a message for the superintendent, asking her to go into the apartment with her passkey. When the superintendent entered, about four P.M., she saw a body wrapped in a carpet. Blood was splattered all over the back of the door, and there were two sets of bloody footprints on the floor. She called the police, who found Madson's wallet, a bloody Banana Republic T-shirt, and two plates of rice in the refrigerator. A bloody household hammer was on the table by the door.

By Tuesday night Jeff Trail's parents had been contacted—they had been at the hospital where one of Jeff's sisters was having a baby—and a metro-wide missing-person report had been filed. Trail was not identified as the body in the rug until Wednesday morning. Identification was made by the tattoo of the cartoon figure Marvin the Martian on his left ankle, although he was carrying his wallet, with his identification and picture. His face was badly beaten.

Trail had been hit from behind, and his face had been bludgeoned multiple times with a hammer. His Swiss Army watch had stopped at 9:55 P.M. Cunanan and Madson had vanished. To the horrified disbelief of all who knew him, Madson immediately went from being the supposed victim to being a suspect for murder. "My first thought: it's Madson," says Minneapolis police sergeant Robert Tichich, of the homicide division. "It's his apartment. There's a body in there. There's no way to pin it on Cunanan as opposed to Madson."

As a result of Madson's new status, his parents weren't even told he was missing until late Thursday afternoon. Instead, the police staked out the parents' house. Between Tuesday and Friday, when Madson's red Jeep Cherokee with a Vail, Colorado, bumper sticker was spotted moving erratically on Interstate 35 going north (speeding up and slowing down, as if the driver, presumably Madson, was trying to attract attention), there are no reported sightings of Cunanan or Madson. On Friday afternoon, the two stopped to eat at a diner near Rush Lake, in Chisago County, about an hour's drive north of the Twin Cities.

"From Tuesday early A.M. till Saturday, it's a big gray area," says Investigator Todd Rivard of the Chisago County Sheriff's Department. The Minneapolis police believe that the two may have gone to Chicago, and there are reports that a receipt for a Chicago parking-lot ticket from early that Friday was found in Madson's Jeep. "I think there's a good possibility they were out of town during that week," says Tichich. But the Chicago police have kept such a tight lid on their case—possibly to protect the reputation of the influential Miglin—that they won't share any information. "We got no reports, not even verbal; we heard nothing," says Rivard.

Madson's body was found in tall grass at the edge of Rush Lake by fishermen on Saturday morning, May 3. He had been shot three times, through one eye, in the head, and in the back. A .40-caliber Golden Saber bullet was found in his chest. His car keys were on the ground, but his Jeep was gone. According to Investigator Rivard, Madson's body showed no sign of restraints, and his only defensive wounds were in his fingers—possibly he raised his hands to deflect a shot to the face.

Meanwhile, according to Jon Hackett and Trail's coworker Jerry Davis, the Minneapolis police did not take Cunanan's voice message off Trail's phone for a week, although both Trail's and Madson's friends informed them that the major link between Trail and Madson was Cunanan. That same week Hackett found a box of ammunition in Trail's closet that matched the .40-caliber bullets Madson was shot with.

Another box of the same bullets—with ten missing—and an empty holster were also found in a duffel bag in Madson's apartment. The police asked Monique Salvetti to identify the bag. "Have you looked at the identification tag?" she asked, indicating a label that was enclosed in a grip around the handle. When they opened the tag in front of Salvetti, there was the name of its owner: Andrew Cunanan.

It was not until two months later, in late June, that the police recovered Cunanan's toiletry kit from Madson's apartment. They had also overlooked a pair of blood-spattered Levi's, size 36, which were heaped in a corner near the sleeping area. (Madson was a size 32.) By then, any shred of evidence was crucial, because the police had not been able to match any of the fingerprints taken from the various crime scenes and vehicles with the sole thumbprint they had of Cunanan from his California driver's license. Since he had no criminal record, he had never been fingerprinted by the police.

What the police had not overlooked, however, was a pair of handcuffs, which led Sergeant Tichich to confirm that there was evidence in the apartment "to corroborate S&M activity. It was well-known that Madson was involved in S&M, and so was Cunanan, and that it had gone on a long period of time." Nevertheless, nationwide attention began focusing on Cunanan only after the next killing.

Lee Miglin's body was discovered by the police under a car in his garage off the Miracle Mile in Chicago on Sunday, May 4. The murder was brutal and had grisly, ritualistic overtones: Miglin's hands and feet were bound, and his body was partially wrapped in plastic, brown paper, and tape. His face was taped except for two airholes at the nostrils. His ribs had been broken, and he had been tortured with four stabs in the chest, probably with garden shears. His throat had been cut open with a garden bow saw. According to friends, however, the autopsy revealed no sexual molestation.

There had been no forced entry into Miglin's Gold Coast town house. His wife, Marilyn, had been out of town, and the message she left, that she would be returning early Sunday morning, had been played. When Miglin did not appear at the airport to pick her up, she went home to find a door open and what looked like a gun in the bathroom. She called the police.

The murderer had slept in Miglin's bed, left a half-eaten ham sandwich in the library, bathed in the sunken bathtub, and shaved in the white-marble bathroom, leaving beard stubble on the floor and a toy gun on the sink, almost as if to taunt the police. The dog, a Labrador named Honey, which had been there the whole time, was calm and unharmed. Between $8,000 and $10,000 in cash and several of Miglin's suits were missing. "There was a horrible feeling in the house," says the writer and socialite Sugar Rautbord, a close friend of Marilyn Miglin's, who went immediately to the residence. "Everywhere you turned, there was evidence. We couldn't touch anything."

The garage, from which Miglin's Lexus had been taken, is across an alley, separate from the town house. "It was like being back in Vietnam, a real battle scene, a highly emotionally charged environment," says Miglin's partner, Paul Beitler. "I saw people's lives destroyed in front of me."

Lee Miglin and his wife—a former dancer who founded a cosmetics company and became a Home Shopping Network celebrity—were much loved in Chicago for being modest, philanthropic, self-made. "Lee epitomized the American Dream," says Beitler. "The man never had a failure." The son of a Lithuanian coal miner in southern Illinois, Miglin rose from selling pancake mix out of the trunk of his car to become, with Beitler, the developer of some of the biggest buildings on the Chicago skyline; on his own, he developed much of the commercial area at O'Hare Airport. There is even a smart shopping street on Chicago's Near North Side named Marilyn Miglin Way. On that street, her boutique faces Versace's.

Few, including Andrew Cunanan, who often traveled to Chicago and never forgot a name, could miss the crowing billboard on the Kennedy Expressway into the city from O'Hare depicting the Wizard of Oz's Emerald City: IF MIGLIN-BEITLER HAD MANAGED EMERALD CITY, DOROTHY WOULD NEVER HAVE LEFT. Moreover, in Cunanan's San Diego apartment there was a 1988 *Architectural Digest* featuring Beitler's house.

After the Miglin murder, rumors started flying around the Hillcrest area that Andrew Cunanan knew Duke Miglin, twenty-five. Certainly the younger Miglin was someone Cunanan would have liked to brag about knowing: he was handsome, drove a fast car, and flew airplanes—he had spent two years at the Air Force Academy—and his father was a multimillionaire. The rumors, in the form of a quote from a Hillcrest bookseller, promptly appeared in the Minneapolis *Star-Tribune*. The same day, however, the bookseller, Bruce Kerschner—who later told me that he had merely confirmed that he had heard the same rumors—claimed in a press conference that he had been misquoted.

"We have no idea how Duke Miglin's name surfaced. We can say with absolute certainty that neither Duke nor anyone in the family knew Cunanan," says Paul Beitler. "We sat him down and said, 'Okay, here's where the rubber meets the road. Tell us now if you have ever had a homosexual relationship, a secret life.' He has told us unequivocally he's not gay and he has had no gay relationship." According to Sergeant Tichich of the Minneapolis homicide division, the Chicago police haven't gone near Karen Lapinski's report to the FBI that Cunanan had told her that he was going into business with Duke Miglin. "It's just sitting there."

Meanwhile, a Chicago male prostitute has alleged to law-enforcement officials that he had a rendezvous in a Chicago apartment with Lee Miglin and Andrew Cunanan.

The Chicago police did not find Madson's Jeep—illegally parked, with multiple tickets, "85 paces" around the corner from Miglin's house—until midnight on Tuesday, May 6. There was no blood inside, but there was a tourist pamphlet with a line drawn around the North Side's gay Boys Town area, and newspaper clips about Trail's and Madson's murders. By then, it appears, Cunanan, the presumed driver of Miglin's dark-green Lexus, was far away. An activated car phone in the Lexus was used three times the following week in Pennsylvania.

On Friday evening, William Reese did not come home from work on time. Finns Point National Cemetery in Pennsville, New Jersey, where he cared for the grounds, is a remote historic site where Confederate prisoners were held during the Civil War. It is not far, however, from a junction of several highways, including a bridge route to Delaware and a turnpike to Philadelphia.

Knowing Reese to be punctual, his wife drove from their home in Bridgeton, New Jersey, to check on him. When she arrived at the cemetery, she saw a dark-green Lexus but no sign of her husband's bright-red 1995 Chevy truck. The door to the caretaker's office was open, and a radio was playing. She called the police.

They found Reese in a pool of blood on the concrete floor of the basement. He had been shot once in the head with a .40-caliber bullet, which later proved to have come from the same gun that killed Madson and Versace.

Meanwhile, police did not search Cunanan's San Diego apartment until after this fourth killing. By then, he was apparently on his way to Miami to strike again.

According to professionals who study the psyches of serial killers, intriguing questions surrounding this case can be answered by understanding the traits that many of the killers display. For example—motive. "For all I know, this violence came out of the blue," says Sergeant Tichich in Minneapolis. If Madson was not an accomplice in Jeff Trail's murder, why would he have stayed in his apartment so long with Cunanan and the dead body? "There's all this evidence they tramped around in blood and had taken measures to conceal this body," Tichich says. "You have to believe that Cunanan was able to control Madson for extended periods of time without possibility of escape."

But wouldn't Madson try to escape? "It's not surprising David stayed with him and he sat with the body for two days. Not at all," says Chicago police captain Tom Cronin, a graduate of the FBI Behavioral Sciences Unit. "It makes perfect sense to David: this guy's got power over me, I can't leave. It is to a degree the Stockholm syndrome. These sexually sadistic offenders have that ability to control people—not necessarily physical control. Many times it's just out of fear."

Trail and Madson had gone far beyond what their friends thought necessary in placating Cunanan. Is being a nice person a weakness? "Yes," says Gregg McCrary, a former special agent of the FBI's Behavioral Sciences Unit, "when you're dealing with a pathological, sexually sadistic offender." It is not by accident that a person like Cunanan constantly seeks to put people in his debt. "They have a sixth sense of who they can manipulate and control," McCrary says. "Their interpersonal skills are so strong and their ability to target these victims, to understand their needs, to meet these needs and fulfill them, is so developed that in return these victims always feel obligated."

But when does murder come in? "When he realizes that in spite of his best efforts, he is not getting what he wants. He's not going to get this guy back, for example, so he can either forget about it and walk away from it or—those predisposed to homicidal violence—kill just to settle the score. Homicide is an attempt to regain control over the situation."

"They don't get dumped. They go to great pains to win someone back just so they can dump back in the future. They're control freaks," says Cronin. "Their behavior is such that they corral people into making them the center of attention."

What triggers the violence? "The trigger can be anything—to him, at the moment, it's rational," says Cronin. "It was the straw that broke the camel's back—you don't know what else is on the camel's back. The first killing he probably fantasized for years. These people are very good at planning things out." Often, says Cronin, they consider themselves much smarter than the police.

Sergeant Tichich acknowledges how hard it would have been to prove, beyond a reasonable doubt, that Cunanan acted alone in the killing of Jeff Trail. "You've got the murder weapon there. You got the body, bloody clothes—everything you could basically ask for in a murder case is there. The only thing you don't have is a video recording of what happened. And in this case, that's about what's necessary."

Sex is often a strong element in these crimes. The offenders need to act out their sadistic fantasies, says McCrary, and they repeat them until they get them right. "Typically, they have compliant victims—they begin with sex partners who were complying with their fantasies. They get someone to go along with bondage and torture until the victim won't go along anymore, so the sadistic offender is not satisfied. By the time they reach their late twenties and early thirties, they've developed their sadistic fantasies. They're really vibrant at this point, and they need to act out these things, and they can't find people to go along with them. So now they find an unwilling victim to abduct, rape, or murder. There's a much higher rate of homicide if torture is acted out against the will of the other individual."

McCrary says the motives here can be mixed—both sexual gratification and the extortion of money. What was done to Lee Miglin, for example, "is a window into [Cunanan's] fantasy." Both Miglin and Trail were wrapped up, but "the hammer to the face [of Trail] is very personal. The destruction of the face is many times the personality of the victim—they want to destroy the person outright. The mask is depersonalization."

Could Lee Miglin's murder have been completely random, as his family maintains? "Why would Cunanan go to Chicago, find Miglin, and torture him without some motive?" asks Chisago County investigator Rivard. He wouldn't, according to McCrary and Cronin. "I'd say it's highly probable that he knew Miglin," observes McCrary. "Would this guy let some stranger in off the street? The answer is no. Either [Cunanan] knew of the guy or knew his son. The idea that he just picked him up off the street and then killed him is bizarre—not the most likely scenario."

Despite Cunanan's reputation for pathological lying and drug dealing, none of the scores of people who saw him out in the bars and restaurants night after night, loud and laughing, thought he was capable of violence. Yet there were signs that he was perfectly capable of it. I spent one revealing afternoon in Rancho Bernardo, the retirement community pressed between freeways in the foothills northeast of San Diego. There I found the life to which Andrew Cunanan was really accustomed. I visited the neat white stucco complex he called home and, after ringing a few doorbells, entered the small rented condominium on the second level facing a golf course where he had lived with his mother between 1991 and 1994.

Then, instead of Armanis and Ferragamos, he wore the red apron of a Thrifty drugstore cashier and actually did an honest day's work. But it didn't take long for neighbors to reveal to me that Andrew had once slammed his mother against a wall so hard that he dislocated her shoulder.

The parish priest, Father Bourgeois of San Rafael Church, told me, "He had some really weird moments—not normal as a son. To inflict physical pain on your mother—he did bruise her arm and dislocate it. She was wearing a sling." Father Bourgeois blamed the behavior on drugs. Cunanan's mother, he said, had explained that, at eighteen, "Andrew went up to San Francisco when his father left, joined the gay community, and became someone totally different."

Lots of young men leave home in a similar way without ending up on the FBI's Ten Most Wanted list. But Cunanan soon began a long, slow slide into sadism and desperate, attention-grabbing gestures that were rarely called into question. In November 1996 in Minneapolis, for example, Cunanan was far more upset that David Madson had a new boyfriend than he let on. Madson, typically, thought they could all just be friends. To call attention to himself at a party Madson was hosting in his loft before an AIDS benefit, Cunanan set a paper plate piled with napkins on fire and then walked away from the table.

One guest at the party reportedly revealed that when he and Cunanan had gone to his apartment the night before, Cunanan bit him so hard on the chest that he threw him out.

Three months before Cunanan left San Diego, he said to his roommate, "Erik, I'm unhappy." Greenman says, "Then he's up and gone. He'd give you a glimpse, and then he wouldn't."

"He seemed a little lost," says his friend Michael Moore. "Jumpy." He would assemble people "for a several-hundred-dollar dinner and then walk away to buy magazines on cars and architecture and read them at the table." Toward the end, he said, Cunanan was down-and-out.

Although Cunanan had invited the guests to his farewell dinner the night before he left for Minneapolis, he said he had no money to pay for it. Friends picked up the tab. Greenman told me that Cunanan had recently gone on a wild spending spree. In a six-month period, from approximately October to April, he had spent about $85,000, including $15,000 from Blachford, the money he got from the sale of the Infiniti, the funds from a loan he took out, and charges on his credit card. At the time of his death, he reportedly owed $46,000 to Neiman Marcus.

Now thoughtful friends are asking themselves whether they should have allowed Andrew to get away with so much for so long. "It breaks my heart. None of us could see it, or wanted to see it, or wanted to help," says

Tom Eads. "I feel a lot of guilt." Both Eads and Greenman received numerous presents. Cunanan gave most of his clothes away before he left for Minneapolis. He gave a watch off his wrist to Eads, saying, "Have it. This is just my beach watch. I've got my Cartier." Eads accepted the gift, he says, "even though in my heart of hearts you knew he shouldn't be doing this."

No one called Cunanan on his lying, either. A friend from San Francisco says, "I see now that I sent a strong signal to him: it's all right if you don't tell the truth about yourself. I'm not here to judge you. I'm here to see that you're funny and inventive, or whether you ever bore me. And if you do, we probably won't be friends." Why would you do that? I ask. "Because it helped the moment."

In the aftermath of the Versace murder, a media maelstrom engulfed the case. Hundreds of sightings were called in from all over the country, and fear gripped the communities where Cunanan had spent time. In San Diego a story had it that Cunanan was possibly HIV-positive and killing for revenge. The police warned that he might be disguising himself by dressing as a woman. After Cunanan's suicide, the police were investigating a possible connection between him and the absent owner of the houseboat where he died, Torsten Reineck, the proprietor of a gay bathhouse in Las Vegas. The police told me Cunanan had visited Las Vegas with Madson last spring.

On August 31, 1997, Cunanan would have been twenty-eight years old. Sadly, he never heard the emotional plea released the day he died by his longtime friend Elizabeth Cote, whose little girl was his goddaughter: "Grimmy says she loves her Uncle Monkey and hopes you'll remember that always. Your birthday will soon be here and the day after, someone else who loves you will be five years old. Please let those be days of relief." The message ended with *Dominus vobiscum*. Andrew Phillip Cunanan had once been an altar boy.

UPDATE: Since Andrew Cunanan killed Gianni Versace and then himself in 1997, the murderer and his victim have both become far more famous, living on through broadcasts on HBO II and Court TV, which regularly rerun programs about the infamous crime that I became so involved in chronicling. Moreover, the mansion where Versace was gunned down in South Beach, since sold off by the Versaces, has become a major tourist attraction. My claim that Cunanan and Versace had indeed met in San Francisco prior to the murder, as I discovered while doing the reporting for the *VF* piece, briefly catapulted me into the media frenzy surrounding the story, and I subsequently expanded the article into a book. *Vulgar Favors: Andrew Cunanan, Gianni Versace and the Largest Failed Manhunt in U.S. History* became the basis for the cable-TV coverage.

The Versace murder and its surrounding stories have had many reverberations. As a result of the costly mistakes, as well as information gleaned from the way the manhunt was conducted, the FBI, to its credit, changed the way it investigated crimes involving gays. But the crime also took the glow away from the South Beach area for stars who had bought homes in Miami. Both Sylvester Stallone and Madonna sold their big properties there.

Not long before Gianni Versace died, his house of couture was hoping to realize hundreds of millions of dollars by taking its stock public. Naturally, those plans had to be put on hold. Donatella Versace, Gianni's younger sister, ascended to the difficult position of chief designer and stumbled for a few seasons before making her mark, publicity-wise at least, by creating the un-dress Jennifer Lopez wore to the 2001 Academy Awards. Versace's clothes have always been known to be flamboyant and hot—"hooker chic" to some. Yet the family has pioneered the use of celebrities as "friends," dressing them (remember Chelsea Clinton's makeover?), flying them to its shows, and putting them up for free. The firm maintains an over-the-top, outrageously expensive lifestyle as its chief marketing tool. Madonna even boasted once that Donatella dropped diamonds into her pockets. Another perk was the Miami mansion, where prominent fashion editors were able to stay as nonpaying guests.

The family has also sought to protect its holdings by pushing Gianni Versace into the pantheon of all-time-great designers. But purists were appalled and eyebrows were raised at the Metropolitan Museum of Art in New York in December 1997 when the Costume Institute there mounted a grand retrospective of his work. A similar exhibit was displayed in 2003 in London. The Versaces have also fought hard to protect Gianni's image, going so far, in 1999, as to force a publisher to drop a book on Versace's life already in galleys and set for publication. The author claimed that the family had threatened legal action against his sources. Meanwhile, the longtime companion of Gianni Versace, Antonio Amico, was paid off early to go away; Donatella has also separated from her husband, Paul Beck.

Despite the plummeting sales of luxury goods after 9/11, the profligate lifestyle set by Gianni and continued by Donatella Versace has been hard to rein in. The London *Times* reported that although the couture house lost money for three years after Gianni's death, papers they filed show that the Versaces paid themselves $41 million in dividends. They raised some cash by auctioning off the contents of the Miami mansion in 2001 and selling Gianni's twenty-five Picassos, but in 2002 the company posted a loss of $8.5 million and is carrying more than one hundred million dollars in debt. In 2003 Versace closed boutiques, slashed employment, and tried to restructure its debt. Amid reports of feuding between Santo and Donatella, a new financially savvy CEO quit after just three months. Rumors abound that the company is for sale. In 2004, Donatella's daughter, Allegra, turns eighteen and stands to inherit the fifty percent share of the House of Versace that her Uncle Gianni left her. As the majority shareholder, she would be in a position to call many of the shots.

Meanwhile, Andrew Cunanan's fatal wish to be celebrated continues in surprising ways. Not only is there a novel based on Cunanan in the offing, the National Endowment for the Arts has also granted the former director of the La Jolla Playhouse and two others $35,000 to begin writing *Cunanan: The Musical.*

Part V:

Fame and Infamy

Notes from the Celebrity-Industrial Complex V

The old distinction between fame and infamy (fame that is earned versus fame that is unearned) is constantly blurring. And because the media is so powerful, its grasp so insistent and seductive, we are all too rapidly getting a sense of the impact of the values of celebrity: the preceding story about Andrew Cunanan graphically illustrates the point.

Since I started reporting on the worlds of entertainment and politics, we've moved from a society that admired entertainers with talent, and politicians with intelligence, to a culture in which the goal is just to achieve fame. Being famous now, increasingly, has less and less to do with talent or with doing anything real, thoughtful, or subtle. It's based on doing something extreme or sexual or violent that grabs the attention of the largest audience.

Michael Jackson, whose career clearly illustrates the trajectory from fame to infamy, is the ultimate creature of fame. His talent was originally undeniable as he grew up in the incubator of worldwide celebrity. Perhaps because of this, his narcissism is now so grotesque that—quite apart from his demonstrably inappropriate sexual behavior with little boys, which has cost him dearly—his behavior is aimed mostly at attracting public attention. He is addicted to the rush of it; one wonders if he could live without it. He is not above dangling his baby from a balcony to get noticed, or dancing on the hood of an SUV the day he is arraigned on charges of sexually molesting a thirteen-year-old. He is the saddest, most tragic—and, unfortunately, dangerous—of clowns wandering the world in his white pancaked face.

One of the strongest themes I have sought to convey in this book is that there are real tragedies of fame. I think of Michael Jackson as one. His insecurity over his appearance reflects a society told millions of times over that we aren't pretty enough or, in his case, white enough. His fame put him on a pedestal so high that no one could reach him. His celebrity distorted every interaction he had with other people. It blinded the mother of the child who shared Jackson's bed in 1993, as it did the far less sophisticated family that brought sexual molestation charges against him in 2003. "They've been seduced away from the family by power and by money and by this guy's image," said the boy's father of his son and former wife in the first case. Fame changes everything—especially at the Jackson level.

I now have reported on Michael Jackson four times, each time driven by my dismay at what the media was letting him get away with. When the first sex-abuse charges against him surfaced, in 1993, he was one of the most beloved icons in the world and I was a fan of his music and dancing. I didn't know just how difficult it would be to get a sense of his reality, or lack thereof.

It is not easy to enter the distorted world of such an elusive icon. Jackson's celebrity was such that he at first intimidated authorities, who were reluctant to prosecute him for child molestation on the basis of one child's word, even though the evidence appeared as solid as a rock. Jackson ultimately had the resources to pay more than $25 million to the first boy—the alleged victim—and his family and to circulate a steady stream of cash to potential accusers. (In fact, despite the Jackson camp's spin, the authorities did find other apparent victims who declined to come forward.) That kind of money does not change hands over a nuisance suit. To quote Arnold Schwarzenegger, when the charges first surfaced of his fondling and humiliating women on the sets of his movies: "Where there's smoke, there is usually fire."

Yet, despite these facts, ABC News and Diane Sawyer—high-level network sources trusted by most Americans—mistakenly reported, before an audience of over thirty million (in a 1995 interview with his then bride Lisa Marie Presley, that basically amounted to a publicity bonanza for a new album Jackson was releasing), that the superstar had been cleared of all charges of sexual abuse. The statement was simply not true and I felt duty bound to report it. Jackson's case was still open. It is just one more example, potentially devastating, of the artificial reality that powerful people can use the media to create. Even more serious, Jackson has gone on to become a father of three and has announced his intention to "have" more children, at least two each from a different continent. (He has frequently stated he wants more children than his father's nine.) Meanwhile, he has been allowed to treat both the original and most recent child-abuse allegations as thwarted attempts to blackmail him for money.

Michael Jackson reached the point where he didn't have to answer to anyone. He was a "genius," whose album "Thriller" sold more copies than any before it. And the money he made for his backers made his happiness the top priority of many in the music industry. He came to believe that he could act exactly as he pleased, responsible to nothing but his inflated ego. Today, his thinking is so deranged and his isolation so complete that, I discovered, he was willing to pay hundreds of thousands of dollars to put voodoo curses on his enemies.

Meanwhile, people who got in Jackson's way—at least during his golden days—have received more than curses. They are subject to threats and intimidation. One of his targets is Victor Gutierrez, a Chilean journalist who was beaten up and was then successfully sued by Jackson for slander. Yet the book he wrote, *Michael Jackson Was My Lover—The Secret Diary of Jordie Chandler*—which contained extremely explicit material about Jackson's behavior with Jordie Chandler (the boy to whom Jackson paid all the millions)—has never been challenged.

My third report on Jackson—detailing his deteriorating finances, his empty charities, and his myriad plastic surgeries, which have left him with a prosthetic device in place of the tip of his nose—was prompted by his dangling his then eight-month-old son, Prince Michael II (nicknamed Blanket), from a German hotel balcony. In the aftermath of these shenanigans (timed conveniently to take advantage of the February 2003 TV rating sweeps), Jackson commanded no less than seven hours in a single week of prime viewing time. In the run-up to the invasion of Iraq, the pictures of the infant swaying from that balcony were telecast as often as details from Baghdad. The incident received major coverage. Jackson's desperation to have his name on everyone's lips put his baby at risk to give the media the kind of sensational story it craves. Michael Jackson is the embodiment of the trajectory from fame to infamy. There is a difference.

Report from the Planet Michael: Michael Jackson

"He hasn't been cleared of anything!"

PART I • **JANUARY 1994**

The tarantulas were out, crawling under the firefighters' boots. Overhead, planes were swooping down low between the ridges, dropping streams of bright-orange flame retardant. As the raging fires threatened to reach Neverland, Michael Jackson's 2,700-acre fantasy, neighboring moguls were up on the hillsides straining to see through binoculars. Hours earlier, the exotic animals from Jackson's private zoo had been evacuated. At any moment a capricious ill wind could send everything up in flames. Neverland, like Michael Jackson himself, who was thousands of miles away on his aptly named "Dangerous" world tour, was feeling the heat.

In August 1993, a thirteen-year-old boy had accused the thirty-four-year-old Jackson of sexual molestation, charges the singer vehemently denied. By the time of the fire in October, he was canceling performances right and left for various maladies, but his lawyers promised he would nevertheless show up to be questioned. By November, however, the encroaching criminal investigation, the civil suit brought by the boy, and the nonstop screaming headlines had shattered the fragile pop idol's image and his grip. On November 12, cutting short his tour, Jackson abruptly fled Mexico for a secret drug-treatment location, touching off shocking reports—of missing medical records, of a disappearing witness, of dispatches alleging that the star was suicidal and was never coming back. Jackson's lawyers fought to keep the civil suit from going forward, but on November 23, a California judge ordered that Jackson would have to stand trial.

The child's case against Michael Jackson started with a car breaking down. In May 1992, Jackson, suddenly stranded, contacted Rent-a-Wreck, Los Angeles' hip car-rental agency. The owner called his wife, a beautiful dark-skinned former model, and told her to get right over there. Jamie (not his real name), her twelve-year-old son from an earlier marriage to a Beverly Hills dentist and part-time screenwriter, was, like millions of kids the world over, a big Jackson fan. Jamie had met Jackson in a restaurant when he was five and had sent him a fan letter. In return, he had received free tickets to a Jackson concert. Now Jamie—with his mother and his six-year-old half sister—once again made contact with the mythic, androgynous Jackson, the powerful multimillionaire and self-contained entertainment conglomerate.

Even by Hollywood standards, the weirdness of Michael Jackson, who has been a professional since the age of five, is legendary. He is as well-known for the cosmetic alterations that feminized his African American features as for having the biggest-selling album of all time. But he has always been protected by the armor of his celebrity. He is such a highly prized corporate moneymaking machine, such a valuable *product*, that almost no one, least of all those CEOs who make millions off him, has ever questioned why this reclusive man-child with no known history of romantic relationships and an estimated worth of $150 million lives a fantasy life in the company of children.

Immediately after their meeting, Jackson began calling Jamie almost daily, despite all his commitments. He was about to launch his first concert tour in four years, to fifteen countries, and he did so by grandly announcing the creation of a World Council of Children "to provide children with a forum to express their unique vision for healing the world." His mission, he said, was to work for all youngsters. "I want to tell the children of the world, You're all our children, each one of you is my child, and I love you all." While on tour, Jackson began calling Jamie from different points along the way—the conversations would sometimes last an hour. Jamie, who is fine boned, delicate, and dark like his mother and who looks much younger than he is, was thrilled to be the object of his idol's attention.

But some consider these long-distance conversations about video games and Neverland to be the beginning of an overwhelming seduction that ended in August 1993 when Jamie graphically described, first to a psychiatrist and then to the police, exactly how Jackson had repeatedly sexually molested him. Case number SC026226, filed September 14 in Los Angeles County Superior Court, a civil suit brought on behalf of Jamie, charges sexual battery, battery, seduction, willful misconduct, intentional infliction of emotional distress, fraud, and negligence. "These sexually offensive contacts include but are not limited to defendant Michael Jackson orally copulating plaintiff, defendant Michael Jackson masturbating plaintiff, defendant Michael Jackson eating the semen of plaintiff, and defendant Michael Jackson having plaintiff fondle and manipulate the breasts and nipples of defendant Michael Jackson while defendant Michael Jackson would masturbate."

Jackson's first call inviting Jamie to Neverland, in Santa Barbara County, a scenic two-and-a-half-hour drive north of Los Angeles, came two days after the star's famous interview with Oprah Winfrey, which aired February 10, 1993. The Oprah interview was the culmination of a three-week global media blitz that had Jackson performing in rapid succession at the Clinton inauguration, at the Super Bowl, and on the widely televised American Music Awards. That first weekend, Jamie, his sister, and his mother slept in the guesthouse, which is so far from the main house, where Jackson sleeps, that paparazzi cannot get the two in the same telephoto lens.

Apart from the private zoo, the giant sundial made of flowers, the merry-go-round that plays "Like a Virgin," the miniature choo-choo train, the hall filled with every video game imaginable, the theater stocked with nearly every film and videocassette ever made for children, the pool, the staff of fifty who cater to their employer's every whim twenty-four hours a day, Michael offered Jamie and his sister a special trip to Toys 'R' Us after closing time to select a shopping-cartful of presents. Those were the first of dozens of video games, action figures, watches, jackets, and other delights that Michael would lavish on the children. Jamie's mother eventually got diamonds and rubies as well. When Michael invited the family to his playground again the next weekend, Jamie, of course, was eager to return. Like most guests at the ranch, Jamie had to sign a confidentiality agreement that he would not speak to the press or write about anything that went on there. This time, before they returned home, Michael took them in his limo to Disneyland, where they got special treatment.

From that point on, Jamie and his mother and sister spent virtually every weekend with Michael. (The mother and Jamie's stepfather were mostly estranged.) Quickly, Jamie began to withdraw from everyone else, no longer playing with other kids. Eventually, he stopped speaking to his father and six-year-old half brother, even on the phone. He and Michael were quickly labeled "inseparable." They played with slingshots and squirt guns. From the balcony of Michael's condo in Century City, they threw water balloons onto passing cars.

In March 1993, Jamie spent four days at Neverland. Eleven-year-old Brett Barnes was also there. He subsequently told KNBC-TV—as did ten-year-old Wade Robson—that he, too, had slept with Michael but that nothing had happened: "It's a huge bed." Also there that weekend were the Cascio brothers, Eddie and Frank, nine and thirteen, who would travel alone with Jackson in the fall on his "Dangerous" tour. Michael, Jamie, and the other boys would stay up until all hours, their senses assaulted by music, video games, and films.

On March 28 a private jet was sent to pick up Jamie, his mother and sister, and Jackson at the Santa Monica Airport and fly them to Las Vegas, where they stayed in the Michael Jackson Suite at Steve Wynn's Mirage Hotel. It was the first night Michael and Jamie would share a bed, Michael wearing sweats, Jamie wearing pajamas. Michael had rented *The Exorcist*, and Jamie got scared. His mother and sister stayed in another bedroom in the suite. The next night the two wanted to sleep together again. But a confrontation ensued, because Jamie's mother objected.

At this point, insiders who believe the case against Jackson claim, Michael began to cry, telling Jamie's mother, "This is about being a family, not making judgments." He declared his love for each of them and pleaded, "Why don't you trust me? If we're a family, you've got to think of me as a brother. Why make me feel so bad? This is a bond. It's not about sex. This is something special." He then said Jamie could sleep wherever he wanted to. That did it—Jamie's mother was won over. From that night on, for more than three months and with few exceptions, she allowed the two to share a bed. Michael essentially moved in and lived with Jamie in one room of the family's small, unpretentious house in Santa Monica Canyon while his little friend went to school.

Jamie has said that sexual touching began at Neverland in April. It started with cuddling and kisses. Michael began to "rub up against me." He later allegedly told Jamie that their being together was fated "in the cosmos." By this time, on visits to the ranch, Jamie was staying regularly in Michael's bedroom, with his mother and sister still in the guesthouse. Both buildings are locked at night and heavily patrolled by security. Michael's bedroom is connected by a secret staircase to a special guest room, the Shirley Temple Room. Former employees of the ranch report that many boys are invited to sleep in the Shirley Temple Room but that, afterward, the staff often finds the bed untouched. Jackson has such a penchant for privacy that the floor outside his bedroom is wired so that whenever anyone comes within five feet of the entrance, *ding-dong* noises go off.

Over time, Jamie says in a leaked, confidential Los Angeles Department of Children's Services report, Michael graduated to "kissing me on the mouth. . . . One time he was kissing me and he put his tongue in my mouth and I said, 'Don't do that.' . . . He started crying. . . . I guess he tried to make me feel guilty." When Michael took the family on a trip to Disney World, in Florida, he "continued to rub up against me quite often," Jamie said.

In May, Jackson and his adopted family jetted to Monaco to the World Music Awards, where Jamie and his sister were widely photographed, usually beside Michael at Prince Albert's table or on Michael's lap. Most thirteen-year-old boys don't spend hours being held on men's laps, but people at the table guessed that Jamie, who was dressed exactly like Jackson, was no more than nine or ten.

"The little boy was loving every minute of it, getting so much attention," said a woman who was there. Jackson, heavily made up as usual with white pancake makeup, wore a hat and mirrored glasses to shield his eyes, and covered his nose and mouth with his hand. "His nose looked like a wax model with most of the wax melted away," the woman said. He barely spoke to anyone other than Jamie and his sister, and drank only Evian water, which his bodyguard poured, after first wiping the glass with his handkerchief. At one point, Jackson sent the mother and two friends off in a limousine with a lot of cash and credit cards and told them to buy whatever they wanted.

According to the Department of Children's Services report, Jamie said things "really got out of hand" in Monaco. "Minor stated Mr. Jackson told him that Mr. Jackson's cousin masturbated in front of him and that masturbation was a wonderful thing. He coerced minor to bathe with him and later, while laying next to each other in bed, Mr. Jackson put his hand . . . under minor's shorts and masturbated minor until minor had orgasm at which point Mr. Jackson cleaned the semen with a tissue saying 'Wasn't that good?' This occurred several times; however, Mr. Jackson began eating minor's semen, then 'began masturbating me with his mouth.' Minor denies ever oral copulating Mr. Jackson or any anal intercourse."

The family flew home via Paris and Euro Disneyland. They made a further trip to Disney World, which Jamie recounted to the Department of Children's Services. "At the end he [Mr. Jackson] had me suck on one of his nipples and twist the other while he [Mr. Jackson] masturbated himself.

"Minor stated Mr. Jackson told minor that minor would go to Juvenile Hall if he told and that they'd both be in trouble. Minor also said Mr. Jackson told him about other boys he had 'done this with' but he didn't go as far with 'them.' [Jamie gave authorities the names of four other boys Michael allegedly told him about. Macaulay Culkin's name appeared in the report, but he has denied any wrongdoing on the part of Jackson.] Minor stated Mr. Jackson tried to make him hate his mo. and fa. so that he could only go to Mr. Jackson."

Jamie began missing many visits he would ordinarily have had with his father, the Beverly Hills dentist and would-be screenwriter, who is remarried and who has a son with his current wife. In the beginning, patients say, the dentist bragged about his son's friendship with Jackson. Having sold one screenplay, he seemed eager to continue in show business. Jamie, who had given him the idea for the screenplay, which was made into a movie, wanted to be a director. The dentist seemed pleased that Michael and Jamie were going to spend five days together at the father's house, sleeping in a bedroom they would share with Jamie's half brother.

Then Jamie's father saw Jackson and Jamie in bed together. They were fully clothed, but his suspicions were aroused. Michael and Jamie told him, he has said, that they couldn't stand Jamie's mother and that she hated his current wife. They seemed to be playing the parents off against each other. Jamie's father eventually came to believe that because of Michael, "there is no family anymore." Jamie's mother, with whom the dentist had always enjoyed a friendly relationship, scoffed at his concerns.

In early June the father saw his former wife and their son at a school graduation and angrily demanded, "What's going on with Michael?" They argued, and the father did not see his son again until mid-July. By then he was feeling desperate, since he knew that his former wife was planning to take Jamie out of school so that they could go with Michael and a tutor on the "Dangerous" tour in the fall. One day the father broke down and began to cry while treating a patient who happened to be a Beverly Hills lawyer: Barry Rothman.

Rothman agreed to represent the dentist, whose relations with his former wife had become acrimonious. A custody battle was brewing, and legally the father was not in a strong position: he had never paid Jamie's mother child support and he owed $68,000. When the father became more and more irate and demanded a meeting, the mother confided in Jackson, who in turn called *his* lawyer, Bertram Fields, to intervene.

Fields did so aggressively, even though minor custody disputes are hardly what he, as one of show business's most visible litigators, normally gets paid $500 an hour for. Fields called in the private investigator-negotiator-forensic audio specialist Anthony Pellicano. The flamboyant Pellicano, who also writes on the side, is a goon and a bully who fights dirty. But if he's on your side, he is an invaluable ally, a trusted advisor, a canny investigator.

On July 9, Jamie's mother and stepfather met with Fields and Pellicano in Pellicano's office on Sunset Strip. After listening to long conversations that the stepfather had secretly taped of himself and Jamie's father concerning the father's suspicions, Pellicano drove over to Jackson's Century City condominium, where Jamie and his sister were visiting. He questioned Jamie alone for about forty-five minutes as to whether anything sexual was going on between Michael and him. Jamie said no.

Meanwhile, Jamie's father, through his attorney, went to a Beverly Hills psychiatrist and, without disclosing any names, explained the situation hypothetically, including a mention of what the psychiatrist called the "condoning attitude" of Jamie's mother. He wanted to know if his son might be the victim of child abuse. In a written reply, the psychiatrist offered the opinion "that reasonable suspicion would exist that sexual abuse may have occurred"; he concluded that "psychotherapeutic intervention" was indicated for everyone involved.

Such would not be the case. Instead, the fighting continued. On July 11, Fields, acting as an "intermediary" between the father and the mother, assured them that Jamie would be given to his father for one week's visitation. During the course of that week, Jamie's side alleges, the boy admitted to his father that sexual touching had occurred between him and Michael. Convinced that his son had been "brainwashed," the father refused to give Jamie back and demanded a meeting with Jackson. On July 12 the mother signed an agreement stating she would not take the boy out of Los Angeles County without the father's consent. That wasn't enough for the father, however, and the mother began taking legal steps through *her* lawyer, Michael Freeman, to force the dentist to give Jamie back. The father, meanwhile, repeatedly threatened to go public with his information.

Fields, at this point, stepped aside and "let Anthony deal with it." On August 4, a meeting of Jamie and his father with Jackson and Pellicano took place on the top floor of the Westwood Marquis Hotel. The only thing the two sides agreed on is that the father read Jackson parts of the criminal code about reporting child abuse. Money was never mentioned, although Fields and Pellicano, who say they suspected extortion from the beginning, were constantly asking the father and his attorney, Barry Rothman, what it was they wanted.

That night Pellicano and Rothman got together in Rothman's office, and Pellicano heard for the first time what Jamie's father did want: $20 million (for a trust fund, Jamie's camp says, to be set aside for the boy's use only). Pellicano refused.

After inconclusive phone conversations, a second meeting took place in Rothman's office, on August 13, with Jamie's father present. Pellicano offered the dentist a $350,000 script deal. He suggested that the father and son could foster their relationship by writing scripts together. The father refused.

On August 16, Michael Freeman, the lawyer representing Jamie's mother, informed Rothman that he would be filing papers early the next day to compel the father to turn over the boy by seven P.M. Rothman asked for time to inform the dentist, who was performing eight-hour surgery. Freeman refused.

On August 17 came the denouement. Jamie's father, desperate that he would lose his son, made an early-morning appointment with the psychiatrist to whom he had posed the hypothetical situation: Mathis Abrams. During a nearly three-hour session, Jamie told Dr. Abrams for the first time the full extent of his alleged sexual relations with Jackson. By California law, such an accusation must be reported to the appropriate authorities, who then automatically begin an investigation. A police sergeant and a social worker from the Department of Children's Services interviewed Jamie and found that his story was consistent. The therapist told the authorities that he felt the boy was telling the truth.

Meanwhile, Michael Freeman, the mother's lawyer, had filed the custody papers and obtained a court order to have Jamie returned to his mother by seven P.M. But the order was held in abeyance by the psychiatrist's reporting of the alleged abuse. Jamie also said that, the week before, his mother had come to get him for lunch and informed him that she was taking him out of the state until the "investigation was completed." He ran away from her and requested that he be allowed to continue to live with his father. He told authorities that his mother liked the "glitzy life" and that he was afraid she would allow Jackson to see him again. Jamie also told the police that he was glad his father had finally "brought all of this out in the open"; he was ashamed but relieved. When authorities told Jamie's mother what he had told them about Jackson, she reportedly broke down and said she couldn't believe how stupid she had been.

At first, Children's Services wanted to take Jamie into custody. Its report recommended that the mother be questioned about "her ability to protect minor" and that the father be questioned about the discussion of money to keep the whole thing quiet—which Jamie had also talked about. Ultimately, Jamie was allowed to stay with his father.

Pellicano, who says he had no idea that any of this was going on, had not heard from Barry Rothman since August 13, when his $350,000 offer was rejected, so while Jamie was in Dr. Abrams's office, Pellicano was calling Rothman. He says he was determined to tape the attorney without his knowledge and get him on the record about the $20 million. Pellicano tried his best to make Rothman admit that he wanted $5 million each for four screenplays, but Rothman avoided discussing the matter. About 11:30 A.M., Rothman faxed Pellicano a letter, formally refusing the $350,000 "to settle and release all civil claims our clients have a right to assert against your client." Pellicano faxed Rothman back what Jamie's side characterizes as a "cover your ass" letter: "I *do not* recognize any civil claims against my client whatsoever. We *have not and will not submit* to the extortionate attempts you and your client have subjected us to." That day was the first time the question of extortion was raised.

On August 20, Jackson, who had been informed of Jamie's charges, left for Asia to continue the "Dangerous" tour, sponsored by Pepsi-Cola. Anthony Pellicano went with him. On August 21 and 22, the police executed a search at Neverland and the Century City condo and carted off several boxes of material. The story broke on KNBC's evening news on August 23. The media war had begun.

Jackson's defense: "If it's a thirty-five-year-old pedophile, then it's obvious why he's sleeping with little boys. But if it's Michael Jackson, it doesn't mean anything," sums up Anthony Pellicano. "You could say it's strange, it's inappropriate, it's weird. You can use all the adjectives you want to. But is it criminal? No. Is it immoral? No." Bert Fields, Jackson's lawyer, agrees. "Michael never had a childhood. He was on the stage from the time he was five, and while he's a highly intelligent person, he has a lot of childlike qualities. He really lives the life of a twelve-year-old." Fields believes that Michael's behavior is that of *any* normal eleven- or twelve-year-old boy. "One of the things he has done—the things *I* did when I was eleven or twelve, probably all of us did—was to have sleepovers. So he'll have kids stay over at his ranch or wherever he is. And almost always he has their parents along on all these things."

Pellicano readily admits that Jackson has shared his bed many times with little boys over the years. "If you hide something like that, then people are going to be even more suspicious, and my view of this whole thing is just to tell the truth. He did sleep in beds with little boys. There's no question about it. He's got a gigantic bed." Pellicano isn't bothered by admitting that Jackson slept with Jamie at Jamie's house at least thirty nights in a row, either. "They *invited* Michael to stay there. Michael didn't crash their house. He didn't say, 'I want to stay here.' They *wanted* him to stay there."

According to Pellicano, there was no cause for alarm in Jackson's having a friend like Jamie. "If Michael has no sexual preference one way or another, male or female, to my knowledge, and the parents of the children are allowing this, you have to look at it in the context—especially at the ranch. They go out and they play and they go on the rides and they have water fights and do all this stuff. And then they kind of like crash. Now, Michael is always fully dressed." Even at Jamie's house? "When [Jamie] went to bed, he had pajamas on, and sweats, and Michael had sweats and pajamas on. Michael goes to bed with his *hat* on. I'm serious." Adds Pellicano, "It would make you nuts if you didn't know Michael. It would make you crazy."

Bert Fields says he suspected that the whole thing was a setup from the beginning. Furthermore, he doesn't think anyone will come forward to corroborate Jamie's story. "We've talked to every child we know of who knows Michael—and had to go back many, many years—and nobody says anything like this ever happened." He says that, from early on, Jamie's stepfather said that he thought the boy's father "wants money."

At some point, in an effort to help his wife, the stepfather had secretly recorded three long phone conversations with the father and reported back to Fields and Pellicano. On the tape, the father threatens to "ruin Michael's career" and implies that he has the proof to do so: "When the facts are put together, it's going to be bigger than all of us put together, and the whole thing is going to crash down on everybody and destroy everybody in sight." Jamie's father says Michael "is an evil guy. He's worse than bad, and I have the evidence to prove it." (Pellicano distributed the tape to the media to bolster his side, but it is crudely edited, full of erasures, and at times actually seems to help the father's case.)

On the tape, the stepfather, who appears to be a longtime friend of the father's, tries to play the mediator. When the dentist threatens to "blow the whole thing wide open," the stepfather asks: "And does that help Jamie?"

"That's irrelevant to me. The bottom line to me is, yes, his mother is harming him, and Michael is harming him; I can prove that, and I *will* prove that, and if they force me to go to court about it, I will [*bleep*] and I will be granted custody, and she will have no rights whatsoever. . . . It cost me tens of thousands of dollars to get the information I got, and you know I don't have that kind of money. . . . I'm willing to go down financially."

"Do you think that's going to help Jamie?"

"I believe Jamie's already irreparably harmed."

"Do you believe that he's fucking him?"

"I don't know."

Later, the father asks the stepfather if he's ever tried to talk to the mother about Jackson's coming into their lives. "If Michael Jackson were just some thirty-four-year-old person," asks Jamie's father, "would this be happening? No. They've been seduced away from the family by power and by money and by this guy's image."

After listening to the tape with the mother and stepfather, Fields and Pellicano believed that the father had Jackson spend time at his house only so that he could bug the room the star and Jamie shared. "And Michael, innocent that he was, went over, and I think spent a week at the father's house in the bedroom with the boy," says Fields.

After being told by Rothman that serious criminal conduct may have occurred, Fields raised that possibility with Jackson. "Michael's response was completely inconsistent with guilt. When I told him what he said, he was completely unafraid of any tape that might have been made during that week. It was not the attitude of somebody who was worried about what was on the tape."

Anthony Pellicano took the spin that would become his mantra: "They're all dysfunctional. You have a dysfunctional father, a dysfunctional stepfather, a dysfunctional mother, and possibly a dysfunctional child." He also decided to go right over and question Jamie. "I went in there with an attitude that I was not going to prove that Michael was innocent. I was going to prove that Michael was guilty. Because if such a thing could occur—and it never would in a million years—I have to protect my client."

Pellicano is famous for taping people—often secretly—but he didn't tape his talk with Jamie. "Absolutely not. You have to understand, that was a whim, and I could have. I had no idea what this boy was going to tell me."

According to Pellicano, Jamie told him a lot in forty-five minutes. "He's a very bright, articulate, intelligent, manipulative boy." Pellicano, who has fathered nine children by two wives, says he asked Jamie many sexually specific questions. "And I'm looking dead into his eyes. And I'm watching in his eyes for any sign of fear or anticipation—anything. And I see none," Pellicano says. "And I keep asking him, 'Did Michael ever touch you?' 'No.' 'Did you ever see Michael nude?' 'No.' He laughed about it. He giggled a lot, like it was a funny thing. Michael would never be nude. . . . 'Did you and Michael ever masturbate?' 'No.' 'Did Michael ever masturbate in front of you?' 'No.' 'Did you guys ever talk about masturbation?' 'No.'

"'So you never saw Michael's body?' 'One time, he lifted up his shirt and he showed me those blotches.'" Then Pellicano asked Jackson to come downstairs. "And I sit Michael next to him and go through exactly the same thing," he says. Pellicano claims they both maintained that nothing had happened, and Jamie began to disparage his father. "He's talking to me about his father never wanting to let him be a boy and never wanting to let him do the things he wants to do. 'He wants me to stay in the house and write these screenplays.' . . . And he said to me several times during this conversation, 'He just wants money.' I said, 'What are you talking about?'"

Then, Pellicano claims, Jamie told him the story, confirmed by Michael, that when Michael was over at his father's house, the dentist told Michael he really didn't have the room for him to stay there. "Why don't you build me an addition?" the father apparently suggested. When he checked with the zoning board and found out he couldn't put the addition on, "he asked Michael just to build him a whole new house." (Larry Feldman, Jamie's attorney, who was hired by the family calls the story "ludicrous and factually incorrect.") According to Pellicano, he learned that the dentist wanted to close down his practice and become involved in screenplays with Michael.

After attempting to work out a deal, Fields left town, putting Pellicano in charge. "Bert gives me an absolute free hand when I'm involved," Pellicano says. "This is problem solving. This is what I make my money at. This is why I have the reputation I have, because I solve problems."

Pellicano's version of the August 4 meeting at the Westwood Marquis (between Jamie and his father and Jackson and Pellicano) differs totally from that of Jamie's side. Pellicano says that as soon as the father and Jamie walked into the room, they both hugged Michael. "He's shorter than Michael," Pellicano says of the dentist. "And he's got his head underneath Michael's neck, and he kisses Michael, and he's got his eyes closed." Pellicano was astounded. "If I believed somebody molested *my* kid and I got that close to him, I'd be on death row right now."

The father began to read the psychiatrist's letter, which cited the criminal statutes that applied to child abuse. "Jamie was looking down, and he pops his head up and looks at Michael like 'I didn't say that.' *That* kind of look."

Pellicano said, "You don't have to recite statutes. I know what the statutes are. Are you accusing Michael?" The dentist answered, "This is all about the molestation of my son." "What is it exactly that you want?" The father answered that Pellicano had told his lawyer "you would help me do screenplays." Pellicano denied it, and the father got very angry. According to Pellicano, the dentist pointed his finger at Michael and shouted, "Only he can help me!"

Michael, says Pellicano, was scared. "The father keeps pointing at him: 'I am going to ruin you! I'm going to take you down!'" Pellicano finally told the father to leave, and the father and son walked out the door.

"Did you tape this meeting?" I asked Pellicano. "No. I don't want to be in the possession of a tape that has my client on it. I don't know what anybody's going to say. And you don't tape-record something unless you know what's going on."

Pellicano, who left the meeting puzzled, called Barry Rothman (the attorney for Jamie's father) and told him what had happened. They arranged a meeting immediately in Rothman's office. "The doctor wants to close down his dental practice and he wants to write full-time, and what he wants is this," Rothman supposedly told Pellicano: "Four movie deals, $5 million each."

"And I look at him like he's absolutely crazy. You want $20 million? There's no fucking way that's going to happen. I'm not going to pay $20 million—and for what?" Once again, Pellicano says, his mind races. Maybe Rothman is lying—how do I get this on tape? Later, they go back and forth on the telephone and arrange another meeting with the father at Rothman's office, for August 9.

Pellicano claimed the dentist told him that he wanted to close his practice and work with Jamie, so Pellicano offered "start-up money. And Rothman chimes in and says, 'Wait a minute—we've already told you what we want.' Rothman says the $20 million: 'We want four movie deals, $5 million each.'" As Pellicano described the scene, he looked the father right in the eye: "'It's never going to happen. Do you understand me?' . . . He goes ballistic." This time Pellicano was thrown out.

On the phone, Pellicano offered Rothman one screenplay "at the going rate of $350,000. . . . I wanted to get them to accept it. They would take $350,000, they would have a contract, and the whole thing would be over. I would get them out of my life, and that would be it." According to Fields, "Pellicano was convinced they'd go for some kind of offer, some kind of check, and we'd have them."

But the $350,000 offer was rejected, because, Rothman said, Pellicano originally offered a three-picture deal at $350,000 each, and then he backed down. "I just told you why it won't be accepted, and it can't be, because you offered three to begin with, and he feels he's being slapped on the wrist for an emotional response regarding his child."

Moments later, Pellicano vainly tried to raise the subject of the $20 million: "Listen, the reason I said no to the deal in the office is that he asked for $5 million per year."

Rothman countered, "That's not . . . We're past that point."

"Twenty million dollars—" Pellicano persisted.

"We're past that point."

But Pellicano wouldn't give up, and Rothman, who still seemed eager for a three-picture deal, replied, "You sat across the table from him and said, 'It's not going to be that figure,' and he said, 'Okay, what do you have to say?' That's what he said."

"That's not true!"

"Yes, it *is* true!"

With that, the deal was off.

In last month's *Vanity Fair*, Bert Fields told Michael Shnayerson that he thought the father wanted the matter to remain private. ("He could hardly hope to collect money after it became public.") The father didn't know, Fields maintained, that if he took his son to the psychiatrist, the therapist would be required by law to report the charges to the police. In an interview for this article, Fields said the opposite. "I believe the father knew that when he went to the therapist, it now had to become public." And that was his method of making it public, rather than calling a press conference. "I can't believe I would want *my* child branded for the rest of his life as the child who was molested by Michael Jackson," Fields continued. "If it happened to my child, I would want to see the son of a bitch put in jail. It's much more important to shelter your child, I think."

Larry Feldman, Jamie's lawyer, called the Fields-Pellicano version of events "preposterous," insisting that it was Pellicano, not the father, who introduced the idea of being paid for screenplays to foster a relationship with the boy. "We vehemently deny there is any extortion. At the most, there is an attempt to prevent the type of public circus that has occurred," said the father's new attorney, Richard Hirsch. "The other side is raising the red herring of extortion, which is not a defense to child molestation."

"I'm really foggy on this," Pellicano responded when asked why he was unable to prevent the charges from blowing up in public, "because I don't know what they thought. It doesn't matter now. Because everything else is history. It's been on TV."

. . .

While the civil suit against him goes forward, Jackson remains under criminal investigation in Santa Barbara and Los Angeles counties. But he has not been charged with any crime. A criminal case is far more difficult to conduct than a civil action. In a criminal case, the evidence presented must convince all twelve members of the jury beyond a reasonable doubt. A case such as this one, consisting of one person's word against another's, with no apparent physical evidence, would be hard to prove without corroboration. That is what the police have been focusing on—trying to find other children with whom Jackson might have behaved inappropriately.

Suppose there was another child who claimed to have been molested by Jackson. Would his parents subject him and themselves to the media madness of a celebrity trial? One anguished father who had spent considerable time at Neverland called me in despair over the fact that he had ever allowed Jackson to share a bed with his son. He has no proof that anything untoward occurred, but he claims that he himself was molested by an uncle and kept the secret from his parents for thirty years. That knowledge tortures him, because he and his wife are divorced and he lives so far away that he is rarely able to see his son. He says that his wife, who has custody, told him that if he spoke to the media, he would never see his son again. A week later, after talking to his wife, who was in contact with Jackson's side, he called again, eager to give me a quotation in favor of Michael Jackson. Dealing with such complicated family histories and emotional flip-flops is routine for law-enforcement officers investigating a criminal case.

The major difference between civil and criminal charges, however, is that a criminal charge can send a person to jail. But is it likely that *any* jury will put a star of Jackson's magnitude behind bars? "The celebrityhood of this will affect every aspect of the investigation and prosecution. It puts pressure on the police; it puts pressure on the DA; it changes everything in a trial—it introduces an *x* factor," says the former Los Angeles district attorney Ira Reiner. "It usually helps the defendant. Juries are starstruck like people generally, and like to be friends of celebrities. It's not impossible, but it's extremely difficult, to convict celebrities of crimes."

Nevertheless, Jackson may have to take the Fifth Amendment in a civil suit, which he faces whether or not criminal charges are filed. Although Jackson cannot be jailed for charges brought in a civil suit, he may have to pay damages. His lawyers lost their big battle to keep him from being questioned in the civil suit while the criminal investigation is going on.

On November 23, 1993, a Superior Court judge in Los Angeles denied their request and set a trial date for March 21, 1994.

In the course of the hearing, Bert Fields, Jackson's civil lawyer, misinterpreting information hastily given to him by Jackson's criminal attorney, Howard Weitzman, told the judge that a grand jury in Santa Barbara had issued two subpoenas for witnesses: "You can't get closer to an indictment than that." Weitzman appeared amazed at this disclosure; he later contradicted Fields, and within forty-eight hours, Fields was no longer solely in charge of the civil case. Fields has always maintained that a criminal trial for Jackson could be fatal: "The stakes are going to jail and ruining his life, and his life is essentially over if he's charged and convicted."

In ruling in Jamie's favor, the judge honored the California law granting injured minors a speedy trial: "It's a tough little statute."

Once a trial date had been set, speculation grew that Jackson would never return to the United States. "He hasn't sent any money out of the country," says Fields. "He isn't moving to Switzerland. He plans to come back to testify."

According to Eddie Reynoza, a featured dancer on the *Thriller* video, Jackson "had little boys around for nine years straight, twenty-four hours around the clock. People in show business couldn't understand how long it took to get the talk going. The public is one hundred years behind on this." Reynoza acknowledges, however, that people close to the star "looked the other way. They were afraid of being fired." As for the children's parents, Reynoza claims that some of them, like Jackson employees, were showered with gifts. "He would buy five Cadillacs at one time. He gives homes, Jaguars, Cadillacs, trips for their birthdays—like a fairy tale out of the movies."

Reynoza claimed Jackson had become increasingly "weird and freaky . . . worried about his face." Although Jackson admits to only two nose jobs, Reynoza says, "The whole inside of his face is artificial implants. He told me, 'I can't go out in the sun. My face would fall off.'"

Reynoza believes that Jackson's drug abuse is the first step in an escalating series of medical roadblocks. "There's no way in hell he's going to appear at a trial with that little boy. He'll end up in a mental hospital. Next thing will be a nervous breakdown. Don't be surprised. . . . You're going to see a lot more of his people quitting. They don't want to get involved in all the media."

The Michael Jackson story is reverberating in some rarely seen parts of the world of celebrity. The man on the telephone, Paul Barresi, former porn star, personal trainer, police informant, and hustler, sounded outraged: "All these people coming out of the woodwork, screaming for the sake of morality and asking for thousands of dollars! Well, society is responsible—it thrives on the repugnant. The tabloids pay *thousands*!" He should know. He was selling a story about Michael Jackson and little boys at Neverland to four British tabloids more or less simultaneously. By secretly tape-recording them, photographing them, and giving their names to the police, he had also betrayed the people who had asked him to put them in contact with the tabloids.

"All these people" are a French couple, Philippe and Stella Lemarque, who cooked at Neverland for nearly a year before they were dismissed and who say they were eyewitnesses to scenes in which Michael Jackson took sexual advantage of young guests, specifically Macaulay Culkin, who has denied that anything went on between him and Michael. The Lemarques described, on tape, Jackson's alleged modus operandi: keeping the kids up all night with sound-and-light shows, games, and videos until they were so overstimulated that they barely noticed his fondling.

Through Barresi, the Lemarques had tried to sell their story a few years ago to the *National Enquirer* for $100,000 but were told that it would take too much investigation to prove and was therefore legally tricky. But now that Jamie's charges had broken, the Lemarques were out hawking again, and they had upped their price to $500,000. To the sex-industry veteran Barresi, the milieu of Neverland was "a perfect situation for a pedophile. Michael Jackson is able to have that fantasyland and could overwhelm kids from dysfunctional families; they're perfect prey." Barresi wanted to make one thing clear, however: "I take no sides. I'm in this strictly for the money."

Meanwhile, Splash News Service, which brokers information about celebrities to the tabloids, sold the highly confidential Department of Children's Services report, which had actually been given first to Diane Dimond of *Hard Copy*. Revenues from the report made up a tidy part of the $100,000 that Splash has reaped so far on the Jackson story.

Yet not until August 26 did the story that was mesmerizing the world make page one in Jackson's hometown, and then, thanks to Pellicano and Jackson's criminal attorney, Howard Weitzman, the first two days' coverage in the Los Angeles *Times* played up the alleged extortion more than the molestation charges. Only on the third day did the *Times* publish a response from the police as to whether anyone from Jackson's camp had reported any extortion attempt. No one had. Even then, the paper made only slighting mention of the Department of Children's Services report. The paper did report that Jesse Jackson had urged the *Times* to use more restraint concerning these child-molestation accusations. During the month of October, the *Times*, which has never been aggressive in its reporting on the Hollywood community, ran no stories on the case. A lot of people simply did not want to believe that Michael Jackson could molest little boys, and the tepid establishment-press coverage reflected the public's repugnance and ambivalence.

As much as in a political campaign, media manipulation is crucial in a volatile case like this. Pellicano worked tirelessly to shape the coverage, with mixed results. Early on, in his most controversial action, Pellicano introduced to the TV news cameras two young boys who said that they were close friends of Michael Jackson's and had shared a bed with him but that he had never done anything to them. Many people then thought that Pellicano's effort to clear Jackson had backfired. "Do you know an adult now who is not absolutely convinced that Michael Jackson did it?" said a prominent criminal attorney. "Pellicano ruined it."

Anthony Pellicano's greatest strength seems to lie in getting people *not* to talk. Larry Feldman charges that Jackson's side has deliberately used Pellicano "to be out front and make slanderous charges about [Jamie] and his parents." He further states in court documents: "Muzzling independent witnesses, while allowing defendant's investigator to say anything he wants in a declaration for the press, is not justice."

Cabell Bruce, a producer for *Hard Copy*, tells of going up to the front porch of a woman who works at Neverland and trying to talk to her. "She literally started shaking, her eyes filled with tears, and all she could say was 'Call Mr. Pellicano.'" Diane Dimond, also of *Hard Copy*, complains that every time she finds a source who has been close to Michael Jackson, the response is "Mr. Pellicano has asked us not to say anything."

Pellicano went as far as to offer to pay a tabloid journalist to tell him who had leaked the Department of Children's Services report to Splash. When the journalist refused, Pellicano pointedly said, "You're not even a citizen" and "I don't want anyone to get hurt in all this." There were also reports that Jamie's father had found a bug on his home phone and that he was roughed up at his office. Pellicano denies that he had anything to do with this: "If I had wanted him roughed up, he would have been roughed up."

Dimond, who along with local KNBC has broken more developments in this case than anyone else, says she has received messages via other reporters from Pellicano: "Tell Diane Dimond I'm watching her." "Tell her I hope her health is good." Pellicano denies that any threats were made.

Given all the bad reports about Jackson, one might assume that the public would be barraged with a resounding campaign *for* Michael Jackson by his Hollywood friends. But with the exception of two statements by

Elizabeth Taylor and a few brief unsigned ones from his music company, Sony, the silence has been deafening—from his manager, Sandy Gallin; from his powerful movie agency, Creative Artists; from his dear friends David Geffen, Michael Milken, Steve Wynn, and Diana Ross.

In September, and again in November, Michael's brother Jermaine and their mother, Katherine, told the press that the allegations were false. Sister La Toya, on the *Today* show, said that she *hoped* the allegations weren't true. (Her husband-manager let it be known that her price for talking to the tabloids ranged from $25,000 to $40,000.) "Every single person I've contacted on Jackson's side or in his family has wanted money," says Dimond. "They say, 'I'd like to tell you something about Michael. He's a dear sweet boy, and for $5,000 I'll come on and tell you this.' It absolutely has impeded me from presenting a full Jackson side of the story."

Most surprising was the unsolicited proposition *Hard Copy* got from a representative of Michael Jackson's father. For $150,000 Joe Jackson would appear on the show to talk about Michael's troubles. The price quickly dropped to $50,000, but negotiations broke down because the producers wanted Katherine Jackson, too, and her husband couldn't guarantee her signature on a contract. The relationship between father and son had come down to a tabloid-TV deal; there is virtually no one Michael Jackson knows who does not view him as some sort of big-bucks ticket to ride. Certainly in his own twisted family, he has, from an early age, been leaned on. And the adorable, sensitive little one with the most talent has been taught to manipulate the media, even lie about his age as an eight-year-old. Says ABC News *Day One* correspondent Michel McQueen, who has dealt extensively with Jackson family members, "They think the truth is whatever they can convince someone of."

Starting in their early days with Motown, the Jackson Five were packaged as God-fearing, all-American, and squeaky-clean. But even words such as "dysfunctional" don't begin to describe the real Jackson-family dynamic. The cruel, violent, and ambitious father would rouse his kids out of bed at two A.M. to perform and tell little Michael that there were people in the audience with guns who wanted to shoot him. (If he didn't move fast onstage, warned his father, they'd find their target.) His mother, a fervent Jehovah's Witness, was a sweep-everything-under-the-rug-and-prevaricate-about-it type whom Michael clung to and adored. The various siblings had multiple marriages and pregnant girlfriends on the side; loose-cannon La Toya, with her public allegations of physical and sexual abuse by her father, posed nude in *Playboy*. The Jacksons alone could provide several straight seasons of *Geraldo*.

"When the Jacksons, none of whom have much education, became famous in the 70s, there were not that many prominent blacks—there was no Colin Powell, no Maxine Waters, no Walter Washington or David Dinkins to be role models. They were the ones on the cover of *Life*. They were the people who represented black America," says McQueen. "But when black America didn't need to reflect itself in them anymore," most of the Jacksons could not accept that time had passed them by. Even today, they treat people visiting the family home in Encino (which Michael owns seventy-five percent of) as if they were visiting the White House. Before McQueen and her ABC crew were allowed to inspect the property, they were asked to put on identifying hospital bracelets provided by Jackson-family security.

Throughout his life, Michael has been the sensation, the supreme object of attention, despite his parents' strict insistence on equality among the six brothers and three sisters, despite his father's beatings to disabuse him of any notion of superiority. He was closest to two of his sisters, Janet and La Toya, and not at all macho like his brothers, but he was the only one who stood up to their father, whom he called "the devil." Conventional wisdom has it that Michael Jackson never had a childhood—that's why he loves being a child. But a woman who observed him closely during the early years disagrees: "He loves childhood because he was a child star. He loves to remember it. Michael is narcissistic in the extreme."

Often isolated from other kids when he was growing up, she says, he learned everything he knew from TV, and "everything he saw on television that represented class and glamour was white." He reportedly recommended that an eleven-year-old blond, blue-eyed white boy play him as a child on the miniseries *The Jacksons: An American Dream* and in Pepsi commercials. His isolation, a severe case of adolescent acne, and his resentful brothers' taunts about his "big nose" caused him to insulate himself further, especially from their sexual exploits with women. One of the most terrifying experiences of his life, apparently, occurred when he was barely a teenager and his brothers threw a willing woman at him.

In business, however, he became, even at a young age, very shrewd and highly competitive, and today he is often described as "cutthroat." He can read a complex contract and has always taken an active role in managing his work. But his isolation has left him with a career instead of a life. "Socially, you cannot be with Michael Jackson," says a recording-industry fixture who knows him very well. "You can if you're willing to talk about his career. He wouldn't know what to do at a mixed dinner party." The woman says, "He's like a skyscraper built on eggshells."

When Michael finally left home in 1988, at age twenty-nine, he had already passed through an intense relationship with the tiny, twelve-year-old actor Emmanuel Lewis, whom he carried around everywhere like a baby. His biographer Randy Taraborrelli reports that the friendship ended shortly after the two checked into a posh Los Angeles hotel as father and son. On one leg of his 1988 "Bad" tour, according to Taraborrelli, Jackson took along a ten-year-old California boy named Jimmy Safechuck, on whom he showered gifts and whose parents got a $100,000 Rolls-Royce from Michael. His manager at the time encouraged him to break off the relationship, because it looked bad.

Life at Neverland appears to be that of the court of a scared, isolated child emperor. Conversations with half a dozen people who have lived and worked there reveal that security is so tight that employees are not allowed even to take a walk on the grounds—whether or not Michael is in residence. He requires attending twenty-four hours a day, but when staff members are hired, they are told immediately never to look him in the eye or to engage him in conversation. Yvonne Doone, who was a cook there for nine months in 1990, explains why: "Whenever he was in a room, all eyes were always on him, all ears were always on him. He can never be ordinary. He can never be someone else in the room. . . . He pays other people to supply protection because he can't trust." She describes life at Neverland as "a radiating circle of fear."

Fame, eccentricity, and money have always shielded Michael Jackson from dealing directly with anything he doesn't like, and if things don't go his way, he is subject to panic attacks. In the past, according to Taraborrelli, Jackson has been secretly hospitalized several times for such attacks, disguised as respiratory ailments. Taraborrelli says he cannot imagine Jackson withstanding a police interrogation. "I think he'll just start to cry. He has created his own world so that he never has to deal with ordinary life, and he won't be able to."

By November, reality was becoming such a nightmare that Jackson couldn't go on. It was then, his side argues, he began taking such quantities of painkillers that he couldn't function. Meanwhile, the police searched the Jackson-family home in Encino, looking for evidence in the child-abuse case. Among Michael's things they reportedly found a nude photo of a little boy. Was it that news that so upset him he called his old friend Elizabeth Taylor for help, or was it the fact that he was next scheduled to play Puerto Rico, a United States territory, where the police might question him? Amid rumors that he was suicidal, Taylor jetted to his side and in a dramatic late-night heist helped spirit him out of Mexico to an undisclosed clinic somewhere in Europe. Says Pellicano, "I used decoys all over the place."

By the time Jackson's attorneys held a press conference the following Monday to reiterate that he was not faking his drug addiction and that he had every intention of coming back to testify, rumors were rife that Jamie had given the police a description of Jackson's genitals and that the police wanted to examine him. The story turned out to be true, and by November 19, the police, apparently concerned that he might be having the alleged telltale markings on his genitals altered in Europe, raided both his dermatologist's and his plastic surgeon's offices, looking for his medical records. They were gone.

So was a key witness, Norma Staikos, the duenna of Neverland, who had made the arrangements to bring children there. Without informing the police, she left the country for Greece, triggering speculation that she, too, was on the run. Howard Weitzman said, "I know she's coming back, and I've told this to the police. To use the word 'flee' is egregious."

Those in law-enforcement circles had long believed that there would be no indictment without an airtight case. As evidence piled up, the Los Angeles District Attorney's Office informed Weitzman that it wanted to question Jackson. Meanwhile, the performer's attorney Bert Fields antagonized authorities by sending a letter to the police commissioner claiming that officers were using intimidation and scare tactics with children they were questioning.

Nothing, it seemed, could stop the avalanche of horrific developments. Pepsi had already said that once the "Dangerous" tour was over, it no longer had a corporate connection with Jackson. NBC put the *Jackson Family Honors* special on hold. Jackson had abruptly dropped out from doing the theme song and video for the film *Addams Family Values*. (When the movie was released, there was a scene in which a kid sees a Michael Jackson poster and recoils in horror.) *People* magazine's November 29 cover read, MICHAEL JACKSON CRACKS UP.

On November 23, the gossip columnist Liz Smith went to the heart of the matter: "With the fate and future and reputation of Michael Jackson on the line, I'm told Sony Records is playing it safe. . . . Sony doesn't want all its eggs in one basket, and so there is a concerted effort to throw a lot of resources behind the already blazing career of Michael Bolton."

Sic transit musica mundi.

PART II • **SEPTEMBER 1995**

On June 14, 1995, some 60 million people tuned in to see Diane Sawyer interview Michael Jackson and his bride, Lisa Marie Presley, on *Prime-*

Time Live, on ABC News. The widely advertised "no holds barred" session—the capstone of a $30-million marketing campaign for Jackson's new double album, *HIStory*—was the first Jackson has given since being accused of child molestation by a thirteen-year-old boy in August 1993.

The last time Jackson had talked about the charges was in December 1993, on live satellite, without reporters present. He complained bitterly that the police had humiliated him by taking photos of his private parts, to verify descriptions of marks on his genitalia given by his accuser. That portion of the satellite telecast, along with Jackson's angry new video, *Scream,* and other taped segments, took up a lot of the *PrimeTime* broadcast. When the show ended, many with detailed knowledge of the case were appalled by what Sawyer and ABC News had allowed Jackson to get away with.

Controversy raged for days over the way ABC had bent network news standards to accommodate Jackson's many demands, but this may be the least of the singer's worries. Sources close to the family of the boy allegedly molested have said that they are considering whether Jackson's specific on-air references to the case breached the contract negotiated in which Jackson paid his young accuser an enormous settlement to drop the charges. (Anything other than a general denial of the allegations by Jackson is said to be a breach of contract.)

Two years ago I interviewed dozens of people close to the case for an article that came out before the settlement and before the district attorneys of Los Angeles and Santa Barbara counties announced, in September 1994, that in the absence of victims willing to come forward to testify, they would not file criminal charges against Jackson. (They also stated that the case could be reopened anytime before the statute of limitations ran out, in 1999, and added that their investigation had uncovered allegations of sexual misconduct on the part of Jackson with two other boys.)

Although Diane Sawyer proclaimed on air that "we have called everyone we can call, we have checked everything we can check," she and the *PrimeTime* team, giving no one but Jackson a say, left crucial areas unreported or incorrectly reported. For example, Sawyer allowed Jackson to state that he had been "cleared" of all charges and that he had settled by paying "reportedly in the neighborhood of $15 to $20 million."

Sawyer did not bring up the fact that, for a long time, prosecutors believed that the boy who settled would take the stand for them. According to individuals familiar with the case, the boy definitely would have testified had the Los Angeles district attorney, Gil Garcetti, moved more quickly to indict Jackson. But the boy himself, according to sources close to the case, was considering going into the witness-protection program—

such was his fear of the retribution he would suffer by publicly alleging that Michael Jackson was a pedophile. He had reason to be afraid.

His family claims that a few weeks before the case was settled, the boy and the housekeeper were nearly run down near their home by a speeding car. The car also came at them in reverse. The boy's attorney, Larry Feldman, was protected for several months by guards from the United States Justice Department after having received numerous death threats and had pornographic graffiti sprayed on the walls of his law-office building. The boy's father received a dead rat in a box at his home. The witness-protection program fell through, however, when neither state nor federal authorities offered it and the boy realized that he might end up living his life like a prisoner.

While Jackson has gone on to marry and become the stepfather of Elvis Presley's grandchildren, Jackson's close involvement with the boy ultimately ripped the boy's floundering family apart. After the settlement, the second marriages of both his parents ended in divorce. The boy no longer sees or speaks to his mother, whom he blames for allowing Jackson to become so intimate with him. He has not seen his eight-year-old sister in two years, or his stepfather, who essentially raised him. Now fifteen, the boy lives with his stepmother. He is not in therapy. He continues to have a relationship with his father, who was accused by Jackson's side of extortion but whom authorities declined to prosecute, saying there was not enough evidence—another fact not mentioned by Diane Sawyer. The boy's father and stepfather, once friends, are now suing each other.

Herewith a fact check of the interview:

> **DIANE SAWYER:** How about the police photographs, though? How was there enough information from this boy about those kinds of things . . .
> **JACKSON:** There was nothing that matched me to those charges.
> **SAWYER:** So when we've heard that there was this marking of some kind . . .
> **JACKSON:** No markings.
> **SAWYER:** No markings?
> **JACKSON:** No.

The Santa Barbara district attorney, Tom Sneddon, who has seen the photographs of Jackson's genitalia, was upset enough after Sawyer's interview to speak to me on the record. "Regarding the markings," Sneddon says, "his statement on TV is untrue and incorrect and not consistent with the evidence in the case."

Others familiar with the evidence are more forthcoming. They say there are definite markings on Jackson's genital area that match the accuser's description and substantiate the child's charges of sexual intimacy. (Jackson admitted to Oprah Winfrey in February 1993 that he suffers from the skin disorder vitiligo, which causes discoloration.) According to the sworn affidavit of a law-enforcement photographer, there is a dark spot on the lower left side of Jackson's penis.

Affidavits of law-enforcement officers filed in Santa Barbara Superior Court detail the tense circumstances of December 20, 1993, when District Attorney Sneddon, Jackson's lawyers Howard Weitzman and Johnnie Cochran, Santa Barbara County sheriffs, various doctors, a police photographer, and a Jackson photographer convened to have pictures taken of an "enraged" Jackson's nude body. Sworn affidavits recall a "hysterical and completely uncontrollable" superstar who had to be physically restrained by one of his doctors, whom he slapped while another one was trying to hold him down on the couch. Jackson tried to impede the photographers' work ("I've said I have vitiligo; so what? What more do you need? Why do you have to examine me?") and at one point told law-enforcement officers, "Get out of here. . . . You're assholes." Later, Jackson flatly refused to complete the series of photographs previously agreed upon.

The boy who had accused Jackson of sexually molesting him, according to those familiar with the evidence, was able to draw—first for the district attorney, then for his own lawyers—an accurate picture of the dark spot on Jackson's penis. The boy's drawings were sealed in an envelope and clearly postmarked on a postal meter before the police ever photographed Jackson.

According to these sources, the boy's drawings were an accurate match of the photographs.

> **JACKSON:** The whole thing is a lie.
> **SAWYER:** Why did you settle the case, then? . . . Can you say how much?
> **JACKSON:** It's not what the tabloids have printed. It's not all this crazy, outlandish money. No. It's not at all.

The boy got "in excess of $25 million," according to sources close to the family, and his parents were also paid off in the millions. The money, distributed in one lump sum, was handed over without Michael Jackson's ever being put under oath for a civil deposition, which could be used in a criminal trial.

People close to the investigation say that Jackson's lawyers, who kept putting off any depositions, agreed to settle the night before Jackson was to have been put under oath. At one point, Jackson's lawyers even argued in court that Jackson might have to take the Fifth Amendment in the civil case to ensure that nothing he said there could be used against him if the criminal case went forward. In answering a civil case in which five former bodyguards accused Jackson of firing them because "they knew too much," Jackson did invoke the Fifth Amendment on the subject of alleged child molestation. The suit, dismissed since the *PrimeTime Live* interview, was not mentioned by Sawyer.

> **JACKSON:** Also, the idea, it just isn't fair what they put me through, because there wasn't one piece of information that says I did that. And anyway, they turned my room upside down and went through all my books, all my videotapes, all my private things, and they found nothing nothing nothing that could say Michael Jackson did this. . . . Nothing nothing nothing . . .
>
> **SAWYER:** Nothing. I got nothing. As you may or may not know, we have called everyone we can call, we have checked everything we can check, we have gone and tried to see if what we heard before is, in fact, the case. I want to ask you two things. These reports that we read over and over again that in your rooms they found photographs of young boys—not adults.
>
> **JACKSON:** Young boys, children, all kind of girls and everything.
>
> **SAWYER:** Then, that they found photographs, books, of young boys who were undressed. . . .
>
> **JACKSON:** No, not that I know of, unless people sent me things that I haven't opened.

According to District Attorney Tom Sneddon, "The idea that there are not any photos or pictures or anything is pure poppycock. In the search, Jackson said, they didn't find anything unless it was 'something somebody sent me.' The statement there were no books or photos of nude children on his premises is incorrect. That is not truthful."

Investigation sources say the police found a lewd, commercially published hardcover book of black-and-white photos of nude boys aged about seven to twelve "at play" and, according to one, that book "is often found in the home of pedophiles." There was also a picture of a nude little boy, scantily draped with a sheet, found in Jackson's bedroom.

> **SAWYER:** Any other settlements in process now or previously with children making these kinds of claims? We have heard that there

is one, not a case that the prosecutors would bring in court, but once again, you're talking about shelling out—

JACKSON: That's not true. No. No. No, it's not true. I think—I've heard everything is fine and there are no others.

Law-enforcement sources, however, confirm that there is another boy who has a lawyer and is currently negotiating a settlement with Jackson. Of the boys mentioned in the district attorney's press release who accused Jackson of sexual misconduct and who are unwilling to testify, Sneddon says, "The status regarding these two is basically the same."

SAWYER: I guess, let me ask this—and I'm trying to think how to phrase it, though. I can hear out in the country people saying— and you've been cleared of all the charges, we want to make that clear—people saying, Look, here is a man surrounded by things that children love. Here is a man who spends an inordinate amount of time with these young boys.

"Michael Jackson has not been cleared," says District Attorney Sneddon, who calls Diane Sawyer's announcement that he had been cleared "a glaring mistake." He adds, "The state of the investigation is in suspension until somebody comes forward." At one point, Sawyer said, "None of the employees who claimed to have seen questionable things had a story that could be confirmed by a child." Again, Sawyer is contradicted by law-enforcement sources. Two years ago, Jackson's personal maid, Blanca Francia, told the police, the *Los Angeles Times*, and the tabloid TV show *Hard Copy* that she had seen Jackson a number of times in the nude with young boys and found a picture of an apparently nude boy in Jackson's room. Under oath she also said she found Jackson in bed with several boys, and a young boy with him in the same sleeping bag. She discovered $300 in the boy's pocket (which he had admitted Jackson had given to him).

How, I asked Sneddon, does Michael Jackson get away with all this? "Why not?" he answered. "What's the downside? Who is he going to get more exposure from, your article or the TV interview? They have to read your article. To *listen* to him, all they have to do is push a button. He's got this huge public-relations train behind him—they're able to contour public opinion any way they want. There's no downside for him." The attorney Danny Davis, who represents the boy's stepfather in his civil suit against Jackson, says, "From Oprah to his public denial on satellite to the

Sawyer interview, this strange person is controlling a major network. He understands money and major networks."

Adds Sneddon: "I see injustices every day in my business." But things are so shameless in Jackson's camp that Epic Records, his label, has sent out a press release saying that sales of Jackson's new album—which at fewer than one million units in the United States, at press time, are not nearly meeting expectations—would save small black mom-and-pop record shops in various parts of the country!

Liz Smith has reported that Jackson wanted Princess Diana to be with him on the Sawyer interview, to commiserate about the sufferings imposed by tabloid coverage, and that he queried the British embassy in Washington about being knighted by the queen for "his work with little children." According to an observer, he actually was working behind the scenes to see if the queen would knight him right there on *PrimeTime Live*. That was one demand that was not met.

The credibility of ABC News was seriously undermined when it was learned that ABC had swapped the airing of ten TV commercials for Jackson's new album—ads between $300,000 and $1.5 million—for rights to "future Michael Jackson music videos." Such videos, which have never been of any commercial value in network TV, are usually provided free. According to the Bloomberg Business News service, which broke the story, the commercials ran in the week between Sawyer's interview and the release of the album. ABC News disavowed any prior knowledge of the deal, which ABC Entertainment said had been made after the interview was set.

Executives at CBS and NBC said that Jackson's handlers had clearly been looking for a "package." (In the interest of full disclosure, my husband, Tim Russert, is Washington-bureau chief of NBC News, with no responsibility for prime-time programming.) A producer from one network told me, "It's difficult to pretend there was no quid pro quo in the ABC deal. Jackson's people approached a bunch of us. Basically they said, 'Come back to us with a proposition, and not just what you can do with your news division—that is not enough.'"

In addition, Sawyer had get-togethers with Jackson and Presley before the expensively produced interview, which is not her usual practice. She posed with them for stylized publicity stills, published in *TV Guide* and sent to newspapers around the country. And contrary to news-show procedures, the air-conditioning remained on loud while Sawyer interviewed Jackson, causing a strange background noise. The cool air was necessary, veteran sound technicians say, because the lights on Jackson were so hot that his thick pancake makeup and lipstick would have melted otherwise, and his false eyelashes would have come off.

"My interview was entirely in my hands," Sawyer told me. "I decided what questions to ask. No one ever said to me, 'Don't ask that. Do ask that.' I felt my primary mission was to cover the serious charges. If I didn't get to some questions of Lisa Marie or the video, well, that's that. The questions I wanted to ask were the serious questions."

"I have no idea what the purpose of her show is," District Attorney Sneddon wondered, out loud, after watching Sawyer's interview.

P A R T   I I I   •   APRIL 2003

"David Geffen, be gone! Steven Spielberg, be gone!" The witch doctor cursing Michael Jackson's enemies and blessing the tarnished King of Pop himself in a voodoo ritual in Switzerland in the summer of 2000 had promised that the twenty-five people on Jackson's enemies list would soon expire. The voodoo man later assured one observer that Geffen, who headed the list, would die within the week. But Geffen's demise did not come cheap. Jackson had ordered his then business advisor, Myung-Ho Lee, a United States–educated Korean lawyer based in Seoul, to wire $150,000 to a bank in Mali for a voodoo chief named Baba, who then had forty-two cows ritually sacrificed for the ceremony.

Jackson had already undergone a bloodbath. The pop star, said to be $240 million in debt, had paid six figures, for a ritual cleansing using sheep blood, to another voodoo doctor and a mysterious Egyptian woman named Samia. She had come to him with a letter of greeting from a high-ranking Saudi prince (purportedly Nawaf Bin Abdulaziz Al-Saud, now the chief of intelligence of Saudi Arabia) and had taken an eager Jackson to her basement in Geneva. As Jackson later told associates, he saw with his own eyes piles of $100 bills that Samia said totaled $300 million. It was "free money," she said; he could have it, and she could also get him a villa and a yacht. She arranged to have three men fly from Switzerland, at Jackson's expense, to Neverland, his luxurious California ranch, to discuss further deals. When the hex delegation arrived at Neverland, Jackson asked Lee to authorize $1 million in cash to be brought to the ranch. Lee refused, but Jackson obtained the money by other means. Lee found out about it only when a $20,000 bill came for an armored truck.

Jackson, in turn, sent Lee to Geneva to check out yet another voodoo doctor, whose specialty was pulling money out of thin air. At the Hôtel d'Angleterre, the voodoo man produced a show of sound, lights, and pigeons before leading his visitors one at a time into the bathroom, where the tub was full of cash amounting, he claimed, to $50 million. When they asked where it had come from, he said, "The U.S. Federal Reserve." There was just one catch: all this money would disappear unless Michael Jackson paid thousands of dollars for the blood of a number of fowl and small animals for yet another ritual. The sacrificial animals were already assembled at a location on the French-Swiss border, waiting to die to make Jackson's wishes come true. Lee was horrified and left in disgust.

What could possibly be next in the most bizarre celebrity story within memory? Now, two and a half years later, we know: a dangling baby; hysterical claims that Tommy Mottola, the head of his record company, is racist; and a string of lawsuits. In a few years, the principal on a $200-million loan Jackson has with the Bank of America will be due. To pay that off without selling his most valuable asset, the Beatles song catalogue, he will have to earn about $400 million before taxes, a virtual impossibility. Michael Jackson's career has been taking a steep downward slide since 1993, when he was accused of sexually molesting a thirteen-year-old boy. He paid at least $25 million to settle the civil suit brought by the boy, and barely escaped being arrested. Now forty-four, Jackson is long past the prime earning age for a pop star, and each album since his record-breaking *Thriller* in 1982 has cost more to produce and sold fewer copies than the one before. In addition, as his career has stalled, his freak factor has risen. Routinely referred to in the tabloid press as "Wacko Jacko" and characterized in his hometown newspaper as a "dancing personality disorder," Michael Jackson is off the charts.

Who has not seen photos or footage of a hyped-up Jackson playing to the crowd in Germany last November by dangerously dangling his squirming eight-month-old son, whose head was covered with a towel, over the balcony railing of his hotel room? No one seems to know where this apparently white baby, Prince Michael II, came from. Four months earlier, Jackson had just suddenly appeared, baby on board, at a Siegfried and Roy show in Las Vegas. After the overwhelmingly negative public reaction to the dangling, however, it was clear that he had gone too far. The next day Jackson apologized to the press and, to demonstrate that he was a normal, caring father, took his two oldest children, the original Prince Michael, now five, and his daughter, Paris, four, also both apparently white, to the Berlin Zoo, with dozens of photographers in tow. He had covered the children's heads with brightly colored gauze scarves resembling burkas, and they at times appeared unprotected in the frenzy;

the scene prompted another round of outcries from the tabloids for an investigation into child endangerment.

Just the week before, Jackson had testified in a civil suit in a court in Santa Maria, California, near Neverland. He was monosyllabic, dazed, and disheveled, and the tip of his nose seemed to be missing, because of exaggerated amounts of plastic surgery. At one point he appeared to fall asleep on the stand. The next day he showed up four hours late. Among the papers filed in another lawsuit was his monthly budget, which includes a $10,000 charge from a Beverly Hills pharmacy.

In early December he appeared in court again in Santa Maria, as a defendant in a $21.2 million civil suit brought against him by the European concert promoter Marcel Avram, who blames him for the failure of two canceled, back-to-back concerts to celebrate the new millennium. That time I was there to see him.

Jackson's choreographed arrivals in a black Ford van at the courthouse in Santa Maria, a working-class town fifty miles north of Santa Barbara, were made with the solemnity ordinarily associated with the Popemobile. Some days an aide would open an umbrella as the star stepped out into the sun; other days were two-umbrella days, designed to shield him from cameras and reporters. Jackson was always flanked by security and greeted by a crowd of several dozen mostly older fans, some of whom had brought their kids to get his autograph. When Jackson was not on the stand, he sat in an anteroom off the courtroom and spoke only with children, as if he were Santa Claus or the Dalai Lama.

Up close, Jackson's appearance is amazing. He wears a black pageboy wig, and his face is caked with white makeup, which conceals a prosthesis that serves as the tip of his nose. One person who has seen him without the device says he resembles a mummy with two nostril holes. He uses red lipstick and perfume, pencils and dyes his eyebrows, and has black eyeliner that looks as if it's tattooed on. He also appears to have white makeup on his hands; his clothes, right down to the crests on his ties, suggest a wealthy private-school boy or a young member of European royalty. The first day I was there, he was wearing a black jacket, a white-on-white tuxedo shirt, and a silk tie. He had only a sock on his left foot, but he was able to walk unassisted. As soon as it was time to enter the courtroom, however, Jackson fell onto a pair of crutches and started limping markedly. We were told he had been bitten by a spider. During a break I went up and asked him if it had been a tarantula. "Oh no, I love tarantulas. I keep them in my reptile house," he replied, referring to Neverland's private zoo. The spider that bit him, he said, came "whoosh" out of the "bush" near his house. "I had to have the house fumigated." It turned out that a brown recluse spider had bitten Jackson on the hand and leg, causing them to swell.

Inside the courtroom, Judge Zel Canter, a portly man with horn-rimmed glasses who seemed starstruck, consulted his lawbooks and let the attorneys argue over tiny points, often in front of the mostly white, female jury. At such times, Jackson, on the stand waiting to testify, would bob his head to a silent melody, tap the mike occasionally to be sure it was on, and make a show of sharing the court reporter's candy—behavior one would expect of a twelve-year-old. "Can I have another Jolly Rancher, please?" he asked during a sidebar. At one point he waved to two photographers in the back, and the next day he made devil's horns with his fingers and other mischievous gestures. When Avram's lawyer Louis ("Skip") Miller objected to his antics, Jackson's own skillful lawyers, Steve Cochran and Zia Modabber, told the judge that spectators in the courtroom had been baiting their client, although I saw no evidence of that. When a video was shown of Jackson singing at one of the two charity concerts whose costs were in dispute, he sat straight up to watch it, clasping his hands and batting his eyes like a schoolgirl.

Known to insiders as an aggressive businessman with dreams of becoming an entrepreneurial mogul like Merv Griffin, Jackson, on the stand, was a reticent mix of dissociation and amnesia. He said over and over, "Could you repeat the question, please?" and "I don't recall." Once, after Skip Miller posed a difficult question and Jackson's lawyers again rose to his defense, Jackson said to the judge, "I've been holding it a long time. I really have to use the restroom." Later, in frustration, Miller asked him, "Have you had any memory problems—memory lapses, say—since your deposition was taken in early June?" Jackson replied, "Not that I can recall."

Jackson described himself as a visionary and compared himself to Walt Disney, who had let his brother take care of the books. When he was asked if he was acquainted with his well-known former public-relations guru Howard Rubenstein, who had charged him $10,000 a month for two years and whom Jackson had introduced to a crowd in Rubenstein's own home with lavish praise two years earlier, he replied, "I barely know his name. I've kind of heard of it."

This bizarre behavior often works to his advantage. The crazier Jackson appears, the more he is indulged and excused and not judged as a middle-aged man with serious obligations and responsibilities. The photographer Harry Benson, who has worked extensively with him, told me, "Michael Jackson is about as crazy as Colin Powell. He knows everything he is doing. He holds his baby over the balcony and everybody goes crazy, but he's in every newspaper around the world." A former publicist of Jackson's added, "Michael doesn't think bad publicity is bad—he thinks more is more. He just doesn't want to be forgotten." Asked if Jackson capitalizes on his weirdness, the Santa Barbara district attorney, Tom Sneddon, who led part of the child-molestation investigation against Jackson in 1993 and 1994, says, "Of course. It's deliberate. I think it's frustrating that people let him get away with it. He's playing the fool and he fools people, but he doesn't fool everybody." Sneddon was disgusted by the tactics Jackson and his lawyers used in Judge Canter's courtroom. "Any other judge would have thrown his ass in jail."

The contractual dispute at the heart of the trial in Santa Maria, which started last November, concerns two benefit concerts Jackson gave, in Munich and Seoul, in June 1999; the Seoul concert alone lost millions, because of dismal ticket sales and wild cost overruns, which Avram blames on Jackson. Although the concerts were advertised as part of Jackson's selfless contribution to the Nelson Mandela Children's Fund, Unesco, the Red Cross, and his own Heal the World Foundation, Jackson was at one point slated to receive a $1-million coexecutive-producer fee, as well as the sponsorship money and TV (including cable) and video rights.

Avram, who was contractually responsible for the costs of the benefit concerts, realized how much he would be out of pocket, but he assumed he would make the money up with two additional scheduled concerts celebrating the millennium. The jury must decide whether he or Jackson is responsible for not putting them on. The charities that were slated to benefit and that generated so much fawning publicity for Jackson overseas were the real losers. A contribution of only $100,000, put up by Avram, was made to Mandela's charity; he let Jackson present the check so that the entertainer could continue to cast himself as a savior of children.

In the 2000 *Guinness Book of Records*, Michael Jackson is cited for the most charities supported by a pop star—thirty-nine—and he constantly flies around the world picking up lifetime-achievement and humanitarian awards. In fact, that was why he was in Germany when he dangled the baby. However, as Roger Friedman reported in his Fox 411 on-line column in February 2002, "the last tax filing available—for 1999—shows Jackson giving no money to other charities at all and receiving no donations from others." The Heal the World Foundation's Web site appears not to have been updated since 1996, and the charity Earth Care, which his brother Jermaine announced on *Larry King Live* this past January, does not appear to be active. In 1998, Britain's Charity Commission shut down Heal the World, which had not made a donation in three years. According to London's *Daily Mail*, the commission concluded, "The name had been so disfigured by the actions of Michael Jackson that it was not worth continuing to run the organisation in any form."

Inside Edition recently reported that the only donation Heal the World made in 2000 was a transfer of $100,000 to the Heal the Kids Initiative, which Jackson began with gadfly Rabbi Shmuley Boteach, author of *Kosher Sex*. That $100,000 is so far unaccounted for, and the New York State attorney general's office has served Heal the Kids with a notice of failure to comply with filing requirements. Jackson's latest benefit song, "What More Can I Give," recorded in the wake of 9/11, was shelved by his own advisors when the news broke that he had given the production rights to a gay-porn director and producer. Nevertheless, last Christmas, Jackson announced that he was forming yet another children's charity, to be kicked off with yet another benefit concert. So far that charity has not even been named. (Jackson's representatives did not respond to repeated requests for comment.)

In the stunningly beautiful Santa Ynez Valley, part of California's Central Coast wine country, there are constant rumors that Neverland, Jackson's 2,700-acre headquarters, is for sale, but local real-estate agent Joe Olla says that almost no one who can afford it would want the amusement park, with its toy railroad and private zoo, and all the other expensive facilities Jackson has added. "Those things might even give it a negative value," he says, declining to speculate on the ranch's worth—which others estimate at between $26 and $30 million—because "some foreigner could come in and, because it's Michael Jackson, double it."

Jackson, the valley's most famous resident, is well-known to the members of every jury pool in Santa Maria. He hires county firefighters for Neverland's own fire department and sometimes employs off-duty and retired police officers in security jobs. Neverland, which costs $4 million a year to run, is organized into thirteen departments, so it is a source of potential revenue for everyone from snake handlers (Jackson has a blond serpent named Madonna) to owners of antiques shops, where Jackson spends thousands of dollars at a time in late-night visits with his children. He also makes visits to Toys 'R' Us in Santa Maria with boys who are sleeping over at Neverland. When Jackson's millionaire neighbors fly over his estate in their private planes in the evening, they report, the amusement park is always up and running. "Employees who have seen him in close contact say he's gotten stranger and stranger in the last two years," a well-connected resident told me. But his employees rarely talk to outsiders. "They're all scared to death they'll be sued. He has a large legal team."

"I used to see him riding down the road in an old pickup once in a while," the former Hollywood gossip queen Rona Barrett, who is a neighbor, told me, "but not lately."

"When Michael Jackson first moved here, everyone was thrilled," says Pat Murphy, author of *Santa Ynez Valley Secrets*. Residents would see him around town with his face in bandages or covered with a surgical mask. "They felt he was giving a lot of local people work, and they really need it. Then out came the confidentiality agreements—we had never experienced that in the valley. They were sworn to secrecy, and people started to say, 'Why so secret? What do we have to be silent about?' Over time, people became more suspicious." Jackson, she hastens to add, has always been generous with local children.

"When Michael Jackson first moved to the valley," Murphy concludes, "he was a very nice-looking African American man with brown skin. Now he's become a white woman."

"I have an adage," says William Hodgman, head of the sex-crimes unit of the Los Angeles District Attorney's Office, which investigated the Jackson sex-abuse allegations in 1993. "The higher the profile, the stranger are the phenomena." Fame twists everything, he explains. "It's all that money swirling around in all different ways—especially with the tabloids, which were often three steps ahead of us. Information was bought and sold; documents disappeared. It's all part of the wildness of celebrity."

A member of the prosecution team says it still gnaws at him that Michael Jackson never came to trial. "Just to get started, we needed victims willing to testify, and it appeared to us there were tender young boys, called Michael's 'special friends,' who ran back a decade," he told me. "We had a 'special friend' identified every year for ten or twelve years. They were all prepubescent boys between about eight and twelve years old, and as soon as they started sprouting whiskers—whoosh—they were out the door," he added. "They were generally cute boys, along the lines of the Macaulay Culkin variety. Some refused to talk to us; others lied when they did. Ultimately we needed people to come forward. We could not send a kid up there one-on-one against Michael Jackson."

As I first reported in 1993, Jackson had slept in the same bed with the then thirteen-year-old Jordan ("Jordie") Chandler (whom I called Jamie in my January 1994 article to protect his privacy as a minor) thirty nights in the boy's small Los Angeles room. Jackson's camp even admitted that— and the boy alleged that Jackson had engaged in acts such as oral sex and mutual masturbation not only there but also at Neverland, at Jackson's "hideaway" apartment in Century City, in Monaco, and at Disney World. The only other two boys willing to testify had not had relationships as intense as Jordie's with the King of Pop. One was the son of a former maid of Jackson's; the other, in Santa Barbara County, claimed Jackson had fondled him, but with his clothes on. The parents of that boy refused to let their son testify. "Silence was purchased with regard to at least one of those other boys," the prosecutor says. "Michael Jackson's sort of wealth buys an awful lot of favors." Jackson arranged for permanent residential visas in the United States for an Australian boy and his parents. The night Jackson had met this boy, the star asked the parents if he could go off alone with him, and he did not return him until the next morning. "If those same circumstances occurred with an average person, the parents probably would have called the police," says a source formerly close to Jackson. "But because it was Michael Jackson, they acted like they were honored."

At the time of the Jordie Chandler (Jamie) accusations, Jackson had Anthony Pellicano, known as the private detective to the stars, who cultivates a Tony Soprano image, working for him. When the police wired Jackson's maid Blanca Francia, whose son was one of the boys involved in the investigation, according to someone on the prosecution team, they heard Pellicano beg her not to go to the police with her information. Other former employees reported threats and harassment from Pellicano, and some still cower when they speak of him.

Last November, Pellicano was arrested by FBI agents, who found explosives in his safe, "strong enough to bring down an airplane," after an informant fingered him as the person who had hired a tough guy to put a bullet through the windshield of the parked car of a Los Angeles *Times* reporter working on a story about the actor Steven Seagal and the Mob. A dead fish was left on the car, as well as a rose and a cardboard sign saying STOP. *Vanity Fair* contributing editor Ned Zeman, who published a Seagal story in the October 2002 issue, says a man confronted him with a gun, pointed it at his head, and pulled the trigger. The gun was empty. Zeman has no idea who the man was. (Pellicano has said he has no involvement with Seagal.) The former reporter Rod Lurie told me that Pellicano had phoned him thirty-five times over a six-month period to get him to kill a piece he was writing about the source-gathering techniques of the *National Enquirer*. Lurie was mysteriously hit by a car while riding his bike. Very few knew of the accident, but Pellicano was one of the first to call to console him. Diane Dimond, who aggressively pursued the Michael Jackson story for the TV show *Hard Copy* starting in 1993, told me, "My home was vandalized, my car was broken into, and our defense documents were stolen. Paramount [which owned *Hard Copy*] gave me bodyguards."

Victor M. Gutierrez, a Chilean journalist who in 1996 brought out an astounding book on the child-molestation case entitled *Michael Jackson Was My Lover: The Secret Diary of Jordie Chandler*, alleges that, in the course of his investigation, Pellicano, who is a major character in the book, visited him and told him, "Consider yourself dead!" Gutierrez says he was attacked outside his apartment in Westwood, Los Angeles. "After I got beat up on the street by three guys, Pellicano stopped in a black Lexus, looked at me, and laughed. He came with a girl, and she started to laugh." Gutierrez adds, "He made my life miserable with threats to my family, to me. He was always bragging about his contacts in the FBI and CIA." (Repeated calls to Pellicano's lawyer for comment went unanswered.)

I tracked Gutierrez down in Chile, where he had moved after losing a slander case brought by Jackson and declaring bankruptcy before his book could be published. Gutierrez had gone on *Hard Copy* and said he had seen a videotape of Jackson having sex with a minor. He could not produce the tape, and he unsuccessfully invoked California's shield law protecting journalists from having to reveal their sources. The jury in Los Angeles ordered him to pay $2.7 million in damages, according to a Jackson lawyer, "to send a message to the tabloids." Gutierrez told me he had first learned about the purported tape from someone in Jackson's extended family.

Jackson doesn't let much go by, but he has never sued over Gutierrez's minutely detailed book, which took four years to research and contains shocking, utterly scatological details about Jackson, including his bizarre use of tampons and enemas. It also names a number of underage boys with whom he allegedly had sexual contact. The sources close to the prosecution I interviewed for this article were all familiar with the book and believed it was an essentially accurate portrayal of Jackson's relationship with Jordie Chandler. The book—which no United States publisher would touch after the slander judgment—was first published privately in Chile, and all the copies soon disappeared, although it is still a collectible on Amazon.com. Two prosecution sources told me they had heard that Jackson had people buy up all the available copies.

Gutierrez describes a passionate love affair and numerous sexual trysts between Jackson and the boy, day by day, week by week. The book quotes former employees who corroborate details of Jackson's allegedly illicit behavior and who also spoke to the authorities. It is heavily illustrated with fragments of official documents from the case as well as pictures of Jordie, the room where he and Jackson slept together, even his report card. Gutierrez reproduces a drawing, made at the height of the case, by a distraught Jordie, who pictures himself committing suicide by jumping from the roof of a building, with the caption "Don't let this happen." There is also Jordie's description of Jackson's genitals and distinguishing marks, and mention of three-way sex with a second boy. At one point, according to the book, when Jordie saw Jackson's mottled testicles, he told him, "You look like a cow!"

Gutierrez, painting a damning picture of Jordie's family, tells how his divorced parents continually turned a blind eye on the obviously sexual nature of Jackson's relationship with their son. His mother received expensive gifts from Jackson, including a $12,000 Cartier bracelet. His father began to negotiate for money from Jackson even after a psychiatrist told him he had "already lost" his son. Gutierrez concludes, "Jackson's sexual conduct with Jordie was not the error that brought Jackson down. His error was underestimating Evan [Jordie's father], who turned out to be a vocal and aggressive negotiator, in contrast to the other parents, who acquiesced, exchanging silence for houses, luxury vehicles and a few hundred thousand dollars."

When authorities were looking for evidence to match Jordie Chandler's description of Jackson's genitals, search warrants were served on Jackson's celebrity dermatologist, Dr. Arnold Klein, and the entertainer's controversial plastic surgeon, Dr. Steven Hoefflin—known for doing *Playboy* Playmates' breasts—to secure Jackson's medical records. The records had been removed, and neither the doctors nor Klein's attorney would reveal where they were. As a result, Klein was subpoenaed to appear before a grand jury in Santa Barbara County. Subsequently he did make himself and his assistant available for depositions. Klein's assistant, it turns out, was Debbie Rowe, Jackson's future wife and the woman who carried his two oldest children. At the time, according to sources formerly close to Jackson, Rowe was known mostly as a "biker babe."

Rowe told authorities that she and Klein flew around the world to minister to Jackson. She gave him massages and rubdowns and was familiar with his body, so she could identify any markings on his buttocks (the descriptions of which have been deleted in the copy of the affidavit I found). Jackson's scalp had been badly burned when his hair caught on fire during the filming of a Pepsi commercial in 1984. According to the affidavit, "A biopsy of Jackson's scalp revealed that Jackson has Lupus, an auto-immune disease which causes hyperpigmentation or hypopigmentation (darkening or lightening) of the skin."

At the time Jackson's hair caught fire, he began using painkillers, which have led to his having to go through detox more than once. "I had always been told he was just so medicated," a former Sony employee told me. "Half the time you don't know where what he says is coming from."

Dr. Klein also diagnosed Jackson as having vitiligo and acne. Beginning in 1990, he prescribed "skin lightening cremes, Solaquin Forte, Retin A and Benoquin." Klein's deposition also describes Jackson's lupus as causing darkening of the skin and dark skin blotches: "Dr. Klein diagnosed Michael Jackson as having Discoid Lupus on his face and scalp and as a result, Jackson must avoid all sun exposure."

Again according to the affidavit, in April or May 1993 (early in Jackson's relationship with Jordie Chandler), "Jackson told Dr. Klein that he had gotten Benoquin on his genitals and it burned. Dr. Klein told Jackson not to put Benoquin on his genitals." Jackson was already wearing a prosthesis on his nose, because of the lack of cartilage resulting from extensive plastic surgery. If too many blood vessels are cauterized in the face, and blood is prevented from flowing to the skin, medical professionals say, the skin can turn black and eventually wither away or fall off.

Body dysmorphic disorder is the name of the psychological disturbance in which those afflicted become obsessed with how they look and with how they are perceived by others. "If Michael Jackson had ever come to me, I wouldn't have treated him," says Dr. Tina Alster, a nationally recognized dermatologist in Washington, D.C. "He doesn't have a realistic view of how he looks. I get a number of these people, and I send them to someone for psychological evaluation. Michael Jackson is an extreme and very public example." She adds, "He's suffering on a number of fronts."

Michael Jackson wants to be seen as "Walt Disney, Mozart, Elvis Presley, and you've got to throw Fred Astaire in there, too," a man very familiar with the pop star's world told me; he offered a hypothetical Jackson attitude: "'The rules that apply to the common folk do not apply to me. I can get away with whatever I want to because I am Michael Jackson. I not only walk forward, but I can walk backward as well.'" Michael, the man says, is haunted by the ghost of Elvis Presley, whom he considers the King only "because he's a white person with a black person's voice." Since Elvis starred in movies, Jackson desperately wants to make films, too, but he won't play Vegas, Elvis's other stomping ground, no matter how many millions he's offered. "He thinks, I'm bigger than Elvis, so I'm bigger than performing in Las Vegas." Jackson even took the step of marrying Lisa Marie Presley, the King's daughter, but they divorced twenty months later.

The informed source says that Jackson thinks, "They don't understand me—the genius. They don't give me my due, because I'm black, so maybe I'll try to become white." This sense of injured merit, which clings to Jackson wherever he goes, causes him to make grandiose announcements about projects that never come off.

For example, there was the press release last spring that he was creating Neverland Pictures and that his partner would be the Indian movie producer Raju Patel. Before that, there were two film-company ventures, yet not one film has been produced. In 1999 it was announced that Jackson would star as the poet of horror in *The Nightmare of Edgar Allan Poe*, but so far no plans for production have emerged. Jackson also proposed plans to construct a giant resort near Victoria Falls, in Zimbabwe, and a huge Majestic Kingdom theme park with a botanical garden and a nightclub in Detroit. Then there were his plans to aid in the marketing of a soft drink named Mystery and to buy the British royal family's yacht, *Britannia*. Kingdom Entertainment, Jackson's partnership announced in Paris with Saudi prince al-Waleed bin Talal, was to be a "family values" global entertainment empire, including a theme-park home for all the British cattle afflicted with mad-cow disease.

In 1998, Jackson announced plans to build a $500-million World of Childhood amusement park in Poland, one of his favorite countries, thereby "creating some 12,000 new jobs and transforming Warsaw into a pop attraction," as *The Guardian* of London reported. Just twenty miles away would be a sort of Polish Graceland, on an island in a lake, where the new king would reside in a baroque castle, which was being overseen by the director of Warsaw's Royal Gardens, who, according to *The Guardian*, "is ready to believe the account of Jackson's aides, that the child abuse allegations were the work of an American religious sect enacting revenge for his refusal to sign up."

Some journalists have openly ridiculed the never-ending string of press releases. In May 2000, Tim Nelson of the Saint Paul *Pioneer Press*, on hearing that Jackson was taking "the helm of a $100 million Korea-based venture fund that will invest in entertainment-oriented Internet companies," listed nine other Jackson projects and asked readers to guess which ones were "actually in the pipeline." His answer: "All of them! Every one! Coming soon to a vacant lot near you!"

Then there are the strategic friendships Jackson has so carefully cultivated, starting with the paranormalist Uri Geller, who taught Jackson the fine points of telekinesis. They met through Mohamed Fayed, the chairman of Harrods in London, who believes that the CIA and Prince Philip had Princess Diana and his son, Dodi, killed. Then there is Marlon Brando, who gave Jackson acting lessons and was reportedly paid $1 million to blather incoherently at Jackson's thirtieth-anniversary concert at Madison Square Garden in 2001. Liza Minnelli's latest husband, David Gest, has known Jackson since they were children, and Jackson and his greatest pal, Elizabeth Taylor, were at the altar in March 2002 as a best man and a maid of honor at the Minnelli-Gest wedding, which featured thirteen bridesmaids in black. Over the years Jackson has showered Taylor with diamonds and $10,000 bottles of perfume. Gutierrez relates in his book an anecdote, told by Jordie's father, of how Taylor once climbed onto a hospital bed next to Jackson's and threw a tantrum to get the painkillers she demanded.

In various court papers there are references to Jackson's exorbitant medical expenses. During the Avram trial, a document that was flashed on the screen showed that two doctors in Munich who were owed 480,000 marks ($264,000) had threatened to go to the press over nonpayment until Avram picked up the bill.

In addition to the Avram case, Jackson is currently being sued by two former employees, Myung-Ho Lee, who has a company called Union Finance & Investment and who managed Jackson's finances from 1998 to 2001, and Kathleen A. Kelly, an investment banker who, in 2000, went to work for Jackson International, the company formed to make deals and investments for the pop star. Both charge that Jackson stiffed them.

On January 31, 2003, Sotheby's filed suit against Jackson for $1.6 million for two nineteenth-century French paintings—one of a cupid and the other of a woman holding a boy and a sheep—he had purchased the previous October. After failing to come up with the payment, Jackson tried to renege on the sale, because, according to his people, the purchase "no longer fits into Michael Jackson's collection." Sotheby's demanded that he pay. This saga is similar to one involving a $1.9-million Vacheron Constantin watch that Jackson took home in December 1999 from the Beverly Hills jeweler David Orgell, who was forced to sue the pop star for nonpayment in July 2000. Jackson tried to return the watch, which, the jeweler said, came back with scratches and food particles on it. Orgell refused to accept it. A year later, in June 2001, Orgell's lawyers announced that the case was settled. The very next day Jackson reportedly used the watch as collateral for yet another loan from the Bank of America.

But these are just the tip of the iceberg. Financially, Michael Jackson is under siege.

In 1998, according to the court filings, Jackson had cash on hand to cover only two more months of his expenses, which then appeared to be running north of $1.2 million a month. Since 1995 he had burned through $90 million in loans advanced by NationsBank, which later acquired the Bank of America, and he was on the verge of signing a "securitization" of himself through the music publisher Charles Koppelman, in order to sell investors bonds based on his future earnings.

He dropped that idea, however, when Myung-Ho Lee persuaded him to remain a private entity and helped him in December 1998 to secure a new Bank of America loan for $140 million. By mid-1999, according to court papers, Jackson had "exhausted the $140 million loan . . . and needed additional funds for his divorce settlement." (Debbie Rowe, his second wife, was scheduled to get $10 million over several years.) Lee then obtained another loan, of $30 million, for Jackson. When that also disappeared in a flash, Lee had to get a further loan of $60 million in December 2000, with the stipulation that Jackson must immediately pay down the previous, $30-million loan.

The reason the bank had no qualms about advancing such colossal sums was that Jackson had precious collateral to borrow against: his one-half share of the Sony/ATV music catalogue, which owns the publishing rights to 251 Beatles songs as well as more than 400,000 other tunes, from "Tutti Frutti" and "Heartbreak Hotel" to "Like a Virgin," all administered by Sony for a very large fee. (The Beatles songs are immensely profitable, but I am told that the others are less so, largely because of Sony's high administration costs.) Sony guaranteed the bank loan, but the company has the sole right to buy Jackson's share should Jackson ever default on the loan, which comes due in about three years. That means Jackson cannot shop around for the highest bidder, and he must submit to an accounting with Sony at a date arranged by him and the music company. The accountings of record companies have been a particularly volatile subject with artists since the industry began, and Sony has steadily been acquiring other song catalogues of which Jackson owns half. So even though Jackson shrewdly acquired the Beatles' publishing company in 1985—after hearing from Paul McCartney that it was on the market—for a sum of $47.5 million, and then sold half of it to Sony in 1995 for $90 million, Sony is holding all the aces.

But the valuable catalogue is only part of the financial story of Michael Jackson and Sony. Jackson took three years to produce his latest album, *Invincible*, which was released in October 2001 and has sold 2 million copies domestically, according to SoundScan, and 4 million abroad—a very respectable number, but far short of the hoped-for profitability, because of the enormous costs involved in producing it. *Invincible* is the most expensive album ever made: Sony advanced Jackson approximately $40 million to make it, insiders say. In addition, Sony spent $25 million to market it, and both sides are negotiating the music for the last record due on his current contract. Everything seems to indicate that Sony wants out. "He's a drain, a money pit," a former Sony official told me.

Jackson's financial woes with Sony may help explain his amazing protest last summer outside Sony headquarters in New York with the Reverend Al Sharpton, when the entertainer accused then Sony chairman Tommy Mottola of being racist. "He's very, very, very devilish," Jackson had said in Harlem earlier that day, in an obvious move to embrace the black brotherhood. Jackson claimed that Sony had not done enough to promote *Invincible* and was giving him short shrift because he was black. What Jackson really wanted, Sony suspected, was to be let off the hook for the record's production costs, among other things, and the company was able to hit back hard, because Mottola not only had a reputation for being close to a number of hip-hop artists but had been married to Mariah Carey, who is part black. A Sony executive quoted in the New York *Daily News* suggested that Jackson's career had been derailed by the sex-abuse charges and that he was incapable of taking responsibility for his own shortcomings. "When you're an artist, you blame everybody but yourself," Charles Koppelman told me. "He wasn't happening. You have to blame someone? You blame your record company."

On February 6, 2003, ABC broadcast a two-hour Jackson documentary produced by Britain's Granada Television, featuring the correspondent Martin Bashir—he claimed to have had eight months of unfettered access to the King of Pop, who decorated himself with diamond brooches and royal crests for his interviews. The day after the broadcast, Jackson declared that he had been betrayed; he filed complaints with Britain's Independent Television Commission and the Broadcasting Standards Commission, saying he had been "unfairly treated" in the program. But in fact Bashir had allowed him to get away unchallenged on a number of serious points. For example, Jackson freely admitted that he still sleeps with young boys in his bed, but he clearly left the impression that little girls are also included and that the relationships have never been of a sexual nature. In the hundreds of interviews I have conducted, I have yet to hear about any female child who has shared his bed.

Furthermore, he claimed that Debbie Rowe, who gave birth to his two oldest children, did so as a gift to him. "You need to be a daddy," he said she told him. (In fact, the two never lived together as husband and wife, and, as noted earlier, Rowe is slated to receive millions as part of her divorce settlement.) Jackson, however, went on to horrify viewers by recounting how he had wrapped newborn Paris in a towel—placenta and all—and taken her home to bathe her. As a result of the documentary—

which showed disturbing images of Jackson forcing his children to wear animal masks in public and manically jamming a bottle into the mouth of his crying baby, whom he calls Blanket—Santa Barbara district attorney Tom Sneddon was deluged with media inquiries. To cap matters, Jackson announced on the show that he hoped to obtain two more children from each continent.

The ABC broadcast, seen by 27 million, and Jackson's declaration that he had outtakes of Bashir's interview that would prove Bashir's hypocrisy toward him set off a TV feeding frenzy. Fox reportedly paid Jackson $5 million for the outtakes, which were shown with footage of Debbie Rowe stating that she would have five more children for Jackson "in a heartbeat." The deal was partly negotiated by none other than F. Marc Schaffel, the gay-porn producer responsible for the shelving of "What More Can I Give." The following week, among Fox, NBC, and ABC, which rebroadcast the program with an added commentary, seven prime-time hours were devoted to Michael Jackson. Meanwhile, Granada TV sold the original show around the world for millions and declared that not a penny would go to Jackson personally but a portion of the profits would go to a British children's charity. One published report suggested that Jackson was paid for the original interview. On NBC's *Dateline*, a plastic surgeon claimed that Jackson had had as many as fifty operations on his face.

Meanwhile, as the Avram trial stretched into February, Jackson had another one to look forward to, with Myung-Ho Lee, his former financial advisor, whose legal representatives, O'Donnell & Shaeffer of Los Angeles, had submitted to the Superior Court of California in Los Angeles County voluminous records of Jackson's expenses and budgets as part of their complaint. Among the outstanding amounts said to be owed during the period October to December 2000 were $114,847 to the Hôtel d'Angleterre (which apparently couldn't take it out of the millions in a certain bathtub), $99,831 to "Celebrity Costumes," and $845,000 designated "Payroll." The dermatologist Arnold Klein was owed $15,000; Mickey Fine Pharmacy in Beverly Hills was owed $62,645; and John Branca, one of Jackson's attorneys, who is said to take a five percent commission on many of the pop star's contracts, was owed more than $250,000. The total loan draw for the period was $4,435,000.

Jackson's expenses for the period of January 1, 2000, to March 3, 2001, were detailed as well, including $75.62 for Slurpee-machine maintenance at Neverland, $3,216.23 for gas for ranch vehicles, and $1,919.83 for candy and soda for the theater and amusement park. The documents even reveal news of Bubbles, Jackson's much-publicized chimpanzee. The animal's trainer was getting $9,900, and its annual boarding fee was $6,000. Jackson's in-flight costs for watches and goods purchased on Swiss Air were $10,681.36. The Oxford University event of 2001 cost $90,563 for Jackson's travel alone. Thousands and thousands of dollars were itemized for limousine services, video purchases and rentals, and equipment services. The tab for three months at the Four Seasons Hotel in New York, billed under the name of Frank Tyson, Jackson's handler, who was born Frank Cascio and went around the world with him as a little boy when the sex-abuse charges first surfaced, was $43,117.20.

"All of us are products of our childhoods. But I am the product of a lack of a childhood, an absence of that precious and wondrous age where we frolic playfully without a care in the world," Michael Jackson told the audience at Oxford in March 2001 in the lecture he delivered to announce the launch of the Heal the Kids Initiative. Jackson's anger and resentment toward his cheerless, driven, and adulterous father are well-known. "I began performing at the tender age of five . . . [and] there was no respite from my professional life."

The speech was partly a critique of the parent generation "that has witnessed an abrogation of the parent-child covenant" and partly a plea to "parents undistracted by the lust for luxury and status" to make their children primary in their lives—this from a man who was televised going on a $6-million shopping spree. "If you don't have that memory of being loved, you are condemned to search the world for something to fill you up." He enunciated the primary purpose of Heal the Kids: "Our goal is simple—to re-create the parent-child bond, renew its promise, and light the way forward for all the beautiful children who are destined one day to walk this earth."

Reading these impassioned words, I cannot help but recall the six "wishes" that Jordie Chandler said that Michael Jackson had told the then thirteen-year-old to repeat three times a day:

1. No wenches, bitches, heifers, or hoes.
2. Never give up your "bliss."
3. Live with me in Neverland forever.
4. No conditioning.
5. Never grow up.
6. Be better than best friends forever.

Now that Michael Jackson has three children of his own—children who are growing up with no mother, who live under constant camera surveillance, whose diets are prescribed, and whose faces are wrapped when they venture out in public—it will be interesting to see one day how they remember their father.

UPDATE: Be careful what you wish. As I write this, I have spent just two days inside an intense media blitz following my latest ten-thousand-word article on Michael Jackson (published in the March 2004 *Vanity Fair.*) The piece followed the latest charges of sexual molestation against Jackson. This time, the alleged victim was a thirteen-year-old and there would be no civil payoff. As this book was going to press, Jackson had been arrested and was facing trial on seven counts of lewd behavior toward a minor and two counts of administering an intoxicating agent with intent to commit a felony.

Now, because of my allegations about Jackson's drug use and his giving wine to children, I suddenly find myself in the highly ironic position of becoming part and parcel of the kind of celebrity phenomenon I describe in this book! Although the story has not yet appeared on the newsstands, it has been characterized as a "bombshell" and has driven entertainment news shows and tabloid TV into a frenzy. When I entered the *Vanity Fair* conference room in our New York headquarters to be interviewed by *Entertainment Tonight,* I found twelve people to supervise the two-camera shoot. *Extra, Access Hollywood, Inside Edition,* and almost every single hour of Fox cable and MSNBC requested time with me after I was first interviewed by Katie Couric on *Today* and, twenty-four hours later, by *The Early show* and CNN's *American Morning.* Later that day, the Jackson family held a news conference to denounce the article but never addressed any of the specific, serious allegations I had made. These included Jackson's allegedly giving wine in soda pop cans to the thirteen-year-old cancer victim. (Jackson called the white wine "Jesus Juice" and the red wine "Jesus Blood.")

Now I watch as panels of "legal experts" debate how what I wrote will play before a jury. Some have clearly never read a word of the article, and both Greta von Sustern and Geraldo Rivera, who came under criticism in my Laci Peterson article, have gone out of their way on their Fox cable shows to try to undermine the credibility of my reporting. Both have charged that my latest story is merely a rehash of my previous reporting. But if we have heard it all before why is it causing such a sensation now?

Celebrity obviously continues to reign supreme on television. As the Democratic primaries unfold, terrorist threats ground airline flights, and the debate over weapons of mass destruction in Iraq continues, the issue of whether or not Michael Jackson fed "Jesus Juice" to children trumps them all. Maybe because it is such a powerful cautionary tale of the dangers of celebrity. Maybe because people actually do sense—despite Michael's many defenders on television—that something terrible has occurred. Still, there are those who see all the attention given this case as completely misplaced: "You are so intense about your work," a friend of mine cautioned me. "He's just a pop entertainer." She was telling me that I was wasting myself on such subject matter. Yet the fact is I am writing about allegations of pedophilia: At least two young boys' lives have been unalterably changed, and not for the better, by knowing Michael Jackson. This is a story of how power can corrupt and corrode. To me, Jackson represents all that fame and the power of celebrity have been allowed to distort in our society.

Ray Chandler, uncle of Jordie Chandler (the real name of Jackson's first victim), told me that Jordie's whole family was ruined as a result of Jackson's relationship with Jordie and that the $25 million they received did not assuage the wounds. Jordie cannot have a normal life. Sooner or later, he is always recognized as "the Michael Jackson kid." Jordie has never again spoken to his mother, whom he holds responsible for putting him in harm's way. His father, Evan Chandler, has divorced his second wife and become a recluse, obsessed and distraught over the claims that he was nothing but an extortionist.

Meanwhile, as the circus continues, the Jackson family has consistently tried to play the race card, refusing to address specific allegations in my article but claiming that I am trying to "lynch" Michael Jackson. It is desperate strategy. The Nation of Islam, now so close to Michael, plays the same intimidation games (attempting to scare off potential witnesses and other possible victims who might come forward to testify against Jackson) that Anthony Pellicano did in 1993 in the Chandler case. Yet throughout all the sordid details, the insatiable media beast, condemned to satisfy 24/7, records the lives of all involved as a great and lurid pageant. The real truths that Michael Jackson's story reveals about our society and celebrity are being lost.

Part VI:

The Empty Hotel Room

Notes from the Celebrity-Industrial Complex VI

I wanted to end this book not with shame or sensation but with a reminder that there is such a thing as real talent, achieved through hard work and perseverance—and also that there is life beyond public acclaim and recognition. Margot Fonteyn, the great prima ballerina who died in 1991, allowed me into her humble *finca* in the Panamanian *campo* and never expressed the slightest regret for having given up everything—her career and the world where she was held in such high regard—for the great love of her life, her late husband, Tito Arias. He did not make life easy for her at all, but Fonteyn—an old-fashioned talent whose existence was less fraught and complex than those of the Tina Turners and Madonnas of today—described her life before Tito, as a famous person traveling the world alone, in an incredibly poignant way: "I have lived my life," she said, "in what I call the empty hotel room."

At the end of her days, away from the lights and glamour, living there on her small farm, it was not a room to which she wanted ever to return.

Last Dance: Dame Margot Fonteyn

"I've spent an awful lot of time in what I call the empty hotel room."

May 1990

Champagne bubbles fizzled at the left-center power banquette in Manhattan's Russian Tea Room, where two of the most famous ballerinas in the history of the planet were dining together, *prima assoluta* to *prima assoluta*. Dame Margot Fonteyn, now seventy, was recalling the glory decades when a single ballerina could dominate the world of dance, as she did. Next to her was eighty-five-year-old Alexandra Danilova, who had appeared at the Maryinsky Theater when there was still a czar, and then trouped all over the Western world as the star of the Ballets Russes. "Choura, you look beautiful," Dame Margot exclaimed to the carefully coiffed Danilova. "It is our trade," Danilova replied in heavily accented English, barely batting the blue-shadowed eyelids that precisely matched her dress.

Just then, as if on cue, another icon of dance appeared to surprise Fonteyn—Roland Petit, director of the Ballet de Marseille, who fell head over heels for her in Paris during World War II. It was he who turned the beautiful ballerina into an international fashion plate, taking her to Dior, who outfitted her until he died and she moved on to Saint Laurent.

"Margot, your hair is white," Petit said with real surprise.

"Yes, it's such a relief," Fonteyn replied with a sigh.

"Margot, we must talk. I will phone you."

"But I have no phone," Dame Margot demurred.

"Well . . . Surely, you must come to Paris. We will do some work together. I will take you to the couture." Petit was making a valiant effort to connect, but Fonteyn chose not to notice. Instead she laughed. "Oh, I don't go to the couture anymore. My life is radically different. I live on a farm with cows."

Dame Margot Fonteyn, the dowager empress of ballet, could live in any world capital she chose, but, to the bewilderment of her friends, she spends most of her time alone on a small Panamanian *finca* with four hundred head of cattle and five dogs. She had been in New York for only a couple of weeks to coach the dancers of the American Ballet Theatre in Frederick Ashton's *Birthday Offering*, a work she first starred in in 1956, when she was the reigning diva of the Royal Ballet. Two days after dining with Danilova, she quit Manhattan for home, a remote farmhouse at the end of a dusty, unpaved, unnamed road.

It takes an hour and a half traveling west from Panama City to reach the humble pueblo of El Higo, which is where the rutted road to Dame Margot's house meets the main highway. On the left a gaudily graffitied butcher shop is attached to an outdoor *cantina,* or tavern. On the right, flying a tattered Panamanian flag, is the rundown headquarters of the *policiá*, past which Fonteyn's manservant, Buenaventura Medina, a strong and stocky Panamanian in his mid-forties, swings the gray Subaru station wagon. He waves to barefoot children, and stops a few hundred yards later to pick up Dame Margot's laundry from a woman living in a tiny shack that is decorated with a piece of white picket fence covered with vibrant hibiscus and bougainvillea. The fence has been liberated from the nearby fairgrounds, run until recently by General Manuel Noriega's officers, who, it is said, populated their *feria* with livestock stolen from local ranches. The little piece of picket fence is the neighbor's revenge.

Buenaventura accepts the laundry in an orange plastic clothes basket and begins honking cattle off the road. Given the milieu, one would hardly guess that these placid creatures swishing flies with their tails are actually descended from sperm acquired from David Rockefeller's prize herd.

Dame Margot lives half a mile on, in a simple four-room house constructed of gray bricks, bricks of the old "colonial" size, made by hand of cement and horse manure over several years' time by an old man in a neighboring town. It is a house without air-conditioning or ceilings, topped with a roof of corrugated aluminum. Macho roosters strut and squawk in front of the veranda, baby chicks scamper after their mothers and feed on macheted coconuts scattered by Buenaventura at the bottoms of clumps of palm trees. About a hundred yards across a carpet of crabgrass is a corral, and beyond the corral a mile or so of hilly red earth and parched jungle leading to a stretch of isolated beach on the Pacific. The whole scene is one of timelessness and languor.

And yet here at the door is Dame Margot, smiling her dazzling take-a-bow smile, an impeccable colonial lady of the old order, gracious, charming, slightly aloof. Her carriage is flawless, the famous line of her back intact, the discipline from thousands of hours of practice and rehearsal immediately apparent despite a limp that causes her to move with caution. It's not difficult to guess that this is a woman who often had the world at her feet. In heat that surely must surpass 103 in the shade, Dame Margot wears a vintage couture houndstooth skirt with a black velvet waistband, a white T-shirt, and around her neck two strands of marble-size pearls. (Most of the other jewelry was auctioned at Christie's last year for needed cash.) She looks exotic even amid this vegetation.

"I have never wanted to live to be old, so old I'd run out of friends or money," Dame Margot says later. She is sitting on the veranda, where all her meals are taken, or rather picked at. "If one lives too long, one runs out of both."

Her husband, the controversial Roberto ("Tito") Arias, died in November, and no one seems to understand why she would want to go on living here. Arias was a paraplegic, the victim of an attempted assassination in 1964, a few weeks after he had been elected to the Panamanian national assembly. Despite his disability they had lived a cosmopolitan, international life for more than twenty years. The devoted Fonteyn, who didn't retire until she was sixty, took him with her on tour or visited him as often as she could in their Panama City apartment. ("Life was a constant struggle to keep him from being bored," she says.) In 1983 they moved to the farm, where Arias amused himself with the technicalities of cattle breeding. It is a primitive place. Dame Margot can call out to Panama City but no farther on a portable phone, and for long-distance communication, she must be driven down the road to a small beach-front hotel run by a crusty, bewhiskered Russian merchant-seaman emigré—the only other European in the area.

Since Buenaventura spends at least half the week in Panama City, Dame Margot is usually quite alone now, in bed by eight, twirling the dial of her little world radio, tuning in first the BBC news and then the news from Australia and the Voice of America. "I feel I ought to keep informed because out here how else would I know anything?" Not that she yearns for urban life. "I know from having just stayed in New York that I could never live again with all that height and concrete. I like the fact you can take the grapefruit off the trees here. I've spent an awful lot of time in what I call the empty hotel room, and I *hate* cement and concrete. I like being on the ground. Besides, this is my home—where else would I go?"

The last several months have been perhaps the most difficult of Dame Margot's life. During 1988 and 1989 she underwent three complicated operations in Houston that culminated in a hip replacement. The ballet world was rife with rumors that she had cancer, but Fonteyn refuses to comment about the exact nature of her illness. An examination in February, however, revealed no recurrence of the previous problem. It was during her absence for a checkup last winter that her beloved husband, born of one of Panama's great political families, had to be taken to the hospital. A day after he was operated on for cancer, he died. A few weeks later, on December 20, 1989, the United States invaded Panama and Dame Margot was isolated on the farm with a Filipino houseguest who read her Bible stories while American jets flew overhead. From her beach, one can see the island where General Noriega had a house, one of the places, locals claim, where he kept his Brazilian witches.

Fonteyn and her husband had known Noriega for years. Just last summer Arias, who was both the son and nephew of former Panamanian presidents, scandalized his family by running for national deputy as the candidate of a party sympathetic to Noriega. He lost badly. Today, Dame Margot downplays the relationship, dismissing her husband's candidacy as just another attempt to avoid boredom. Of the general she says, "You can be clever without being wise. I think General Noriega was clever but not wise."

Fonteyn has been involved in Panamanian political life for decades, if only as an interested observer. "She knows a tremendous amount," says the former United States ambassador to Panama Ambler Moss. In the years after her husband was shot, she was literally his voice. His paralysis prevented him from speaking above a faint whisper that was barely understood except by Fonteyn and Buenaventura, and she "translated" his words for friends and colleagues. "Even after he was shot, in a wheelchair and barely intelligible, people still consulted him about politics," says Moss. "It was an interesting role—a kind of political guru." And Fonteyn made it possible for him to function—taking care of him, speaking for him. "He had a wonderful brain," she says now. "I can't tell you what he would have had to say about recent events in Panama."

Years before Noriega ascended to the presidency, but when he in fact controlled much of the country as the head of the intelligence services, he would often lunch or dine with Arias and Fonteyn. "Noriega was the kind of person who wanted to feel important," Buenaventura explains. "He knew Margot and Tito were very important, so he wanted to know them, to be close to them." "Noriega was fascinated with Margot's fame," says Louis Martinz, one of Fonteyn's closest friends and now the international media spokesman for the new Endara government. "But when she retired, he lost interest."

Even so, Noriega threw a showy birthday party for her in 1983, with a two-tiered cake featuring reclining porcelain ballerinas on a bed of bright-green shredded coconut. He was too shy to dance Panamanian folk dances with her, so Louis Martinz did. And in 1987, Dame Margot dragged a bewildered Rudolf Nureyev, who was visiting her in Panama, to meet the general. "At least Noriega gave the impression that he knew such things as art existed," she says now, although she is not a defender. "Nine times out of ten, foreign invasions are not justified, but this time I think the U.S. did the right thing. There was no other way."

"The sweetest sound I ever heard was that of the American bombers," says Gerasimos Kanelopulos, a friend of Dame Margot's and the owner of the Argosy, a lively Spanish-English bookstore in Panama City. Kanelopulos and a few other friends, including Louis Martinz, have come to Saturday lunch. "Look, did you ever see that old TV show, *The Twilight Zone*?" Martinz asks. "Well, that's Panama—the twilight zone." Martinz was an admirer of Roberto Arias's uncle, the charismatic and eccentric Arnulfo Arias, who was three times elected to the Panamanian presidency and three times deposed, with American approval. He recalls that Arnulfo—a Rosicrucian who followed the stars and spoke of a philosophy of concentric circles—had a certain affinity with Noriega, who would at times give incomprehensible speeches about interlocking triangles.

As the lazy lunch of unintentionally organic beef, fish, rice with coconut, and tropical vegetables turns into an eight-hour affair—washed down with pitchers of Buenaventura's icy sangria—Fonteyn and her friends trade the latest firsthand anecdotes about Noriega, the new government, the state of the canal, Dan Quayle, and the United States Southern Command. The consensus of this well-informed group is that Noriega never thought the United States would come after him. He had lost touch with reality by mixing too many religions—"Catholic and Buddhist and his Brazilian voodoo." Basically he was caught because he couldn't get his mojoes working right.

But so what? Let the gringos worry about Noriega. "He is not a priority in our minds now," declares Dame Margot's stepson, Roberto junior. "This is a country of hear no evil, see no evil," his former wife, Elba, adds. This is Panama, after all, a poor land settled by pirates whose progeny became bankers, a country that has few important exports, a country that before Noriega wrecked the economy had gained what strength it had—apart from the canal—by being a safe haven for drug money.

"If you try to find a clean business in Panama, it doesn't exist," a former CIA chief there says cynically.

Margot Fonteyn first saw Panama in 1955, shortly after she married Roberto Arias. They had met eighteen years earlier, when she was a hardworking teenage ballerina with the small Sadler's Wells ballet. Each May the company went to Cambridge to perform at the theater that John Maynard Keynes had built for his dancer wife, Lydia Lopokova. Tito was a Cambridge undergraduate, the son of Harmodio Arias, a brilliant Panamanian lawyer and self-made man who himself had been educated at Cambridge on a special scholarship the Panamanian congress made possible for poor boys from the provinces, and had gone on to serve as president of his country.

Fonteyn, who began life with the ordinary English name of Peggy Hookham, was the reserved daughter of a British father and a half-Brazilian mother. She spent her first eight years in England and then sailed from the United States to Shanghai, where her father was employed as the chief engineer of the British Cigarette Company. By the time she was fourteen and enamored of the dance, Peggy Hookham had left school, and she and her mother returned to England to learn once and for all if she should seriously pursue ballet. After ten minutes of auditioning in her bare feet, she was accepted by the director of the Vic-Wells (later called the Sadler's Wells, and then the Royal Ballet), Ninette de Valois. She was only fifteen when she was made a full member of the company, and seventeen when she danced Giselle. By then Margot Fonteyn (her stage name taken from her mother's maiden name—Fontes) was a star, with an extraordinary onstage aura that mesmerized audiences. "I realized," said her first partner, Robert Helpmann, that "she had the curious quality of making one want to cry."

The morning after she met Roberto Arias, Fonteyn herself was in tears. "I got up and I walked across the room and I had this really strange sensation. So I went back and sat on the edge of the bed. Then somehow it came into my mind about people walking on air when they're in love. Not till then did I remember this person I had seen the night before. And then I said, 'Oh, that must be it.'"

And that *was* it for many years. The mysterious and reticent Tito sailed for Panama for summer vacation and out of her life. There were other loves, of course. Margot Fonteyn was always awash in roses. She knew practically every major celebrity in Britain—there were sailing parties with Olivier, dinners with David Niven. "I have a side to me that likes to party and dance all night," she says. And yet she worried about becoming "an old ballerina," ready for retirement at age thirty-five with no place to go and no one to love.

Incredibly, she felt this way even in 1949, when she and the Sadler's Wells company visited New York and took the town by storm. Curtain calls took twenty minutes. The parties were nonstop. Their tour set box-office records, and Margot Fonteyn made the cover of *Time*. The following year she made the cover of *Newsweek*. New York was Fonteyn's turning point. "I think I won New York by smiling," she once said, and America, suddenly dance-hungry, was smitten. The United States made her ballet's biggest star. "She lit up the stage," says Robert Gottlieb, who saw those first performances in New York and many years later edited her autobiography and her book *The Magic of Dance*. "Her curtain calls alone made your heart jump."

It was during a New York season in the early 1950s that Roberto Arias reappeared, without warning. He had just been named Panama's ambassador to the United Nations, and one night he came to the theater where Fonteyn was performing. The next morning she was awakened by a phone call saying he was coming by for breakfast. Over coffee, Dame Margot recalls, he said, "'You're going to marry me and be very happy.' And I said, 'You're crazy.'" He was then married to someone else, with three children under the age of seven. A few minutes later, he took off for the airport.

A hundred roses were delivered to her hotel by his chauffeur. There was a diamond bracelet and a fur coat that was too big. His limo was at her disposal. Since they had last seen each other, Arias had woven a rich tapestry of powerful international contacts. While still in school, he had, quite by chance, been responsible for getting FDR's mother, Sara Delano Roosevelt, out of Paris before war was declared in Europe and had thus earned the gratitude of the entire Roosevelt clan.

Arias had become a maritime lawyer for Aristotle Onassis, and also the owner of a tabloid newspaper, *La Hora*. In *La Hora* he gave the Panamanian upper class the nickname it is still known by: *rabi-blancos*, or "white butts," from the name of a white-tailed Panamanian bird.

"They were a very political family," sniffs a Panamanian matron when asked about the Ariases. "They were always running for office or trying to get power. That was their thing." In the words of another Panamanian, "Tito is the reflection of an era, when the traditional oligarchy ran the country." But he seems also to have been something of a rogue. "He got away with murder all his life—there was business he was doing that was not very straight," says his sister, Rosaria Arias de Galindo, the publisher of the Panama City daily *Panama América*. She thinks that people protected him out of respect for their father.

"When you talk about Tito Arias, you have to talk about Churchill—he was a close friend of Churchill's. When he'd go to the States, he'd be with these senators and movie stars—John Wayne, Elizabeth Taylor," says his cousin the Panamanian national deputy Lucas Zarak. "In the entire world there are few people who had as many good connections." Zarak, who is a nephew of Arnulfo Arias's wife, thinks that "Tito tried to be a little bit of everything in his life—a little bit of a playboy, a little bit of a smuggler. He liked that people talked about him—it didn't matter how." Zarak remembers the time—shortly before he was shot—when Arias was campaigning for deputy and in an elevator, by chance, ran into a political opponent who was also a friend. "Tito asked him how it was going and the man said not so good because he was running out of money. So Tito reached into his pocket and counted out $5,000 and gave it to him. Even when he was a little boy, he was always in trouble because he spent more than his allowance."

"They literally broke the mold when they made Tito," says Louis Martinz. "When people would gossip about him, I'd say, Stop it. Stop comparing him to a human being. Pretend he's from Mars. The same standards don't apply to him."

But he was, in any case, definitely the man for Margot Fonteyn.

"This was the only person I felt I could be married to. I thought, The only way I will always have an interesting life is with this man—it certainly won't be boring," she says. On February 5, 1955, they were married in a chaotic civil ceremony in Paris and then honeymooned on a yacht in the Bahamas.

Arias soon became Panama's ambassador to Great Britain, and Fonteyn, elevated to a Dame of the British Empire, eagerly began the rounds of the diplomatic life. In January 1959 the Ariases made a private visit to Cuba, where Castro had just come to power. A few weeks later, the couple "went fishing" together off the coast of Panama to meet up with a waterskiing skiff that was sinking because of the arms it was filled with. Arias had begun a revolution that couldn't shoot straight. What followed was a debacle featuring a band of Cubans—led by a nightclub owner—landing at the wrong time in the wrong place, Arias and Fonteyn being separated on two different boats, gunfire that caused the death of one of Arias's *compadres*, and Arias's eventual escape to the Brazilian embassy—but not before he left behind a briefcase. In the next few days the Panamanian press had a field day with the news that documents in the briefcase showed that in addition to the help from his left-wing Cuban friends, Arias had received $682,850 from John Wayne for a "shrimp business." Dame Margot ended up spending a night in a Panamanian jail, in a VIP cell decorated with roses grown by the warden. At the time, *Life* magazine labeled the insurrection "one of the funnier fiascos of recent history."

Fonteyn remains mum on the subject of her husband's political and business deals, and it's clear that the Arias family has always tried to protect her, even though its members often took a dim view of his activities. Lucas Zarak recalls, for instance, that Arias was arrested twice for bootlegging. "You know, when you get right down to business with those political things and revolution . . . with Tito they were all very stupid—they were so impractical," says his sister. "But I remember my father telling me once—when I went to see Margot, who was dancing in Chile—'No matter what you tell her, remember she is his wife.' I always had the impression that the relationship between man and wife had absolutely nothing to do with the relations a man and woman can have with the rest of the world."

Not long after the abortive coup, Arias was back as the British ambassador, under a different Panamanian president. There were weekend visits to Churchill at Chartwell, where Viscount Montgomery jokingly offered his services for Arias's "next revolution." Or they'd dash down to Monte Carlo for trips on Onassis's yacht, where Arias had a brass plaque with his name outside his own private stateroom. When he couldn't bear the gloom of the English climate, he'd bolt suddenly for Panama. On one of these visits, he showed up at a fancy party wearing a white linen Panama suit after they had gone out of fashion. When asked why, he replied, "Because I'm the white sheep of the family." Such sallies delighted Dame Margot, who remembers him also as the "most charitable man imaginable. He once got a telegram from an old lady friend that said, 'Darling Tito, could you please wire me $300. I've got a banker on the hook and if I can have three new dresses, I think I can snag him.' He wired the money immediately."

Roberto Arias was shot five times in June 1964. The assailant was a close aide who thought he had been double-crossed politically. At the time of the murder attempt, Margot Fonteyn was dancing at the Bath Festival in England. She was forty-five, and two years into her historic partnership with Rudolf Nureyev, who was still in his twenties. He had defected in 1961, and their magical stage relationship had developed almost immediately. Nureyev and Fonteyn were rumored to be carrying on offstage as well (rumors she always denied), and there were also rumors that the Arias marriage was on the rocks and that Arias had a roving eye. But some of their friends dispute these claims. "He *did* spend all her money and she *did* have problems with him," says Queenie Altamorano, who would often visit Arias when Fonteyn was away, "but she's a very devoted human being and she doesn't change her mind easily. Her life was Tito."

Her professional life was Nureyev. "At first I didn't want to dance with him. It was a big challenge because I was so much older," she remembers now. "Then everyone said this gave me renewed life and everything. Probably it did—I don't know. After we did the first performance and it was such a tremendous success, I thought it would be sensible to retire, on that high point. But somehow or other, fate doesn't always do the things that might be sensible. Fate leads you to do other things. And I'm a great fatalist."

Driven by the necessity of caring for her husband, Fonteyn, who never earned any sort of big money until she danced with Nureyev, maintained a killer schedule, flying back and forth to Panama for a few days from halfway across the world.

The ballerina who had planned to stop performing at thirty-five danced for twenty-five years beyond that.

Like most Panamanians, Rosaria Arias de Galindo, her sister-in-law, reveres Margot Fonteyn. She is thought of as something close to a saint for her dedication to her difficult and restless husband, who, despite his infirmity, would think nothing of deciding to go abroad from one day to the next, changing countries at whim, usually needing a ticket for Buenaventura as well as other expensive care. Margot Fonteyn paid all the bills with nary a word of complaint. "One day we found out she had pneumonia," says Arias de Galindo. "She refused to stay in the hospital, so she came here. She was thrilled to be wearing one of my nightgowns. She herself could never undress at night because Buenaventura or someone had to come into the bedroom two or three times a night to turn Tito. Something so human as being naked underneath a nightgown she could never experience." Señora Galindo shakes her head in disbelief.

Once, in order to attend a New York party at a penthouse, Arias had himself hoisted up the fire escape in his wheelchair. "He was always very macho," says one of Fonteyn's closest friends in New York, the publicist and balletomane Donald Smith. "He would just continue doing what he wanted to do. If he decided he wanted to go swimming, a car would have to be hired for the afternoon to take him to the New York Athletic Club around the corner. Then someone would have to be hired to help put him in the pool. An afternoon could end up costing $600 or $700."

"He was an extremely strong, opinionated man—she really did play the role of the acquiescent wife to a very, very great extent," says the American Ballet Theatre codirector Jane Hermann. "Tito made the decisions." "She would be ravenous after a performance, but she would always cut Tito's food first and feed him first," says Louis Martinz. "She had no identity of her own when Tito was around." Yet Donald Smith recalls the look of utter amazement on Dame Margot's face when he blurted out one day how sorry he was for her—"you whose whole life is motion being tied up with someone who can't move." "Oh, Donald," Dame Margot replied, "it's so much harder for you. You see, I love him."

On the recent documentary of her life broadcast on PBS, she confessed, "Until I married Tito, I had absolutely no idea who I was offstage. And then I married him and I knew—I was Mrs. Tito de Arias." In her autobiography, there is a passage that goes even further: "Real life often seemed so much more unreal than the stage; or maybe I should say my identity was clear to me only when I assumed some make-believe character," she writes. "It was so easy for me to step out into the limelight through the plywood door of Giselle's cottage and suffer her shyness, ecstasy, deception, and madness. . . . But when I left the stage door and sought my orientation among real people, I was in a wilderness of unpredictables in an unchoreographed world."

"Come on, Merengue darling. Come, my little boy. . . . I love you so much." Fonteyn's big Labradors are the center of attention on the ranch now. Four dog beds were the only furniture on the veranda for a long time, and were often mistaken for chairs by visitors who tried to sit in them. There is a fifth dog, but she almost never associates with the other four, since she sleeps with the mistress. She used to sleep with Arias, but since his death has switched beds. "I once asked my husband, 'Who shall I take care of when you're gone?'" Dame Margot says. "My husband loved the dogs very much. They kept him company. If I left here, who would take care of my dogs?"

The wound of Arias's death is still very fresh. "You know, I was just happy being with him—it didn't matter what he was doing or where he was." After lunch, while guests are still seated at the table under the thatched *ramada*, Dame Margot is briefly in tears up on the veranda with her friend Gerasimos. He has brought her gifts of the cheeses and chocolates she loves. She has brought him the autographs of Rex Harrison and Stewart Granger she garnered in New York for his collection, plus the signed Christmas card from King Hussein of Jordan. ("That brave little king" is one of her heroes.) She herself collects nothing—the tributes and tutus are packed away in her brother's house in England. Only the prizes won by Arias's cattle are on display in the living room here. In her bedroom there are a few family portraits and ballet books. That's it.

Rail thin, Fonteyn no longer exercises, "since it used to be a process that led to something—the stage—and it no longer does." Nor does the most musical of dancers ever listen to a note. "I haven't quite figured it out, but I think it has something to do with motion."

Later, sitting in the dark after the guests have left, she admits that she doesn't like to look back and that praise makes her feel uncomfortable. "Since I never saw myself dance the way others saw me—three-dimensionally—I have no idea what they felt when they saw me. I can't possibly know. Seeing myself on film is two-dimensional—it's not the same, so I'm always at a loss to know what to say. All I was ever trying to do was what was expected of me. And I always felt inadequate."

"Is the door to the stage completely closed now?"

"I don't think the door is closed; I just don't miss it. At least when you are taking care of a herd of cows, they don't come up and ask you to dance *Swan Lake* all the time."

Late in the afternoons, Dame Margot will pile the dogs into the station wagon and ask Buenaventura to drive her to the beach. "There's here and there's the rest of the world," she declares. She's right, of course. On this utterly deserted stretch of white sand and scalloped maroon and orange-colored shells, it hardly seems to matter what intrigues and plots are being hatched nearby or even far away. To walk through the sand, Fonteyn leans heavily on Buenaventura—who encourages her: "You need the exercise." Most of those celebrated thigh muscles are gone now, and she who once airily covered acres of stage space like so many fluttering rose petals must measure every step. But then Buenaventura goes into the water, and as Dame Margot Fonteyn stands alone, watching a brilliant sunset begin to streak the horizon, the shape of her famous line and carriage suddenly takes hold; unconsciously, effortlessly, she becomes a frail and valiant ballerina silhouetted against the sky.

UPDATE: Margot Fonteyn died less than two years after this *Vanity Fair* article appeared. She had cancer when I interviewed her but did not publicize her illness. In the course of my reporting, I learned that Tito Arias had a young mistress from an old Panamanian family who stayed with him when Fonteyn went off to dance—for many more years than she ever cared to—in order to pay the family's bills. On the day Arias died, the young woman was so distraught she committed suicide. Although this information might have added a juicy tidbit to my article, I left it out. I could not bear to hurt Margot Fonteyn, who to me was a paragon of dignity and fortitude. I am not sure that I would be able to keep information like that hidden today.

ACKNOWLEDGMENTS

Vanity Fair has an outstanding staff of hardworking pros who have helped me to see all these pieces to fruition and to give me this fabulous experience of looking at fame up close. I begin with the two famous editors in chief I have worked for, Graydon Carter and Tina Brown, who believed in me and sent me off to parts unknown to meet the amazing people in these pages. It is not easy to do investigative reporting and go up against powerful interests and people, but Graydon has thrown the weight of the magazine behind me and allowed me to follow the story wherever it leads; my grateful thanks also to the quiet power, the quintessential managing editor Chris Garrett. Getting long, complicated pieces into print, often with crashing deadlines, is a team effort. My deepest gratitude goes to my selfless, outstanding editors throughout the time I have worked for *Vanity Fair*, Wayne Lawson, Katrina Heron, and Sharon Delano; the Legal Eagles who say yes much more often than no, Robert Walsh, Jerry Birenz, and Rich Bernstein; Ellen Kiell and her wily production staff, who find extra space for me; all the awesome researchers under John Banta and, formerly, Pat Singer; the very talented people on the visual side, especially David Harris and Susan White; not to mention the many brilliant photographers who have illustrated my work and thus enhanced it; copy editor Peter Devine; the dedicated director of public relations Beth Kseniak and her staff; Punch Hutton, for knowing everything; Heather Fink, the inexhaustible Olympic infochamp, who has never not been able to find anything I have ever asked for; ditto for Cindy Cathcart and the library staff; Michael Hogan, my techno guru; Lindsay Bucha, who typed many of the manuscripts for me in her off hours and is always ready to assist with a smile. Thanks too to the *Vanity Fair* offices in Los Angeles, London, and Paris, who are unfailingly helpful whenever I land there; also to David Friend; and finally to my gifted writing colleagues at the magazine who have always been generous and gracious to me whenever I have needed guidance from them. I should also thank Mr. Si Newhouse, who runs the rare company that rewards creativity and enterprise and pays all these incomparable people.

In the creation of this work, there are more than a thousand people who gave me their time and told me their stories and who helped me to put together all the facts that make up my reporting. Obviously they are the glue that holds everything together, and they have my profound thanks. I am sure there are those who wished they had never spoken to me, but hopefully they are a minority.

George Hodgman has been the inspirational editor of this book, overseeing every detail, always going the extra mile. He has been terrific to work with. So has the whole crew at Henry Holt beginning with John Sterling and Jennifer Barth, Maggie Richards, Elizabeth Shreve, Kate Pruss, copy editor Susan Joseph, and art director Raquel Jaramillo. My agent, Amanda Urban, also has done her usual bang-up job getting this project up and running. I also want to thank Mark Fowler for his legal work, Becky Bucha and Chrystyna Dattilo for helping to type the manuscript, and Supurna Banerjee for her help.

I am blessed with dear friends who also happen to be unbelievably smart and totally "get" the subject matter. Jill Abramson has an overwhelming workload, but she always had time for me to talk about this book and to offer her clear insights; the same goes for Katrina Heron, who is no longer my editor but whose judgment, like Jill's, I prize. The irreverent Blair Sabol always cuts to the chase, and Sally Bedell Smith has patiently listened to me expounding for years as we walk around the track at St. Albans School. I salute her stamina and value her feedback. Laura Handman is another kind friend who is never too busy to be generous with her astute legal advice. Jurate Kazickas, Janet Maslin, Christy Ferer, Kazuko Oshima, and Suzanne Wright have always been wonderfully supportive of my work.

David Leyrer is a new friend who knocked me out with his witty analysis of celebrity culture—he came along at precisely the right moment.

Finally, my deepest gratitude is to all my family, my Kappa sisters, and wonderful old friends in California—Go Bears!—who are used to me crashing in and out of their lives as I pursue deadlines. And, finally, thanks to Tim and Luke in Washington, my two great guys, who have lived through a series of my temporary obsessions with quite a cast of characters over the years. Their humor and equanimity keeps the intense mom sane. God bless you all.

About the Author

Since joining *Vanity Fair* in 1988, MAUREEN ORTH has interviewed superstars and heads of state and has made headline news with her investigations of murders (Gianni Versace) and scandals (Michael Jackson). Her first book, *Vulgar Favors,* appeared for three weeks on the *New York Times* bestseller list. She has written for *Newsweek, New York, New West, Vogue, New York Woman,* the *Washington Post,* the *New York Times, Rolling Stone,* and *Esquire.* From 1983 to 1984, she was a network correspondent for NBC News. She is married to Tim Russert, Washington bureau chief of NBC News and moderator of *Meet the Press,* with whom she has a son, Luke.